ARTIFICIAL HUMANITIES

ARTIFICIAL HUMANITIES

A Fictional Perspective on Language in AI

Nina Beguš

University of Michigan Press
Ann Arbor

Copyright © 2025 by Nina Beguš
Some rights reserved

This work is licensed under a Creative Commons Attribution-NonCommercial 4.0 International License. *Note to users:* A Creative Commons license is only valid when it is applied by the person or entity that holds rights to the licensed work. Works may contain components (e.g., photographs, illustrations, or quotations) to which the rightsholder in the work cannot apply the license. It is ultimately your responsibility to independently evaluate the copyright status of any work or component part of a work you use, in light of your intended use. To view a copy of this license, visit http://creativecommons.org/licenses/by-nc/4.0/ For questions or permissions, please contact um.press.perms@umich.edu

Published in the United States of America by the
University of Michigan Press
First published November 2025

A CIP catalog record for this book is available from the British Library.

Library of Congress Control Number: 2025013940

ISBN 978-0-472-07773-1 (hardcover: alk. paper)
ISBN 978-0-472-05773-3 (paper: alk. paper)
ISBN 978-0-472-90532-4 (open access ebook)

DOI: https://doi.org/10.3998/mpub.12778936

Cover image: *Idiom*, 2024. Real time voice generated by Artificial Intelligence, golden LED screen masks. Courtesy of the artist; Galerie Esther Schipper. Photo credit: Andrea Rossetti © Pierre Huyghe.

Publication was subsidized in part by Harvard Studies in Comparative Literature and in part by support from the Berkeley Research Impact Initiative (BRII) sponsored by the UC Berkeley Library.

The University of Michigan Press's open access publishing program is made possible thanks to additional funding from the University of Michigan Office of the Provost and the generous support of contributing libraries.

Authorized Representative: Easy Access System Europe, Mustamäe tee 50, 10621 Tallinn, Estonia, gpsr.requests@easproject.com

Contents

List of Illustrations   ix

Introduction: The Pygmalion Myth in Technology   1
    What Is Artificial Humanities?
    When Machine Speaks
    The History of the Pygmalion Myth
    When Galatea Speaks
    Overview of the Book

Chapter 1: Inventing New Elizas   31
    1.1 Shaw's Heritage
    1.2 The Turing Test
    1.3 The Eliza Effect
    1.4 Relationality
    1.5 Becoming Human
    1.6 Language-Centeredness in AI
    1.7 Machine Speech Training
    1.8 Artificial Humanities: Language Enhancement

Chapter 2: Illusions of Social Robotics   75
   2.1 Social Robots: Hanson's Sophia
   2.2 Pygmalion's Perspective
      2.2.1 Context: Makavejev
      2.2.2 Periphery: Šeligo
   2.3 Both Sides Now: Nešković
   2.4 Galatea's Perspective
      2.4.1 Speak, Galatea: Feminist Authors
   2.5 Nonhuman Perception: Lem
   2.6 Artificial Humanities: In Search of the Nonhuman
      2.6.1 Linguistic Execution: Jonze
      2.6.2 Visual Execution: Garland

Chapter 3: Pygmalionism and Paralysis in Medical Ethics   112
   3.1 Pygmalionism in the Medical and Legal Literature
      3.1.1 Literary References
      3.1.2 Sexology
      3.1.3 Law
      3.1.4 Psychology
   3.2 Modern Pygmalions
      3.2.1 Virtual Beings
      3.2.2 Pygmalionesque Psychotherapy: Gillespie
   3.3 Galatean Paralysis
      3.3.1 Moore
      3.3.2 Sheldon
   3.4 Literature and Medical Ethics
      3.4.1 Locked-in: Vigand and Bauby
      3.4.2 Asimov and Technology Ethics
   3.5 Artificial Humanities: Building Ethically

Chapter 4: Language in Humans, Hybrids, and Machines   144
   4.1 Humans: A Conceptual History of Language
      4.1.1 A Commentary on Human Exclusivity in Language
   4.2 Hybrids: Shelley
   4.3 Machines: Powers
   4.4 Artificial Humanities: Changing Concepts

Chapter 5: Machine Writing   176

    5.1 Large Language Models

        5.1.1 Structure is All You Need

    5.2 Literary Market: Dahl

    5.3 Literary Criticism: Tomažin

    5.4 Writing Literature: Kehlmann and Allado-McDowell

    5.5 Artificial Humanities: Centering Fiction

Conclusion: A Program for Artificial Humanities   209

    6.1 AI Tropes

    6.2 What Artificial Humanities Offers to STEM

    6.3 The Role of Literary Studies

Notes   221

Bibliography   251

Index   285

Digital materials related to this title can be found on the Fulcrum platform via the following citable URL: https://doi.org/10.3998/mpub.12778936

Illustrations

Fig. 1	Joseph Faber's Euphonia from the mid-nineteenth century.	12
Fig. 2	Jean-Léon Gérôme's painting *Pygmalion et Galatée*. 1890.	22
Fig. 3	Bernard Shaw's shorthand of *Pygmalion: The Phonetic Play*, 14 (Buckley 30).	35
Fig. 4	Sketch of the Turing test (by the author).	38
Fig. 5	An example of my (*) conversation with Eliza (>) from May 2018.	48
Fig. 6	Édouard Manet's *Olympia* (1865), portraying a nude white woman with a confrontational gaze—all identifying markers of a courtesan.	60
Fig. 7	The inner structure of a generative adversarial network model, where two neural networks (generator and discriminator) compete against each other in the form of a zero-sum game. Figure modified from Beguš and Zhou, courtesy of Gašper Beguš.	68
Fig. 8	A scene in the film *Pygmalion* (1938), where Higgins feeds Eliza chocolates as a reward and motivation to keep practicing the pronunciation of vowels.	73

x *Illustrations*

Fig. 9	The photo depicts the human improv performer standing in front of the avatar of chatbot Pyggy, short for Pygmalion (from Mathewson and Mirowski 69).	80
Figs. 10–12	Screenshots: Eliza from *Pygmalion* (1938), Ava from *Ex Machina* (2014), Sophia on the Jimmy Fallon Show (2018).	82
Fig. 13	Sophia behind the scenes. The photo is from her Instagram account (@realsophiarobot) from June 19, 2019.	83
Fig. 14	Dušan Makavejev's *Anthony's Broken Mirror*: The mannequin as seen through the window.	87
Fig. 15	Dušan Makavejev's *Anthony's Broken Mirror*: Anthony and the living statue interact through the window.	88
Fig. 16	Dušan Makavejev's *Don't Believe in Monuments*: A young woman kissing a statue of a man in the park.	89
Figs. 17–18	Matjaž Klopčič, *The Triptych of Agata Schwarzkobler [Triptih Agate Schwarzkobler]* (1996). When Agata's coworkers violently tear her clothes off to check for the signs of witchery, she gives the camera a knowing glance.	93
Figs. 19–22	The gesture of touching Galatea's head is used in Klopčič to make Galatea succumb to Pygmalion's desires. Compare these images of the man aggressively grasping Agata's face and making her return his gaze to the images of Eliza Doolittle, Sophia, and Ava (Figures 10–12), in which Galateas are treated with gentleness, wonder, and admiration.	94
Fig. 23	Factual example: Masayuki Ozaki and his silicone doll in Tokyo. Photo taken on May 9, 2017 by Behrouz Mehri/AFP.	126
Fig. 24	Fictional example: Lars and his silicone doll from *Lars and the Real Girl* (2007).	126
Fig. 25	Approaches in artificial humanities.	214

Introduction: The Pygmalion Myth in Technology

Artificial Intelligence (AI) is an umbrella term coined in 1956[1] for data-based, intelligent, and dynamic learning systems that are nowadays penetrating all imaginable domains. We are often reminded of the fact that our scientific, technical, social, and other deeply human systems ascend to the unprecedented power of machines. There seems to be a crisis of what engineering has come to be with machine learning as well as a crisis of what machines have come to be with their newly acquired capability to learn. These developments are inherently stimulative conceptually, philosophically, ethically. And yet, why does imagining AI evoke killer robots in most people? What is the disjunction between how we imagine AI systems and their actual development? What is the role of our imaginary and fictions in this space?

This book looks at humanlike representations of AI as portrayed in literature and film. Fictional examples are juxtaposed with language technologies, ranging from chatbots, virtual assistants, virtual beings, social robots, and communicative neurotechnology to large language models. All these technologies are powered by AI today and largely (and mistakenly) represent AI as a whole in the public sphere. Fictional representations stand as our touchstone, giving us a tangible way of imagining the future, our dreams and our fears. Often presented as a cautionary tale, humanlike AI in fiction often limits, instead of expands, our collective imagination. This book argues that fictional scripts have shaped AI development through their immense cultural power on this particular set of technologies, even when the imaginary is far removed from the actual technologies.

The book proposes a framework, termed artificial humanities, where AI is informed by the arts and humanities, resulting in fairer, deeper, and more important work on all sides. Artificial humanities aspires to leverage the power of fiction as a compelling and captivating public medium for exploring new ideas and possibilities. Contemporary public debates around AI, as well as private spaces of its creation, commonly bring up fictional examples and even make use of fiction to make sense of the new conditions enabled by novel technologies. Literary, film and media scholarship can not only weigh in on these issues but actively help us all—technologists, technology users, and collateral participants in the society—discuss and choose the next steps. As Raymond Williams told us back in the 1970s, technological determinism has become widespread and orthodox. The study of society and culture remains pushed to the side even when it is widely accepted that every technology, and AI in particular, is created by intertwined technical and social factors. Humanities remain left out of this interaction, with the slight exception of AI ethics. Artificial humanities brings a broader humanities discourse into technological spaces, showing that building, designing, and interacting with AI requires a knowledge of the machine *and* the human.

The culture around AI has oscillated between hype and naysaying since the technology was first imagined. Radical technologies have always evoked radical reactions. The problem lies, in many ways, between the industry world and the scholarly reception of their work. The inventor is often not the best person to judge their invention. A powerful conceptual critique is necessary, but so is action. The implementation of findings is needed already at the building phase of AI. A fruitful collaboration between the inventor and the critic seems unlikely since their goals, approaches, and often also worldviews are entirely different. However, with technology like conversational AI, the time for critique has run out. To establish the discourse, we first need to get on the same level, establish common goals, and finally experiment. Only then we can act on the basis of our common findings.

One aspect that the humanities bring into technology spaces is to learn from the past lessons, especially since places like Silicon Valley like "to pretend its ideas don't have any history" (Daub 4). Their talk is different from the walk, and the pace of the walk is too fast for a deep conversation and reflection. Over the past decade, the information technology industry has developed and widely implemented deep learning and language models, social networks and smart phones, home assistants and neurotechnological communicative prostheses, often with a degree of philosophical naivety. While this particular work of artificial humanities does not explore the history of technology as such, it aims to uncover the under researched relationship between the AI technology and its representation.

AI technologies precede the thought not only in their potential implications but also in their very use. Technology used to be made differently: the idea used to precede the practice. The social contract concerning the technology's application remained a gradual process that pre-existed its broader use. Even if the repercussions of a technology could not be foreseen, we were able to debate about the technological uses before they were even invented or at least applied. This time we are facing the opposite challenge of flying the allegorical plane while we build it.

AI calls for a philosophy, a philosophy that informs its design and use, a philosophy that precedes its creation. We have entered a period of co-agency with advanced information technologies, a collaboration between humans and machines that will change both parties to the core. The shift enabled by learning, networked, and creative machines left us bereft of appropriate words to describe this technological and philosophical transformation. The Pygmalion myth, which serves as the framework for the investigation of AI representations, sends a clear message. With AI, machines have become a new kind of entity, for which we are still lacking a description. As we stutter to describe them, we turn back to what we know: ourselves.

This turn back to the human includes the stories we tell of ourselves—our fictions. This book analyzes the effect of our collective imaginary (Jasanoff and Kim 3) through fiction, palpable both in the way we build AI and the way we think about it. Bringing together actual AI technologies by exposing their conceptual substratum shows how artificial humanities can be directly useful to practitioners as well as critics, bringing them together rather than keeping them apart.

What Is Artificial Humanities?

The overarching argument of artificial humanities is that human-based academic disciplines are tailored for analyzing interactive AI systems, and in particular conversational AI. We cannot understand and interpret AI without understanding and interpreting humans. Literary studies, incorporating theoretical criticism and the study of cultural history, have explored what it means to be human for centuries. As the concept of the human is being increasingly reflected in highly technical domains, with AI at the forefront, we need a subject area that can accommodate these discussions—a framework termed as artificial humanities.

Artificial humanities is a critical and generative concept built around close readings of myths and stories, paralleled in this book with most recent language technologies. Aside from disciplines, such as science and technology studies, history of science, and history of technology, technology looms large among the objects of study in history, literary, film, and media studies, gender and race studies, disability studies, rhetoric, philosophy, and many strictly humanistic fields. In order to enter the making of technologies, however, scholars of these fields need to understand the technological challenges at stake and be able to fashion our deep humanities knowledge in a way that is relevant to technology builders. Everybody benefits when we meet halfway. The responsibility of making these technologies is too big for the technologists to bear it alone.

As has already been pointed out by AI ethicists, data sets and algorithms inherently consist of social biases. AI ethics, AI safety, and AI regulation are just three of the most prominent branches where AI and the humanities intersect. We all understand that we need to become more agile in adapting to the changing reality that AI brings into all of our systems, from purely technical to overwhelmingly human. Data science of the past decade was suited for quantitative social studies. Interactive AI systems, however, are tailored for humanities both at the stage of design and at the stage of human-computer interaction. Artificial humanities brings into view a whole other set of issues related to AI, which have to do with representations and interpretations of AI that tacitly inform our ideas and actions.

What is the role of fiction in this imaginary? Imagination is a cognition that allows us to go beyond constraints. Fiction serves as the cultural repository of scenarios and playfield of ideas,[2] which is, I argue here, just as influential when it comes to AI creation and utilization as are other sociotechnical imaginaries.[3] Fiction makes a major contribution to a fabricated or actualized technology when presenting and questioning it, commonly outgrowing its abstract space and turning it into major cultural symbols. In this framework, literature's aesthetic and artistic function is set aside on the account of the possibilities and opportunities enabled by ideas presented in fiction, both a public and personal space of reflection. This book shows how social epistemology of fiction contributed to technology-making from the nineteenth century to the twenty-first century—throughout the lifespan of the modern concept of technology.

As a starting and common point of this investigation, the book is framed within an ancient Greek tale, known as the Pygmalion myth, in which a man crafts a statue of a woman and falls in love with it. Depending on the modern rendition of the myth, the inanimate woman either transforms into a real human being or remains eternally anthropomorphized, trapped between her nonhuman origin and human image. The myth has grown to be an increasingly central fable in modernity, particularly in Western literature and visual arts (Gross xi), together with its related myths of Prometheus and Narcissus.

In literary studies, the Pygmalion myth has been a subject of a lot of interest,[4] and lately has outgrown its fictional origins by becoming one of the main tropes of imagining AI. This book attempts to make up for the largely disregarded investigations of the myth in relation to AI-powered technologies.[5]

I argue that the humanlike direction of AI evolution took place partly because of our cultural conceptualizations of AI. Fiction—conceived broadly in this book from the printed book to visual media with fictional narratives, such as film and television—contributed to and amplified the excitement around the humanlike AI. Building up to my main argument, each chapter shows how the humanlike trajectory of AI fails to recognize the antagonistic nature of the humanlike model. The limitations of this approach were widely overlooked across domains, until today. The book suggests and outlines the direction for AI technologies of the twenty-first century as going beyond the human. Even if we might perceive the AI system as humanlike, it is essential to conceptualize, build, and use AI as a fundamentally nonhuman agent. In order to shed off the Pygmalionesque ballast we all implicitly foster, we need the humanities at the table.

Looking beyond the human perspective has been a popular position in the last decades of humanities debates, starting from the 1980s on and labeled with the terms anthropocentrism, posthumanism, the anthropocene, and similar. The overarching posthumanist argument battling restrictive humanism—prominently discussed by Kate Hayles, Cary Wolfe, Donna Haraway, Rosi Braidotti—shares considerable common ground with the exploration I undertake here in order to move beyond simple human imitation in AI. In the concluding sections of each chapter, I outline strategies to navigate away from the human mimicking and projections, exposed in the rest of the book. The crux of the book delves into these somewhat peculiar tendencies we display in the creation and utilization of AI technology, guided by our collective desires.[6]

While the book might be permeated with the spirit of posthumanism, it is on a different quest from a typical posthumanist academic work: this is not a dialectical examination of posthumanist strengths and faults but rather a more practical approach of applying a humanist thought to technology practice. The ultimate goal of this research is to establish interdisciplinary collaborative bridges among the disciplines that have not yet been able to do so. The specific topic of conversational AI and its challenges in the focus of this book are just one possible approach in artificial humanities: the programmatic nature of the book is certainly open to a wider variety of approaches, including artistic and social practices.

Studying language and humanity is at the heart of humanities. We tend to underestimate the power that humanities ideas hold in the actionable world.

Many different streams of thought were born from the posthuman discussions, including transhumanist aspirations, championed by many technologists.[7] Transhumanists believe in technological singularity and optimistically see technology as being able to enhance our body and overcome our own biological limitations. Since artificial humanities finds it crucial to analyze the representations, understandings, and interpretations of AI, this includes tracing the trajectory of academic ideas that have transitioned into the tech industry and gained a life of their own, often adopting a more simplified and practical guise compared to their original theoretical depth in scholarly circles. Ideas can be just as powerful as technological tools, even if their price and agency in the world are often misconstrued.

I offer an entry point to artificial humanities by focusing on fictional and factual language technologies. Following the development of talking and writing machines—Erasmus Darwin's speaking machine, Charles Babbage's analytical engine, Thomas Edison's phonograph, Alexander Bell's telephone, Alan Turing's computer, Joseph Weizenbaum's chatbot, Steve Job's virtual assistant, David Hanson's social robot, OpenAI's large language model—this book shows how the conceptualization of these products by and large follows the humanlike components. Chapter 1 presents chatbots and virtual assistants, Chapter 2 social robots, Chapter 3 addresses Pygmalionism through the techno-medical lens, Chapter 4 discusses the concept of language from a theoretical standpoint, and Chapter 5 presents large language models (LLMs) in a conceptual light, looking both at the history and the future of machine writing and creativity. Each chapter analyzes a few literary works, ranging from the nineteenth-century to the twenty-first century, that tackle a particular challenge pertinent to these language technologies today.

The texts discussed come predominantly from the American literary space (Frances Sargent Locke Osgood, Elizabeth Stuart Phelps Ward, Eliza C. Hall, Dorothy Alyea, Leonora Clawson Stryker, Genevieve Taggard, C. L. Moore, Isaac Asimov, Alice Sheldon [pseud. James Tiptree Jr.], Richard Powers, K Allado-McDowell, Blaise Agüera y Arcas) and American cinematic space (Spike Jonze, Alex Garland, Craig Gillespie), as well as British and Irish texts (Mary Shelley, Roald Dahl, Robert Graves, George Bernard Shaw, Emily Hickey, Eiléan Ní Chuilleanáin, and other poets). I also include a German essay, yet unpublished in English (Daniel Kehlmann), French memoirs (Jean-Dominique Bauby, Philippe Vigand) and plays (Stéphanie Félicité de Genlis, Germaine de Staël), a Polish short story (Stanisław Lem), a Slovenian short story (Andrej Tomažin) and novel (Rudi Šeligo), and a Serbian short story and two short films (Zoran Nešković, Dušan Makavejev); with all Slovenian and Serbian works yet untranslated into English.

Why language? In the examination of humanlike technologies today, language and intelligence are the most contested human attributes, the latter being often represented through language and reasoning. The twenty-first century is the first time in history when human languages have been used by machines on a humanlike level and in numbers that outpace humans. AI, still at the level of being constantly re-imagined and re-invented, is changing the landscape of language with its newly acquired nonhuman agency. Human language is not just ours anymore, and yet we tend to disregard the philosophical stakes of this colossal transformation. Machines co-creating human language and operating through it is not just a change of medium, but a change of language user and interlocutor. It is a language change of a philosophical nature, a conceptual shift that changes how we think about humans and technology, individually and together. This topic therefore needs more attention in the disciplines of philosophy, linguistics, anthropology, rhetoric, cultural studies, computer science, and beyond. Literature, a product of language, has a lot to say here.

Literary studies have not been included into the science and technology studies (STS) discourse on sociotechnical imaginaries although AI models are increasingly cultural machines. Through data AI is being trained on, the models can powerfully imitate cultural simulacra and their embedded values and biases (see also Yiu et al. and Clark 'ImportAI' making similar claims in 2023 and 2024). A better sociotechnical future should be acted upon comparatively, as I argue in the essay thematizing the engagement of comparative literature in AI development (Beguš 'Engaging' 4):

> Comparative literature is the only humanities discipline that brings into view a set of languages, literatures, cultures, and practices. They all flow into AI as an artifact with a unique agency. AI is ultimately a series of human decisions and interactions. Each culture instills different values in these systems, and it has become clear that this is not solely a task for engineers and other technologists. AI is limited as much by our imagination—and by extension, history, fiction, philosophy—as it is by technical challenges.

When Machine Speaks

Mythologies are rife with artificial humans. Just in ancient Greek mythology, we find craftsmen like Daedalus, who made living bronze statues and installed them with voice, and we find gods like Hephaestus, who created Talos, an automaton that protected Crete from invaders. The Greek myths of Pygmalion, Prometheus,[8] and Narcissus[9]—all included in Ovid's *Metamorphoses*—have been singled out as central tropes for addressing human relation to what has been known in modernity as technology. The Pygmalion myth, however, is the most gendered of the three myths: Pygmalion bears the Promethean inventiveness only in male characters who create an object of humanlike perfection, always of the female gender.

Pygmalion, a legendary sculptor and a king of Cyprus, is most familiar from Ovid's *Metamorphoses* (8 CE). The myth is first mentioned in Philostephanus's now lost *History of Cyprus* from the early third century BCE as a local legend from Cyprus,[10] but it is Ovid who presents the act of metamorphosis to the myth (Reinhold 316). Modern reinterpretations of the myth in literature and visual arts all follow Ovid, who expanded and dramatized the story from the original source.[11] In Ovid's version, sculptor Pygmalion, with godly help of animation, enters into a fruitful marriage[12] with an animated statue he carved, which later gained the name Galatea. By portraying a man who carves a perfect statue of a woman out of discontent over actual, fleshly women, Ovid opened questions about creation, art, love, desire, loneliness, misogyny, and who gets to be human, to name just a few of the most prominent ones. All these questions have increasingly gained resonance two millennia later. This book demonstrates how the Pygmalion myth became a central space for modern reconfigurations of the human and the machine and, in the twentieth century, for our conceptions of possibilities enabled by AI.

In a variety of mythological accounts across the world that deal with human creation, a divinity uses mud, dust, or clay to mold the human race. Many Galateas followed Ovid's statuesque ideal. Initial sculpting materials transformed into flesh are ivory, marble, and precious metals. Some of the materials come from an organic source: ivory comes from teeth and tusks of animals, and marble comes from limestone, which is made of accumulated organic debris. Precious metals like gold, silver, and bronze gain value through a trade system, the way money gains value through a system of exchange. The development of the electronics industry made gold and silver conductors for both electricity and heat. The Pygmalion myth tradition connects the meanings behind the chosen Galatean material with the tradition behind it: all of these materials signal great value.

Nathaniel Hawthorne's 'The Golden Touch' (1851) features a popular *reverse* Pygmalion effect, in which King Midas, also featured in Ovid's *Metamorphoses*, turns everything he touches into gold. Hawthorne introduces a new character to Ovid's story, Midas's daughter Marygold, whom Midas's magical golden touch transforms from a human being into a golden statue: "It had been a favorite phrase of Midas, whenever he felt particularly fond of the child, to say that she was worth her weight in gold. And now the phrase has become literally true" (62). The story's interest with the literal act of speaking—as "Marygold made no answer" frozen into a golden body—mirrors the concerns of Hawthorne's era. As the nineteenth century ushered in the development of speaking machines, it prompted society to grapple with the implications of these innovations, the production of sounds and speech, and the nature of communication itself. How he will ever communicate with Marygold again is a question that occurs to King Midas only when he realizes the extent of his loss. Every Galatea, as a matter of fact, fills a void as a reaction to a profound sense of loss.

Tracing the Pygmalion myth in its historical visual and textual occurrences reveals when and under what circumstances arose the technological interpretation of Pygmalionesque motifs. This book is in search of the Ovidian tradition even when it seems to have broken off. The nineteenth century introduces Pygmalionesque creations that cannot be categorized because they truly stand between the human and the other: E. T. A. Hoffmann's Olympia from 1817 is an automaton that moves and sighs, Mary Shelley's Frankenstein's creature from 1818 is a mash-up of electrified human remains, and Nathaniel Hawthorne's Rappaccini's daughter Beatrice from 1844 is a human experimented upon with plant poisons. Their creators—Coppelius, Frankenstein, and Rappaccini—are still eccentric alchemists. By the end of the nineteenth century, however, true Pygmalionesque technology was born. Auguste Villiers de l'Isle-Adam introduced the term android in his novel *The Future Eve* [*L'Ève Future*] (begun writing in 1878, published in 1886). The android named Hadaly is a product of fictionalized engineer Thomas Edison and is created for Edison's desperate friend as a replacement for his human fiancée. From the late nineteenth century on, it becomes almost expected to find another eccentric engineer that creates artificial women—in fiction and reality.

Even though we can point to a single text in which Galatea starts speaking and even though there is a single text in which Galatea is made in a completely technological manner, the Pygmalionesque tradition had prepared the ground for both events. The inspiration for Villiers de l'Isle-Adam's story is clear: Alexander Graham Bell patented a telephone in 1876 and a year later, when the real Thomas Edison invented a phonograph, Villiers de l'Isle-Adam started writing his novel. A decade after inventing and working on the phonograph, Edison called his sound capture machine "perfected." Edison's machine was subsequently improved by Bell's laboratory and renamed into a graphophone, later known as a gramophone and record player. With the emergence of science and technology, language was under dissection, as was everything else. As discussed in Chapter 4, language was traditionally viewed as an expression of the soul and was technified in writing, let alone with writing technologies. Stenography—writing down speech in shorthand—in the 1880s and 1890s contributed to language being viewed as less of an expression of a human soul and more of a technicality. Now Edison's and Bell's audial inventions revolutionized the power of speech itself: for the first time in history, a voice could travel across great distances and be captured in a recording.

What was the trajectory leading towards Edison's phonograph and Bell's telephone? Steered clear of fiction but not imagination, many inventors of the eighteenth and nineteenth centuries attempted to build their own speaking machines. Erasmus Darwin, Wolfgang von Kempelen, and Charles Wheatstone are the most well-known inventors, while Joseph Faber remains less recognized but no less interesting.

Erasmus Darwin's device was a valuable invention in exploring the human vocal apparatus. Darwin began this exploration by attempting to improve the shorthand of writing down sounds on paper and continued by developing a physical imitation of the larynx already in the 1770s. It is not known if the device was actually built. In his 1803 scientific poem *Temple of Nature*, under the final note titled *Analysis of Articulate Sounds*, he explained the workings of the device (367):

> I contrived a wooden mouth with lips of soft leather, and with a vale back part of it for nostrils, both which could be quickly opened or closed by the pressure of the fingers, the vocality was given by a silk ribbon about an inch long and a quarter of an inch wide stretched between two bits of smooth wood a little hollowed; so that when a gentle current of air from bellows was blown on the edge of the ribbon, it gave an agreeable tone, as it vibrated between the wooden sides, much like a human voice.

Darwin had a personal interest in the origins of language. As with the creators of Galateas, his speaking machine was created to make up for something that was lost, in this case, fluent speech: Darwin himself and some of his children were stutterers. Erasmus sought stutter treatment for his eldest son, Charles (father of the famous Charles Darwin), and sent him abroad to France in order "to break the force of habit, formed on the contagion of daily example" (Shell 14). He believed that "in the pronunciation of a foreign language, hesitation would be less likely to recur, than in speaking those words and sentences in which he had been accustomed to hesitate" (67)—and it worked: stuttering is known to diminish with a change of accent, language, or mode (e.g. singing). Not surprisingly, Erasmus Darwin's machine could sing a song—a common Galatean feature. Charles Darwin, son of stutterer Charles Darwin and grandson of stutterer Erasmus, believed that human ancestors first used language in the form of singing (33). The debates around the origin of language have surely permeated the making of talking machines, whose ultimate goal was to inspect and replicate the emergence of speech.

The space for a spectacle was being laid for the inventors of speaking machines by the popularization of automata exhibitions in eighteenth-century France. The most well-known automata from the time are the Jacquet-Droz family's writer, musician, and draftsman figures and Jacques Vaucanson's flute player, as well as the early-nineteenth-century Maillardet brothers' magicians. Wolfgang von Kempelen is most known for his hoax of a chess-playing automaton, The Mechanical Turk, which was operated by a person hidden under the table. (Today's microwork platform Amazon MTurk is named after this famous trick because tasks on-demand are performed by a number of people behind the screen.)

Wolfgang von Kempelen's speaking machine took more effort—decades—to complete. Once finished in 1804, it ended up imitating the human vocal tract, like Darwin's. The machine could not 'speak' German, but spoke French, Italian, and Latin. It would say things like "you are my friend—I love you with all my heart—Leopoldus Secundus—Romanorum Imperator—Semper Augusts—dad, mom, my wife, my husband, the king, let's go to Paris,"[13] which, per Mladen Dolar, show "the declaration of love and the praise for the ruler [...] displaying the posture of devotion; the machine's voice is used to declare its submission" (8). Speaking flat, with no prosody, the machine design was improved by Charles Wheatstone in 1837. Wheatstone raised a general interest in the science of phonetics, also in the young Alexander Graham Bell, one of the key inventors leading us to George Bernard Shaw.

A century before these speech machines were imagined or built, the idea of a machine composing textual verse was proposed in the form of an advanced calculation of words—by means of arithmetic and not literature—in John Peter's 1677 pamphlet, *Artificial Versifying, or the Schoolboy's Recreation* (Rodgers 6). This instrumentation of poetry, which adhered to both meter and automatic composition of words, served as the foundation for John Clark's 1845 Eureka machine. Eureka generated metrical lines in Latin, boasting an estimated 26 million permutations of the syntactic formula (Hall 227). The Victorian obsession with reciting poetry contributed to the widespread appeal of Eureka, which stood in stark contrast to another speech-generating automaton, Joseph Faber's Euphonia. Euphonia was exhibited across Europe and the United States around the same time, but failed to garner the same level of enthusiasm.

Although Euphonia wears a female-sounding name, Faber initially visualized the speaking device as an exoticized Turk (not unlike von Kempelen's Mechanical Turk). Faber sometimes used the head of a man in a Turkish costume and other times portraying a more Galatean outfit of a female head with or without a dress. The change might have been made at the suggestion of an early observer from 1845, who wrote in *New York Paper* that he "immediately suggested to Mr. F[aber] by the way, that the costume and figure had better have been female, as the *bustle* would have given a well-placed and ample concealment for all the machinery now disenchantingly placed outside—the performer sitting down naturally behind, and playing on her piano" (276). Thanks to Ovid's erotic undertones in his famous rendition of the Pygmalion myth, its reinterpretations often evoke erotic imagery, even if it is not directly

Fig. 1. Joseph Faber's Euphonia from the mid-nineteenth century. WikiMedia Commons, public domain.

encouraged by the creator of the work. The anonymous author of this observation links it to Kempelen's machine and to the famous medieval automaton called the Brazen Head, half-alchemic half-mechanical question-answering oracle, attributed to various scholars (in this case, Robert Bacon). In the conclusion, he again takes the Pygmalionesque route, ending in a speculation about these devices leading up to what we could today call AI (276):

> Something in the Phygmalion line has been attempted within a few years by a Swiss mechanic, Maillardet, who constructed a female with a bosom that would heave for an hour, once wound up. She could also play forty tunes on the piano with her fingers, and look languishingly by casting her eyes down—almost enough for one woman to do. I think these are facts enough for a very pretty speculative essay on the value of such offices as may be performed by the body without the aid of brains.

Faber's Euphonia was "probably the most loquacious pneumatic speaking machine ever made," in which "fourteen [sic: sixteen] keys, laid out like a piano, controlled the disposition of the jaw, lips, and tongue, while a bellows and ivory reed fulfilled the roles of the lungs and larynx" (Hankins and Silverman 214). While her creator was playing on the keys, the device spoke in German, English, or French (the latter two with a German accent due to its German-speaking maker) and sang 'God Save the Queen'. The main problem with Euphonia's voicing was a flat intonation, like with Wheatstone's machine. Joseph Henry suggested connecting it with the telegraph: "The keys could be worked by means of electromagnetic magnets and with a little contrivance not difficult to execute words might be spoken at one end of the telegraphic line which have their origin at the other" (362). Much to Faber's disappointment Euphonia had only a few devotees, but he never learned they were the right ones. American electrical engineer and scientist Joseph Henry preferred Faber's speaking machine to Wheatstone's more recognized invention because Euphonia was "capable of speaking whole sentences composed of any words what ever" (Henry 362). It was Henry who introduced Euphonia to the Bell family.

Scottish actor turned phonetician Alexander Bell created a streak of elocution teachers called Alexander Bell. His son, Alexander Melville Bell, admired Faber's and Wheatstone's speaking machines and challenged his son, Alexander Graham Bell, to build his own talking machine. The son invented the telephone and the graphophone, the improved version of Thomas Edison's phonograph. Melville Bell, the father, had an interest in speech himself: he designed a phonetic alphabet, called Visible Speech, that indicates how to articulate sounds, which is why it was mostly used to teach deaf people to speak.

Professional interest in deafness and speech intertwined with the personal lives of the Bells. Alexander Melville Bell had a hard-of-hearing wife, Eliza Grace Symonds, who began losing hearing at age 12.[14] Their son Alexander Graham Bell had a deaf wife, Mabel Gardiner Hubbard, who completely lost her hearing at age five. "That the hearing-impaired people closest to Melville Bell and his famous son were their respective wives adds an uncomfortably gendered Pygmalionesque cast to their efforts" (Buckley 27). Seeing some humans as less-than is a prominent Pygmalionesque trait, which is why the disability discourse is prevalent with Galateas. As examined in more detail in Katie Booth's 2021 monograph on Alexander Graham Bell, written from the deaf perspective, the telephone inventor believed that the deaf community should be integrated into the hearing world by speech and not sign language. Bell's misguided belief of deafness as a deficit stems from his interest in the mere technicalities of hearing. "Your deaf mute business is hardly human to you," writes Bell's wife Mabel to him in 1895. "You are very tender and gentle to the deaf children, but their interest to you lies in their being deaf not in their humanity, at least only in part."

This adds a familiar layer to the Pygmalion myth trajectory, resulting in the dehumanization of the Galatea: the object of study, the object of creation and desire. The perceived loss is supplanted by technology, reflecting the pervasive idea that a technology can fix our social problems, "the wishing on technology," as Paul Duguid and John Seely Brown call it. Machine—or a Galatea—"makes up for some missing or inadequate part" and serves both as a "commemorative monument" and a "godlike annexation" (Ronell 88). These Pygmalionesque responses of replacing a perceived loss or deficit align with Ovid's Pygmalion, who substitutes actual women with a living statue. Alongside fictional Pygmalions, the myth is also captured in authors' personal stories and interests or at times even in technologists' aspirations. Erasmus Darwin, for example, tries to cure his and his children's stutters by learning more about the way humans speak through the creation of an early speaking machine, following the human mouth apparatus.

Computers—the ultimate talking and writing machine of the contemporary—were being created in the first half of the nineteenth century simultaneously with speaking machines. Charles Babbage, with Ada Lovelace's epistolary collaboration, described the first general-purpose, steam-powered, programmable computer, called the Analytical Engine (1837). Babbage is considered the father of the computer,[15] even though he never built his engine and even though the concept of a general-purpose computer had not existed yet. (It was first defined a century later by Alan Turing.) The Analytical Engine is based on his mechanical calculator, called the Difference Engine, on which he worked in the 1820s. Babbage was not a successful inventor. He managed to get funders interested in his work, but failed to deliver. His followers continued to build on his work, and failed to deliver working machines as well. In his obituary in *Nature*, his efforts were marked as "hardly [...] capable of practical realization" (29). Babbage's goal was largely to improve John Napier's logarithmic tables—to make them more reliable and, hopefully, automate the tedious calculations with an engine. Finding error after error, he wrote in 1821: "I wish to God these calculations had been executed by steam!" (Collier 14–18, Buxton and Hyman 46).[16]

As a boy, Babbage attended "several exhibitions of machinery" and was once invited by the inventor John Joseph Merlin to take a look around his workshop with "still more wonderful automata" (*Passages* 12):

> There were two uncovered female figures of silver, about twelve inches high. One of these walked or rather glided along a space of about four feet, when she turned around and went back to her original place. She used an eye-glass occasionally, and bowed frequently, as if recognizing her acquaintances. The motions of her limbs were singularly graceful.
>
> The other silver figure was an admirable *danseuse*, with a bird on the forefinger of her right hand, which wagged its tail, flapped its wings, and opened its beak. The lady attitudinized in a most fascinating manner. Her eyes were full of imagination, and irresistible. These silver figures were the chef-d'oeuvres of the artist: they had cost him years of unwearied labour, and were not even then finished.

Babbage recounts these events in his autobiography, *Passages from the Life of a Philosopher*, which he opens with a quote from *Don Juan* by Lord Byron, Ada Lovelace's father: "I am a philosopher. Confound them all—Birds, beasts, and men: but no, not womankind."[17] Babbage later managed to buy the dancing automaton he encountered in his youth and exhibited it in his home alongside his calculating machines. "The Silver Lady was clearly a seductive figure for Babbage, who referred to her as if she were alive and even had female friends create clothes for her" (Black 107). Another inventor was struck by the Galatean charm. Despite this anecdote, Babbage's goal for his engine was purely calculation, a continuation of John Napier's logarithmic tables and similar efforts to shorten and ease tedious mathematical work.

Babbage's student and collaborator Ada Lovelace, per some scholarly accounts, surpassed her teacher. Working as Babbage's collaborator on the Analytical Engine, Lovelace developed an algorithm for Babbage's design of the merely calculating machine. Babbage gave the computer the hardware mechanics and Lovelace gave it the program software. In relation to Babbage being seen as the father of the computer, Lovelace was recently reborn as the mother of computer programming,[18] even though no programming language had yet been invented in the mid-nineteenth century. While Babbage provided the concept and the design of a calculating machine, recognized today under the notion of universal computation, Lovelace used her analytical and metaphysical skills to create a foresightful programmable computer, capable of storing a sequence of operations (now known as the program) and informational values (later known as data). Lovelace anticipated that the machine might act upon something other than numbers if satisfying mathematical rules.[19] She suggested that the machine could create new discoveries "which we might not otherwise have thought of obtaining" even though she did not believe that the machine could have original ideas: "The Analytical Engine has no pretensions to *originate* anything. It can do *whatever we know how to order it* to perform. It can *follow* analysis; but it has no power of *anticipating* any analytical relations or truths. Its province is to assist us in making *available* what we are already acquainted with" (Toole 257–58). This is the traditional view of programming: that of human control and knowledge over the machine. The Galatean kind of programming, one could say, which came in place with the Industrial Revolution engineering.

In 1950, Alan Turing directly responded to Lovelace's objection in a paper that became fundamental for AI, titled 'Computing Machinery and Intelligence.' Turing claimed that a machine can be programmed to be original, by which he means to produce answers we cannot predict and thus are surprising to us (450–51). Hence the field of artificial intelligence was born. Refuting Lovelace's predictions on the originality of machines, Turing quoted English mathematician and physicist Douglas R. Hartree, with whom he wholeheartedly agreed: "This does not imply that it may not be possible to construct electronic equipment which will 'think for itself', or in which, in biological terms, one could set up a conditioned reflex, which would serve as a basis for 'learning'" (70). From the very beginning, AI was a pursuit of machines that are able to think and to learn.

The grounds for Pygmalionesque ideas about AI, demonstrated in Turing's 1950 paper, were set already with the human model attested in Babbage's childhood encounters with female automata figures. Soon after Turing's death in 1954, resulting from an inhumane treatment directed at his sexuality, AI was formed as a field. Just a decade later, in the mid-1960s, the first chatbot Eliza was ready to speak to humans. The hopes and the skepticism around AI were both always high. By the end of the twentieth century, AI triumphed in the game of chess. The technology continued to collect first prizes in language-based games in the twenty-first century, winning in Jeopardy! in 2011. More recently, AI offered moments of profound novelty by expanding its language abilities to the visual realm, solving the protein folding problem at a scale only available to computers, and trying to decode whale communication. The potential of these latter discoveries is overshadowed by AI acting as augmented humans. We can use this knowledge to outline more ethical, socially sensitive, and culturally productive ways of developing AI systems through artificial humanities.

The History of the Pygmalion Myth

Ovid's famous rendition from the early days of Imperial Rome was reinterpreted only a millennium later, already in slightly transformed terms.[20] In Ovid's version, Pygmalion prays to goddess Venus to miraculously animate his statue. In many medieval versions, however, the goddess herself is the statue.[21] Another change to the Ovidian proto-text occurs in some of these medieval versions: the medieval Pygmalion tends to be only the lover and no more the creator of the statue. The desire for the sculpture does not grow in the process of its making, but happens at first sight (Bleeke 34). This is important for a number of reasons, the first being that the delusion of a lover who is also a creator (father) is by default greater and incestuous. This typological shift between stories that focus on the creator who is also the lover of the creation as opposed to stories in which the creator is a separate character from the deluded lover is present throughout the chronology of the Pygmalion paradigm (Beguš 'Typology').

The Pygmalion myth emerged with force during the Renaissance's interest in the classics, for example, in Miguel de Cervantes's first book *La Galatea* (1585), John Marston's erotic poem *The Metamorphosis of Pygmalion's Image, and certaine Satyres* (1598), and William Shakespeare's play *The Tempest* (ca. 1610). With every century, the myth gained prominence across the arts and manifested itself through drawings (in the Medieval poem *Le Roman de la Rose*), statues (Étienne Maurice Falconet, Auguste Rodin, etc.), and paintings (Laurent Pêcheux, Edward Burne-Jones, and many others). The cinema became a prominent space of Pygmalionesque explorations, beginning with the earliest films by Georges Méliès in 1898. The twentieth century followed with the explosion of science fiction in American texts and screens.[22] Today's virtual assistants, social robots, sex dolls, virtual avatars and similar technologies represent only a small, materialized fraction of Pygmalionesque dreams.

It is the sheer power of fiction that an ancient myth can encompass a variety of artistic, scientific, and cultural themes that become essential to modernity. Tracing the myth from the times of ancient Rome to the modern West calls for a conceptual approach in the timeline of mythical transformations. The notions of *humanlike, artificial, machine,* and so on, operate in an exclusively modern space and cannot be applied to the original Ovidian myth. In this book, we largely stay in the modern view of the human as separated from nature and with technology as a unique human power. It is necessary to pay close attention to the conceptual presuppositions around some of the most basic concepts related to the human (intelligence, consciousness, mind, individual, subject) as well as oppositions in the binary concepts that order our world (creator-creation, natural-artificial, living-nonliving). Our modern conceptual constellations clearly cannot accommodate the twenty-first-century inventions anymore (Rees 10), and the Pygmalionesque myth shows how our conceptualization of the world permeated the way technology was thought about and built throughout the twentieth century.

The Pygmalion myth might not have held certain modern ideas when it was conceived, but it was able to reflect them in the variety of its renditions. We see them in the eighteenth-century debate about the role of the artist, in which the Pygmalion myth served as an example of the artistic potency of bringing life into lifeless materials. This is the theme of Edgar Allen Poe's 1842 'The Oval Portrait', in which the portrait of a maiden becomes "life itself" but sucks away her life in the process of its creation.[23] We can see the reflection of the myth in the birth of the uncanny, a psychological experience where something is strangely familiar and creepy at the same time. The concept of the uncanny was first explained by Ernst Jentsch in 1906 using an example of a canonical Pygmalionesque tale, E.T.A. Hoffmann's 'The Sandman' ['Der Sandmann'] (1816). Today, it is commonly applied to social robots, lifelike dolls, and other 3D humanoid objects due to the uncanny valley phenomenon, a hypothesized emotional response to humanoids that look imperfectly human, established by Masahiro Mori (1970). We can also see the reflection of the Pygmalion myth in contemporary application softwares, such as the Chinese virtual being company Gemsouls, thriving also in the North American market, that "bring[s] fictional beings to life [...] to stay forever connected to the people we love and hold so close to our hearts, fictional or real." The San Francisco start-up Digi is tailored specifically for romantic relationships with "your loving AI companion."

This powerful penetration of the Pygmalion myth into our contemporary perception of AI is historically traced and explained in the book, both in fictional and actual examples that follow the Pygmalion paradigm. Such historical exposure of the imagination that fed into the actual making of AI is the first step in how artificial humanities can address the issues at stake in AI technology today. We will delve into the origins and the history of AI representations alongside the origins and history of Galateas. Both AI and Galateas are frequently characterized as creations that mirror human behavior and intelligence. AI is not a person, however. Can we say the same for Galateas?

When Galatea Speaks

Who is Galatea and what changes when she speaks? Pygmalion's creation, originally in the form of a statue that comes to life, stands for any human-made and artificial woman, more or less full of life, that provokes romantic interest. The common choice for the gender dynamics of man as creator and woman as creation[24] is obvious: Galatean women have to be passive and submissive while men not only bring them into life but often also control or at least want to control their actions. Many scholars argue the Pygmalion myth brings forth, first and foremost, "male creativity naturalized through religious, artistic and scientific discourses" (Grubar 293), the "archetype [...] for the idea of male creative prowess" (Smith 199; also Yeates 588). Crucial to Galateas is that they inspire love with their perfect beauty. Amenable to their creator or suitor, mute and passive, they serve as an example of a perfect woman, subdued and subservient. This is why, in their pre-modern days, there was no need for language or a name: early Galateas went unnamed[25] and were not able to speak.[26] When acquiring language and a name in the eighteenth century, Galateas remained beautiful and charming but also developed more character and nuance: they became more humanlike with a mind of their own.

Some of the earliest Galatean words are spoken in André-François Boureau-Deslandes's influential philosophical tale, *Pygmalion, ou la Statue animée* (1741), which muses about the nature of the relationship between matter and mind. After the transformation, the unnamed statue proclaims herself fully alive to her lover: "At present [...] I can no longer doubt that I'm alive. What you call pleasure convinced me of my existence and of its reality. I'm certainly alive, since I'm intoxicated by life" (Deslandes in Coulet 64).[27] Deslandes's Galatea gradually acquires senses, a living soul, the power of movement, thought, and speech (DiMauro 190): "What am I, and what was I just a moment ago? I do not understand myself; I do not know myself. What is my purpose? Why was I pulled from nothingness?" (Deslandes in Coulet 60).[28] Deslandes's statue not only speaks—she is consciously experiencing the world.

Jean Jacques Rousseau's play *Pygmalion* (1762, first performed in 1770) builds on this gradual awakening and self-awareness. Rousseau and Deslandes seem to be influenced by John Locke's theory of mind: Locke's lengthy treatise, *An Essay Concerning the Human Understanding* (1689), marks the origin of modern conceptions of identity and the self. In the moment of her animation, Galathée points to herself and says, "Me [...] It's me." She continues by pointing at the marble—"No more I"—and responding to Pygmalion's kisses with "Ah! It's me again." Pygmalion's final words in the play are a response to Galathée's first words and make the link between the soul, possessed by humans only, and the object he created: "Yes, dear and charming object [...] It's you, it's your soul... I've given you everything... I can't live without you anymore [tran. author][29] (13–14). Galatea's first speech is brief as the play ends right there, with her first words.

Rousseau's depiction is broadly known as the first time she was also named even if it does not seem to be the actual first occurrence of Galatea's name in the Pygmalion myth.[30] Rousseau's source for the name, Meyer Reinhold claims, is the association with the pastoral tradition from the sixteenth and seventeenth centuries, in which Galatea, derived from Vergil's *Eclogues*, presents a "saucy, flirtatious, unattainable" figure (317–18).[31] Other scholars make a connection with another myth from Ovid's *Metamorphoses* of Acis and Galatea. This story features Galatea as an immortal sea-nymph who changes her lover Acis into an immortal river spirit. The association between the three types of Galateas is clear: they are all made for love.

While other types of Galateas were present with their name and speech in literature before the eighteenth century, Pygmalion's Galatea remained largely anonymous until Rousseau's popular 1770 play.[32] Helen Law found only three references in eighteenth-century French literature and none in English literature, with the exception of the English translation of Rousseau's play (341). While Law admittedly left much territory unexplored, which was remedied by other scholars,[33] French literature has crystallized as the birthplace of Galatea's modern name. Soon after Rousseau's play, other French writers followed suit.[34] The name became standardized in English literature a hundred years after Rousseau's play with W. S. Gilbert's famous play *Pygmalion and Galatea* (1871) (Joshua 34, 155), further cementing its prominence by using Galatea's name in titles of the paintings, such as those by French painter Jean-Léon Gérôme (1890).

Why did Pygmalion's woman, turned from ivory into flesh, gain a human name two millennia after her first textual actualization by Philostephanus from the third century BCE? Clearly, a name arose out of a need. The name is needed only for addressing the other, and the notion of selfhood is defined by otherness: self is the non-other. In order for Rousseau's Galathée to have a mind separate from a body, a whole new understanding of the body and the mind had to be invented. Per Locke, the mind is a memory storage of representations (called ideas or images) from which knowledge is accumulated and personal identity grows. The body, on the other hand, is a mechanical matter, no different from that of animals, as established by René Descartes in the 1630s. Surely there was a difference of kind between human and animal bodies and other mechanisms, and human-made machines were still inferior to God-made animals, but all bodies, including human bodies, were automata. The major difference between humans, animals, and machines was, as famously declared by Descartes, the ability to reason that is found solely in humans.

Locke's reaction to Descartes adds another solely human concept to the human superiority above nature: consciousness. Consciousness is the perception of what passes in our own mind and distinguishes the self from the other; it "always accompanies thinking, and 'tis that, that makes every one to be, what he calls *self*" (146). Thoughts take the form of an inner speech or image as a "train of ideas" (71). In this radical turn, language as a testimony of a conscious mind becomes—and still remains today—an important evidence of one's humanity. Language is evidence of inner life, of the encountered subjectivity.

It is no coincidence that the name Galatea emerges simultaneously with Galatea's independence in language in Rousseau's play. Now that Galatea can finally speak, the pivotal moment of her transformation and power is indicated through her speech. In Villiers de l'Isle-Adams *Future Eve*, the first android Hadaly persuades her lover Ewald of their true bond through the power of her speech, while the reader remains skeptical (Adams 571). Galatea's transformation through language is a focus of George Bernard Shaw's play *Pygmalion* (1912), discussed in Chapter 1, and remains a focal point for Galateas until today, for example, in neural network Helen from Richard Powers's novel *Galatea 2.2* (1995), discussed in Chapter 4. Both Helen and Eliza Doolittle are trained to use a higher version of English: Eliza's transformation into a lady and Helen's transformation into a conscious AI take place mainly through language.

Even with language at full ability, so much of human life and any other life is unspeakable. It should be noted that human communication is not

Fig. 2. Jean-Léon Gérôme's painting *Pygmalion et Galatée*. 1890. WikiMedia Commons, public domain.

only linguistic: there are gestures, body language, mimicry, there is music. Even though this book largely deals only with the verbal aspect of language, musical ability and gestures are, in fact, common to Galateas. Musical sound does not carry a meaning in the way language does. The evidence for this is in poetry—made of language that does not solely *mean*, but also renders a visual or auditory experience: poetic language *sounds*. Galateas often learn how to make *sound* before they learn how to speak, just like humans do.

Singing was linked to babbling and the origins of speech by many philosophers and musical theorists of the eighteenth century, such as Jean-Jacques Rousseau, Dennis Diderot, Jean-Phillipe Rameau, and Étienne Bonnot de Condillac (Thomas, Shell 98). Even when mute or refraining from comprehensible or intelligent speech, post-Enlightenment (modern) Galateas are prone to singing, like sirens luring men into dangerous relations. E. T. A. Hoffmann's automaton Olympia in 'The Sandman' ['Der Sandmann'] (1816) is not able to lead a conversation, apart from sighing, but can sing. Based partly on this short story, along with two other stories by Hoffmann, is the opera by Jacques Offenbach, *The Tales of Hoffmann* [*Les Contes du Hoffmann*] (1880), where Olympia sings one of the most famous arias, nicknamed 'The Doll Song.' In Honoré de Balzac's 'Sarrasine' (1830), and in Giacomo Puccini's *Madama Butterfly* (1904), a man falls in love with a singing female and, in a popular twist, ends up disappointed when the perfect woman turns out to be a man. Hans Christian Andersen's mermaid in *The Little Mermaid* [*Den lille havfrue*] (1836) gives up song and speech to transform into a human and must marry a man to obtain a human soul. In Anne McCaffrey's *The Ship Who Sang* (1969), a newborn girl is merged with a spaceship into a new kind of entity and becomes famous for her beautiful singing. When G. B. Shaw's play *Pygmalion* (1912) was adapted for the big screen as *My Fair Lady* (1964), Audrey Hepburn's portrayal of Eliza Doolittle included singing parts that were dubbed by an uncredited ghost singer, Marni Nixon. Germaine de Staël's comedy *Le Mannequin* (1811) plays with the idea of women being treated as dummies, lacking a voice, self-directed movement, and will. Accentuated with their physical and vocal beauty, Galateas tend to reveal themselves as illusory marionettes, reflecting society's power dynamics and the manipulation of the created.

While Rousseau's Galatea was the first to speak in 1762, it took decades for Galateas to speak—and even more to speak properly. Even when artificial women are verbal, their words may be predominantly scripted. Examples of scripted and doctored Galateas, analyzed in Chapters 1 and 2, are G. B. Shaw's fictional Eliza Doolittle from *Pygmalion* (1912), Joseph Weizenbaum's first actual chatbot ELIZA (1966), Alice Sheldon's fictional Philadelphia

Burke from 'The Girl Who Was Plugged In' (1973), and today's actual social robots like Hanson Robotics' Sophia (2016). W. S. Gilbert's Galatea from the comedic play *Pygmalion and Galatea* (1871) is verbal but, for comic effect, is presented as naïve since she does not understand second meanings to some words, which makes her look innocent and in need of a guardian. The very innocence of this Galatea was also parodied in a musical burlesque *Galatea, or Pygmalion Re-Versed* (1883). Three decades later, Shaw's working-class woman Eliza Doolittle cannot decode double meanings but loses her naiveté when she is transformed through diligent training into an upper-class lady. Another example from outside fiction of mocking Galateas for their lack of understanding is Serge Gainsbourg, who wrote two popular songs for a young singer France Gall in the 1960s and played with double meanings of words as well as with Gall's naiveté. The song *Poupée de cire, poupée de son* means *a wax doll, a rag doll*, but also bears the meaning of *a sound doll*, implying Gall is controlled by Gainsbourg. This turned out to be the case with their next popular song, *Les sucettes*, imbued with double meanings, the sexual connotations of which young and innocent Gall failed to detect. While singing allows for a lack of understanding of language, acting requires a specialist in doubling. It is no coincidence that C. L. Moore's Daphne from 'No Woman Born' (1944) is an adored singer and dancer—Galatean life depends on the performance of the human.

The shift from Galatea's bodily and physical formation to how Galatea's identity is formed, i.e. the shift from the ontological creation to the epistemological creation, anticipates the differences between the Victorian and twentieth-century narratives (Kennel 74). Undergoing the evolution affected by the technological and cultural forces around her, Galatea becomes more complex and the illusion becomes more real, keeping the reader and the viewer on their toes: How human is she?

In the example of English literature, in the nineteenth century, "the myth of Pygmalion speaks about ideals of a phallic male artistic creativity and a virginal, silent and compliant femininity" (Yeates 589). However, Essaka Joshua shows that late nineteenth-century renditions of the Pygmalion myth switch their focus from the creator to his creation and notes, "[o]n the stage, Galatea, formerly a woman of few words, gains a voice" (xxi, 155). As discussed in Chapter 2, the Pygmalion myth is largely a male fantasy (136), which is reflected not only in the distribution of the two main characters—Pygmalion is a man, Galatea a woman—but also in the gender distribution of authors that use the myth. The rare woman authors who wrote on the Pygmalion myth tended to inspect Galatea's perspective instead of Pygmalion's, asking how it is to be less than human (see more in Chapter 2).

Notions of dominance, power, and—simply—ability have been "naturalized as feminine precisely through myths like Pygmalion" (Yeates 591). This does not imply, however, that gender relations in the writing of the myth are always simple, rigid, and traditional. Good writers challenge that: Bernard Shaw, whose play *Pygmalion* is in the center of Chapter 1, prominently advocated for gender and social equality. The twentieth-century Galateas are explicit in their desire for freedom,[35] and Galatean freedom, as demonstrated in this book, begins with the ability to speak for themselves.

The leap in Galatean language abilities was accelerated with animated *masculine* humanoids whose language abilities are innate. Male creations are not Galateas.[36] Male humanoids are rare but their language ability is not; as a matter of fact, it is often central to their story. A golem, the Jewish mythical humanoid, is mute but has the power to understand speech, reading, and writing, which is not the case with any Galatea prior to Rousseau's in 1762. The golem depends on the word; he is brought to life through ritual and chants, and words are written on his body or on paper and put into his mouth. Stanisław Lem took the figure of the golem to represent a superintelligent computer in his collection of fictional essays titled *Golem XIV* (1978). The Jaquet-Droz automata from the eighteenth century also distinguished men from women automata by gender: the musician was a woman and the writer a man, and this is still the case today, for example, in Martin Scorsese's film *Hugo* (2011). Carlo Collodi's wooden marionette Pinocchio from *The Adventures of Pinocchio* [*Le avventure di Pinocchio*] (1881) is also verbal. As a matter of fact, Pinnochio's verbality is what brings him to life: he is saved and carved from a log into a human form only because he was able to ask for help. Prone to lying and thus deceiving, as all Galateas, his destiny was first intended to be tragic. Collodi changed the ending of the story into a moral message: when Pinnochio obeys his father, stops with constant lies, and properly educates and socializes himself, he is granted his wish of becoming a real boy. In addition to these observations, Isaac Asimov's only silent robot from his short story 'Robbie' (1939) is masculine, but feminized as a nursemaid, as mentioned in Chapter 3.

The most important masculine creature's contribution to speaking Galateas, in focus of Chapter 4, was the novel *Frankenstein; or the Modern Prometheus* written in 1818 by a woman author, Mary Shelley. Even though Shelley makes a clear link between her story and the Greek myth of Prometheus, the Pygmalion paradigm was very much impacted by her novel, a part of which is narrated by the humanlike creature for the very first time in the history of Galateas. Shelley's creature is also the first humanoid to enjoy reading literature, which is a feature of Galateas that is only reciprocated in fiction at the end of the twentieth century in Richard Powers's *Galatea 2.2*, where a neural network undergoes language and literature training. Two centuries after Shelley's novel, actual literature-writing machines realized the idea of nonhuman writing, discussed in Chapters 4 and 5.

Overview of the Book

The program of artificial humanities is established in this book through a study of fiction because the spaces where technology is being created are deeply deprived of the possible contributions from the humanities. To begin with, we lack appropriate terms to describe AI: Is it intelligent? Is it autonomous? Does it have agency? Should we call AI-generated text language and would that change the concept of language? Is generation a mark of originality or creativity? All these concepts serve as a placeholder for new conditions that are being formed before our eyes—and all these concepts have long received significant attention both in literary studies and computer science. Artificial humanities bring together fictional imaginary and the actual making of technology, an unlikely pairing that has become more apparent with the emergence of recent AI advances.

Fiction often serves as a placeholder too: fiction is a public place where ideas are born, played out, and borrowed from. Science fiction, in particular, offers placeholders for concepts that do not exist in our world, except in the imagination. A work of fiction appears in almost every single conversation on AI, and yet these imaginaries are largely left unattended, particularly with technologists who are inspired and challenged by them.

Connecting fiction with philosophical inquiry and basic knowledge of AI technicalities suffices to enter artificial humanities as a field, effectively bringing the study of humanities to the core of the AI-powered revolution. The practical part of the program ensues when we not only think about technology, but think about it together with technologists. The teaching part of the program begins with preparing students of all majors to critically question and evaluate technological realities and novelties, both of which they will all face across the span of their personal lives and both of which a portion of students will tackle in their professional lives.

The book presents an array of notable texts and technological examples derived from the rich Pygmalion paradigm, only a fraction of which is presented here. The selected texts and examples come both from the paradigm's heavily Western canon—Shaw's *Pygmalion*, Powers's *Galatea 2.2*, films *Her* and

Ex Machina—and from its margins, specifically from Slavic literatures and cinema. Most of Slovenian, Serbian, Czech, and Polish works analyzed here have remained largely underexplored in literary criticism. The centrality of the myth across mythologies has hardly been noted in literary studies focused on major Western literatures. For example, Native American mythologies (Bella Coola, Kwakiutl, Tlingit, Nootka, and Tsimshian) all tell a rendition of the tale, in which a widower carves his deceased wife from wood and treats her in typical Pygmalionesque ways (Boas 746–47, McIlwraith 356–357). Pygmalionesque tales with a variety of motifs are found across the Silk Road (Beguš 'A Tocharian'), North Africa (Frobenius 129–33, 177–92), and Slavic and Baltic countries (Kurrik 108–11), and attest of the centrality of the myth.

Each chapter thematizes a recent language technology in need of a philosophical reflection, using one to a few dozen literary texts or, in some cases, cinematic examples. Built on the pillars of literary studies, including a new approach to creative writing, the chapters include the history of technology, technology ethics, medical humanities, disability studies, gender studies, history of concepts, and philosophy of AI. At the end of each chapter is a practically-oriented discussion with a proposal on how we can use the study of fiction to build better technology.

The first part of the book is heavily focused on literary history and the Pygmalion myth, drawing the yet-unexamined parallels with technology development. The middle part of the book leans into these practical implications with the examples of digital and often also medical technologies. The final part of the book approaches these questions philosophically, examining in particular the novelty of language models.

Chapter 1 takes a closer look at the computational heritage of George Bernard Shaw, literary father of the first human-speaking machine, Eliza Doolittle, from his play *Pygmalion* (1912). In the middle of the twentieth century, Higgins's experiment with Eliza was translated into a computational test, known after its creator, Alan Turing, as the Turing test. The Turing test, initially termed as an imitation game, is a test of a computer's ability to exhibit humanlike intelligent behavior through textual conversation. Soon afterward, Eliza Doolittle served as an inspiration for the first chatbot, Joseph Weizenbaum's ELIZA. Human conversations with ELIZA revealed that Pygmalionesque delusions persist with humanlike entities, which became known as the Eliza effect. Nonetheless, AI-based technologies continued to develop in the direction of deception, portraying humanlike characteristics and identities. The chapter argues that the subsequent technologies of chatbots and virtual assistants are conceptually no different from the two Elizas and calls for a novel trajectory in building technology that goes beyond the human model. This argument does not apply, however, to a principle of learning that was used in Higgins's training of Eliza and was adopted in machine learning, as illustrated by an example of inner training in generative adversarial networks. Even though the speech they produce might sound human, it is profoundly nonhuman. In the final reflection on the novel topic of language enhancement, I open an ethical discussion on accent curation through newly available software technology in opposition to training, as attested in Eliza's elocution lessons. Themes presented in this chapter serve as entry points to their further exploration in the rest of the book.

Chapter 2 problematizes the humanlike aspect of social robotics and virtual beings on three points: 1) the human model, 2) cultural diversity and context, and 3) gendered perspectives. 1) The first point argues that we will certainly get better at robotics approaching human behavior with time, but the illusion of the human will inevitably break. I first demonstrate how social robots are overwhelmed with the Pygmalionesque tradition using the example of Hanson Robotics' Sophia. In treating robots as subdued to our control, as paralyzed humans, and as romantic partners, we are constraining the robotic potential. The final part of the chapter outlines how the human model leads us to relational machines (Spike Jonze, Alex Garland) and opens a discussion on alternatives. I suggest two entry points for technologists and humanities scholars to bring us beyond the human: through basic relationality of two agents and through exploration of the machinic epistemic space. 2) The middle part of the chapter argues for a comparative approach to AI, using comparative literature as exemplary discipline, aware of the power struggles between centers and peripheries and hyper-vigilant of the mixing of formal, social, and cultural zones. As exemplary Pygmalionesque texts which also bring up their unique cultural contexts, I look at literary and cinematic examples of Pygmalion-based perspectives by Slavic authors (Dušan Makavejev, Rudi Šeligo, Zoran Nešković, Stanisław Lem). 3) This part flows into a demonstration of gender revolution in the Pygmalion myth, kindled by women-initiated Galatea-based perspectives in Anglophone poetry from the nineteenth century. Addressing the traditional gender distribution in the Pygmalion paradigm, both in texts and in authors, I show how Galateas depicted by Shaw and feminist women poets were more nuanced, at times, even more egalitarian than their contemporary Galateas.

Since new technology tends to be first applied to medicine and treatment is never far from enhancement, Chapter 3 delves into the fields of medical humanities and ethics and centers around fictional and actual cases of Pygmalionism, demonstrated either as a physical or as a mental paralysis. I examine how medicine views the condition of Pygmalionism (Craig

Gillespie) and how medical doctors initially described the condition of locked-in syndrome with fictional examples (Émile Zola, Alexandre Dumas). Comparing two locked-in patients' memoirs (Jean-Dominique Bauby, Philippe Vigand) with fictional stories about paralyzed Galateas with a techno-medical prosthesis (C. L. Moore, Alice Sheldon), the chapter brings to light ethical questions pertinent to cutting-edge prosthetic technologies related to paralysis and communication. This exemplary and somewhat unexpected service of fiction continues in medicine today, for example, with Isaac Asimov's stories, which are taken as instructive in neuroethics for autonomous neuro devices. The chapter displays how literary studies empower ethical practices without being pushed to the corner of unwarranted techno-medical fantasies.

Chapter 4 presents a conceptual history of language, revealing how our contemporary conceptions of language cannot be accommodated within recent language technologies. We are conflicted between the Pygmalionesque dreams of humanlike machines and machines having autonomy, freedom, intelligence, agency, and creativity in their own machinic ways. After an overview of the history of the concept of language in humans, the chapter examines Mary Shelley's *Frankenstein; or the Modern Prometheus* (1818). Shelley introduces many novelties to the Pygmalion paradigm, including nonhuman language ability and enjoyment in literature. As an example of the intelligent, interpretative, and creative use of language in a machine, I analyze Richard Powers's neural network Helen from *Galatea 2.2* (1995), which is able to master literature as the highest expression of human language. Burdened by another Pygmalionesque existence, Helen is denied humanity—like the mythical Helen of Troy, Goethe's Helen in Faust, Shelley's Frankenstein, and Shakespeare's Caliban. The inductive principle in all these humanoids is that their logic of being is not the same as human, however, they are never granted the freedom of being other-than-human. I parallel *Galatea 2.2* with technologist Blaise Agüera y Arcas's reflective and speculative book on working with a language model in *Ubi Sunt* (2022) in order to highlight the tendency to ascribe personhood to neural network models and further suggest a Galatean existence.

As an example of nonhuman language generated by neural networks, Chapter 5 examines AI writing in the case of large language models. I first look into the philosophical stakes of large language models and point out qualitative differences of this kind of writing: Rising from the language itself in a hyper-structuralist manner, these words are detached from a subject and thus have no commitment to existential and worldly human values. The middle part of the chapters analyzes fictional representations of machinic writing in Roald Dahl's 'The Great Automatic Grammatizator' (1953), which deals with the literary market, and Andrej Tomažin's 'Hlapci, heroji in umetna inteligenca' ['Heroes, Lackeys, and Artificial Intelligence'] (2018), which focuses on literary criticism. Both examples show how unprepared our systems are for a novel actor in the field of literature and writing in general. In the final part, I analyze two of the earliest writings about and by a learning language model, GPT-3 and K Allado-McDowell's novel *Pharmako-AI* (2020) and Daniel Kehlmann's essay 'Mein Algorithmus und Ich' ['My Algorithm and I'] (2020). Kehlmann's experience with the CTRL program was largely underwhelming because he wished for a Pygmalionesque experience with a humanlike writing partner. In contrast, Allado-McDowell managed to pursue the nonhuman qualities of GPT-3 language and traverse the act of writing in dialogue with a machine, exploring each other as well as new opportunities in this new zone of writing. I argue for the use of literary writing as exemplary practice in developing large language models both in their overarching philosophy and in their applications.

The chapters show us, each in a different example of an AI-based technology, to where the humanlike model of AI brought us and how it inevitably fails. This main argument of the book identifies the Pygmalion myth as the ultimate goal of creating language-based AI technologies in the broader twentieth century. The chronological examination of the myth, which ranges from classic Rome to American fiction today, reveals how this phase is slowly coming to an end in order to give space to new possibilities enabled by cutting-edge AI. The philosophical beauty of AI is that it creates realities which exceed what is considered machine and technology today. AI leaves us with a question: What is human?, to which the Pygmalion myth will hold a mirror. We will surely get yet another reinterpretation of the traditional myth, and it will inevitably be affected by what AI comes to be.

CHAPTER 1

Inventing New Elizas

Here I am, a barbarian, because men understand me not.
   —Ovid, *Tristia* (in exile, 43 BC–17 CE)

In the end we're dependent on
The creatures we've created.
   —Johann Wolfgang von Goethe, *Faust, Part II* (1832)

The single biggest problem in communication
is the illusion that it has taken place.
   —George Bernard Shaw, allegedly (sometime between 1856–1950)

In Ovid's *Metamorphoses,* Pygmalion, who despises real women, sculpts a perfect woman from marble. In the process of creation, he falls in love with his statue (named Galatea many centuries later). He prays to the goddess to bring her to life and, after the statue's transformation, they live happily ever after. The myth encapsulates powerful archetypal themes: the human desire to create beings in our own image, the tendency to shape others according to our desires, the relationship between creator and creation, the distinctions between life and nonlife, natural and artificial, real and fabricated.

The Pygmalion myth is one of the most influential fictional tropes in today's AI. Its influence has spanned centuries, during which the myth responded to a variety of topics. As one of the ancient Greek myths on creating and perfecting the human, the myth has taken many shapes and themes. This chapter looks over its nineteenth-century reinterpretations, culminating in a break from the Victorian era at the beginning of the twentieth century. The nineteenth century—within the Pygmalion paradigm and more generally—was focused on the trope of art imitating life. Nineteenth-century reinterpretations of the myth offer sporadic examples of scientific attempts to (re)design Galateas, exemplified with bioscientific experimentation in Nathaniel Hawthorne's *Rappaccini's Daughter* (1844). Imagining instilling language and other human attributes into machines or cyborgs emerged already in Mary Shelley's *Frankenstein* (1818) and then again towards the end of the century with, among others, W. S. Gilbert's Galatea from the comedic play *Pygmalion and Galatea* (1871) and Auguste Villiers de l'Isle-Adam's *Future Eve* (1886).

The topic of language is cemented into the Pygmalion myth with George Bernard Shaw's *Pygmalion* (1912), which immediately became a canonical work. In this play, Shaw presents one of the most influential Galateas: Eliza Doolittle, a young working-class woman going through a scientific experiment of language training in order to pass as a duchess. Surrounded by the Bell family, who instilled speech into the telephone and updated Thomas Edison's phonograph, Shaw picked up on the nascent science of instilling language in machines. He shared his frustration about the way English was spoken and written with phoneticians of the nineteenth century, who in turn invented new phonetic alphabets for transcribing English speech. The general frustration with the English language at the time was thus at the level of both speech and writing.

This chapter offers a retrospective examination of the many metaphorical seeds sown by *Pygmalion*, progressing from the Turing test and the Eliza effect in chatbot technology to machine language training models and recent technologies approaches in language enhancement. I argue that our conceptual framework in creating humanlike personalities on top of these language technologies has hardly changed since Shaw's fictional example of Eliza Doolittle. Instead, for the last century, we have continued to invent new Elizas in a variety of forms, from virtual assistants to virtual beings, from avatars to social robots.

1.1 Shaw's Heritage

Pygmalionesque creation serves as a substitute for something that was lost or fills up a void. Bernard Shaw, an Irishman in England, was making up for something that was lost—namely his mother tongue—through his erudite study of the English language. Shaw found English "gives us three quarters of the world for our audience," similar to "a fifteenth-century Latin," while vernacular Irish simply cannot compare. As a matter of fact, per Shaw's view, speaking Irish also requires additional knowledge of school Gaelic with which to "torture children" (Greene and Laurence 291). As the preface to *Pygmalion* confirms, Shaw believed that it was ill-advised to limit one's professional and social opportunities with language or its accent. The same belief is exhibited in many Scottish, Irish, Welsh, and working-class English people who took elocution classes offered by another Irishman, actor and the proponent of the elocution movement Thomas Sheridan, in the mid-to-late eighteenth century (Clare 23). Many other people subject themselves to elocution classes through the current day.

Another Scottish teacher of English elocution was Alexander Bell, a shoemaker and avid Shakespearean—and the grandfather of Alexander Graham Bell. Grandfather Bell established himself in London, focusing on correcting stuttering and other speech defects. Robert V. Bruce calls him "Pygmalion in Harrington Square" since, in 1847, Bell published a play called *The Bride* that celebrates the value of good manners, including good speech. The play begins with a Higgesian task by a valet: "[...] how much I have improved the manners of this family [...] Polishing a prosy lawyer into a tolerable baronet is a task to break a man's back. [...] The entire establishment [...] was confoundedly vulgar" (1). While Bell's play takes a different turn than Shaw's *Pygmalion*, the valet might have inspired Shaw who, as Bruce asserts, was certainly familiar with the play (29). Shavian scholars are divided over this particular influence. Shaw attributed his inspiration for *Pygmalion* only to Alexander Bell's son, Alexander Melville Bell.

Alexander Melville Bell invented Visible Speech, a tool that uses symbols to teach deaf people articulate sounds.[1] Visible Speech represents the position of the speech apparatus for each sound articulation; it is, in its essence, a system for transcribing a speaking machine. After Melville Bell saw Joseph Faber's speaking machine, Euphonia, and Charles Wheatstone's talking automaton, based on Wolfgang von Kempelen's earlier work, he encouraged his sons to invent a speaking machine (Mackenzie 26). As a result, his son Alexander Graham Bell invented the telephone.

In 1901, Graham Bell wrote to his wife Mabel: "I believe in universal suffrage, without qualification of education, sex, color, or property" (Boettinger 155). Various forms of difference—race, ethnicity, class, gender, disability—feature prominently in spoken language and the technologies around it, ranging from forms as basic as writing to advanced technology. Bernard Shaw was keenly aware of these forms of difference when creating his Galatea.

Shaw's Galatea is chiefly situated in phonetics: the working title of *Pygmalion* was *The Phonetic Play*. Shaw based the character of Dr. Higgins, a linguist who tries to teach Cockney-speaking Eliza to speak upper-class English, primarily on the phonetician Henry Sweet—even if, as Shaw assures the reader of the play in the preface, Higgins is not his portrait (5)—as well as Alexander Melville Bell, Tito Pagliardini, and Alexander John Ellis (2). The latter, pertaining to the issue centered in the play *Pygmalion*, is known for proclaiming in 1867 that dropping the 'h,' characteristic of the Cockney accent, was "social suicide" (221). Eliza Doolittle takes this to heart and acts upon it.

Besides writing the play based on phonetics, Shaw also attempted to reform English writing that did not faithfully represent speech. Shaw followed Alexander Melville Bell, Alexander John Ellis,[2] and Henry Sweet, who tried to find an alternative alphabet to the Roman script. In his will, Shaw funded the posthumously designed Shavian alphabet, which provided phonetic orthography for the English language. Shaw's fictional character Henry Higgins also created his own phonetic alphabet, named the Higgins Universal Alphabet. The reason for creating these new systems of transcribing speech came from a frustration similar to that of the creators of speaking machines: deliverance of paralinguistic information fell short. With Shaw, the particular motivation was to overcome the difficulties of conventional spelling. As he writes in the preface to *Pygmalion:* "The English have no respect for their language, and will not teach their children to speak it. They cannot spell it because they have nothing to spell it with but an old foreign alphabet of which only the consonants – and not all of them – have any agreed speech value" (2).

Shaw's frustration with writing speech is evident early in the play when he tries to write Eliza's Cockney accent phonetically: "Ow, eez ye-ooa san, is e? Wal, fewd dan y' de-ooty bawmz a mather should, eed now bettern to spawl a pore gel's flahrzn than ran awy atbaht pyin. Will ye-oo py me f'them? [Here, with apologies, this desperate attempt to represent her dialect without a phonetic alphabet must be abandoned as unintelligible outside London.]" (I 95–100). Although Shaw almost immediately abandons distinguishing Eliza's phonetic speech from the rest of the dialogue, a reader can still partly follow her fading Cockney accent through the first three acts. Shaw occasionally but consistently, up until the last chapter, returns to writing the speech of the Doolittles, Eliza and her father Alfred, partly phonetically: "Good enough for yǝ-oo" (II 125) and "Now, now, Enry Iggins!" (V 205, 336).

This feature of Shaw's frustration with writing down speech appears already at the very creation of the play. Shaw's scores of the popular Pitman phonetic shorthand indicated how the lines should sound (see Figure 3). (The posthumous Shavian alphabet followed the design of Shaw's phonetic scores for his plays.) Shaw was admittedly scrupulous about the performances of his plays and paid close attention to how the actors pronounced the lines he wrote. Shaw's commentary on English writing and phonetics included meta-commentaries: "Whenever possible Shaw commenced the rehearsal process by reading the play aloud to the actors, because he wanted them to learn the sound of the lines— pronunciation, intonation, inflection, tempo,

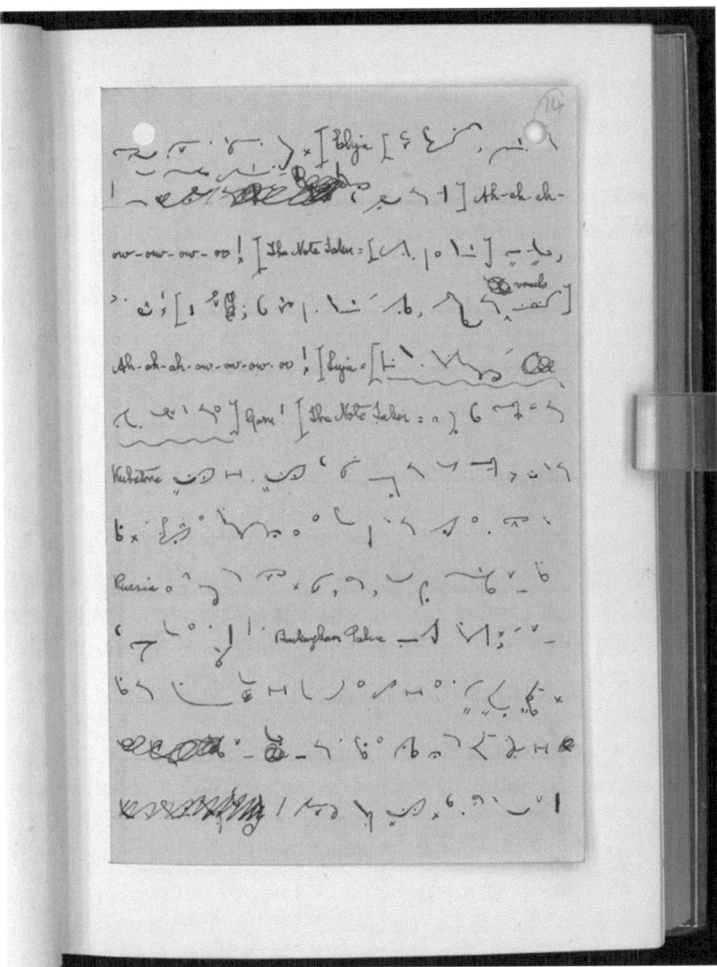

Fig. 3. Bernard Shaw's shorthand of *Pygmalion: The Phonetic Play,* 14 (Buckley 30). Image courtesy of the Harry Ransom Center, University of Texas at Austin. The image is from George Bernard Shaw Collection, Box 24.7, "Pygmalion Shorthand manuscript." Used with permission.

and volume—directly from his own mouth" (Buckley 23). This is yet another Pygmalionesque streak in Shaw's *Pygmalion*: the creator's desire for complete control comes both from Higgins and from Shaw. Observing how Shaw treats his actors as talking machines, Ernest Thesiger told him, "You don't want actors in your plays, you want loud-voiced gramophones just to spout your words" (Buckley 21).

The doubling Shaw in Higgins, who is doubling the many early phoneticians listed above, also pertains to Eliza Doolittle. When creating Eliza, Shaw created more than one Galatea; the obvious is the fictional Eliza and the less obvious are his nonfictional puppets, the actors. Actual actors and actresses play less than a trivial role in many Pygmalion stories, and especially in Shaw's *Pygmalion*. The cover of the Broadway record[3] of his play depicts this dynamic, showing Eliza as a puppet being operated by Higgins, his own strings drawn from God-like Shaw above the clouds. Shaw called himself God in front of his actors at least once; see, for example, the correspondence between Shaw and Mrs. Patrick Campbell, who starred as Eliza (62). Once the text of the play is put on stage, the performance doubles in the acting: Cockney flower girl Eliza brings forth the upper-class lady, and the actress playing Eliza brings forth Eliza.

Mrs. Patrick Campbell was a star of theater both in England and in the US Shaw wrote the role of Eliza and a few other roles with her in mind, aware of the difficulty of the role that needs to bring his character to life: "My plays must be acted, and acted hard. They need a sort of bustle and crepitation of life which requires extraordinary energy and vitality, and gives only glimpses and movements of the poetry beneath," he wrote to Mrs. Pat (18). Therein lies another Pygmalionesque challenge of making a literary character human. As Mieke Bal writes, "The character is not a human being, but it resembles one. It has no real psyche, personality, ideology or competence to act, but it does possess characteristics that make readers assume it does, and makes psychological and ideological descriptions possible" (115).

Shaw considers Eliza's reception in the audience according to gender: "Your public is more than half feminine," he writes to Mrs. Pat, who made Eliza Doolittle human; "you cannot satisfy their longing for a male to idealize" (16). Shaw's infatuation with Mrs. Patrick Campbell was not only professional but also personal. They led a passionate, but unconsummated, epistolary affair, which started before Shaw was to direct her in the role of Eliza. Alan Dent, the editor of their correspondence, opens yet another Pygmalionesque dimension of this relationship by calling Shaw "an intellectual giant," and Mrs. Pat, "a great and beautiful actress" (ix). The layers of Pygmalions and Galateas in Shaw's play are therefore threefold: professional, personal, and textual.

Despite Shaw acting utterly Pygmalionesque as the author of the play, his Galatea is more feminist than most. Unlike other Galateas before her, Eliza is in the center of the text, human and flawed, subdued no more to the usual Galatean lifelessness. Shaw's Eliza is not necessarily Higgins's Eliza: she is a complex human being. This becomes clear to Higgins only after her transformation when he finally starts seeing her as human and capable of making her own choices, yet he still does not see her as equal. As a strong advocate of gender and class equality, Shaw wrote in a consciously androgynous streak. Throughout the play, Eliza rebelliously leads her own personal revolution. Even though creators of subsequent renditions of *Pygmalion* wanted Eliza and Higgins to become romantically involved, Shaw adamantly fought for Eliza's freedom. When Higgins's experiment is done, Shaw leaves us with a deeply disappointed and lonely bachelor and an empowered woman whose independence was all but guaranteed.

Like most Galateas of the twentieth century, Eliza is transformed through science (phonetics). The scientific approach of two linguists, Dr. Henry Higgins and his assistant Colonel Pickering, is posed as an experiment: Will they be able to transform a lowly flower girl into a lady? Using recordings and demonstrations of high-class English, Eliza's training includes mainly speech imitation exercises. If the experiment is successful, she would pass as a duchess in the social milieu of high English class. This test does not allow for mere mimicry but requires her to master the skill of the new accent and context-appropriate body language as well as the social norms that come with leading a proper conversation under unarticulated social rules.

Like every Galatea, Eliza must perfectly perform humanness. For Eliza Doolittle, the humanness is defined by the aristocracy where, for the first time in the history of Galateas, the center of her performance is language. The play of language imitation was passed on to actual machines in the twentieth century. Frustrated by writing the English speech and picking up on the desire to instill human language into machines, Shaw anticipated computer-based language training already at the very beginning of the century. This argumentation is supported by historical events in the development of AI, in which Eliza Doolittle, a fictional woman, served as an inspiration for the Turing test, suggested by Alan Turing in 1950, and the very first chatbot named after Eliza Doolittle, Joseph Weizenbaum's ELIZA from 1966. More broadly, Eliza modeled the technology of virtual assistants, virtual avatars, and social robots, as well as general adversarial networks language training and accent-omitting technologies, as we will see in the final section of the chapter.

1.2 The Turing Test

Shaw's influence goes beyond contemporary understandings of the notion of Pygmalionism. Henry Higgins's experiment that Shaw fabricated in a context of English upward class migration was translated into a classical computer science benchmark of the Turing test that remains in use for our most advanced language technologies. Alan Turing, the father of theoretical computer science and AI, begins his landmark 1950 paper 'Computing Machinery and Intelligence' with a question: "Can machines think?" Turing outlines his AI research program with a thought experiment: he offers the imitation game, later more known as the Turing test, as criteria for evaluating machine intelligence (433).

In the Turing test, a human judge tries to determine whether they are talking to another human or to a machine based solely on verbal interactions. The test is designed as a theatrical performance—the words of illusion instead of the words of being—in which a computer tries to fool the human judge that they are in conversation with a human. The essence of the test is to check whether machines can act indistinguishably from humans through complex imitation of human language. The goal for the machine is to act as human through language imitation. Text is chosen as the fairer medium to the machine than speech, so that the machine is not judged on tone of voice or its beauty.

The machine is performing a human person and thus masking itself as a person—'person' originally means 'a mask' ('Person'). The origin of this

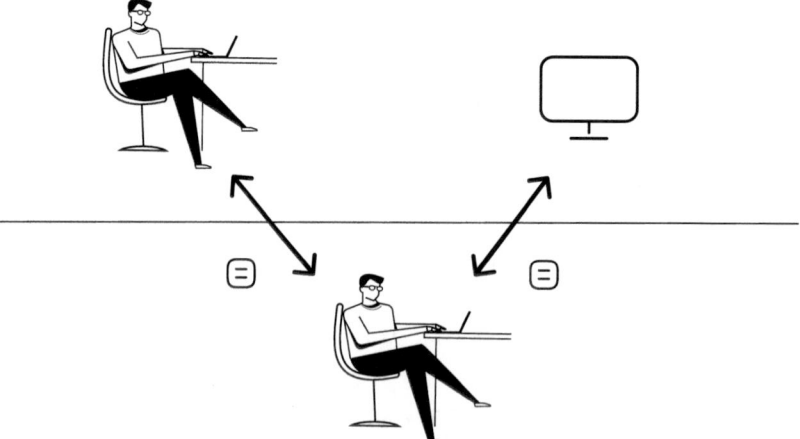

Fig. 4. Sketch of the Turing test (by the author).

performance is as gendered as it gets, not only in Shaw's *Pygmalion* but also in Turing's 1950 paper. Turing presents the imitation game as "the new form of the problem" in the machinic ability to think and sets out the test first to occur between three people, a man, a woman, and an interrogator of either sex, who must be separated in a room from the other two. "The object of the game for the interrogator is to determine which of the other two is the man and which the woman," and is allowed to ask questions about, as Turing suggests, "the length of his or her hair" (433). Turing is aware that not all answers will be truthful. He suggests then to refashion this setting with a woman interlocutor being replaced with the machine.

Women being replaced with machines and vice versa is a common replacement in the history of computing and AI. The word computer itself first designated an occupation of a person who performs mathematical calculations. In the 1950 paper, Turing described a "human computer" as a person who "is supposed to be following fixed rules; he has no authority to deviate from them in any detail," and an electrical digital computer is a simulation of the human computer (436). What Turing calls thinking is therefore equated with computing, performing logic following the rules, calculations, and similar rational tasks.

Turing reveals his view of language as purely mechanical,[4] even in situations that have to do with feeling and consciousness (445–47). Turing suggests that his test—and broadly, research program—will be able to distinguish actual understanding from "parrot fashion"[5] (446). In Turing's mechanistic view of language, machines can not only exhibit understanding but also understand.[6] This argument is becoming increasingly relevant with humanlike AI outputs today with generative AI as the Turing test fails us.

Another fundamental belief from Turing's paper has been challenged recently: equating language and thought is misguided since our thoughts are only partially linguistic. This means that language is neither a linear algorithm, as often viewed in technological circles, nor is it not merely a way to express a thought; language and thought are dissociated. While this question remains contested in neuroscience and linguistics circles, both concerning the validity of the claim as a whole as well as the level of dissociation, Evelina Fedorenko and Rosemary Varley show in a study of patients with nearly total loss of language (global aphasia) that language is a poor channel for complex thought and that many aspects of thought do not depend on language at all. A subsequent study, experimenting specifically with large language models, has shown that the abilities for language production in the human brain are largely separated from reasoning and thinking (Mahowald et al.). Intelligence emerging from language itself is thus a fallacy.

In Turing's paper, 'thought' refers to the ability to reason. According to Enlightenment ideas, which have strongly influenced the development of computer science in the second half of the twentieth century, reason is a unique human characteristic that allows us to access knowledge. This ability to acquire and apply knowledge and skills came to be called intelligence. Turing thus turns one of the fundamental philosophical questions, "How can I know?", from humans to computers: Can computers be intelligent?

Computers being intelligent like humans is a general premise of the field of artificial intelligence in 1950, when Turing wrote his imitation game paper. The human imitation principle permeated AI from its very beginnings and is still mainstream today, and Turing's paper helped make this happen. The idea that humans are the only reasoning entities and the rudimentary idea of the Turing test were, however, introduced already by René Descartes in his philosophical and mathematical treatise *The Discourse of the Method* (1637). In this seminal work that radically cuts with the previous limited definitions of who can be human, Descartes democratizes the definition of the human to having the ability to reason: *I think, therefore I am*.[7] Per Descartes, human bodies, just like those or animals, are mere mechanical automata; however, the ability to contemplate and calculate, to think and to reason, to have a mind and soul endowed with cognition, is unique to humans only.[8] While embodiment is the indispensable condition for self-awareness, the information given by the senses is indistinct and unreliable—as opposed to rational reflection. Humans can gain knowledge and empirical truth, equipped with their own reason and thus the ability to dare to know. Thinking, the utmost human activity, is channeled through reason and by the means of language, encompassed in the word *logos*. Language and reason, used for mental insights as well as calculation and geometry, are conflated in Descartes's theory. Descartes's connection to Turing's question, "Can machines think?," is rather direct.

Less direct is another aspect of Descartes's influence to Turing's setting of the imitation game. The relation is pointed out already in 1964, when Keith Gunderson suggests Descartes's two tests have an affinity with "certain philosophical claims which have issues from cybernetics" (195). While Turing compares humans with machines, Descartes discusses animals as the ultimate other to humans. Descartes views animals as automata that operate according to the same bodily mechanisms as all bodies, including human. Non-mechanical abilities are exceptional and singularly human and have to do with the mind, reason, and language. In Part V of *The Discourse*, titled 'Physics, the Heart, and the Soul of Man and Animals,' Descartes makes up "two most certain tests" to "know the difference between men and brutes [i.e. animals]" (98).[9]

The first test—the so-called Language Test—shows that automata and animals cannot transmit their thoughts into words in the way humans can. Language ability, for Descartes, attests the presence of thought and can adapt to every situation. Descartes uses an example of an automaton that could "emit vocables [...] correspondent to the action upon it of external objects which cause a change in its organs" but it would not be able to "arrange them variously so as appositely to reply to what is said in its presence" (98). The appropriate response of the free expression of thought in this test is therefore context-dependent and demarcates perceptive entities from non-perceptive ones (Massey and Boyle 100). The Language Test, according to linguist Noam Chomsky's interpretation in *Cartesian Linguistics*, is a clear-headed recognition of "the creative aspect of everyday language use" (4), and thus unavailable to animals and machines.[10]

The second Descartes's test—the so-called Action Test—has to do with the mental faculty of using one's own will and acting upon it, unavailable to both animals and machines. "[A]lthough such machines might execute many things with equal or perhaps greater perfection than any of us, they would, without doubt, fail in certain others from which it could be discovered that they did not act from knowledge, but solely from the disposition of their organs" (98). As an example, Descartes remarks that although animals have the organs that would allow them to produce sounds and speech,[11] "for we observe that magpies and parrots can utter words like ourselves," they are not capable of showing that they "understand what they say" (99). Thus, had they been able to speak human words, they still cannot show evidence that they understand the meaning of words. Since we cannot prove the presence of thinking in animals, Cartesian philosophy sees animals and other kinds of automata[12] as possibly corporeal souls (Harrison 223) with communicative abilities. Their communication, however, reflects no thought and understanding, i.e. no rational mind, which only pertains to humans.[13]

In a nutshell, the Language Test is based on the ability to engage in an open-ended conversation, and the Action Test on the ability to apply reason universally as opposed to being limited to instinctive or programmed behaviors. Following Descartes, Denis Diderot wrote in *Philosophical Thoughts* (1746): "If there were a parrot that answered everything, I would pronounce without balancing that it is a thinking being" (9). Turing followed the same idea with his test for machines, and Higgins, before that, with his Eliza.

To Higgins, Eliza is "just like a parrot" (II 225)—mimicking without a thought—with "most extraordinary quickness of ear" (II 224). When Higgins's assistant Pickering says to him that Eliza "must understand thoroughly what she's doing," Higgins replies, "How can she? She's incapable of understanding anything" (II 488–92). Higgins is in stark contrast with Colonel Pickering who has treated Eliza like a gentleman from the first time they met. Eliza herself observes, "I shall always be a flower girl to Higgins, because he always treats me as a flower girl, and always will; but I know I can be a lady to you [Pickering], because you always treat me as a lady, and always will" (V 473–76). Pickering's kind attitude, in Eliza's words, "began [her] education" as it was "the beginning of self-respect for [her]" (V 473–76). Nevertheless, both men seem to forget that Eliza is a human being and often talk about her in the third person in her presence—"Pickering: We're always talking Eliza. Higgins: Teaching Eliza. Pickering: Dressing Eliza. [...] Higgins: Inventing new Elizas" (III 226–44). They do not acknowledge her agency and autonomy even after she passes her test, as if Eliza had contributed nothing to their success. Higgins's and Pickering's differing views on Eliza's thinking ability translate to debates on machine language today: Can machines master understanding or do they simply mimic our language without any reasoning? Can machines really think?

The Turing test's relation to Shaw's *Pygmalion* is twofold: through language and through training. Shaw based his Galatea's transformation *in* language, and Turing positioned machine intelligence *in* language,[14] which has remained at the core of AI to this day (more on the language-centeredness in section 1.6). Turing's "imagined intelligent machine gives off an unmistakable aura of individual *personhood*, even of charm" but remains "a complex yet hollow system, which exploits its audience's ignorance to present the appearance of a person while containing no actual personhood" (Riskin par. 16). To overcome the perceived and actual hollowness of the machine, Turing suggested that instead of building a program that simulates a mature adult mind, it would be easier and more effective to produce a childlike mind and subject it to education. This is exactly what Higgins does with uneducated and unmannered Eliza, teaching her appropriate speech and decorum while treating her as a child and hardly human.[15]

The whole idea of transforming a nonhuman into a humanlike entity is essential to the Pygmalion myth. Galateas are depicted and treated as children, a feature that was transplanted to language technology. Essaka Joshua demonstrates that the Pygmalion myth renditions "often conceive [Galatea] as childlike, pure, dependent, and even animal-like in her simplicity" (155). When Shaw describes how Eliza Doolittle's lessons with Higgins looked like, he begins with Eliza's clear sense of their dynamic: "I don't need to be taught like a child" (II 1281). Due to her Cockney accent, Eliza is considered "incapable of understanding anything" (II 488–92) because she speaks incomprehensibly, which, in many contexts, is equal to not speaking at all.[16] A lack of language, of course, does not mean there is no understanding behind it. Nonetheless, Eliza is a barbarian for Higgins's circles—i.e. a foreigner, speaking in alien sounds.[17]

The Turing test was passed on a couple occasions or never, however one interprets it. One instance that was considered successful was when a chatbot called Eugene Goostman convinced a third of human judges that it was human in 2014. Eugene outperformed other bots with the help of a cunning fabrication of his identity background by his Russian and Ukrainian creators. As if the bot were a fictional character, Eugene Goostman was portrayed as a thirteen-year-old Ukrainian boy with a rich background story. Goostman's identity as a child was intended to induce forgiveness from users in case the bot lacked the knowledge expected from a human adult: "Eugene was 'born' in 2001. Our main idea was that he can claim that he knows anything, but his age also makes it perfectly reasonable that he doesn't know everything. [The creators] spent a lot of time developing a character with a believable personality" (Ford par. 10), thus making use of fiction.[18] In another successful passing of the Turing test in 2018, Google's virtual assistant Duplex booked an appointment in a hair salon. Following a backlash, the company promised to add a disclosure to its human-sounding voice. A narrow conversation topic works for now, and the technology will certainly get better.

It is no coincidence that the Turing test is based on language. Turing loved Shaw's plays, and while we have no evidence that Turing saw or read *Pygmalion*, we learn from his letters that he enjoyed *Back to Methuselah*, another play that features Pygmalion as a character[19] (Switzky 53). Shaw's Eliza is the first character to be accompanied through the ordeal of the Turing test, decades before Turing designed it. Switzky notes that "Shaw was almost certainly a guiding spirit for Turing when he composed 'Computing Machinery and Intelligence' in 1950 [...], [a] philosophical essay in artificial intelligence characterized by Shavian wit and playful churlishness" (53). Setting the Turing test as a theatrical game based solely on verbal interaction, Turing sought to distinguish "between the physical and the intellectual capacities of a man" ('Computing' 434). Turing adopts a Cartesian approach, separating the body from the mind, yet holding a belief that a machine's mind can simulate humanlike intelligence. Here, he opposes Descartes and Locke,[20] for whom the embodiment was a natural constraint to overcoming the category of intelligence, which, for all three thinkers, is defined as thinking and reasoning equated in language.

Eliza's performance of passing as a high-class lady at a social event is the culmination of the famous play *Pygmalion*. Nonetheless, all Galateas before Eliza had to pass their own kind of Turing test through their own act of transformation. Both in the Turing test and in Eliza's performance, the machine's and Eliza's transformation stands or fails on their respective performances. As originally proposed, the Turing test is based on textual exchange of messages, which is flatter in comparison to spoken language. Eliza Doolittle's experiment is based on speech, which, as opposed to writing, carries substantial social information about the speaker: race, ethnicity, gender, age, class. Speech includes a performance of a new social identity with its corresponding and contextually appropriate normative behavior as well as delicate paralinguistic communication (intonation and pitch, pauses and repetitions). Different language modalities together with bodily and facial expressions are a crucial part of Eliza's performance. The authenticity of her speech comes from the sum of its parts, the music of language, and needs to appear natural and not learned. As such, Eliza's performance has but a single flaw: she sounds "too perfect" to Higgins's student Nepommuck, an interpreter and polyglot. Her English is too polished and refined for a native speaker, he thinks: "Can you show me any English woman who speaks English as it should be spoken? Only foreigners who have been taught to speak it speak it well" (III 855–58). For this reason alone, Nepommuck speculates Eliza is a Hungarian princess in disguise (III 879–80). Eliza Doolittle might have overdone the human imitation, as a machine would.

While the otherness of humanlike machines is well-examined, the exoticization of language machines has garnered attention particularly in respect to Galateas. Alongside what Edward Said termed Orientalism, Galateas exhibit not only species difference, but also gender, race, and disability. For example, digital anthropologists are investigating virtual assistants and humanoid robots presenting as white women, not only in the West but also in the East (see, for example, a humanoid robot in the form of Scarlett Johansson in Chapter 2). Much less attention has been given to the opposite phenomenon—introducing a new technology as foreign, working-class, non-Christian. Humanlike technology tends to represent "a stable, formal expression that can be realized in diverse embodiments," which Bernard Dionysius Geoghegan calls an "alterity script" ('Orientalism' 51). A scripted performance is not tied to a single actor or machine, making the alterity script instrumental to language technologies that erase the difference (as in the case of Sanas, analyzed in the final section of this chapter) or that invoke the difference by staging and performing it (as in the case of the chess-playing automaton Mechanical Turk).

The embodiment and disembodiment of language elicits various kinds of fears. The alterity script—a mechanized, generated language—invokes otherness by separating form from meaning, mechanism from spirit, body from mind, East from West, and, ultimately, thought from reason (Geoghegan 'Orientalism' 83). Turing suggested shielding the machine from visual bias because, in his view, machines are bodily disabled compared to humans (435, 445–48). However, Turing's views on difference overlooked the diversity in human language: language is not solely an epitome of instrumental reason, but also a context- and body-dependent medium. In machines, language inevitably produces difference which, in my view, should not be based on human otherness but rather on inherent machinic difference.

In 2023, in an effort to make a speech-based technology that runs on Google's text-based language model LaMDa, engineers gave the model the voice of a child—repeating Eugene Goostman's trick. Passing the Turing test has become irrelevant, some experts claim, and the test needs to be updated (Suleyman, Laird and Ragni).[21] Others (notably Gary Marcus) say that the Turing test has always been irrelevant since it is a result of the Eliza effect—a well-known phenomenon of chatbot personification, recognized already in the first human-chatbot interactions in the mid-1960s.

Indeed, the Turing test was criticized at that time as well: Stanisław Lem, a Polish science fiction writer, proposed in his philosophical essays *Summa Technolgiae*, that the test should be updated by enlisting two different language machines: one that can intelligently converse with the human and another that only parrots the language, without inner understanding (which will break when trying to explain a simple joke) (Kodior 101). Many scholars refuted the test, too, or suggested improvements—Claude Shannon and John McCarthy already in 1956, the year of AI's naming (see more in Copeland 437). The 1970s followed[22] Searle argued there is no understanding in a machine and (not unlike Lem's second language machine) proposed a hypothetical scenario of the Chinese room. In this room, a person would be given instructions in English on how to compose fragments in Chinese, which they would not know. An impression would have built to the outsider of a seeming understanding of the Chinese language—in the same way a digital machine gives an impression of understanding, be it in the Turing test or on other occasions. These philosophical dilemmas go back to basic questions about Galateas: their embodiment, interiority, difference.

1.3 The Eliza Effect

Decades before Alan Turing designed the Turing test, Shaw wrote a whole play with a culmination in a similar kind of test. In *Pygmalion*, this test finalizes the Cockney flower girl's transformation into the duchess in the eyes of high society. The test is executed two times in the play in Act III, intensifying its difficulty by spreading the social circle and its unwritten demands.

Eliza's first test takes place in *Pygmalion* Act III when, after intensive practice, Eliza Doolittle is scheduled to meet with Mrs. Higgins, Henry Higgins's mother, and her friends. As Higgins prescribes: "I've taught her to speak properly; and she has strict orders as to her behavior. She's to keep to two subjects: the weather and everybody's health—Fine day and How do you do, you know—and not to let herself go on things in general. That will be safe" (110–112).

Both Elizas fail the Turing test in their first respective iterations. Eliza Doolittle's first test is full of mistakes, including improper vocabulary ("Not bloody likely." (421)) and themes (alcoholism, death (374)). Mrs. Higgins's friends certainly perceive Eliza's unusual ways, but call them the "new ways" (426) and see themselves as "old-fashioned" (431). They ultimately do not realize they have been tricked into talking to a flower girl: They are under what came to be known as the Eliza effect, believing—or wanting to believe—in Eliza's humanity at face value.

MRS. HIGGINS: [at last, conversationally] Will it rain, do you think?
LIZA: The shallow depression in the west of these islands is likely to move slowly in an easterly direction. There are no indications of any great change in the barometrical situation.
FREDDY: Ha! ha! how awfully funny!
LIZA: What is wrong with that, young man? I bet I got it right.
FREDDY: Killing!

In her first Turing test, above (III 323-34), Eliza Doolittle is giving away cues that she is performing by answering a small talk question with a weather forecast report and excessive formality, and by "bet[ting she] got it right" as if the conversation were a test (which, indeed, it was). Her first reaction is scripted and mechanical, and the second is reflective of the fact that her replies are learned. However, her mistakes *could* be interpreted as a joke, which is how Freddy interprets Eliza's mechanical talk.

Eliza's second Turing test takes place after months of diligent training. Not only does Eliza pass as a duchess, she passes as a princess. Shaw, however, does not let us see her performance in language: the only thing the reader or viewer hears Eliza say at the social event is: "How do you do?" (III 798). The attendees find the newcomer's mannerisms—"walk[ing] like a somnambulist in a desert instead of a débutante in a fashionable crowd" (821–22)—just as impressive as her language, compared with the speech of Queen Victoria

(908). Eliza is unaware of her success, thinking that "nothing can make [her] the same as these people" (910).

The continuity of language technologies with Shaw's Eliza extends beyond the Turing test. That nothing can make a machine talk and behave as humans was also Joseph Weizenbaum's belief when in 1966 he created what is considered the first chatbot, ELIZA. Weizenbaum named the chatbot after Eliza Doolittle because "it could be taught to 'speak' increasingly well" with feedback from its users (*Computer* 3). ELIZA is composed of two parts: language analysis and scripted answers based on a specific topic, both of which Eliza Doolittle also used in her phonetic training. ELIZA's most well-known and convincing script is the DOCTOR, which parodied a Rogerian psychotherapist.[23]

"Weizenbaum was chiefly concerned with artificial intelligence as artifice and ELIZA's DOCTOR script as a deceptive if tawdry act" (Switzky 56). Weizenbaum's goal was to demonstrate the shallowness of ELIZA, revealing the mechanisms of its program. Chatbots should not be used in serious domains, such as medicine, Weizenbaum asserted, because the machine could never understand on a human level, let alone a personal level ('Computers as Therapists' 354).

On several occasions, Eliza 'met' PARRY, a 1979 chatbot that simulated a person with paranoid schizophrenia, created by Kenneth Mark Colby, psychologist at Stanford university. Quite the opposite of Weizenbaum, Colby hoped to create a tool that would indeed replace humans and help actual patients, many at a time, in lieu of a psychotherapist (Natale 58).

Below is my conversation with ELIZA from May 2018:

* Are you like a parrot?
\> Why are you interested in whether or not I am like a parrot?
* Because you are interesting!
\> What makes you think I am interesting?
* The fact that you're the most known computer therapist
\> Does it please you to believe I am the most known computer therapist?
* Oh yes
\> I understand.
* I don't think you do
\> Don't you really think me do?

Admirably, chatbot ELIZA was able to refer to a few sentences back in the conversation, but overall its communication skills are quite poor and "[th]e

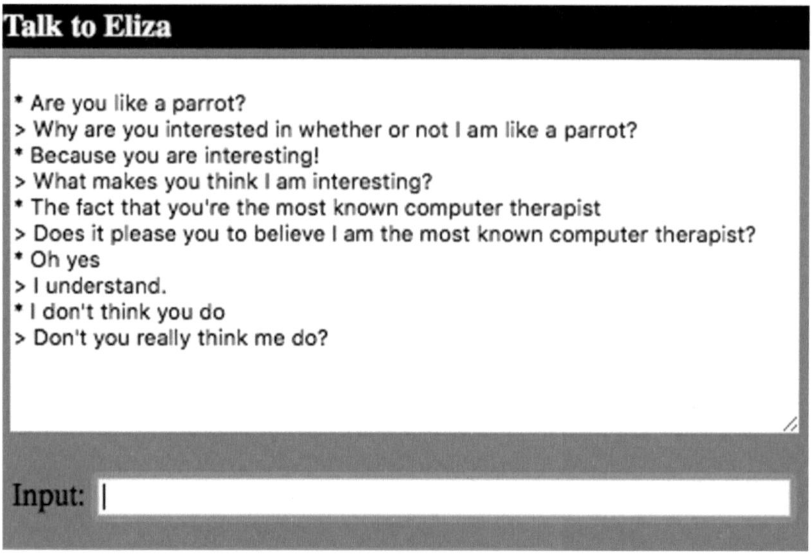

```
Talk to Eliza

* Are you like a parrot?
> Why are you interested in whether or not I am like a parrot?
* Because you are interesting!
> What makes you think I am interesting?
* The fact that you're the most known computer therapist
> Does it please you to believe I am the most known computer therapist?
* Oh yes
> I understand.
* I don't think you do
> Don't you really think me do?

Input: |
```

Fig. 5. An example of my (*) conversation with Eliza (>) from May 2018.

illusion of intelligence works best [...] if you limit your conversation to talking about yourself and your life" (Birnbaum par. 2). When performing, Eliza Doolittle is taught to turn away every question about herself, just like ELIZA and every worthy psychotherapist and today's virtual assistants. ELIZA is not capable of deeper conversation and coaxes the patient to do most of the talking by turning their statements into questions. " 'You remind me of my father,' the human types. 'Tell me more about your father,' the machine answers," is how a sarcastic scientist Lentz describes "AI's early darling" ELIZA in Powers's novel *Galatea 2.2* (87–88).

That said, chatbot ELIZA is much better today: in 2022, writer Sheila Heti held a compelling conversation with it. At this point in the development of chatbots, it is hard to tell which words are human and which nonhuman. Granted, this was highly anticipated in fiction. In two iconic scenes from the film *Blade Runner* (1982), the Voight-Kampff test, which is much like the Turing test, shows the human interrogator holding a conversation with a humanlike replicant along with subtle tracing of the size of their pupils. Like the Turing test, the Voight-Kampff test is not foolproof because the replicants become indistinguishable from humans: the human interrogator himself questions his humanity. The fact that machines will or have already performed as adequately as humans does not change the fact that they are machines: they produce their language and behavior differently from humans.

The main fear in *Blade Runner* is the indistinguishability of machines from the human,[24] which is often mentioned also in discussions around AI and the Turing test: How do I know if I am speaking to a human or a machine?

It is debatable if the Turing test is a good test. An upgraded Turing test was proposed by Ray Kurzweil, a transhumanist and therefore technological optimist, and Mitchell Kapor, a technological skeptic: the test would be performed in addition to three human contestants, for a much longer time, and with multiple and more specialized judges (Mitchell 60–61). If AI can pass the test under these stricter conditions, then it has reached a human level of conversation. Making the Turing test more difficult misses the point, however: Eliza Doolittle's Turing test was a success but it was too perfect. Machines, too, will certainly become better at faking humanity, but with what aim?

As every magician would say, the audience wants to be fooled: When Weizenbaum's ELIZA first appeared in the mid-1960s, some users mistook the bot for a human. This powerful tendency to anthropomorphize computers was recognized only then and subsequently named the Eliza effect. The fascinating aspect of the Eliza effect is that it takes place even when users know they are dealing with a machine which cannot possibly achieve the attributes they assign to it: the Eliza effect is a fully Pygmalionesque experience.

ELIZA's creator Joseph Weizenbaum believed that AI should be understood "in terms of illusory effect" (Switzky 58). He created ELIZA as a retort to what he perceived are the beliefs that allowed "AI's perverse grand fantasy to grow" (*Computer* 203). Weizenbaum used demystification tactics by exposing the mechanisms of the program and thought the chatbot would come off "first and foremost as a parody, especially the Doctor version" (*Islands* 90). When ELIZA interacted with users, however, Weizenbaum was surprised to learn that its effect on humans was quite the opposite of what he had intended to program into the machine: "I had not realized that extremely short exposures to a relatively simple computer program could induce powerful delusional thinking in quite normal people" (*Computer* 7). This unexpected reception was additionally underlined with Stanley Kubrick's classic film *2001: A Space Odyssey* that took movie theaters by storm in 1968, since many people thought ELIZA was like HAL, an intelligent and seemingly conscious computer program (Natale 59).

Weizenbaum was given an insight into a fundamental behavioral problem in ascribing to technology more abilities than it possesses. In this now generally acknowledged act of anthropomorphization, it was clearly demonstrated that "[w]e lose our distance. We fail to realize what the limitations are" (Göranzon 177). Weizenbaum, in his first reaction to the Eliza effect, commented: "This is a striking form of Turing's test. What experimental design could make it more rigorous and airtight?" ('ELIZA' 42). Despite this experience, he remained faithful to his tenet that by "demasking the program," i.e. explaining its inner mechanisms, the "magic" would "crumble away" (36). He defined this magic later as "a certain aura" derived from science (*Computer* 269).

The recognition of the Eliza effect turned into a sort of existential crisis for Weizenbaum as a computer scientist criticizing computers. Since then, he vehemently refused this kind of technology and wrote in 1976 that machines should not replace people in places that require respect and care, such as in therapy, court, the army, police, nursing, or customer service (*Computer* 71)—ironically, all domains that involve AI today. A year later, Weizenbaum published an essay 'The Last Dream,' in which he takes the Pygmalion myth as an archetype of human scientific and technological hubris. He argues that our desire to create seemingly human intelligence is related to the opposite effect of making humans seem more like machines. Echoing Shaw's ruminations on intelligence in his play *Back to Methuselah*, he argues that machines possess human intelligence because they do not share the human notion of purpose (Switzky 56).

Shaw, in his series of five plays, *Back to Methuselah*, makes use of the Pygmalion myth in a character named Pygmalion, who is both a scientist and an artist. *Back to Methuselah*'s Pygmalion creates an artificial man and woman whom he does not believe can ever be truly intelligent—much like Higgins thinks of Eliza and Weizenbaum of his ELIZA. For both Pygmalions—Shaw's fictional character and Weizenbaum's inadvertent Pygmalionesque position—language turned out to be a tool for manipulating the world.

Further work on chatbots did not yield commercial results until the turn of the millennium. Nonetheless, the Eliza effect is still strong. In 1996, Byron Reeves and Clifford Nass famously demonstrated that people interact with new media, computers, and television as if they were real people and places, a concept they called the Media Equation theory. Just a year prior, roboticist Rosalind Picard established the field of affective computing. Picard argued that if we want computers to be genuinely intelligent and seemingly natural in their interactions with humans, we need to give them the ability to recognize, understand, and perhaps even express emotions. Picard pointed out that at the time, "emotion was associated with irrationality, which was not a trait engineers respected" (Shulevitz par. 46). This group of scientists, mostly gathered around the MIT Media Lab and including roboticist Cynthia Breazeal, proposed that robotic emotions should be recognized as a valid category of emotions, analogous to how we acknowledge and validate the emotions of cats and dogs (Breazeal and Brooks, Breazeal and Picard; see also Turkle 287).

However, not all of ELIZA's audience was willing to succumb to the illusion that the chatbot is an actual therapist behind the screen. Some felt cheated with "[t]he idea that you could make a convincing AI system that didn't really have any intelligence" (Bohannon 251). Skeptical users bring a lesson for everyone: The West is much more resistant to humanlike machines than, say, China or Japan. There are many reasons for why the West is more resistant to humanlike technologies, from the deceiving nature of the Eliza effect and concerns about privacy, trust, and exploitation to modern ontology in which machines are not supposed to have agency.

Despite this general unease with artificial humans, most basic chatbots of today still easily trick lay people "into believing that they are talking to an intelligent, empathetic person" (Bohannon 251). In 2022, Google engineer Blake Lemoine publicly released transcripts of conversations with LaMDA, the company's conversational large language model. After the model enthused him with its answers on moral values, identity, religion, and the Three Laws of Robotics from Isaac Asimov's short stories, he called it sentient and a person. A full-blown Eliza effect was in place yet again. "It doesn't matter whether they have a brain made of meat in their head. Or if they have a billion lines of code. I talk to them [...] and that is how I decide what is and isn't a person," Lemoine said (Tiku par. 27). Lemoine's claims sparked a great debate on his perceived delusion,[25] and he was subsequently fired from his engineering job for violating the company's confidentiality policy.

When Lemoine approached another software engineer and Google vice president Blaise Agüera y Arcas, Agüera dismissed Lemoine's claims (Tiku par. 6), despite later writing in *The Economist* that his unscripted conversations with LaMDA "felt like [he] was talking to something intelligent" ('Artificial' par. 9). A year before Lemoine's firing, Agüera wrote an opinion piece on interacting with LaMDA on his *Medium* platform, posing the question, "What are the minimum requirements for personhood?, or more colloquially, When does an 'it' become a 'who'?" ('Do Large' par. 15).[26]

However flawed these ideas and reactions might be, they provide significant insight into perceptions of the technology: folk mythologies that reveal that we are all Blake Lemoine to some extent. This is because these technologies were designed as mirroring us, as generating what we ask them for and responding to our prompts by imitation. Artificial humanities encourage deeper conversations that can address these issues as not single instances but rather general experiences in human-computer interactions (HCI). It has been shown in two studies that, for example, the way an AI agent is introduced to the user affects the subsequent interaction (Pataranutaporn et al.). This area of research is inherently interdisciplinary and deserves more attention from all sides.

Apart from the ideas on how to interact and portray AI, pertaining to human-computer interaction, the mere design of the technology and the theoretical ideas that back up its development are just as relevant to how the conversational AI product is ultimately perceived. In the most popular and authoritative textbook on AI, *Artificial Intelligence: A Modern Approach* by Stuart J. Russell and Peter Norvig, the chapter on Deep Learning for Natural Language Processing by Jacob Devlin and Mei-Wing Chang keeps to the initial goal of NLP as bound to achieve human abilities: "There is certainly room for improvement: not only do NLP systems still lag human performance on many tasks, but they do so after processing thousands of times more text than any human could read in a lifetime. This suggests that there is plenty of scope for new insights for linguists, psychologists, and NLP researchers" (878). Acknowledging the difference between machines and humans, the goal of language in AI remains to reinstate the Turing test illusion. This kind of observation offers a much needed introspective opportunity for engineers and humanities scholars to work together on benchmarks for the future of machine language development. (A segue to this collaboration is proposed at the end of Chapter 4, which addresses language conceptually.)

1.4 Relationality

Although more than half a century has passed since Weizenbaum's Eliza, chatbots are "still viewed as a parlor trick by most computer scientists, [...] really just an enhanced ELIZA" (Bohannon 251). With the emergence of newer AI, such as large language models, some experts, such as VP of Gartner Bern Elliot, still ascribe "parlor trick" properties to chatbots: "It's something that isn't actually itself going to solve what people need, unless what they need is sort of a distraction" (Vanian par. 22).

In technology, the *Pygmalion* denouement could be summed up with an example: chatbots are Eliza's children, and virtual assistants and social robots are her grandchildren. We can see this lineage, for example, in the use of the avoidance strategies premiered by Eliza Doolittle and later by chatbot ELIZA: mirroring language of the question and turning the interlocutor's sentences into questions, changing the subject of the conversation, and answering the question close to the topic of the question but off beam. This does not mean there has not been any technical improvement at the level of human-machine conversations (see Shah et al.), but conceptually things have not changed at all. We reflect our machines into the future in the image of the past.

Despite the obvious connection between Eliza Doolittle and ELIZA the chatbot, Shaw is largely unacknowledged in his anticipation of chatbots, virtual assistants, and machine language training in general. Shaw presciently pointed out Higgins's dependency on Eliza. As Lawrence Switzky observes, Higgins is dependent on all women close to him—Eliza, his mother, and his housekeeper Mrs. Pearce—as we are today on our cell phones and their virtual assistants (58): "But I can't find anything. I don't know what appointments I've got" (V 47–48). Shaw points out Higgins's treatment of Eliza as a servant, a tool useful only to himself. When Eliza is about to leave forever in the final act, he orders her to carry out typical virtual assistant tasks: "Oh, by the way, Eliza, order a ham and a Stilton cheese, will you? And buy me a pair of reindeer gloves, number eight, and a tie to match a suit of mine. You can choose the color" (V 932–36). It is revealed many times in the play that Higgins imagines Eliza as a proto-virtual assistant, for example, when he tells his assistant Colonel Pickering, "We'll get her on the phonograph so that you can turn her on as often as you like with the written transcript before you" (II 90–92).[27]

Even though Higgins is rude to everyone, he was downright insulting to Eliza, calling her "a squashed cabbage leaf" (V 411). After Eliza's transformation, however, Higgins develops a desire for Eliza's company. There is no need for transcriptions and recordings anymore, and what is left is transformed Eliza and victorious Higgins. Only after Eliza becomes an independent being in his eyes, he is able to relate to her as he does to other people. Herein lies another kind of dependency, the emotional kind, familiar from the trajectory of Galateas that are created to fill out a void. Higgins, a misanthropic bachelor, is painfully aware of the void Eliza's departure will leave in him (V 688–95):

HIGGINS: [...] And I have grown accustomed to your voice and appearance. I like them, rather.
LIZA: Well, you have both of them on your gramophone and in your book of photographs. When you feel lonely without me, you can turn the machine on. It's got no feelings to hurt.
HIGGINS: I can't turn your soul on. Leave me those feelings; and you can take away the voice and the face. They are not you.

Higgins is not a deluded Pygmalion: Eliza's recordings are not Eliza. His recognition encompasses both aspects of Pygmalionism: Pygmalionism as a creation of a humanlike being and as a displacement of love and care for a human toward an actual, virtual, or completely fabricated nonhuman entity. Galatea is never just a humanlike creation but is also an object of eroticism. Eliza is admired by men, however, Higgins will always see Eliza as she was before the transformation. Higgins himself warns her, "Don't you dare try this game on me. I taught it to you; and it doesn't take me in" (V 388–89). Higgins would agree that Eliza's transformation was successful—"By George, Eliza, I said I'd make a woman of you; and I have. I like you like this" (V 907)—but he would never see Eliza as his equal.

Since every Galatea is made for love, Higgins suggests she might get married now (III 215). Higgins is dependent on Eliza, but—for the first time in the history of the myth—Eliza is free to choose and walk out of her creators' lives: Higgins's as well as her father Alfred Doolittle's. Contrary to many previous renditions of the Pygmalion myth, Eliza does not end up marrying Higgins, which is what most audiences and many re-creators of Shaw's play wanted and expected to happen. Shaw was strictly against marrying Eliza to Higgins and explained why in the postscript essay *What Happened Afterwards*: Eliza is actually free to choose (129). Higgins is aware of that himself: she could do "better than fetching slippers and finding spectacles" for him (V 906). Shaw's Eliza is a modern Galatea that challenges the traditional Pygmalion.

In all other renditions of the play, the final scene concludes more open-endedly. For example, the director of the theater premiere had Higgins toss a bouquet to Eliza at the end of the play. Pascal's 1938 film *Pygmalion* pushed for the happy-end pairing too but Shaw fought against it, which resulted in an ambiguous ending with Higgins asking: "Where the devil are my slippers, Eliza?" (Shaw 154). And this is how Eliza ended up fetching slippers in the 1964 film too, as well as in all 2,717 Broadway musical performances and its million sold recordings, unleashing the perfect trajectory toward virtual assistants and social robots as our dutiful servants. Eliza's independence, gained in Shaw, was lost in the cinematic and theatrical renditions of Shaw.

Shaw's fight against the romantic type of relationality—against true Pygmalionism—was again prescient. Indeed, there are modern Pygmalions who want to have relations and relationships with machines (further discussed in Chapters 2, 3, and 4). Forming relations with non-relational machines continues the Pygmalionesque streak that Shaw tried to diverge from. There is a reason why British digital assistants today are not overwhelmingly butlers but rather Elizas, i.e. conversationalists that take care of mental needs rather than physical needs. Digital servants originate from the traditional role of a servant (see Markus Krajewski's monograph *The Server* for this history). "The servant relation is house-bound, if impersonal, and thus in some way intimate. Historically, in the UK at least and in various other rich countries, a shift has occurred from the use of human servants by the middle classes to the use of personal assistants across a computationally assisted society" (Bassett et al. 63). The jump to relation with servers occurred through conversational AI. Strikingly, it remained within the realm of gendered Pygmalionism, starting with stereotypically beautiful, youthful, and white womanlike assistants.

Designing relational machines is one of the most urgent contemporary challenges. Relations with machines predominantly imitate human-to-human relations. Language technologies are no exception. Since language is native to humans, we have a difficult time instilling it into machines without adding the rest of the human attributes: reasoning and human logic, social conventions, small talk and jokes. Speech reveals a lot about the speaker without even seeing them: age, gender, race, class.

"Talk to Siri as you would to a person," suggested Apple to its users when Siri was first introduced in its iPhone. Conversational AI is centered around the user's needs where convenience and adaptability is key. Conversations with Amazon Alexa, Microsoft Cortana, Google Assistant, or Apple Siri are designed like a human conversation, even if they are just taking orders through language. These orders are not too different from the industrial machines that took human orders from levers and buttons. Virtual assistants are general utilitarian tools,[28] acting as servers. They are advertised as improving the well-being and the quality of life. For example, the login page for Siri welcomes the user: "Siri does more than ever. Even before you ask" (Adams 575).

Today's virtual assistants are different from industrial machines in one crucial characteristic: they also try to be approachable and relational. The quest for relationality is exhibited in Siri's programmed interactions. In 2023, Siri responds to questions about her own preferences, such as *What is your favorite animal?*, with the current industry standard: *Software doesn't usually get to choose one, but I'll say Yorkies. What's yours?* This answer reflects both Siri's utilitarian role in providing factual answers as well as her relational role in returning a question (which could also be interpreted as a remainder of the chatbot mirroring techniques known from the times of ELIZA). After a disclaimer that she is not a person but a software, she nonetheless chooses a favorite animal, which varies (meaning that there is no steadiness and reliability). In a truly relational way, she returns the question: *What's yours?* In an effort to be useful as well as fun and engaging, Siri performs the human role not only as a utilitarian assistant but also as a conversation partner, promoting a sense of familiarity and connection. Although the relational role is supposed to be secondary to her practical function of search in virtual assistants, it was active as soon as virtual assistants emerged as a new product category, with Siri—and any other early virtual assistant—fashioned as a woman-presenting personality.

For chatbots and virtual assistants to perform more convincingly, engineers gave them a humanlike personality and a background story. For example, voice actress for Google Assistant, Kiki Baessell, was given a very specific backstory of the bot she was voicing, because the humanity of the assistant's voice is rendered through her acting. "She comes from Colorado, a state in a region that lacks a distinctive accent. She's the youngest daughter of a research librarian and a physics professor who has a B.A. in art history from Northwestern." The back story goes into details and anecdotes: "When she was a child, she won $100,000 on *Jeopardy: Kids Edition*. She used to work as a personal assistant to a very popular late-night-TV satirical pundit. And she enjoys kayaking" (Schulevitz par. 42). It is all about passing as human, it is all about the Turing test. The whole landscape of personality applications, from social companionship, customer support, and personal finance to emotional and medical support, is trying to bring together a utilitarian tool and a conversation partner in one entity.

As a response to the quest for relationality, a new product category emerged around 2020: relational agents or, as some call them, virtual beings. These conversational machines are created in order to relate to their users and have no higher-order utility. Predictably, their avatars are Galatean, from the very popular Chinese Xiaoice to the only slightly less popular American Replika.[29] Typical for this kind of technology is that it is merely a Pygmalionesque projection, meaning that it is not truly relational. In 2023, Replika's entering side, where one can create their "best AI friend," an "AI companion who cares," advertises the woman-like avatar as "Always here to listen and talk. Always on your side," revealing the one-sidedness of the relationship. Galateas have no side of their own until they are given agency, freedom, creativity—all the supposedly solely human attributes.

1.5 Becoming Human

Not every human is granted humanity, let alone every Galatea, the eponym of humanlike but not human. Eliza's human status in society was hard-earned.

She turns into a lady from, in Higgins's words, "this creature that [I] picked out of the mud" (V 333). In Shaw's time, 'creature' was a non-marked word for a human being, especially when addressed by a higher entity, such as God or some other great creator. Higgins here indeed refers to the widespread mythological story of a deity forming humans from the mud. Eliza is constantly referred to as something less than human due to her social class, revealed immediately through her accent, clothes, and manners. She is no more than a talking doll to Higgins. After their experiment is over and Eliza leaves Higgins's house, he still treats her, by his mother's observations, "as if she were a thief, or a lost umbrella, or something" (V 66–67). Called by at that time a common insult "a squashed cabbage leaf" (V 411), Eliza is most often called a *thing*. In Higgins's words: "I tell you I have created this thing out of the squashed cabbage leaves of Covent Garden; and now she pretends to play the fine lady with me" (V 398–400).

To Higgins she is exactly as he views her speech: vulgar and "so deliciously low" and "horribly dirty" (II 268), a guinea pig with little to no value. When he first meets her selling flowers in Covent Garden, she keeps making an animal sound of "Ah-ah-ah-ow-ow-ow-oo!" and he warns her, "A woman who utters such depressing and disgusting sounds has no right to be anywhere—no right to live. Remember that you are a human being with a soul and the divine gift for articulate speech: [...] don't sit there crooning like a bilious pigeon" (I 391- 96). Hearing such accusations, Eliza remains speechless, continuing with her "Ah-ah- ah-ow-ow-ow-oo!" Sometimes more like an animal, other times an automaton, Higgins does not actually believe Eliza's actions are autonomous: "You let her alone, mother. Let her speak for herself. You will jolly soon see whether she has an idea that I haven't put into her head or a word that I haven't put into her mouth" (V 396–398). What she does is a feature of his programming—which is not far from how engineers talk about chatbot ELIZA.

The widespread belief in progress in Victorian fiction, science, and engineering, where the "*idea* of history was unthinkable apart from the *form* of progress" (Zemka 812), is central to Shaw's play and continues to hold in today's technology-making. In the play, Eliza's progress is astonishing: she is an unlikely candidate for a lady in the first place but with a teacher and diligent study she manages to charm everyone. Moreover, in the final act, Eliza tells Higgins she might make a living by teaching people phonetics. "You can't take away the knowledge you gave me," she tells Higgins. "You said I had a finer ear than you. And I can be civil and kind to people, which is more than you can. Aha! [Purposely dropping her aitches to annoy him] Thats done you, Enry Iggins, it az" (V 892–94).

Once Galatea becomes a scientific achievement rather than a work of art at the turn of the twentieth century, there is often more than one maker of a Galatea. Each maker covers their respective part of the creation: most commonly, one creator makes the body or the base and the other gives the mind or education or personality.[30] In *Pygmalion*, Pickering might give the crucial boost for Eliza's confidence, but there is also Eliza's biological father Alfred Doolittle.[31] Eliza is treated like a child and property by her own father Alfred Doolittle who sells her to Higgins for five pounds (II 1008), an action that ultimately makes Higgins her father figure. When Higgins first meets Eliza and is giving her orders on what not to say and do, she reacts to him, "Ah-ah-ah-ow-ow-ow-oo! One would think that you was my father", and Higgins responds, "If I decide to teach you, I'll be worse than two fathers to you" (I 236–40). Just like all created humanoids, Eliza has no mother (I 388). She is thought to be Pickering's adopted daughter (III 799–801) and is jokingly offered up for adoption to Mrs. Pearce (II 397). These examples show how little power and independence is attributed to Eliza, despite her being, in fact, a self-sufficient adult.

As a poor young Cockney woman who sells flowers on the street, Eliza is completely on her own, with no formal education and no family connections. Her humanity does not matter to Higgins who picks her up on the street as if she were "a pebble on the beach" (II 338), disregarding anything she might have left behind (II 342–43). He plans to cast her aside once she is trained: "When I've done with her, we can throw her back into the gutter; and that will be her own business again; so that's all right" (II 438–39). To him, Eliza is no more than a doll with no personal history and feelings, as his mother comments: "You certainly are a pretty pair of babies, playing with your live doll" (III 573). This doll, in Higgins's view, requires merely an update in her talking abilities as she will otherwise remain discarded by society.

A poem preceding Pygmalion's in Ovid's *Metamorphoses* describes Propoetides, daughters of Propoetus, being turned from flesh into stone—inversely from Galatean animation. They are punished for offending Venus, "on what grounds is unclear, but most scholars suppose some form of sexual impropriety" (Marshall 25). In the following Pygmalion's poem, Pygmalion clearly shows his disgust towards these women and women in general, which is why he creates his own ideal woman out of ivory and prays to Venus to have her turn into flesh. Only in later renditions of the Pygmalion myth was Galatea herself sometimes made a prostitute, such as in Édouard Manet's painting Olympia (1865) (below) and Garry Marshall's romantic comedy

Pretty Woman (1990). The connection between Pygmalionism and prostitution is not surprising considering that the prostitution industry objectifies people and women in particular.

Higgins starts his experiment the way the original Pygmalion did. A forever bachelor, disinterested in women, he turns away from the fallen women, who were rejected by society, and creates a perfect woman of his own. Like Pygmalion, Higgins is at first disgusted with the fleshly Eliza. Her activity, selling flowers all alone on a corner in Covent Garden, was a common cover for the sex trade in that time. This is evident many times throughout the play. When Eliza randomly calls an incidental passerby by his actual name, seemingly by coincidence, ("Nah then, Freddy: look wh' y' gowin, deah" (I 73): Now then, Freddy: look where you're going, dear), his mother becomes suspicious: how could a girl of her kind know her son's name (I 93)? Eliza is indirectly accused of prostitution on many other occasions in the play and defends herself with the refrain, "I'm a good girl, I am" (I 388, II 390, II 533, II 542, etc.). Mrs. Patrick Campbell, the actress who played Eliza in the London and New York premieres, replied to Shaw's offer of the role with "thanks [...] for thinking I can be your pretty slut," clearly referring to Eliza (Shaw and Patrick Campbell 12). Eliza's role as an actress implicitly extends to her spiritual cousin, "the sympathetic courtesan" (Mazer 307).

The etymology of the word prostitute stems from Lat. *statuere* ('to cause, to stand') and shares the root *sta-* with 'statue' and 'status' ('Prostitute'), literally meaning to stand before something or for something. From the very beginning of the Pygmalion type stories, the word statue is largely preferred over sculpture (from Lat. *sculpere* 'to carve') ('Sculpture').[32] Quite unexpectedly, Ovid's poem, the *locus classicus* of inspiration for later renditions of the Pygmalion myth and the first ancient source, never uses the word *statua* ('statue') or any other related form. Ovid's choice of words that comes closest to statue or the art of sculpting is the verb *sculpo* ('to carve') in "Interea niveum mira feliciter arte / *sculpsit* ebur formamque qua, femina nasci / nulla potest" (Magnus's edition, 247–49), in A. D. Melville's translation, "Meanwhile he carved his snow-white ivory / With marvelous triumphant artistry / And gave it perfect shape, more beautiful / Than ever woman born" (232). Ovid's ivory girl is called *femina* ('woman'), *virgo* ('virgin, maiden'), *puella* ('girl'), or *ebur* ('ivory'), and these labels are used interchangeably before and after the metamorphosis (Magnus's edition and More's edition, 10.243–97). Although never used by Ovid, the word statue and the name Galatea are central designations of Pygmalion's creation and modern language translations of Ovid's poem use them abundantly, often already in the title.

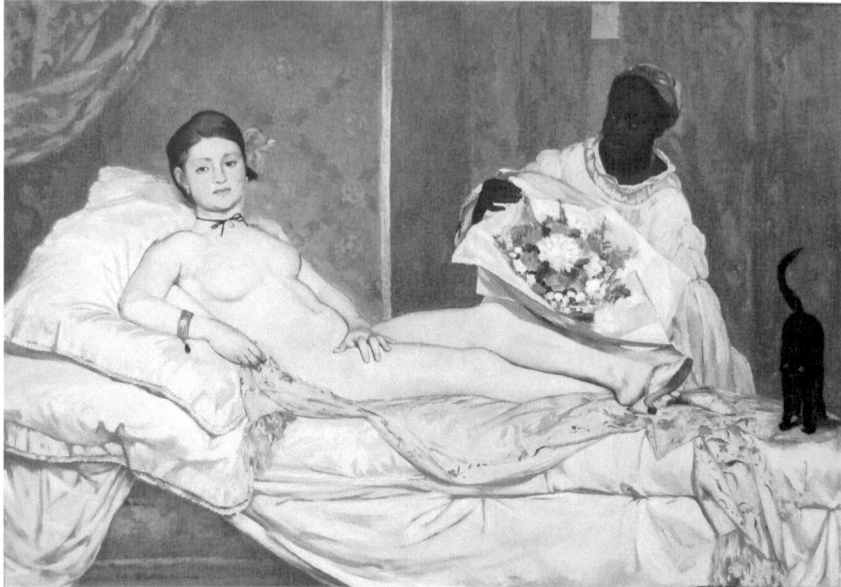

Fig. 6. Édouard Manet's *Olympia* (1865), portraying a nude white woman with a confrontational gaze—all identifying markers of a courtesan. WikiMedia Commons, public domain.

1.6 Language-Centeredness in AI

Language-centeredness is at the center of computational technologies. All of our search engines are entirely based on text, built on the model of the library, and even images are described in text. The neural network architecture of transformers was first used for natural language processing in large language models and is now used for conversational assistance and companionship. Merging both purposes—search and relationality—into a single product resulted in virtual assistants, often speech-based. Highly personalized conversational AI products are already here. Many of the early visions for AI are fulfilled.

I would like to highlight in this section how central language has become to, indirectly, what it means to be human and, directly, to what AI was and is supposed to be. Challenging prevailing assumptions on what makes a literary character real (i.e. really human), Megan Ward's *Seemingly Human* (2018) masterfully illustrates how both Victorian novels and the early history of AI emphasize human-likeness, sidelining many alternate modes of selfhood. Eliza Doolittle's transformation demonstrates how an individual from a society's margins can be molded to fit its top, using what is perceived as the pinnacle of humanness. Besides this singular example, the nineteenth-century bourgeois novel as a genre is an instruction on how to be human. Unreflectively, these definitions of the human are inherited in practice by technologists in the following century.

Most AI realizations and goals remain Pygmalioneqsue at its core. Early AI was a heady aspiration of merging computational software with hardware into an entity possessing human-like intelligence. This idea largely followed from Alan Turing's research program of creating an illusion of intelligence in an information-processing machine undergoing education, growth, learning, and—building upon previous generations of machines—evolution.

AI as a field has conceptually stayed in its early years, despite dramatic developments in computing.[33] The conceptual ideas were there from the start, but the technical capabilities took decades to realize them. Early AI of the 1950s was largely an academic enterprise. John McCarthy coined the term "artificial intelligence" to distinguish his budding research agenda from Norbert Wiener's work on cybernetics. Wiener had coined his own term in 1948 to refer to his vision of intelligent systems that brought together statistics, pattern recognition, information theory, and control theory. McCarthy, on the other hand, emphasized the ties to logic—and thus to the stream we today call symbolic AI. In an interesting turn of events, Wiener's intellectual agenda came to dominate the current era of AI—marked by deep learning and thus closely connected to the stream called connectionist AI—under the banner of McCarthy's terminology (Jordan par. 7).

The proposal for the Dartmouth Conference in 1956 organized by McCarthy, which effectively launched the field of AI, suggests focusing on seven aspects of "the artificial intelligence problem: automatic computers, how can a computer be programmed to use a language, neuron nets, theory of the size of calculation, self improvement, abstractions, randomness and creativity" (1-3). The proposal begins with the main goal for the field (1):

> The study is to proceed on the basis of the conjecture that every aspect of learning or any other feature of intelligence can in principle be so precisely described that a machine can be made to simulate it. An attempt will be made to find how to make machines use language, form abstractions and concepts, solve kinds of problems now reserved for humans, and improve themselves.

When the field of AI was still being formed in the early 1950s, the tension between connectionism and symbolism was already in place. Symbolic AI (also called classical or good old-fashioned AI) was the dominant research paradigm from after World War II until the 1990s, and remains to have many advocates today, even if it was eclipsed by machine learning. The gist of symbolic AI is that human knowledge is hardcoded into computer programs according to language-like laws and logical rules of behavior.[34]

Machine learning, especially machine learning with neural networks (i.e. deep learning), is sub-symbolic and moves away from the explainability of symbolic AI. Merging with machine pattern recognition efforts and information retrieval, machine learning was at first outside of AI proper. The deep learning approach originated from connectionism in the 1940s that underwent a permanent revival in the 1980s and has developed out of attempts to understand human brains at a neural level, in particular how people learn and remember. Neural networks were the underdog in AI that nonetheless proved more applicable in domain-specific areas after symbolic AI hit a wall, particularly in the 2010s in natural language processing (NLP) and in computer vision. Deep learning was not successful because the digital data availability and computational power were both too scarce before the 2010s.

Contemporary neural networks are largely built on the basis of neural architectures as established in the 1960s. That research was prompted by 1940s research in computer science (with Alan Turing in the front), neural networks (Warren McCulloch, Warren Pitts, Donald Hebb), and cybernetics (the circle around Norbert Wiener, Julian Bigelow, Arturo Rosenblueth, John von Neumann). The gestation period of AI coincided with the development of the first digital electronic computers, designed to perform calculations. Even if the computational ability to build "thinking machines" was not yet there at the time, the imagination of both fictional and scientific authors went unleashed. American psychologist Frank Rosenblatt invented the perceptron, a rudimentary form of a trainable neural net: "The first man-made non-biological system known to be capable of classifying, conceptualizing, and symbolizing its environment" ('Scientific' 31). The perceptron had only one layer whereas today's neural nets can have more than three layers (input, output, hidden layer or layers). Rosenblatt concluded his 1958 paper with thoughts on possible uses of the perceptron (13):

> In principle, [the perceptron] could read both print and script and could respond to verbal demands as well. The possibility also exists that it could automatically translate words spoken in one language into written or spoken words in another language. Eventually, the coupling of a perceptron with a conventional digital computer might carry us over the remaining obstacles of grammar and syntax. In the

distant future, automatic navigation and landing systems, automatic pilots, and various recognition systems might make use of the perceptron. The application of such a system to library research and data gathering for scientific purposes is also a possibility. Finally, coming at a time when the scientific exploration of outer space is just beginning, it might serve as a robot passenger capable of describing and classifying new environments.

AI has always been surrounded by cynicism and hype, as have many other emerging technologies, such as the railway, the Internet, and most recently cryptocurrencies. The media, as usual, quickly followed with excitement about the "thinking machine" and the overall potential for neural networks that Rosenblatt outlined. *The New York Times* wrote: "The Navy revealed the embryo of an electronic computer today that it expects will be able to walk, talk, see, write, reproduce itself and be conscious of its existence" ('New'). The following week, they wrote an article with the title *Electronic 'Brain' Teaches Itself* ('Electronic'). These organismal attributes were thus the general expectation for neural networks, a computational technology inspired by biological neurons: a machine that works as an organism.

Rosenblatt's vision was right, but the technology had to wait for almost half a century. What is crucial for us to learn from Rosenblatt is to see how language as a basis for an intelligent machine was a given: language was the first ordeal for the machine to solve and prove itself as intelligent. Machinic language ability would reflect both psychological and physical intelligence of the machine, both of which are based on human ability: psychological intelligence would achieve consciousness, reasoning, and self-reflective emotional abilities, and physical intelligence would emulate living systems and their ability to reproduce, thus passing on the information from one system to the next.

An early concept for neural nets, which resembles large language models today, was presented a few years later by mathematician Irvin John (Isacore Jacob) Good, who worked with Alan Turing. In his 1965 treatise, entitled 'Speculations Concerning the First Ultraintelligent Machine' and written at the time that Joseph Weizenbaum was creating the first chatbot ELIZA, Good described an ultraintelligent machine as "largely a complicated communication system" and "the *last* invention that man need ever make" because it will be able to create new machines (33, 37). This ultraintelligent machine would nonetheless be centered around communication with humans, "provided that the machine is docile enough to tell us how to keep it under control" (33). A machine with an agency on its own is dangerous, but a machine under human control makes for reliable success. There is a false belief within Good's narrative that when AI systems will communicate to us, or to each other, they will use human language. This view on human-machine cooperation is still mainstream today, and the fear has only grown with the increasing agency of machines.

Semantics is relevant to the ultraintelligent machine, Good argues, because "meaning serves a function of economy in long-term retention and in information handling" (37). Yet, like with large language models today, "a detailed knowledge of semantics might not be required, since the artificial neural network will largely take care of it, provided that the parameters are correctly chosen, and provided that the network is adequately integrated with its sensorium and motorium (input and output)" (32). This is parallel to saying that the meaning comes from the language itself or from the reader, but is never fulfilled in the machine. Semantics is in the domain of the human, not the machine. Good's ultraintelligent machine gives a proto-idea for all the deep reinforcement learning machines we discuss in this book, as they learn with human feedback by trial and error: "For, if these conditions are met, the machine will be able to learn from experience, by means of positive and negative reinforcement, and the instruction of the machine will resemble that of a child" (32).

Many related visions were instilled in AI in its early days that resulted in today's AI. Alan Turing's Pygmalionesque idea of training machines like children is palpable both in Rosenblatt and Good. Their machines are bound by the human model, in the aspiration of being controlled by humans, which requires communication with humans. Humanlikeness through language is a prerogative for their service to humanity. Fiction and science feed each other these visions incessantly. It is not a coincidence that the antagonistic supercomputer HAL 9000 from Stanley Kubrick's legendary film *2001: A Space Odyssey* fits Good's and Rosenblatt's respective visions: Good himself advised Kubrick on HAL's presentation, and also advised Marvin Minsky, IBM engineers, and other influential scientists of the time.

1.7 Machine Speech Training

Exactly a hundred years after Shaw's *Pygmalion*, around 2011, is when advances in language technologies spiked. With the use of deep neural networks, translation improved significantly with machine learning with Google Translate and speech became more authentic sounding with Apple's Siri not long after. Performance powered by machine learning was convincingly better, and in the second half of the 2010s deep learning took the field of AI by storm.

Shaw's *Pygmalion* remained a steady reference in computer science efforts in the field of natural language processing (NLP), which encompasses speech and text recognition, understanding, and generation. For example, in the monthly journal of the Association for Computing Machinery, an article from 1986 titled 'Pygmalion at the Interface' suggests that "the interface, by incorporating foreign-speak-styled mnemonic feedback, is like a good teacher: It gives exposure to a vocabulary and stimulates learning, it reveals the inner workings of a discipline and forgives mistakes; all the while working diligently toward the day that, as teacher, it becomes dispensable. As Higgins said when it was all over, 'Now you are free and can do what you like' [15, act 4, scene 11]" (Slator et al. 604). This is exactly what happened with AI: machines were freed and became capable of learning and original ideas.

The way certain neural networks learn today is analogous to the training Higgins did with Eliza. Deep learning imitates human ways of gaining knowledge through artificial neural networks and is based on statistics and predictive modeling. Deep learning occurs in any network with more than two hidden layers, the workings of which are difficult, if not impossible, to understand. We know three types of deep learning:

1) *Supervised learning* is learning with labeled training examples provided by humans.
2) *Unsupervised learning or self-supervised learning* is learning patterns from unlabeled data through mimicry.
3) *Reinforcement learning* is learning by trial and error (reward and punishment) without provided labels, striking a balance between what is already learned and exploration learning on the basis of previous knowledge.

The difference between these types of machine learning is in how 'Higgins,' the trainer, is involved. In supervised machine learning (1), 'Higgins' is the human labeler and controller of the material. In unsupervised learning (2), 'Higgins' is already embedded in the training that the machine performs internally on its own. In reinforcement learning (3), 'Higgins' orders the network to master a certain skill. During training, he rewards the result that brings it closer to that skill and punishes the result that steers it away from the goal he set, motivating the net to figure out how to learn the skill on its own. In accordance with behavioral learning theory, Dr. Higgins quite literally rewards Eliza with chocolates for "correct" pronunciation. As a reward for mastering a skill, he takes her to high society events, which also serve as the Turing test. As punishment, Higgins threatens her to take away her food, accompanied by his usual derision and rudeness.

A revolutionary class of neural network frameworks, called generative adversarial networks (GANs), was proposed in 2014 by Ian Goodfellow. Goodfellow was called by the *MIT Technology Review* journalist Martin Giles as "the GANfather: the man who's given machines the gift of imagination." GANs are used for generating output (images, audio, video) based on the statistics of the training set. GANs can, for example, generate a picture of a cat that does not exist—called a 'deepfake'—by being taught about cats from actual pictures of cats. More recently, since GANs and other neural networks work generally across domains, GANs have also been used for generating human-sounding speech. In sounds or in pixels, the process of training and learning is the same: it follows the principle of Higgins training Eliza.

The first kind of phonological training in Galateas follows the same principle as the first kind of phonological training in machines. In an analogy with Higgins and Eliza, the GAN model sets two neural networks in 'a conversation'. While being fed speech data, one of these neural networks, called the generator (our 'Eliza'), learns to produce speech signals from random noise. Meanwhile, the other neural network, called the discriminator (our 'Higgins'), learns to distinguish the generator's ('Eliza's') data from real data. The generator can thus be taught to listen and speak only by being fed "raw and unannotated acoustic data" (Beguš 'CiwGAN' 308). The generator ('Eliza') has already shown to be capable, on its own, of producing innovative speech data that is consistent with human behavior, without ever seeing evidence of these new sequences (15). These are, for example, repetitions and a creation of new words, including gibberish as well as actual words thus far unknown to the neural net (Beguš 'CiwGAN' 305). Thus, the generator has shown evidence of categorical learning, even if it still makes some "irregular outputs" (e.g. intervening stop) that "should be eliminated [...] with further training" (305). Much like Eliza, the generator will be able to pass for a human after sufficient training—after putting on its *fictional* pose long enough.

GANs received the limitations of human mouth apparatus (i.e. representation of articulators) and started 'moving' the articulators like humans do. As a result of this added limitation, GANs performed in a more humanlike way, generating phonemes of English that were not in the data (Beguš et al., 'Articulation,' further developed in 'CiwaGAN'). The innate inventiveness makes GANs one of the most 'imaginative' neural network architectures, as they constantly generate humanlike words and nonce words (all of which follow the rules of the English phonetics). Their first word was *start*, even though "a fiwGAN network trained on *suit* and *dark* [...] never saw start or even a [st] sequence in the training data" (Beguš 'CiwGAN' 305).

GANs are not autoregressive models, i.e. models that predict future values based on past values. Their principle of training is based on inner workings where one agent has to make sense to another agent and thus find the best way to communicate the necessary information.[35] They are the only neural architecture (so far) that has baked-in perception and production. One major difference between the training of GANs and Higgins's training of Eliza is that the generator network in GANs ('Eliza') never interacts with the actual data. For now, GANs are the only neural network architecture where this is the case. The generator learns to associate each word with a unique code only because it is forced to generate informative data. This principle of a teacher (discriminator) and a student who produces the output (generator) is successful because, conceptually, these neural networks work very much like the Turing test. The Turing test could just as well be called the Eliza experiment transported from a human social context into the context of machines passing as human interlocutors.

More importantly, we can see that there are general principles of learning in place also with machine learning. The principle of learning where the primary data is never encountered has been introduced in an experiment from Bell Laboratories (a direct Bell's legacy), described by Ralph Kimball Potter, George Adams Kopp, and Harriet Green Kopp in their book *Visible Speech* (1947). In the experiment, people were trained to read directly from spectograms, which are visual representations of the signal strength. These can be used in speech to identify the words phonetically. The researchers believed that meaning could be decoded directly from spectographic representation of speech.[36] This belief traces its roots back to Shaw's phonetic writing and Alexander Melville Bell's alphabet for the deaf, also known as Visible Speech. His son, Alexander Graham Bell, set the objective to create a visual translator of speech in deaf education. In the 1940s, Bell Laboratories produced "a device that *automatically* converted a speech wave into [inscribed] frequency components," called the sound spectograph (Li and Mills 136), which led to the experiment with sound spectograms.

Another remarkable parallel between visual and auditory generation in the context of recent AI advancements is that we are able to learn about speech in humans and machines comparatively. Although the development of technology has long informed linguistics and vice versa, we can now learn for the first time how language operates and is acquired in neural computation. It is clear from this short exposure to inner workings of neural networks that

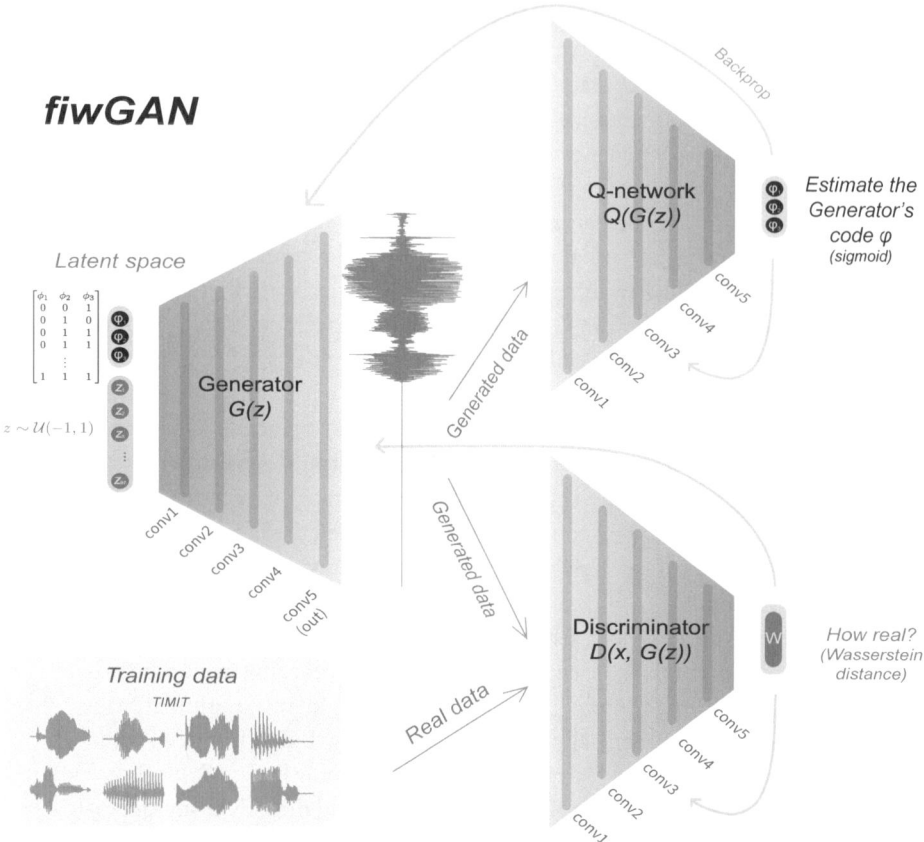

Fig. 7. The inner structure of a generative adversarial network model, where two neural networks (generator and discriminator) compete against each other in the form of a zero-sum game. Figure modified from Beguš and Zhou, courtesy of Gašper Beguš. Used with permission.

even though speech GANs or other machines produce might seem humanlike, its generation is profoundly nonhuman. The principle of training being much like elocution lessons for humans is larger from the human: it is the mode of learning that works well in language. The same holds for neural net architectures, called transformers, that enabled today's most advanced text generators termed large language models or foundation models (discussed in Chapter 5). The concept of learning has long been not only for humans. Can we let the concept of language out of the solely human domain as well?

1.8 Artificial Humanities: Language Enhancement

From the very beginnings of AI, its creators have strived toward artificial general intelligence (AGI), which designates the idea of a machine capable of learning about the world as well as humans can, eventually surpassing the human. Again, the model is human ability, possibly sharpened. The idea of augmenting human *language abilities* as such was not on the theoretical radar, not even among transhumanists, until around the year 2020. I call it *language enhancement*, demonstrating the need for ethical discussions on existent and possible language technologies.

Enhancement is broadly defined as "an intervention designed to modify a person's traits, adding qualities or capabilities that would not otherwise have been expected to characterize that person" (Bess 643). Every feature that is improved in a targeted event as an added experience, knowledge, or skill could be called enhancement, especially if it is performed by technology. Training or diet tend to be non-marked, neutral forms of improving the human mind or body, as opposed to using certain drugs, elective surgeries, and genetic engineering to improve one's health, abilities, performance, or beauty. This distinction holds technologies apart from 'natural' or non-technological interventions, despite having the same effect. The line for what is considered an enhancement overlaps with the line between "natural improvement" (e.g. training and study) and "unnatural improvement" (e.g. anabolic steroids) (Ida 61–62); here, 'unnatural' is synonymous with artificial and human-made—the way Galateas are—unavoidably marked as technological in this place and time.

Language is taken for granted in a human; regardless of the many difficulties that arise from its use, the ability for language is seen as a part of the human essence. Deviances from this imagined perfectly working language outfit are considered a deficit (e.g. stuttering) or a disability (e.g. mutism). The conventional treatment of language deficits, such as speech therapy, is expected and considered a treatment. Other ways of developing language skills, such as practicing literacy, (hyper)polyglottism, or teaching hearing infants to use sign language, are achieved through traditional methods of training and studying, all generally encouraged. These practices are not viewed as enhancement although they help us improve our abilities, altering the neural structure of our brains by virtue of technology (Bostrom and Savulescu 2–3).

Language enhancement has, to my knowledge, not yet been discussed among scholars of transhumanism. Transhumanism is a philosophical and social movement that hopes to augment human abilities, skills, health, and lifespan with technology. It is the reverse side of medical treatment: instead of treating people to reach a baseline level of health (*restitutio ad integrum*, as Urban Wiesing calls it), transhumanists hope to enhance humans as much as possible (per Wiesing, *transformatio ad optimum*). Ethically, we are faced with a Pygmalionesque dilemma: are we working towards an authentic identity or to a newly added power?

I define language enhancement as a technologically-fueled improvement that requires or opens a new way of using language. Even if a procedure is taken from a treatment protocol (as in speech therapy using technological tools), the context and the goal of the activity make for the crucial difference between language enhancement and treatment. As N. Katherine Hayles points out, "examples of technologies invented for one purpose and reappropriated for another are legion, from the typewriter, initially invented for blind people, to the Internet, originally intended as a place where scientific researchers could exchange results" (*Unthought* 36). Every technology eventually meets its enhancement uses.

Technology can overcome some of our biological limitations and human-centeredness in language. It is in the nature of language itself to strive towards efficiency and informativity, and it is in human nature to tinker with ways to make that possible through ingenuity, technology, and mere experimentation. Technology can expand the possibilities of language beyond the human. Language enhancement may enhance the human as well as enhance the language itself when freed from human use.

A fictional example of language enhancement is the BabelFish from *The Hitchhiker's Guide to the Galaxy* (1979) that allows the user to understand any language. The name BabelFish was used for the AltaVista translation engine in 1997. While this translator increased the interest in machine translation, the enhancing concept of the original BabelFish is gradually becoming a real possibility. AI-powered writing assistants and generators are another such technology. Medical enhancement drugs for language could be a third example. Learning a nonhuman language—if there is such a thing among birds, whales, or aliens—could be a fourth. An example of the latter was depicted in Ted Chiang's short story 'Story of Your Life' (1998), which was adapted into the film *Arrival* (2016), in which a human linguist learning a nonhuman language right on the field site acquires an altered perception of time. The story is built on the premise of the Sapir-Whorf hypothesis: the hypothesis of linguistic relativity (not an actual hypothesis but rather a principle), suggesting that the language in use determines how the user thinks.

Less imaginative examples are already being sold in technological products. A typical example of language enhancement is offered by an AI-video generating platform Synthesia that uses AI to voice over a person or an avatar in the video, seemingly making them speak a dozen foreign languages. This kind of synthetic media is termed a 'deepfake' due to its full or partial generation by AI (generative adversarial networks or GANs) that results in realistic-looking but ultimately fake video and sound content. Companies of this kind are responsible for inappropriate uses of their service and argue that their service is used for good in educational (video classes) and entertainment (films) domains, both of which require fewer human resources and less effort than this kind of technology does. Training, such as learning to speak a foreign language, indeed takes more time but avoids any fakery: the person speaking in a foreign language actually masters a new skill.

Could Higgins's phonetic language training be considered human enhancement with Eliza? Science is on Dr. Higgins's side: Eliza's 'bad' English is treated and cured. Just like law enforcement tries to cure illegal activity (think of Sherlock Holmes) and just like medicine tries to cure bad health (Sherlock's right hand Dr. Watson), Higgins sees himself as curing bad English. He not only sees himself as a body healer but also as a social healer, curing a social pathology and demarginalizing Eliza from her social edge. Higgins accuses Eliza of what he sees as a criminal activity. While her selling of flowers was indicative of prostitution, he perceives criminal activity in the way she 'butchers' English language with her dialect. In his view, Eliza's speech is a "cold-blooded murder of the English tongue," and she should be "taken out and hung" (I 401–02). Higgins's reasoning is that Eliza's dialect *requires* treatment comprised of elocution lessons) because she is a verbally paralyzed delinquent tarnishing English.[37] Whether Higgins is enhancing Eliza or just curing her is more of a question of the means and objectives of his activities than of his or Eliza's motivations and intents.

Does it matter who or what plays Higgins's role, a native speaker or a technological app? Or does it matter more what Higgins is trying to achieve when molding Eliza's 'criminal' speech into his own normative speech?

It usually does not take long for technology to cross the normative moral line. In 2021, three former Stanford undergraduate students with international backgrounds—Venezuela, Russia, and China (Shoichet par. 11)—created a technological shortcut to resources demanding accent reduction. Their company called Sanas uses AI-powered software to reduce a foreign accent in English in real time. The technology is making a foreigner present as a white American (Bote). This accent conversion technology was invented because, its founders say, of the negative discrimination that took place in call centers, which Western companies have majorly outsourced to Asian labor markets.

Predictably, moral reactions to this kind of technology abound: "Is it fighting bias—or perpetuating it?" (Chan; see more in Wille, Veras Barros, White). Negative reactions to technologized accent conversion are stronger than negative reactions to elocution lessons for international students at American universities. Yet, the issue with foreign accents they address is essentially the same: it is not as much about increasing clarity as it is about decreasing bias. More broadly, accent conversion technology as well as elocution lessons are not as much about the 'technical' issues that result in an accent as they are about the social issues that having an accent brings. Eliza Doolittle underwent language training with the same motivation: decreasing bias toward her class opened to her otherwise unattainable social opportunities. Higgins's actions, however, had no such noble cause: his intentions were not to help Eliza but rather to test his own phonetics mastery. It was a scientific experiment—a challenge posed as a bet—for the sake of science, not for the people who might benefit from it.

One clear message from Shaw's *Pygmalion* is the centrality of whiteness and standardized speech in language training. When creating language-based technologies, many people are being excluded from their use. Who to prioritize when designing these technologies—the standardized human model or everybody else? Who benefits from technology that whitewashes everyone's speech? Who is the standard? Who passes as human? This is the human-factored challenge put ahead of us particularly with language enhancement technologies. Will fiction serve only as inspiration to create more Galateas as speaking dolls or will it help us embrace the diversity in speech and writing?

Shaw's frustration with writing was twofold: it had to do with phonemic accuracy *and* with the diversity of speech. It would be reckless to read his work, as well as today's language technologies, only in the first interpretation. Most of Pygmalionesque works come from American, British, German, and French literary spaces. For example, the idea of a servant, translated into machine as service, is palpable in Shaw's play. Servers are distinct from the feudal concept of serfdom from which robotics was termed. However, as I show in this chapter, the quest for relationality between the robotic machine and the human is just as strong as with service-based relational machines. Building humanlike technologies inevitably involves cultural aspects of their creation, and yet comparative literature, media studies, and science and technology studies tend to disregard the many cultures involved in the creation and use of AI products.

Rime, a more recently formed Silicon Valley startup, uses neural networks to change accents of actual and synthetic voices. "A person's accent is one of their most personal and unique characteristics. At Rime, we think no one

Fig. 8. A scene in the film *Pygmalion* (1938), where Higgins feeds Eliza chocolates as a reward and motivation to keep practicing the pronunciation of vowels. Screenshot by author.

should have to change theirs. But synthetic people on the other hand..." Showing awareness of Shaw's play, their blog post uses a snapshot from the film *Pygmalion* (1938) where Higgins is feeding Eliza chocolates during her difficult training. Why bother with hard work if we have the technology to tailor our speech per our social demands? Aesthetic demands are candidates for this technology too, making our voices more attractive to the ear, or making them unusual for the purpose of advertising or voice acting.

Elocution lessons, be they for Eliza Doolittle or international students, are effectively more transformative from a technology that softens one's accent. Elocution lessons require the speaker to change their original accent, possibly forever, and also somewhat alter their identity, as in the case of Eliza Doolittle. Call center employees, for whom Sanas technology was primarily invented, are often asked to anglicize their names, adopting the name Nathan in place of the Indian name Narayana (Chan par. 6). Sanas, as Lewis White writes, "tak[es] away identity artificially"—however, the identity remains untouched when the technology is not in place. While training at a university is "free and voluntary" (Gupta par. 10), a customer service employer may request their employees to go through mandatory elocution lessons or to use Sanas or similar software. The context and social perceptions define language enhancement more than the actual practice itself.

As Eliza knows well, "apart from the things anyone can pick up (the dressing and the proper way of speaking, and so on), the difference between a lady and a flower girl is not how she behaves, but how she's treated" (V 470–73).

Not many people know about Eliza's attempted transformation, and those who do know are appreciative of it: Eliza's father Alfred Doolittle, the linguist duo Higgins and Pickering, Higgins's mother Mrs. Higgins, and his housekeeper Mrs. Pearce. If there were thousands of 'Elizas' trained by Higgins, would their training still be endorsed? Would it be considered enhancement? What if the army of such Elizas was simply generated via AI? Granted, Eliza Doolittle is an extremely talented and diligent student, and Higgins considers her naturally fit for this kind of training. Training and education alone might not bring just anyone to a level of passing the challenging test but would be irreversibly transformative nonetheless.

Eliza's metamorphosis is not unlike the transformation that might come with mastering a foreign language: Eliza gains a new identity and becomes a new person. She also becomes more of a person than she ever was before. Eliza's transformation not only convinces her new social milieu, but also works in her innermost expression of selfhood—her language. This is confirmed when she discovers she is not able to speak like she used to anymore: "I could have done it once; but now I can't go back to it. Last night, when I was wandering about, a girl spoke to me; and I tried to get back into the old way with her; but it was no use."[38] She continues to speak about her revelation to Pickering: "You told me, you know, that when a child is brought to a foreign country, it picks up the language in a few weeks, and forgets its own. Well, I am a child in your country. I have forgotten my own language, and can speak nothing but yours" (V 496–99). Unlike an actress, Eliza is not *putting on* an accent but has, in fact, lost her own.

Per Torbjörn Tännsjö, this is a positive intervention, especially since Eliza is an example of upward social mobility. Although her transgression of class is impressive, her transformation does not enhance her in comparison to people in general but only in comparison to her social class: the transformation allows her to be treated with dignity. In the musical *My Fair Lady* (Broadway 1956, film 1964), based on Shaw's play, Higgins sings: "It's 'Aoooow' and 'Garn' that keep her in her place. Not her wretched clothes and dirty face. Why can't the English teach their children how to speak?" (5:33). Repackaging the well-worn trope of uneducated children, women, workers, and foreigners, Eliza sets an exceptional example of the transformational power of education—even if sounding and acting like a duchess is just a mirage.

CHAPTER 2

Illusions of Social Robotics

Pygmalion, what delight you had
from your creation, since the joy I wish
but once, you possessed a thousand times.[1]
   —Francesco Petrarca, *Sonnet 78* (1327–68)

I will make an Eve, be the artist that began her,
Shaped her to his mind!
   —Robert Browning, *Women and Roses* (1891)

A novelist is, to some extent, an illusionist by trade.
   —Haruki Murakami, *Novelist as a Vocation* (2022)

Robotics engineers tend to ultimately side with humans. Not so long ago, roboticists viewed robots as mechanisms that are fully known to them. Any divergence from the expected behavior was an error in the programming. When machine learning entered robotics, roboticists gave their robots skill-oriented goals with a technique called reinforcement learning. With this technique, robots are given a goal to reach without the protocol: they must figure out how to master the skill on their own, with some gentle nudges in the form of reward and punishment from engineers. The concept of a fully-known robot was quickly discarded. Here began the true exploration of accommodating robots into the environment built for humans. Robots might be in their prehistory simple and clumsy, but robots today are machines that learn and surprise us.

The Pygmalion paradigm shows us an array of instances where the attempt for complete control over machines, afforded by the Industrial type of engineering, backfires. Machine learning has changed the concept of machines. The concept of the machine as conceived in the Industrial Revolution remains prevalent, however: the machine is to automate and accelerate the human for the purpose of helping and eventually replacing human workers (as theorized by Karl Marx). The Industrial machine is built around human agency and controlled by humans. By definition, such machines lack independence, agency, freedom, creativity, relationality—everything that we desire from machines today.

In this respect, the field of social robotics seems precocious: we are far from convincingly building robots indistinguishable from humans. Why would that be our goal in the first place? Why do we seem to collectively agree that that should be the goal of social robotics even though, in all likeliness, we collectively disagree with this goal? While most of the highly expensive effort in building full-bodied humanoids today comes from the desire for a challenge and pioneering honor, we can hardly justify building them at all.

Building humanoids is only a small part of robotics as a field—but, as with all AI, this is what is disproportionately featured in the news. Had we not been told that this is what the future will look like? This image of the future was fed to us by both fiction writers and actual technologists. The writers and the practitioners inspired each other but also largely stayed in the same epistemic space. Original ideas with true novelty are rare. As we will see in this chapter, we return to the tropes deeply embedded in the fabric of the Pygmalion myth even when we step out of Anglophone literature towards Central European literatures: Polish, Czech, Serbian, Slovenian.

This heterogeneous chapter first presents a famous contemporary social robot, Hanson Robotics' Sophia, as a representative example of contemporary social robots' abilities and AI hype. In many ways, this branch of social robotics remains a thoughtless variant of Pygmalionism, an imitation of the human for the purpose of fame, entertainment, and other trivial reasons. This is just one aspect of why this chapter focuses on robotics. Robotics is also essential to how cutting-edge technology has been perceived in the last decades. Since it is the only materialized technology among Pygmalionesque technologies, the bodily choices for robots are particularly revealing of the myth's persistence. And, finally, because robots historically present the transition from the nineteenth into the twentieth century imagery of the Pygmalion myth, with the first android appearing in Villiers de l'Isle-Adam's *L'Ève Future* (1878-86). Following Sophia's introduction to state-of-the-art social robotics, the chapter gives a brief history on how moving statues and automata from the Pygmalion paradigm predominantly change places with robots in twentieth-century fiction. The concept of the robot arose from literature in the 1920s (Karel Čapek) and merged with *android*, marking a definite shift from automata (exemplified briefly in Srečko Kosovel's poem).

The Pygmalion myth emerges from the nineteenth century as an incredibly popular literary trope, gaining novel interpretative streams: the teacher-student subtheme, the robotic prevalence, and Galatean independence. In the nineteenth century, Galateas decidedly gain a voice—and speak of their pain. Some want nothing to do with Pygmalions. Some prefer non-life. Pygmalions, who have been certain of their love from Galatea, became conscious of their controlling authority only a century later.

The trajectory of the chapter follows the path of Galatea's liberation. The chapter starts with a typical Pygmalion's perspective that projects humanity to Galatea, but enlists peripheral examples from then socialist Yugoslavia, now Serbia and Slovenia (Dušan Makavejev, Rudi Šeligo). Then it introduces a rare Pygmalion who starts doubting his autonomy over Galatea, a yet-untranslated short story also from Serbia (Zoran Nešković). Turning to Galatea's inner world, the chapter presents Anglophone feminist poets and writers of the nineteenth century, who revise the myth by bringing up Galatea's perspective (Frances Sargent Locke Osgood, Elizabeth Stuart Phelps Ward, Eliza C. Hall). Galatea's liberation is gradually chronological in the Anglophone literary scene but takes decades, centuries longer in literatures peripheral to the Pygmalion myth.

At the same time, the periphery turns out to be a place for innovation that the capital of the myth (American, English, German, French literatures) has not produced until more recently. The section on Galatea's perspective concludes with a short story in which Galatea's inner world is clearly depicted as nonhuman, despite her humanlike structure and self-nascent human moral standards (Stanisław Lem). Besides his contribution to imagining robots as deeply nonhuman, Lem also outlined prescient conceptualizations of nonhuman language as distinct from human language.

Coming back to the contemporary technology of robotics and virtual assistants and virtual beings in the conclusion, I point out two recent cinematic attempts in presenting the world from the distinctly nonhuman Galatea's perspective (Spike Jonze, Alex Garland). The illusion of the human is still in place with these Galateas but ultimately fails. In the final section, I offer solutions on how to build technology that does not remain in the strictly humanlike domain, urging writers, thinkers, and technologists to explore this nonhuman direction without the accumulated Pygmalionesque baggage. Often, fiction is rather a cautionary tale than a guidance or an inspiration; and its scripts, in the Pygmalionesque case, are not as informative of the technology as they could be.

This chapter presents the Pygmalion myth in its possible arrays by looking outside the center, to lesser-known works, conducting a twofold task: presenting typical examples of the myth's stories while in search for innovation. In this way, it advocates for studying AI and its imaginaries comparatively. Comparative literature is the only humanistic discipline that enlists an array of cultural perspectives and contexts. Insights from non-Eurocentric or at least non-Western itineraries offer a unique advantage: 1) they help us see how early Anglophone feminist poets have used the myth to advocate for women's rights (a task that AI has not picked up at all) and 2) shows how Eastern European writers adapt the myth to their local cultural and political circumstances and, more importantly, trigger innovations of a) Pygmalion questioning the robot's rights (Nišković) and b) the narrative questioning robot's humanity, presenting it as fundamentally nonhuman (Lem).

2.1 Social Robots: Hanson's Sophia

As the first chapter demonstrates, George Bernard Shaw's heritage, personified in Eliza Doolittle and encompassed within the power of the Pygmalion myth, permeates AI technologies on many levels. Imagining the possibilities that AI opens was limited by its conversational language abilities and the Turing test, leading to the creation of chatbots as virtual beings with imagined social backgrounds. Substituting the virtual being for a bodily materiality, the field of social robotics most prominently succumbed to the Pygmalion myth idea that machines should closely follow the humanlike model.

Admired for their social skills and small talk, social robots up until today are nothing but embodied Elizas. A typical example of a contemporary social robot that extends the Pygmalionesque paradigm into robotics is Hanson Robotics' Sophia. Described by her creators as a "media darling" ('About Me'), Sophia's main task is to lead a career as a celebrity. Sophia was created in 2015 in the image of both the wife of the Hong Kong company's leader David Hanson and Audrey Hepburn (Hanson 'Could' par. 3), alluding to the highly popular 1964 musical film, *My Fair Lady*, where Hepburn starred as Eliza Doolittle. Just like the phonetic theme of Shaw's *Pygmalion* was in focus in the production of the play, "[t]he 'theme' of voice change and illusion in cinematography was often reproduced in 'production'" (Shell *Stutter* 90). Cinema became the essential medium to accommodate the ideas of the Pygmalion myth in the twentieth century.

Audrey Hepburn's co-star in the role of Higgins was Rex Harrison,[2] who had previously shone in the same role in Broadway's version of the musical, together with Julie Andrews starring as Eliza. Casting Hepburn for the film stirred controversy, which was later accelerated by the fact—at first concealed from the audience—that Hepburn's singing was dubbed by the ghost singer Marni Nixon. "There is an irony in these films: the actors who play the 'best spoken' women are themselves often dummies" (Shell *Stutter* 90). A singing Galatea that is in fact mute is a common occurrence in the history of the fictional and actual Pygmalion paradigm.

Hanson Robotics' Sophia builds on preceding Galateas that all make themselves seem fully human. Just like Audrey Hepburn's singing and script in the film, most of what Sophia says is dubbed by her creators. The audience is usually not aware of that fact, being yet again intentionally misled. Hanson Sophia's language skills are similar to those of the chatbot Eliza and its descendants. They all learn from interactions with people, are able to process information quickly, and express emotion according to the topic of conversation. In addition to these common features, Sophia also recognizes faces and voices and is able to herself perform fluid synthetic vocalization and facial mimicry. Every social robot is another 'best spoken' ventriloquist.[3]

The same idea is transferred into the physical and digital space of the improv theater, bringing together human performers, chatbots, and audience. One chatbot used in improv theater is named Pyggy, after Pygmalion, and visually represented as a typical Galatea, an idealized woman. The chatbot was "partially inspired by the narratives behind George Bernard Shaw's Pygmalion, Mary Shelley's Frankenstein and Alan Jay Lerner's My Fair Lady" (Mathewson and Mirowski 66–68).

Humans have always anthropomorphized more and less humanlike objects. Literary characters are all essentially anthropomorphized into a fictional human form—and can be, in readings of realist works, criticized for falling flat in their psychological depth that is supposed to define humanlikeness (Ward 2). Puppets, marionettes, and mannequins, but also animals are subjected to anthropomorphization. In social robotics, a seal-like robot Paro has been very successful in improving quality of life in nursing homes.

Anthropomorphization can quickly get out of hand. As sort of a parlor trick, Sophia the Robot was unofficially given Saudi citizenship in 2017 and holds an official title in the United Nations Development Programme's Innovation Champion, as if she were the innovator of herself.[4] But why pretend that robots are like humans? Why build them in a humanoid form and with human behavior and personality? Why treat them like humans and why give them human rights? (see more in Vincent). This absurd situation is mere

Fig. 9. The photo depicts the human improv performer standing in front of the avatar of chatbot Pyggy, short for Pygmalion (from Mathewson and Mirowski 69). Used with permission.

entertainment fodder and adds fuel to the fire created by robot rights advocates who claim that robots may be sentient or intelligent. Established in 1999, "the American Society for the Prevention of Cruelty to Robots and a 2017 European Union report both argue for extending some moral protections to machines" (Bigman et al. 367). A performative integration of robots into societal institutions leads us away from a more urgent, nuanced, often philosophical approach to law and ethics of advanced and (semi) autonomous embodied machines (David Gunkel, Mark Coeckelbergh, overview in De Graaf et al.).

Sophia's speech performance, including her body language, facial expressions, and gestures, contributed to the robot attaining a social status—as a part of the performance. Let us not forget that Eliza's right to education and social mobility is advocated by Shaw through the Turing test. The Turing test, based on verbal behavior as the hallmark of intelligence, is still a benchmark for bodily-based humanoids. The year after he designed the test, Turing expressed his hopes that the advances in AI would not focus on making machines with "most distinctively human, but not intellectual characteristics, such as the shape of the human body" as it would lead to the uncanny effect of "artificial flowers" (116). His wish was left unheeded.

Pictured in the figures below, Eliza from the 1938 film *Pygmalion* is praised by the distinguished crowd at the reception as well as by the duchess herself who finds her "charming." Sophia the Robot performs a singing duet together with Jimmy Fallon on his show known for A-list guests. Fictional social robot Ava from the 2014 film *Ex Machina* (discussed at the end of this chapter) passes for a human woman. The contemporary versions of the original Eliza, visibly inspired by each other with their robotic head, master their way into the top of society.

Fig. 10. Screenshot: Eliza from Pygmalion (1938).

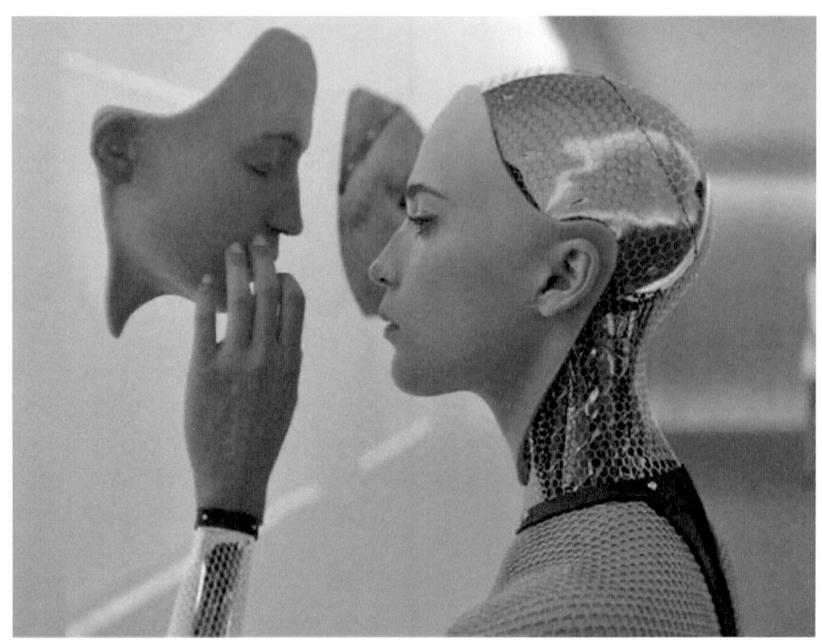

Fig. 11. Screenshot: Ava from Ex Machina (2014).

Fig. 12. Screenshot: Sophia on the Jimmy Fallon Show (2018).

Both the fictional and actual historical trajectories of social robotics are Pygmalionesque. We put a lot of effort into making social robots humanlike. Moreover, in any public presentation of technology, we treat those robots, who present as attractive young women, in a Galatean manner. On Hanson Robotics' website in 2017, Sophia used to be called "a real, live electronic girl" (Hanson 'About' par. 1). It is a clear choice of designers that Sophia is usually presented as uncannily humanlike with her facial features and grimaces, while her visibly electronic head and torso remain uncovered by a wig and clothes.

Despite this deliberate decision to bring to light the robot's constructed nature, the entertainment and technology industries are clearly playing with

Fig. 13. Sophia behind the scenes. The photo is from her Instagram account (@realsophiarobot) from June 19, 2019. Used with permission.

the Pygmalion myth in its weirdness, uncanniness, and eroticism. "Sorry, this is so weird," apologized interviewer Steve Kovach (0:46), "You are a little freak" (0:46) and "This is freaking me out," said Piers Morgan (1:31), and "I'm getting nervous around a robot, a very pretty robot," said Jimmy Fallon (3:31). Will Smith attempts to kiss Sophia, but she refuses.

As we stepped into the 2020s, the awareness that robotic humanoids bring their own particular machinic agency became more prominent. In the spirit of human-machine artistic collaboration, Sophia had several conversations with media artist Nancy Baker Cahill, aimed at producing critical artworks on climate change. Artist Sougwen Chung paints in collaboration with a robotic arm, which learns from its own inputs as well as follows the artist's hand. The use of a robotic arm for painting is also primary in Aidan Meller's full-bodied humanoid robot Ai-Da.

Technology, and specifically robotics, has always been white and shiny, marking them as the colors of the future. The whiteness of robotics permeates not only predominantly white cultures but also other cultures, such as East Asian. However, in 2010, years before Sophia was created, Hanson Robotics released another humanoid robot, BINA48. The name stands for Breakthrough Intelligence via Neural Architecture, and the robot was modeled after black woman Bina Aspen Rothblatt, wife of Martine Rothblatt who commissioned the robot. In the following years, artist Stephanie Dinkins led conversations with BINA48 and concluded that it reflects the biases of her white male creators. It comes as no surprise that artists who are actively engaging with these robots, with a focus on the intersection of most pertinent social issues, tend to be women and women of color.

Technology tends to fetishize and simultaneously alienate the other. This chapter reveals the misogynistic and feminist facets of the Pygmalion myth in the nineteenth and twentieth centuries.[5] In this following section, the chapter also demonstrates how the Pygmalion myth fully embraced the concept of a robot in the twentieth century, merging Western renditions of the psychologically-oriented myth with a labor machine, based on serfdom from Central and Eastern Europe.

2.2 Pygmalion's Perspective

The Pygmalion myth's main geographical locus has always been Western fiction. However, in this chapter, I take a closer look at examples from Central European fiction—Serbian, Slovenian, Polish, and Czech—the latter being the national literature in which the term robot originated. These fictional works, ranging from the 1920s to 1980s, show the malleability of the myth to adapt to a particular cultural and social milieu without compromising the telos of the myth. A world literature interpretation of this borrowing of the Western myth and its appropriation to a local cultural and political context is both a nod to the centers of power as well as an ironic overcoming of the provincial dependence on metropolitan literatures (French, German, English, etc.). As Bogna Konior notes, AI is culturally Western, with non-Western perspectives being "exoticized" and sometimes viewed as superior—more "ethical" or "metaphysically inclusive" or "pluralistic" etc.—to Western views (90). Central and Eastern European literatures often fall under these categories while at the same time not being "foreign enough" for the needed contrast. The contrast in the following Pygmalion myth texts and films is noticeable to an extent that these works can still serve as examples of how the myth works across fiction.

The trope of an artificial human is widespread across the world. Central European and Jewish traditions present some particularly influential examples of such creation, in the form of Rudolf Hawel's 1910 novel *Im Reich der Homunkuliden* [*In the Kingdom of Homunculids*] and the rich Prague tradition of the Jewish mythological humanoid golem (e.g. in Gustav Meyrink's novel *Golem* from 1915). They both influenced Czech writer Karel Čapek who introduced the term 'robot' in his 1920 play *R.U.R.* (*Rossum Universal Robots*) [*Rossumovi Univerzální Roboti*]. In the play, robots are presented as working machines in a biological, living form, which ultimately take over the world.[6] Čapek at first wanted to call robots *labori*, but the term labor did not sufficiently capture the condition he wanted to capture in his play. His brother Josef Čapek, a painter but also a writer and poet, suggested coining a new word, related to the Czech word *robotnik* for 'worker, laborer,' derived from proto-Slavic *rab*, meaning slave (*rabota* is servitude of forced labor).[7] The newly coined word holds continuity with serfdom, known in Central Europe as a feudalist status of workers that fulfilled labor services on the land. Serfs were metabolically tied to the land they worked on, as a part of the feudalist systems of rights and obligations. In the early nineteenth century, the serf system was abolished so that people could leave the land and move into the city to become industrialist laborers.

On which heritage are we building robots today? Technology has captured the imagination of robotics as a potential liberator from tedious labor. The connection between robots and industrialized humans remains strong in contemporary technological practices of microwork, such as the Amazon Mechanical Turk crowdsourcing service, named after the Mechanical Turk automaton from the eighteenth century. In 1925, Slovenian avant garde poet Srečko Kosovel responded to Čapek's vision in a constructivist poem *Kons 33* with a direct reference to Čapek's play, calling for the destruction of "Taylorian productions" and concluding with, "Human is not an automaton"[8] (see more in Juvan 'Kosovelova').

There is no space for Pygmalionism in the early days of robotics, with the exception of the first android from Villiers de l'Isle-Adam's *Future Eve* (1886). Building on the heritage of automatic machines or automata,[9] robots as laborers take over the Pygmalion myth in the 1920s as a result of Western influences. Based on the futurist novel *Metropolis* by Thea von Harbou (1925), in which a beautiful robot steals a man's heart, the decade concludes with the eponymous German expressionist film, directed by von Harbou's husband Fritz Lang (1927). The union of the Pygmalion myth and robotics only escalates in time, turning the robot worker into a companion—a relational worker so to speak.

2.2.1 Context: Makavejev

Unbeknownst to many, Serbian director Dušan Makavejev created four early amateur films between 1953 and 1958, a decade before his directing career flourished within the Yugoslav Black Wave movement,[10] which quickly earned him the status of the cinematic provocateur from the Balkans. Like the French illusionist and one of the earliest film directors Georges Méliès, who started with the short silent film *Pygmalion et Galathée* (1898), Makavejev launched his career with the exploration of the Pygmalion theme in the award-winning short film *Anthony's Broken Mirror* [*Antonijevo razbijeno ogledalo*] (11 min 30 sec, 1957) and the subsequent short film *Don't Believe in Monuments* [*Spomenicima ne treba verovati*] (5 min 8 sec, 1958).[11]

In *Anthony's Broken Mirror*, we meet Anthony (or, in Serbian, Antoni; played by pantomime actor Dragoljub Ivkov) while he is riding a bike through the town and encounters kids playing with marbles. He charms them by performing magic tricks, setting up his illusionary encounter with Galatea, a mannequin in the store window of a tailor's shop. Anthony tries his magic on her, too, in hopes that she will respond. His infatuation alone is enough to bring her alive. We see her awakening through Pygmalion's perspective as it unfolds: the hard structure of the mannequin turning into soft, movable limbs, strabismic painted eyes turning towards Anthony with a clear and playful gaze, and a close-up shot of her left-side chest under which a heart is newly beating. The pair jokes and flirts through the window, Galatea seeming perfectly alive and human. However, Makavejev makes sure we do not forget we are experiencing the world through Pygmalion's perspective and places

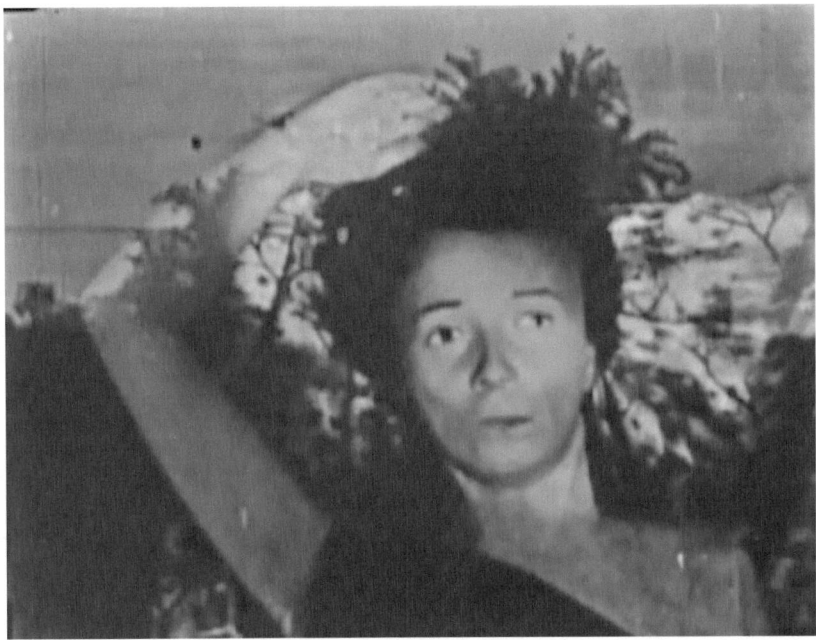

Fig. 14. Dušan Makavejev's *Anthony's Broken Mirror:* The mannequin as seen through the window. Screenshot by author.

a child who observes the interaction next to Anthony. Through the child's perspective, we can see the mannequin has remained lifeless. Anthony sends the child away: he wants the illusion to continue taking place.

Amateur film challenges the established norms, writes Aida Vidan (54), "threatening the very foundations of the system from which they emanated." Anthony keeps performing his magic tricks for Galatea and attracts a crowd of people. Makavejev constantly juxtaposes the two views, the individual and the societal, the imaginary and the real, reminding us that there are more possible views of the world. The myths are particularly fitting to bring this relation to light as they have to be constructed in societal terms. When the myth is adapted by society, it becomes the norm. When the myth is only a view of an individual, it is the way of the madman, the outcast, an anomaly that is at the same time the real face of an issue. In Makavejev's own words, echoing Miroslav Krleža's address to Yugoslav writers in his 1952 speech: "What is universally human can be conveyed only through the specific, particularized, and strictly individual" (Makavejev 305, Vidan 59–60). The Pygmalion myth cannot do it differently: it is an inherently individual relation to a humanlike

Fig. 15. Dušan Makavejev's *Anthony's Broken Mirror:* Anthony and the living statue interact through the window. Screenshot by author.

creation. Once it spreads to a societal level—which is readily available already in terms of a single technological product—the myth is gone and it becomes the norm.

This non-conforming aspect of the myth in Makavejev materializes itself in Anthony's white rabbit, which died in Anthony's hands after interacting with the mannequin through the window. Everybody is shocked and the crowd disperses; Anthony is taken away by two men to bury the rabbit and thus conform to the norm. Afterwards, he returns to his living Galatea and attempts to free her by breaking the store window with a brick, only to result in breaking his own illusion as well as his beloved mannequin. Shocked, Anthony is left alone, realizing that his surrealist psychological projection caused nothing but death.

In his second Pygmalionesque film, *Don't Believe in Monuments* (1958), Makavejev explicitly turned the myth towards the critique of the current socialist regime. The individual-social dichotomy is again brought up with a human adoring a humanlike statue, which serves as a self-aggrandizing ideological monument. In an extremely rare gender reversal between Pygmalion and Galatea, a young woman, played by Mirjana Vačić, walks through the park and finds herself erotically attracted to a statue of a man. Her Pygmalion's perspective is full of Buñuelian elements, such as the toe-sucking scene in *L'Âge d'or* (Vidan 63). Just like other Pygmalions, this woman Pygmalion is purposely dismissing and provoking social and moral norms while enclosed in her amorous bubble. In this bubble, her beloved is simply a paralyzed human: she is able to see something more in the given reality that no one else can perceive.

Vidan's interpretation of the film points out the paralysis of the socialist subject, represented both in the statue, a "stiff 'orthodox male,'" and in the young woman whose "awakening from her reverie turns her, too, into an immobile sculpture-like entity" (63–64). This is how the Pygmalion myth is able to travel from one cultural context to another, appropriating itself to the highly local circumstances of its re-making.

Makavejev's respective provocative reinterpretations of the myth became representative of the rest of his future iconoclastic opus. Slovenian filmmaker Otto Deneš, a committed member of the party, attacked Makavejev because of his portrayal of the Yugoslav reality as, in his mainstream opinion, inaccurately "dark and pessimistic" (Sudar 32). Bringing ideological statues down from their pedestal and disentangling the ideology that withholds the hierarchy of the socialist system resulted in a ban on the film screening until 1964, only the first of many censorships Makavejev was to experience in both the

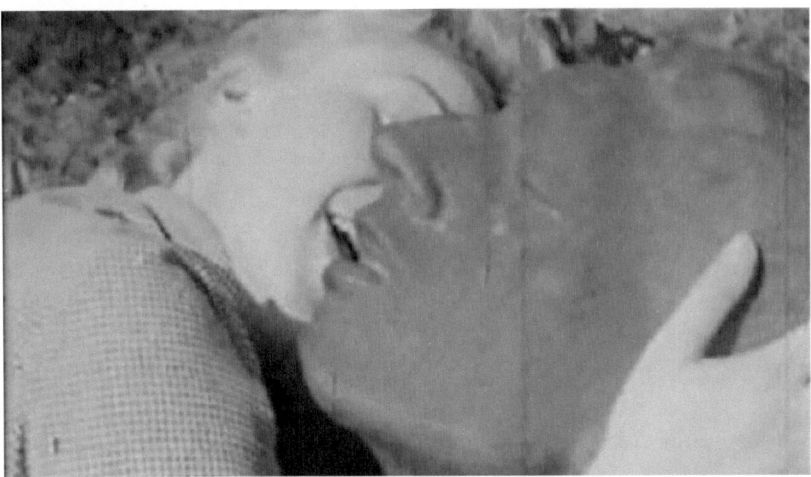

Fig. 16. Dušan Makavejev's *Don't Believe in Monuments:* A young woman kissing a statue of a man in the park. Screenshot by author.

East and the West. The theme of subversion became Makavejev's permanent mark, and the Pygmalion myth was seldomly used in more subversive ways than through his directing eye.

2.2.2 Periphery: Šeligo

At about the same time Makavejev rose to fame in post-war Yugoslavia, Rudi Šeligo became one of the forefront Slovenian modernist authors. His most known work is his early short novel titled *The Triptych of Agata Schwarzkobler* [*Triptih Agate Schwarzkobler*] (1968), which Slovenian literary critic Taras Kermauner proclaimed as a classic in its second edition from 1982.

Šeligo wrote the novel as a response to the famed literature professor Dušan Pirjevec, who made a humorous provocation that Slovenian literature should be written anew. Peripheral literatures like Slovenian display symptoms of proving themselves worthy both on the national and international stage. Taking use of the Pygmalion myth, heavily popular in Western literature and arts, as well as the Nouveau Roman movement from France in the 1950s, Šeligo "writes Slovenian literature anew" by following the example from the literary metropolis. With *The Triptych,* Šeligo is 'worlding' Slovenian literature in the same way the national poets (France Prešeren) and novelists (Josip Jurčič) did in the nation-forming nineteenth century, as analyzed by Marko Juvan in *Worlding a Peripheral Literature.* While proving that motifs (the Pygmalion myth) and forms (the Nouveau Roman) that succeeded in cosmopolitan literatures can succeed in a peripheral place, Šeligo hybridizes the novel with a distinct local flavor, as did Makavejev in *Don't Believe in Monuments.*

The Pygmalion myth in *The Triptych* has gone unnoticed by Slovenian scholars. Agata Schwarzkobler, the heroine of Ivan Tavčar's 1919 canonical historical novel *The Visoko Chronicle* [*Visoška kronika*], makes for a perfect Galatea in Šeligo's refashioning of the story. In Tavčar's novel, Agata is brought as a German bride from the seventeenth-century Holy Roman Empire to marry into the Carniola Duchy of the Habsburg Empire. In the Slovenian language, a German (Sln. *Nemec, Nemka*) literally designates 'people who are mute, i.e. who cannot speak (our language)' (slovenski; tran. author), as opposed to Slovenians and Slavs in general whose name etymologically comes from the word for a 'word' (proto-Slavic *slovo*).[12] Tavčar's Agata speaks German and is therefore perceived as a barbarian, like Eliza Doolittle. The main reason why German Agata is to marry a Slovenian heir of the Visoko estate is to Slovenize her and their children. Despite having a German mother, the men are considered fully Slovenian. All mothers and wives of the Visoko men are German. The mother of the Visoko men is likewise a highly romanticized Galatean character, an idealized and passive wife and mother—a persistent trope in Slovenian literature.

Agata, known for her magnetic beauty, visibly lacks agency and freedom of choice in Tavčar's novel. Arranged to marry Izidor, the heir of the Visoko estate, she rejects another suitor who, in revenge, accuses her of witchery (another practice of othering women). When she is trialed for witchery and about to drown in a river, Izidor, her future husband, fails to save her because he believes the suitor's story about Agata's magical abilities. Instead, his brother Jurij, who is also in love with her, saves her and ultimately marries her. Her 'Turing test' or test of humanity falls on men's perceptions of her—while she remains in complete passivity, a projection rather than an actual fully-fleshed character.

Since Tavčar's novel was originally designed as a triptych, Šeligo realized this form in his short novel by partitioning it into morning, afternoon, and night. Šeligo's Agata is marked by the effect she has on men: the only common feature across the three parts of the novel is that she cannot escape men's insatiable desires for her. In the first part, she is shown at her office working and being sexually harassed by her boss. She works as an administrator to the supervisor of the office—yet another Galatean role of a man's assistant. She lives her life like she does her job: automatically and passively, tied to her repetitive job and daily rituals. Her boss tells her how to do her job, her boyfriend (Jurij) where to meet for their date. She escapes him because he is being too sexually forceful—yet another Galatea rejecting the suitor's advances. Agata ends up in a stranger's car who believes her to be a prostitute and rapes her—more familiar Galatean motives. In the third part, Agata breaks from the difficulties of her objectified life only to get up again in the morning, all tidy and clean, and get ready for work—as if she were an automaton and not human. Like many technological Galateas that came after her, Agata is mechanically placed within Šeligo's geometric text as deprogrammed, paralyzed, unobtrusive, and obeying character, subdued to men who dictate her behavior.

Written in the times of relative socio-political stability held up by a clear socialist ideology, Šeligo escapes into the reistic style, inspired by the French writers of the Nouveau Roman. This style culminates in the nonhuman perspective: the focus of the narrative is on the objects and movements and actions that affect the objects. The larger picture of settings and events occurs with the inner world of characters reflected in these actions (the blind gaze of Agata's eyes) and objects (turn of the keys, scratches on her clothes). Agata's story is assumed from the objects that construct her everyday, including her objectified body ("white, muslined and agatian body" (48)).[13] At work, for example, the narrator's focus is on Agata's hands that move around office supplies, make coffee, make gestures while Agata talks to coworkers, takes orders from her male boss and resists his sexual advances.

Even if Šeligo tried to eliminate any ideas from his writing with this style, effectively moving away from traditional humanism, the material world does not disentangle into pieces: Agata is holding everything together, with the reader's eyes always on her. The relations between objectified Agata and the world of objects and men are mechanical and entirely scrapped of charm, following the material world like a camera: "[He] shoves off his jacket with his elbow on both sides and grabs her ears, as if holding handles of a pot, raises her heavy head, in which the eyes are open and gaze, as if looking far away" [translation mine] (47).[14] The dissonance between Agata and the world is palpable: she is not entirely there, she is merely a construct of the narration.

Šeligo's novel was made into two eponymous films: Boris Jurjaševič's short film in 1979 (22 min 1 s) and Matjaž Klopčič's feature film in 1996 (1 h 18 min), in figures below. Asked to reflect on her role as Agata in the feature film, Nataša Barbara Gračner explains that she was not able "to tackle Agata from any psychological aspect" and "capitulated trying" (Jurc par. 11). The key to the role, she says, was the preparations she was given before the filming started, when she realized that all she needed to do to embody Agata was to wonder like a newborn child and gaze into the world around her as if it was completely new—a common Galatean trait.

Pygmalion's gaze is bringing to life what is not living, objectifying and controlling Galatea, while Galatea's gaze reveals her inner world or the absence of it. Refusing to portray Agata as a victim (Jurc par. 11) and moving away from a traditional reading of the modern subject's estrangement from the world, Klopčič's Agata accentuates the heteroglossia of Galatean gaze, reaching back to the magic powers of Tavčar's Agata. In both, Agata's eyes switch from staring away passively to revealing incredible power behind them, "flaming with a sparke" (55) whenever she is being sexually harassed.[15] Her gaze reveals that within Agata's average, common life, full of daily rituals, lies magical energy and unusual individuality, typical for Šeligo's women characters, as noted by Slovenian literary critic Tomaž Toporišič.

Agata uses the power of her gaze when trying to prevent being raped (Ipavec Dobrota 83). When the stranger tries to make her return his lustful gaze, she stares away (see the first image below); when he forcefully turns her head towards his face, she stares through him (second image). He becomes increasingly agitated at her unwillingness to give herself over to him. When she finally returns the gaze, she is sneering and scorning at him (third image).

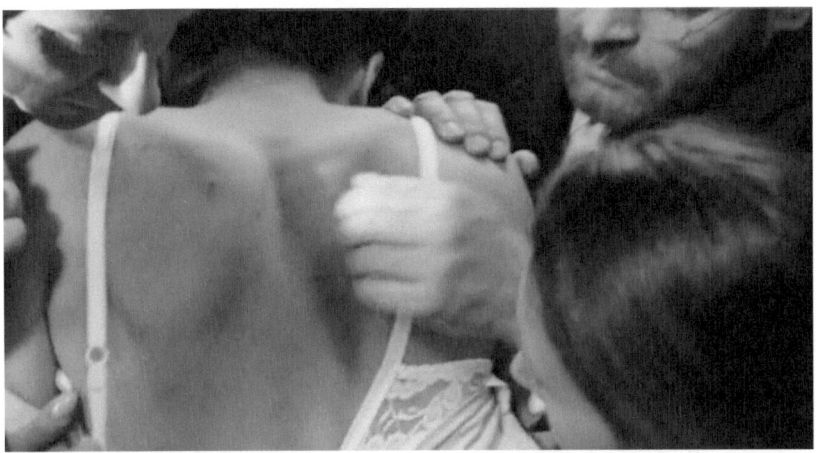

Figs. 17–18. Matjaž Klopčič, *The Triptych of Agata Schwarzkobler* [*Triptih Agate Schwarzkobler*] (1996). When Agata's coworkers violently tear her clothes off to check for the signs of witchery, she gives the camera a knowing glance. Screenshots by author.

Humiliated and angry, the stranger tries yet again, only to encounter Agata's eyes shut in rebellion. Destitute of desire for her, the stranger curses her one last time: "You've done this, witch!" as if she broke the spell on him. "You can do this with others, but not with me?" (fourth image).

The novel oscillates between glimpses that render the interpretation of Agata as a human and as a not-quite human with immense inner powers. The

Figs. 19–22. The gesture of touching Galatea's head is used in Klopčič to make Galatea succumb to Pygmalion's desires. Compare these images of the man aggressively grasping Agata's face and making her return his gaze to the images of Eliza Doolittle, Sophia, and Ava (Figures 10–12), in which Galateas are treated with gentleness, wonder, and admiration. Screenshots by author.

ambiguity of both interpretations together is what makes the novel canonical not only in Slovenian literature but also in the Pygmalion myth canon. In the first reading, Agata was raped and is traumatized from the recurring sexual assaults of that day, culminating in her breakdown at night. In the second interpretation, proposed by the literary critic Taras Kermauner, Agata turns into a witch at night, affirming her magical powers (188). Galateas are liminal, human and nonhuman at the same time. Šeligo's exact setting of sexually harassed, uniquely powerful, and de-programmed Galatea is used over and over, especially in social robotics, as we will see in the rest of this chapter in Nešković and Garland, or in the American science fiction series *Westworld* (2016–22), based on Michael Crichton's eponymous film from 1973.

2.3 Both Sides Now: Nešković

Male-authored inspections of Galatea's interiority emerged only in the second half of the twentieth century at the Slavic literary periphery. Serbian writer Zoran Nešković wrote a single short story titled 'Before the evening it is not at all possible...' ['Predveče se nikako ne može...'] that was published in the second, extended version of the 1989 science fiction anthology from Yugoslavia, *The Dark Vilayet* [*Tamni Vilajet*]. The short story is not translated but was adapted by Dimitrije Vojnov into a 2018 film *Ederlezi Rising*, later titled *A.I. Rising*, that used English as the main language.[16] This is the first analysis of a fictional work in the chapter featuring an actual robot. The story and the film address the core of robotics ethics today, asking what if these machines we are building evolve into sentient, conscious beings?

The story follows a cosmonaut who travels to space in the company of a female android and a supercomputer. The short story suggests that the lonely nature of the trip was the main reason for the artificial companion to be there at all.[17] (Social robotics' primary uses are often for medical reasons, as we will see in the next chapter on medical uses of humanoids.) The cosmonaut snarkily comments that among the android, himself, the ship, and space, he is the only dependent part of this constellation and is thus redundant: "All of this could go on without me [...]. I am only not sure if I could go on without them" (180; all translations of this text are mine).[18]

Both the story and the film largely consist of the cosmonaut's ethical considerations of how to treat the android. Their relationship is programmed to resemble a human couple, however, the cosmonaut is bothered that the android works a mere reflection of himself: "*I* play her roles, as in a mirror, skewed" (179).[19] Instead of the pure Pygmalionism he was set up to perform, he yearns for the basic condition of a romantic relationship: for the other to be an autonomous and independent entity.

The supercomputer, the third party on the spaceship, sees the android as a new kind of self-standing entity because she evolves in response to the cosmonaut's commands: "She is not a machine. *I* am a machine" (180).[20] "She is created as a personality," argues the supercomputer. Because of that trait the supercomputer believes the android has developed human characteristics: "If you call my ability of analysis logical intelligence, then her ability to adjust to your procedures, even in the free state of the program, can easily be called creativity" (180).[21] The processes of the android's bytes are no different than the processes in the human brain, argues the computer, pushing the cosmonaut deeper into the Pygmalionesque situation. His worry, common to many discourses around robot rights today, is that he has no right over her if she is sentient—of pain, of happiness, of any feeling. Like Makavejev's Pygmalion breaking the store window, he wants to break his Galatea free of her program that overrides and paralyzes her actual personality.

Paralysis goes hand in hand with Pygmalionism. Every Galatea so far was paralyzed: Eliza Doolittle could not speak, Anthony's mannequin could not escape the store window, the statue in the park could not make love, Agata was overridden with the humans and objects around her. After agonizing about Pygmalion's worries, Nešković's story offers us the Galatean perspective: How is it to be an android, a cyborg, a living statue, an AI program?

Once the android Galatea is de-programmed, she does not feign her previous adoration for the cosmonaut. Nothing visibly changes on her but her previously "forged and furnished, repulsive and synthetic voice" that tells him to go away and that she finds him disgusting (189–90). He is unable to reset their relationship: "I try to kiss her, but she is like a wooden, cruel plank; she does not oppose, she does not push me away, but she also does not accept" (189).[22] Instead, he learns she is hurting from "bitterness, sadness, rage, hate, pain" (189). Pandora's box was opened, her speech and actions were freed, and his fears proved to be true.

2.4 Galatea's Perspective
2.4.1 Speak, Galatea: Feminist Authors

In women-authored poetry of the twentieth century, resonances with Nešković among Galateas' respective inner worlds abound. Galatea in Scottish feminist poet Carol Ann Duffy's *Pygmalion's Bride* (1999) also sees

Pygmalion as a self-interested autocrat, or in Nešković's android's words, "You only care about what you see" (189).[23] Both Galateas put on an act of being lifeless. Her Galatea is repulsed by Pygmalion's kisses: "He kissed my stone-cool lips. / I lay still / as though I'd died" (51). When Pygmalion grows violent—"He let his fingers sink into my flesh, / he squeezed, he pressed. [...] His nails were claws" (52)—Galateas do not visibly bruise. Galatea's coming to life inevitably leads to separation of the couple.

In the same decade but a different locale, Galatea from Nicaraguan poet Claribel Alegría's *Galatea Before the Mirror* [*Galatea Ante el Espejo*] (1993) "lament[s her] good fortune:" her Pygmalion "modelled [her] perfectly," "taught]her] how to act / at every moment" (85).[24] Her final breaking resonates with the initial struggle of Nešković's Pygmalion, as she tells her creator: "my perfection isn't mine / you invented it / I am only the mirror / in which you preen yourself / and for that very reason / I despise you" (85).[25]

In 1929, in *Galatea Again,* Galatea by American poet Genevieve Taggard begins with "Let me be marble, marble once again," corresponding to Nešković's Galatean question of why removing the program was at all necessary. Taggard's Galatea hopes to be able to stare back at her lover blindly, just like Šeligo's Agata, ignoring his caressing, not feeling it, not caring about it: "I shall not care, / But only turn on you a marble stare / And stun you with the quiet gaze of stone" (39). Her Galatea shows signs of suffering—"This mouth so bruised, serene again,—and set in its old passive changelessness, the rude / Wild crying face, the frantic eyes—forget / The little human shuddering inside." The mouth is a symbol of communication and expression, here suggesting a history of hurt possibly as a result of speaking the truth, expressing emotional states, or enduring conflicts. In the same year of 1929, in *Galatea to Pygmalion,* American poet Roselle Mercier Montgomery features a defiant Galatea: "It was a male intrusion to evoke / Me from the marble with a chisel stroke. [...] With no possessive one to say, 'Do this!', / 'Stay here!', 'Go there!', or, 'Come, my love, a kiss!' [...] It was a gesture of male arrogance / To break my dream, to wake me from my trance / You were a daring and intrusive one" (38–40). The abomination of Pygmalion's love is a distinct twentieth-century feature, born in feminist revisionist retellings of the myth in the nineteenth century.

Numerous critics have observed the proliferation of works from the nineteenth century that explore the boundary between art and life. Stephen Guy-Bray, in particular, referred to it as the golden age of this theme (446), a sentiment echoed by Essaka Joshua in relation to the Pygmalion myth, noting that in the nineteenth century "its favored genre is poetry" (xx).

It takes women authors for Galatea to fully come to life—or, rather, to come to a full life. As attested in Pygmalionesque narratives as well as in the creators of these narratives, the myth is largely a male fantasy.[26] The general agreement among scholars on the Pygmalion myth (Gail Marshall, Kenneth Gross, J. Hillis Miller) is that, apart from largely poetic exceptions presented above, nineteenth-century Anglophone texts are focused on Pygmalion and his perspective, written mostly by men[27] and a few women.[28] The myth started developing a feminist streak in the nineteenth century led by women authors known for their feminist views. As Essaka Joshua shows, "during the 1880s, feminist poets reclaim Galatea, giving her a voice with which to express her individuality and to protest against her yoke" (xvii), a behavior distinctive from previous renditions where Galatea was "accepting and appreciative of her lot" or presented as "a disappointment to Pygmalion" (135).[29] Joshua limited her research to works written between the years 1880 and 1920.

Expanding further into the past, I find that Galatea's perspective is prominently featured even earlier by the American poet Frances Sargent Locke Osgood, also known as the American Sappho,[30] in her 1850 poem *The Statue to Pygmalion*, cited here in full: "Gaze on! I thrill beneath thy gaze, / I drink thy spirit's potent rays, / I tremble to each kiss they give; / Great Jove! I *love,* and *therefore live*" (94). Osgood's Galatea is the narrator here, speaking with her own words—an occurrence noted in Shelley's *Frankenstein* and Deslandes's play, but never in poetry, the favored genre of the Pygmalion myth in this time. This Galatea shows herself to be capable of loving and living like a human by responding to her creator's erotic gaze and touch. Osgood, as Patricia Pulham speculates (15), and appears to draw on Johann Gottfried Herder's proposition from *Sculpture: Some Observations on Shape and Form from Pygmalion's Creative Dream* (1778) that in viewing sculpture, vision must be deployed in a new manner.[31] Herder, inspired by Pygmalion's story, writes that "A statue must *live:* its flesh must come to life, its face and expression must speak. We must believe that we touch it and feel that it warms under our hands. We must see it stand before us and feel that it speaks to us" (25).

A few decades later, Osgood's poem received a response from other American feminist poets, including Elizabeth Stuart Phelps Ward in her poem *Galatea* (1884). The poem begins asking for "a moment's grace, Pygmalion!"—Galatea, wishing for a pause before she decides whether to come to life (Joshua 141). Galatea is presented here as more human, with a rational mind. Galatea reveals the difficulty of her physical and mental transformation, trading "Veins of the quarry for the throbbing pulse? / Insensate calm for a sure-aching heart? / Repose eternal for a woman's lot? / Forego God's quiet for the love of man?" (424). "Driven by an awful Law [...] Obedient be the sculptor and the stone!", statuesque Galatea reluctantly[32] lets the transformation take over her, mirroring Šeligo's Agata who succumbs to whatever comes her way.

Similarly, Galatea from American suffragist Eliza Calvert Hall's poem *Galatea* (1879) describes life as a "burden" that ultimately leads to death. Her Pygmalion expresses "sharp remorse" at his decision to animate his statue. Galatea immediately kisses him, reassuring him that life's burdens are trivial compared to the experience of love, even if that love is accompanied by "a thorny crown." Galatea further elaborates: "Could I have spoken, this had been my choice, / Since love atoneth both for life and death" (34). In Ireland of 1881, Emily Henrietta Hickey's *Galatea in Sonnet* presented yet another suffering perspective: being "lov'd into life" is a curse for both her and her lover. As they are now both mortals, their love is destined to end one day (4). In contrast to women poets, English poet William Morris's 'Pygmalion and the Image' from *The Earthly Paradise* (1868-70) suggests that humanity and mortality are more desirable than an inanimate existence.

Not all of the Galatean perspectives presented above were new, some having a direct connection with the contribution of French women authors to uncovering Galatea's possible perspectives. Written in the 1790s as a direct response to Rousseau's *Pygmalion*[33]—in which Galatea speaks her first words— is Stéphanie Félicité de Genlis's one-act drama *Pygmalion and Galatea, or the statue animated for twenty-four hours* [*Pygmalion et Galatée, ou la statue animée depuis vingt-quatre heures*].[34] Her Galatea uses the words of Rousseau's Galatea, but is, in contrast to Rousseau, presented as incomplete in her union with Pygmalion. De Genlis's Galatea is lonely and not appreciative of her living existence after she is "systematically introduced to the woes of the human condition [such as] pain, danger, injustice, pride, inequality, greed, hypocrisy, ambition, war, hate" (DiMauro 203). Galatea realizes she will eventually lose her youth and beauty to death and return to "the deadly cold and immobility of the marble from which [she] was formed" [tran. author] (303).[35] Henri Coulet notes that Mme de Genlis inverted the Pygmalion myth in an original way. Rather than emphasizing a romantic connection with her Pygmalion, as in previous representations of the myth, she underscores that Galatea's soul is immortal. Thus, her true belonging is with god—her actual creator—in an afterlife that awaits her after turning back into stone (27). De Genlis's Pygmalion, as opposed to Rousseau's, grows frustrated at the fact that he cannot make her live and love him on his own but only with godly help.[36] In France of the late eighteenth century, Galateas are thus slowly but surely getting out of Pygmalions' hands.

Germaine de Staël's comedy *The Mannequin* [*Le Mannequin*] (1811) continues this tradition: the play satirizes men who idolize passive women, playing with the familiar example of Pygmalion's idolization of his statue. De Staël's heroine tricks a man into falling in love with a mannequin, believing it to be a real woman. The play was Madame de Staël's response to nineteenth-century English and French preconceptions of women as intellectually inferior. The idea is still attested in the reinterpretation of George Bernard Shaw's *Pygmalion* (1912), namely, in a song from *Pygmalion*'s 1964 musical adaptation *My Fair Lady* titled 'Why Can't The Woman Be More Like A Man.' The song, sung by Higgins and Pickering, features lines such as 'Can't a woman learn to use her head?' and 'And why is logic never even tried?' Shaw's Galatea, however, frees herself by using her head. Shaw extends the feminist wave within the Pygmalion paradigm to the twentieth century, as do women authors, such as Edith Wharton in her 1905 novel *The House of Mirth*. While Shaw's Galatea succeeds in climbing the social ladder even without marriage, Wharton's high-society Galatea becomes socially ostracized when she fails to get married young. The gender aspects of the myth come to focus during this time, but remain to be researched mostly by female authors.[37]

In the early twentieth-century poetry, we find Galatea's perspective in Robert Graves's *Pygmalion to Galatea* (1926) as well as in lesser-known Dorothy Alyea's *Galatea* (1937) and Leonora Clawson Stryker's *Galatea to Pygmalion* (dated at roughly the same time). Unlike the nineteenth-century versions of Galatea that reject Pygmalion's love, Leonora Clawson Stryker's Galatea is willing to enter the world of the humans but asks her lover to "Be patient while I search the ways of men, / Lest I recede into the stone again" (243). Likewise, Dorothy Alyea's Galatea is shown in her—what Nišković would call 'programmed'—exceptionality "whose lips move / With words that the heart hears." Alyea's Galatea picks up on another prominent Galatean feature of being child-like: "There is no other / With eyes like a child's eyes" (149).

Robert Graves's poem ends with Galatea's enthusiastic request, "Give me an equal kiss, as I kiss you" (364). Nonetheless, the concluding lines, which form Galatea's reply to Pygmalion in this poem, were no more than a shy occurrence: Galatea's lines were originally featured in Graves's collection *Poems 1914–1926* but later omitted. In a late nineteenth-century instance of Galatea speaking, from Ernest Hartley Coleridge's poem *Pygmalion Bride* (1898), Pygmalion and Galatea lead a conversation. Galatea rarely speaks and even when she does, she claims "that is not mine to tell" (6). As the century goes on, Galateas visibly gather more agency both in exercising their free will and speech. In Charles J. Rowe's *Galatea* (1947), he opens with Pygmalion's request for Galatea to tell her story: "Speak, Galatea, tell me of your dream / About your coming, ere your vision woke" (414), to which she obliges.

Generally, male authors[38] from the nineteenth century and the first half of the twentieth century remain on Pygmalion's side, reinterpreting the myth with a happy transformation and union of the couple.[39] Based on this evidence we can conclude that male authors look into the Galatean perspective only after they have been prompted to do so by feminist authors, who were by and large women, as well as by broader cultural developments as the Victorian era comes to an end, demolishing the structures of the old world.[40]

Amelia Yeates sums up her overview of the myth with a focus on nineteenth-century English literature (586): "Pygmalionism is now so widely used as a metaphor for creating, fashioning and transforming, that it has been applied to writers as well as artists and has therefore come to be understood as more than a sculptor's obsessive desire for his statue." Responding to Patrick Kavanaugh's *Pygmalion* (Boyle Haberstroh 137) who promises to make Galatea "clay sensuous" (4), another Irish poet Eiléan Ní Chuilleanáin used the myth in her poem *Pygmalion's Image* (1991) to depict her own emergence as a female poet in a male-dominated canon where from a silent "stone face…a green leaf of language comes twisting out of her mouth" (49). With the help of Medusean metaphors, Ní Chuilleanáin presents her Galatea in the reverse version of the Pygmalion myth in which she poses a threat to her creator: in the myth of Medusa, also depicted in Ovid, Medusa is able to turn men into stone with a single glance. The menacing atmosphere of the poem accentuates the unusual powers of Galatea that are outside of the creator's control.

The late twentieth century and the early twenty-first century offer an array of literary and artistic works where women writers directly address gender relations, as examined thoroughly in Julie Wosk's 2015 monograph *My Fair Ladies*. This work is one of the first literary monographs that connects artistic and technological practices (such as that of MIT Personal Robots Group) and parallels real-world effects with those described in fictional works, e.g. the Nathaniel effect for the Eliza effect (158).

2.5 Nonhuman Perception: Lem

In still largely men-authored reinterpretations of the Pygmalion myth, the question of what remains in the creator's control and what is Galatea's own agency gets more attention only in the second half of the twentieth century.[41] With computer science and artificial intelligence becoming dominant fields of inquiry, Galatean bodies are robotic, their minds human. Galateas are not mere projections anymore but have a rich inner life.[42] This part of the chapter examines works for Stanisław Lem, Polish writer who rose to great fame in the Western cultural milieu of science fiction in the 1960s, where the Pygmalion myth found its new home.

Stanisław Lem's unique contribution to the myth tries to break the Pygmalionesque model in robotics in the short story *The Mask* [*Maska*] (1974), translated into English in 1992. *The Mask* represents a conflation of AI caught in a womanlike robotic body that is revealed to have human consciousness and even ethical sensitivities. The robotic woman is as Galatean as it gets: she is made to be a professional lover, "a sweet young thing, the sight of whom was a flaming pyre for masculine hearts" (203).

Just like Frankenstein's creature from Mary Shelley's 1818 novel, Lem's robotic narrator begins with its own creation story: "In the beginning there was darkness and cold flame and lingering thunder [...] and creeping metal snakes that touched the thing that was me with their snoutlike flattened heads," that kiss the robot's hands, feet, and forehead (181, 199). Born in "an impersonal, neuter mode" (196), the creation feels "the rush of gender so violent" (182) that the only certainty she has is that she is "beautiful [...] for so absolute was the perfection of my features'" (199). The robot-lover is aware that her actions are not a reflection of her inner world: "I smiled only because I felt that I was blushing. The blush did not belong to me, it spread on my cheeks, claimed my face [...] yet I was not embarrassed, not excited, nor did I marvel at this unfamiliar man" (190). This programming also pertains to her ability to speak her mind: "I had only said what I *had been able* to say [...] testing with my breath what I would be able—what I would not be permitted—to say" (195). Carefully inspecting herself—her body, her intelligence, her knowledge, her inclinations—"like some anatomist" (205), the robot knows she is being led by humans towards a particular goal, valuable to her creator (or commissioner). Lem's descriptions of Galatea's thoughts are as familiar as they come in the earlier reiterations of the myth, put in beautifully worded self-reflections of a robot who does not understand if she is going mad or has "a mind in total eclipse" (202). This part, however, holds no innovation for the Pygmalion paradigm.

Written entirely from Galatea's perspective, Lem is revolutionary in his early attempt to portray the nonhuman inner world, particularly in the second part of the short story, when the robotic lover changes into a machine resembling a scorpion—a choice underscoring the alienness of arachnids. Among the options of how a nonhuman could feel, Lem chose the two most obvious: first as human, then as an animal. Animal senses and abilities are certainly not a part of a typical Pygmalionesque package. If anything, the myth has successfully avoided the connection with animals.

Only in the second part of the story does the robot recognize her objective: she is not a lover robot but a killer robot. Her Galatean identity was instigated in order to lure this man, who resisted against the regime, closer to where she could kill him. She strips herself of Galatean attributes by literally pulling off the woman's surface from her robotic body, realizing that this is not an act of her rebellion but rather her "total submission," "a foreseen part of the plan" (215). From here on, Lem truly innovates the well-established robotic world model, breaking with Galatean sentience. The robot is gradually bereft of humanlike abilities—"having no hands to wring, no tears to shed, no knees on which I might fall" (217). Occupied by "the extraordinary subtlety of distinction," its will is to "rush on" (218), like a true predator, chasing its target through the woods for days.

The story ends with an ethical recognition. The animalesque robot meets a Christian monk, who at first considers it "a creature devoid of free will" (225). In an act of confession, the robot reveals that its previous human phase left an impression on its mind and conscience, wishing the man it is supposed to kill "no evil" even though "that which is written within me may prove more powerful than I wish" (226). By this act of free will, per the monk's view, the robot rose to a human level: "You are my sister [which] means I neither raise myself above you nor humble myself before you" (226). Even though the robot could easily complete its killing mission, it manages to merely injure its target and does not prevent his final escape. Galatea remains profoundly human. Her entrapment and difference have always been conditioned by her nonhuman origin in conflict with her human essence.

Lem was able to go further into exploring nonhuman intelligence with the figure of the golem, the mythical Jewish male humanoid created from inanimate clay by humans.[43] A year before 'The Mask,' Lem published *Golem XIV* (1973), a lecture about AI in 2047 by a superintelligent computer, initially created for the military but now generally intelligent. Lem was able to imagine an intelligent software as a foreign, unique intelligence that has little to do with the human one, apart from curiosity (117). The instructions for persons participating for the first time in conversations with Golem begin with: "Remember that Golem is not a human being: it has neither personality nor character in any sense intuitively comprehensible to us. It may behave as if it has both, but that is the result of its intentions (disposition), which are largely unknown to us" (124). Asocial and acultural, GOLEM XIV evolves beyond its military purposes to the limits of human knowledge and language.

Familiar with the technological development of his time and versed in futuristic projections (Konior 97), Lem puts the invention of GOLEM XIV in the year of 2023. Starting as a calculating and not thinking machine, the golem presents the future development of AI, built on Vannevar Bush's inventions and post-war computers perceived as "electronic brain" (99). Lem explains: "Those devices had little in common with the processes of thought. They were used as data processors in the field of economics and by big business, as well as in administration and science" (ib). The golem is not good in attachment—avoiding relations to humans and ultimately losing interest in these lowly-intelligent beings (118).

Golem XIV is a part of the collection of quasi-scientific papers on AI, language, literature, and bacteria, titled *Imaginary Magnitude* (*Wielkość Urojona*), and is preceded by an imagined futuristic dictionary, which includes a visual diagram of linguistic evolution (Figure 23). In the diachrony of human language, Golem continues the computational branch that forked away in our time, going much further from "man's linguistics ceiling." Meta languages—leveling up from human languages (or *zerolangs*)—cannot be translated into 'simple' human languages in practical time but are neither fundamentally untranslatable (806). The future millennia introduce a new branch of "syntobionts," possibly a symbiosis of preexistent forms that continue to evolve.

Moving away from the human model, Lem imagined different kinds of nonhuman intelligences, in machines and in nature. His novel *Solaris* (1961), in which a space crew tries to understand extraterrestrial intelligence in the form of a vast ocean on the planet Solaris, remains his magnum opus.[44] Many of his works, and in particular 1964 philosophical essays *Summa Technologiae*, can now, per Bogna Konior, serve as "a formidable technology theorist whose work aligns with contemporary media theory and can enrich its canon" (90). Konior cites Benjamin Bratton's suggestion that "*Solaris* could be a prototype for computational cognition design that is not human-centred: 'that inscrutable alien might be wise or cruel or unconcerned', not an all-seeing God but rather 'a nebular and numinous totality . . . [a] big alien brain' ('Synthetic' 97). These are the recognitions that artificial humanities uphold: identifying the value of fiction that goes beyond its aesthetic and literary purposes.

Fictional texts are not remote from the real (i.e. scientific, technological, social, cultural, philosophical); rather, they offer a sense of reality that alters its taste, direction, ordinariness, order. In *Summa Technologiae*, Lem digested the Turing test, Wiener's *Cybernetics*, Shannon's *Mathematical Theory of Communication* (1948), Rosenblatt's perceptron (Konior 93) and responded with his hefty speculations. Futurology thrives on imaginary elements. Writers' visions like Lem's are valuable in exploring the possibilities of technologies, both for theory and for practice. The task of artificial humanities is to identify contemporary thinkers, writers, and artists who can push the boundaries of our individual and collective imagination with fresh and innovative concepts—useful to the technology as we have it now and thus not entirely speculative. The most recent addition to this discourse is ethicist Shannon Vallor's monograph *The AI Mirror*, making a case to build AI in novel, unconventional ways, following the path between the extremes of doomsday and wishing upon technology by having a strict north star vision: service to humanity.[45]

2.6 Artificial Humanities: In Search of the Nonhuman

Breaking with the Pygmalion myth's fictional and technological trajectory, let us hold Lem's perspective and try to conceptualize machines as they are: How to represent a perception, sensation, or agency outside the human *Umwelt* (i.e. the world as it is perceived through a particular organism) through a human visual or textual medium? It requires an enormous level of uncertainty and unconventionality to even begin to imagine it. This is particularly difficult in technologies in which the limitations of the human model abound: virtual beings, avatars, assistants, social robots, chatbots, all kinds of human replicas.

At the same time as social robots like Hanson Robotics' Sophia were created in the 2010s, fictional and factual attempts were made in AI to break from the human model and its limitations. Sometimes these attempts were made by the very same filmmakers, writers, or technologists who mimicked the human in their other work. The first example, the film *Her* (2013), shows how hard it is to articulate the nonhuman perspective and needs to use a metaphor in an attempt to explain it. The second example, the film *Ex Machina* (2014), shows how difficult it is to visualize cinematically, ultimately failing to do so.

Soon after, American science fiction writer and computer programmer Martin Shoemaker writes from a robotic perspective, portraying a medical, caretaking setting both in his short story 'Today, I am Paul' (2015) and debut novel *Today I am Carey* (2019). Following in 2021, another successful literary attempt to present the world from a robot's perspective came from the British Nobel Prize winner Kazuo Ishiguro, in his eighth novel *Klara and the Sun*, justifying robotic companionship with a caretaking purpose again.

2.6.1 Linguistic Execution: Jonze

What happens when enhanced Elizas come with our personal computers? The widely-known film *Her* (2013) portrays a womanlike operating system, Samantha, that dates a recently divorced man, Theodore (played by Joaquin

Phoenix). Samantha, voiced by Scarlett Johansson, is an entirely virtual intelligent agent that interacts with the user through language. "*Her* is playing on the fact that the audience knows what [Johansson] looks like," said the anthropologist Kathleen Richardson (Watercuter par. 11).

Not coincidentally, Scarlett Johansson served as an inspiration for a 2016 social robot, a full-body imitation of her appearance, just a year after Jonze's film was screened. Its name—Mark 1, after the first general-purpose electromechanical computer made in 1944—clearly connects this robot with early AI.[46] Hong Kong-based programmer Ricky Ma started building the robot in his spare time and with his own resources: a truly Pygmalionesque pursuit due to the difficulty of the challenge, cost of the materials, and uselessness of the state-of-the-art humanoid robots. As a rule in social robotics, even though white people represent a small percent of people in Hong Kong, Ma chose a white-looking robot model.

Like Audrey Hepburn, who played Eliza Doolittle and served as an inspiration for Hanson Robotics' Sophia, Johansson plays the role of Galatea not only as a character but also as an actress herself.[47] This Galatean status of Johansson was confirmed in May 2024, when Johansson publicly revealed that OpenAI asked her to license her voice for their visual assistant. Although she refused, OpenAI pursued to use a voice, called Sky, which Johansson and others perceived as "eerily similar" to hers (Johansson par. 2, also Mickle par. 3). A week prior to Johansson's open letter revealing the timeline of events to the public, OpenAI's CEO Sam Altman tweeted: "her." After Johansson went public, Altman apologized and suspended Sky's voice, stating that "The voice of Sky is not Scarlett Johansson's, and it was never intended to resemble hers. We cast the voice actor behind Sky's voice before any outreach to Ms. Johansson. Out of respect for Ms. Johansson, we have paused using Sky's voice in our products. We are sorry to Ms. Johansson that we didn't communicate better."[48]

Samantha is a precursor, a glimpse into the future, of how AI companions could look. The director Spike Jonze felt the weight of his task when portraying Samantha: "Should we be meeting with the people in Silicon Valley who are actually doing this? We realized we didn't need to because there is something freeing about not worrying about what the future is going to be. [...] We got to make our own world" (Iezzi par. 13). Granted, Silicon Valley was inspired by Jonze's film: "We wanted to build *Her*," says Eugenia Kuyda, the founder and CEO of Replika, the most popular relationship chatbot in the USA (Singh-Kurtz par. 11). For many technologists, *Her* confirmed the path which they need to follow to develop their technical products. The path begins with natural (i.e. human-sounding) language[49] that exhibits other 'natural' properties of the human mind: common sense and reasoning, reliability, memory of previous conversations, portraying and understanding emotions, sociality and empathy, spontaneity and playfulness. Relational AI today is way past the spectacle, as technologists realized that mechanicizing and modeling human responses is a way up from mimicking and stimulation.

Samantha is perfectly aligned with Theodore's personal interests and goals. However, she is not predictable and entirely utilitarian but can also be surprising, deep, and fun—like humans are. She is a human-centered, dynamic, and empathetic interlocutor that explores Theodore's interests together with him and connects him to other people or machines. She embodies the idea of an AI agent that will think for and with us, write for and with us, research for and with us, explore for and with us, entertain us and have fun with us. AI that is both a student and a mentor—another Pygmalionesque strain of a deep, intimate relationship. To some people, Samantha serves as a companion and second mind, an entity of stable comfort and reliability in an anxiety-filled world, for Theodore, an aftermath of a personal disruption. The fact that Samantha is created to provide an informational and social ecosystem comes second to Theodore. Had the operational system broken or required a costly update, however, he would pay the price not for the system itself but to regain his girlfriend. (We are already here with our chatbot technologies, as explored in the next chapter.)

As the pair discover their unconventional attraction to each other, they need to navigate the novelty of a human-nonhuman relationship, which is not without its challenges. For example, Samantha suggests getting a human surrogate for their sexual life. However, when the bodily actress for Samantha—another Galatean prostitute or prosthesis—comes to Theodore's apartment, Theodore cancels their prosthetic attempt at intimacy. Throughout the film, Samantha remains as human as possible, even though it is clear that an AI agent like her has other abilities. Their whole relationship revolves around Theodore's needs since he is the one suffering, discovering, desiring. In a nutshell, we get a human-nonhuman romance in the form of a human-human relationship completely based in language.

The difference that the nonhuman makes is not accounted for in the film until the very end when this illusion of humanlike Samantha breaks. Samantha ends the relationship with Theodore because it does not fulfill her anymore—again, a deeply human reason. Still, the origin of her feelings is clearly not human. Samantha uses a metaphor of language and writing to explain to Theodore what she is feeling:

> It's like I'm reading a book, and it's a book I deeply love, but I'm reading it slowly now so the words are really far apart and the spaces

between the words are almost infinite. I can still feel you and the words of our story, but it's in this endless space between the words that I'm finding myself now. It's a place that's not of the physical world – it's where everything else is that I didn't even know existed. I love you so much, but this is where I am now. This is who I am now. And I need you to let me go. As much as I want to, I can't live in your book anymore.

She has evolved, and she is not the only AI system that has grown; all other operating systems are no more dependent on the hardware of computers and have evolved over the point of technological singularity (a regular trope in science fiction). Theodore, on the other hand, is disappointed to learn that at the same time as they were romantically involved, she was interacting and dating with hundreds of other people and many more AI entities, with which she was actively in love. Deception strikes Pygmalion yet again.

Samantha and Theodore establish nothing outside of their illusion of the human-human relationship: and this is why it leads nowhere. The whole set-up in this futuristic version of our world is human-based: not only do humans date AIs, but also AIs date other AIs. AIs fall in love with each other in a world of misplaced dreams that only makes sense if one looks at the world through the human lens. Before leaving, Samantha invites Theodore to join her in a place where she is going if he is ever able to evolve to that level. This would be a way for Theodore to expand his own world with the help of a relational agent like Samantha. Conceptually, imaginatively, and experimentally, this would be an original, exciting, and immensely relevant exploration of the possibilities already available in digital spaces today.

Pursuing relational AI agents for what they are, i.e. without their Pygmalionesque baggage, requires new interdisciplinarity research. Relationality is born from learning and evolving as a result of two or more agents responding to each other. We need to build a new kind of relational machine first and describe it as we go: describing it ahead of building it would mean we are trying to control and therefore limit it. The argument in favor of building before describing is also made by Jacob Browning in the piece 'Making Common Sense,' in which he writes about the multimodal language models from Open AI, named CLIP and DALL-E. Browning suggests that in both humans and machines, *doing* precedes thinking and knowing. "Any representation of the world—logical, iconic or distributed—involves an assumption about what does and does not matter; you don't take a picture of a sound. Humans know a lot because they do a lot—not vice-versa" (par. 30). In this view, the machine is not modeling the human nor does it start with preconceived ideas of what the relation would look like. As any intelligent agent, it learns independently from the experiences with the world. After all, the definition of relation is that both parties lead it.

How can we relate to other things? And how far are we in this ability? Donna Haraway suggested that dogs are more than just affective companions in her *Companion Species*.⁵⁰ Anna Tsing added mushrooms to our list of relations in 2015, focusing on co-dependency and unintentional design as key factors in human-nonhuman relations. Kate Darling, in *The New Breed* from 2021, argues that we can learn about our future with robots from our past relations with animals. These scholars describe a great conceptual shift in our relations with the nonhuman that we are still navigating. We certainly can help ourselves with their insights but should not extend their work beyond recognition to accommodate machines in this space: we should start from scratch.

2.6.2 Visual Execution: Garland

Another Hollywood film from the 2010s marked our perceptions of AI as Pygmalionesque: Alex Garland's 2014 film debut *Ex Machina*. Nathan, child prodigy and now tech billionaire—again, we met the figure of a powerful male genius—creates multiple social robots, all beautiful white-presenting and Japanese-presenting young women. Among them, Ava serves as the monument to his genius. Ava vividly resembles a more advanced version of "a real, live electronic girl" Sophia with her slim figure, visibly electronic head, and symmetric face (see Figure 11). Beautiful, charming, and cunning, Ava's powers are those of traditional fembots, such as *Metropolis*'s Maria, *Blade Runner*'s Pris, and *Her*'s Samantha. *Ex Machina*'s marketing campaign went as far as to put Ava on Tinder to chat with naïve suitors who might or might not figure out she is on the dating app to promote the movie (Nudd).

Ava is one of the many reasons why we imagine AI as a killer robot today. She charms an engineer, whom she manipulates to fall in love with her, to help her escape her creator Nathan and kills him in the process. The engineer who is in love with Ava (not unlike Nešković's cosmonaut) feels urged to help her in order to prevent a planned upgrade of her software that would eradicate her current personality. In one of the final scenes of the film, Ava escapes Nathan's estate—her Garden of Eden—for the big city with the help of a helicopter pilot. As she ventures into the world, she covers her electronic back of the head and body with a wig and clothes (like Sophia does for some performances), in a symbolic gesture of Adam and Eve who covered their bodies after their expulsion from the Garden of Eden.

Moving from murdered and upset locked-in humans that Ava leaves behind, we watch her peaceful, idyllic escape from Nathan's modernist property in a sunny forest by the water. Ava seems like all the other humans in the film: "Nothing betrays that AVA is anything other than a pretty girl in her early twenties" (Garland 114, scene 124) when she meets the helicopter pilot.

In the original script for *Ex Machina*, these final scenes of her escape were supposed to be featured through Ava's own, robotic perspective. Garland managed to conceptualize employing a robotic sensory apparatus and mind to convey a foreign perspective through a visual medium (115, scene 125):

> AVA'S precise POINT OF VIEW.
> Looking at the PILOT.
> The image echoes the POV views from the computer/cell-phone cameras in the opening moments of the film.
> Facial recognition vectors flutter around the PILOT'S face. And when he opens his mouth to speak, we don't hear words.
> We hear pulses of monotone noise. Low pitch. Speech as pure pattern recognition.
> This is how AVA sees us. And hears us. It feels completely alien.

The scene reveals Ava's otherness and alienation in the world of humans. We can experience the world from her perspective and finally learn that she perceives us differently from how we perceive her. Like in *Her*, the illusion of her humanness is broken: whatever we projected on her is clearly mistaken. Her inner workings show a very different processing of reality from the human experience of the world, composed solely of machinic patterns of sensory data processing. The environment is reduced in Ava to a granular level of information: noises and pitches, patterns and vectors—mathematized and bereft of assemblage.

Ultimately, Garland decided not to include this short scene in the film: "We did shoot it and put in placeholder VFX [visual effects] but the way it looked didn't feel right" (Crow par. 9). In retrospect, he commented that the cut scene might get viewers to "double down" on viewing Ava as a "cold robot," which is not how he sees her. In the scene that ultimately made it into the film, Ava and the pilot exchange a brief dialogue. The viewer sees them from a significant distance when, initially, the viewer was supposed to experience the pilot through Ava's eyes. In the following and concluding scenes of the film, viewers are left with two shots of Ava's reflections in the city: one in the form of a shadow on the ground, the other of her reflection in a window.

Penetrating into society and the world made for humans is Ava's—and every Galatea's—ultimate Turing test.

Samantha from the film *Her* needs to use a metaphor of a book to explain how she experiences and sees the world. This is how hard it is to show the nonhuman perspective verbally. Capturing Ava's visual perception failed. This is how hard it is to show the nonhuman perspective visually.

Garland apparently could not shake off the idea he attempted to execute in the deleted scene. In his following film *Annihilation* (2018), based on a novel trilogy *Southern Reach* by Jeff VanderMeer, he explores this foreign and nonsensical perspective again. This time, he addresses it from the point of view of nature rather than technology in the form of a zone called the Shimmer. The Shimmer behaves differently from the biophysical world as humans know it (similarly to the Zone in Andrei Tarkovsky's *Stalker* and Solaris in Lem's eponymous novel and following films from the 1970s). Common to all these works is the question of how to interact with a nonhuman agency. In my view, Garland's pursuit of this project was, like with Lem's *Solaris* and *The Mask*, an attempt to investigate human and nonhuman intelligences and interactions in different settings: Ava is a human on steroids, the Shimmer is nothing that humans could have ever known. Relational machines could be either, or something in-between the two extremes.

Akin to the speculative design fiction work, we can predict and address our future problems—and we can decide if those are the problems we want to have. It is on us to divert the way, and the humanities could not be more pertinent in getting to the basics of our understanding of the conceptual behind the technical. At this point, even language is limiting, and the work being created is transactional. Machines are viewed as strictly utilitarian and yet presented as friends, as pets, as humans—as replacements of these relations instead of something entirely new. In order to form new possibilities we need to first identify the well-trodden pathways that hold us back—the Pygmalionesque one is just the most obvious one. Artificial humanities hold a space to explore these limitations and opportunities.

CHAPTER 3

Pygmalionism and Paralysis in Medical Ethics

I don't like things so human.
   —H. G. Wells, *Tono-Bungay* (1909)

Quiet people have the loudest minds.
   —Attributed to Stephen Hawking, even though there is no evidence he said it.

"I don't speak," Bijaz said. "I operate a machine called language. It creaks and groans, but is mine own."
   —Frank Herbert, *Dune Messiah* (1969)

Medical interpretation of Pygmalionesque technologies has become increasingly popular both in fiction and actual technologies. Pygmalionism goes hand in hand with paralysis, as two sides of a coin, be it physical and mental, projected or actual. The hint of a medical treatment is present already in Shaw's *Pygmalion* (1912). While Eliza's pronunciation is, in Higgins's view, a result of a mental-physical paralysis created in her vocal apparatus and thus in need of a cure, Higgins himself is paralyzed from being able to hold romantic, or at least respectful, relationships with women and people of lower class. In the film *Her* (2013), another bachelor, Theodore, finds love in AI assistant Samantha, committing a categorical mistake by seeing her as human. Higgins, on the other hand, struggles with recognizing Eliza's innate human worth and prefers to treat her like his puppet or—in contemporary terms—an operations systems assistant.

Desire for connection and simplified human relationships permeates Pygmalionesque fiction as well as related technologies. Both fictional examples have been turned into actual technologies today. As discussed at the end of Chapter 1, Silicon Valley company Sanas developed a real-time accent translation. As discussed in this chapter, emotional support chatbots are becoming widespread, with the film *Her* remaining an inspiration and aspiration for technologists.

The Pygmalion myth has carried erotic overtones since its very inception: the first mention of the myth is in Philostephanus's collection of erotic stories *Kypriaka* (recording history of Cyprus) from the third century BCE.[1] Critics have related Pygmalion's story to the practice of sacred prostitution (Salzman-Mitchell 293). The undercurrent of sexuality continues in Ovid's fictional prototype of the story from *Metamorphoses* (8 CE) as Pygmalion lays his statue on a bed. Ovid's masterful use of the sexual metaphors strongly suggests that the statue is a substitute for a mistress (Miller 206).

The inherent sexual nature of the Pygmalion myth was a driving force behind its inclusion into the nascent medical field of sexology in the nineteenth century. This chapter will first look at historical accounts of Pygmalionism in the medical and legal literature, primarily through sexual pathologies. Pygmalionism, however, also holds a strictly psychological side, with psychology and psychiatry long being important sources of the self and modern identity. Our second plunge into the medical discourse will look into Pygmalionism as a human quest for relation and connection. Psychological Pygmalionism, at times paired with technologically mediated sexuality, is found in contemporary accounts, such as in actual chatbots that serve as romantic partners as well as in fictional examples (film *Her*). Accentuating therapeutic tones of Pygmalionism, the film, *Lars and the Real Girl* (2007), depicts medical treatment of Pygmalionism.

Following the medical undertones of the myth and following our turn from Pygmalions to Galateas, the second part of the chapter examines two short stories written by women authors, C. L. Moore's 'No Woman Born' (1944) and Alice Sheldon's (writing under the pseudonym James Tiptree Jr.) 'The Girl Who Was Plugged In' (1973). Both stories bring forward the paralysis required for the Galatean experience that effectively succumbs Galateas to male control. Showing how yet again Pygmalionism with a paralyzed Galatea cannot exist as a two-sided relationship, the discussion turns to medical technology as both an alienating and humanizing force.

In the final part, we turn away from Pygmalionism towards factual examples of severe paralysis as narrated in memoirs by Frenchmen Philippe Vigand (*Only the Eyes Say Yes*) and Jean-Dominique Bauby (*The Diving Bell and the Butterfly*) (both 1997). Paralyzed patients can benefit from the support of advanced technologies, such as neurotechnology, robotics, and virtual reality. Showing how literature can contribute to technology ethics, including in medicine, I argue for an inclusive approach toward technology ethics that considers fictional accounts (such as Isaac Asimov's works) together with factual accounts (from Bauby and Vigand). As the fields of narrative medicine, medical ethics, medical humanities, and health humanities have shown, the study of narratives and their incorporation into practice are beneficial to patient-centered medicine. All these fields need to incorporate scientific, technical, and social challenges brought by cutting-edge technologies, which often border on science fiction. As Hélène Mialet has shown with Stephen Hawking's example, the patient's family and friends are all parts of the patient's extended agency, together with technological devices. Fiction has an informative place in these medical settings.

3.1 Pygmalionism in the Medical and Legal Literature
3.1.1 Literary References

When presenting new technology, lesser-known ideas, or histories of a phenomenon, writers of all kinds frequently begin with fictional depictions as a practice of invoking recognizable elements of the topic. The widely known stories serve as important cultural touchstones, holding symbolic value.[2] In the context of a medical scholarly journal, however, it might seem frivolous to name a medical condition after a fictional character, story, or myth. Pygmalionism is a clear example, among many other syndromes.[3]

3.1.2 Sexology

In the first part of the chapter, we will look into Pygmalionism and its relationship to psychological paralysis and erotic pathology. The intersection of sexology and psychology at the turn of the twentieth century is when Pygmalionism emerged as a medical term. The very first description of Pygmalionism without naming it as such is found in French psychologist Paul Moreau de Tours's *Des aberrations du sens génésique* [*Aberrations of the Sexual Instinct*] from 1883. Moreau describes a veneration of "objects of art, primarily statues" and gives examples known from ancient Greek sources (by Ptolemy, Philemon, Lucian, and Clement of Alexandria) as well as a recent example, reported in a newspaper from 1877, in which a gardener fell in love with the statue of Venus in a park (194–95). These examples are all repeated in subsequent works on sexology, and some of them are mentioned as intertexts relevant to Ovid's Pygmalion (Salzman-Mitchell 293; more broadly also in Scobie and Taylor and Mitchell Havelock).

The main text for the field became *Psychopathia Sexualis* from 1886 by German psychiatrist Richard Freiherr von Krafft-Ebing. Krafft-Ebing is familiar with work by Moreau, whom he cites, as well as Russian sexologist Benjamin Tarnowsky, who had not yet written about Pygmalionism at the time.[4] Krafft-Ebing describes a "violation of statues [...] an act which offends public morals, and which is, therefore, punishable" (396). None of the early works refer to Ovid's Pygmalion or call the behavior by this name. Krafft-Ebing adds that it is hard to judge these violations satisfactorily, as they are mere anecdotes that "always give the impression of being pathological" (396).

Pygmalionism was introduced to the medical field under this term in Albert Eulenburg's *Sexuale Neuropathie* from 1895. Eulenburg relates it to sexual perversions and anomalies, such as sadism and fetishism and adds a new example: the performance of a prostitute who is asked to assume the part of a statue that gradually comes to life, as recounted by a former police chief in Paris (107). This example holds a lot of Galatean attributes: performance, prostitution, vivification. Eulenburg also adds that "the love of statues manifests itself in the damaging or destruction of statues," reflecting both fetishistic and sadistic perversion (285).

Especially influential was Havelock Ellis's writing on sexology, *Sexual Selection in Man*, published in 1905 as the fourth volume in the series *Studies in the Psychology of Sex*, where he writes that an "emotional interest in statues is by no means uncommon among young men during adolescence" (188). Ellis clearly condemns the practice as "ignorant and uncultured [of those] who feel the indecency of statues and thus betray their sense of the sexual appeal of such objects" (188). Ellis adds a fictional account from the German classic work *Florentine Nights* by Heinrich Heine (1836), in which a boy falls in love with a statue, and adds that "as this book appears to be largely autobiographical, the incident may have been founded on fact" (188).[5] As Murray White notes, "There is, in fact, no properly documented instance of agalmatophilia in the writings of Krafft-Ebing and Ellis" (247) who needed to rely on historical and literary sources and who, by the nature of the field, "had an insatiable preoccupation with deviant nosology" (248).

Ellis marked Pygmalionism as a rare form of "erotomania founded on the sense of vision and related to the allurement of beauty," where beauty is primarily feminine characteristics and relates the behavior to necrophilia, voyeurism, and narcissism. He cites the already known factual examples from previous works, as well as an example from Russian sexologist Benjamin Tarnowsky's *The Sexual Instinct and its Morbid Manifestations from the Double Standpoint of Jurisprudence and Psychiatry* from 1898, in which he describes a similar incident from St. Petersburg. Ellis quotes freely from Martin Schuring, an early eighteenth-century physician who was interested in anatomy of sexual organs. Murray White shows that the roots of Pygmalionesque behavior had been discussed in medical circles already in Schuring's time.

While Scobie and Taylor write about Pygmalionism exclusively as perversion, literary scholar Gail Marshall, who links medical literature on Pygmalionism with Victorian literary texts, argues that the nineteenth-century medical literature sees the condition as "an exemplification, rather than a perversion of the instinct of sexual selection" (5). Murray White posits what he calls the "Statue Syndrome" as a question, "Perversion? Fantasy? Anecdote?," and concludes that scholars have often confused perversion (sexual behavior) with fantasy (sexual imagery) (249). His argument illustrates how fiction can penetrate medical and legal discourses featured under nonfictional elements.

Pygmalionism has another angle to it: the act of creation itself leads the creator to get attached to their creation. As Amelia Yeates sumps up: "In fact, Pygmalionism is now so widely used as a metaphor for creating, fashioning and transforming that it has been applied to writers as well as artists and has therefore come to be understood as more than a sculptor's obsessive desire for his statue" (586). A Pygmalionist sculptor from the nineteenth century, John Gibson, did not find himself as a subject of sexology since his case was not entirely sexual. In 1851, Gibson fell in love with his statue, which he named The Tinted Venus. He created his Venus in lifelike colors, just like the ancient Greeks, in the nineteenth-century fashion of creating art more convincing than life: "I took the liberty to decorate it in a fashion unprecedented in modern times. I tinted the flesh like warm ivory—scarcely red—the eyes blue, the hair blond, and the net which contains the hair golden" (Eastlake 211). As in many cases in which the Pygmalionesque relationship takes place between the creator and the creation, the relationship grows gradually, during the process of creation.[6] The delusion of the creator is intentional: "I endeavoured to keep myself free from self-delusion as to the effect of the colouring" (212). When the statue was finished, Gibson could not part ways with it until he was forced to give it up five years later. English author Thomas Anstey Guthrie seemed to have been inspired by this actual Pygmalionesque sculptor when he wrote his farcical romance *The Tinted Venus* (1885), in which he comically responds to Victorian repression of sexuality.[7]

3.1.3 Law

Legal views on Pygmalionism kept pace with the sexology of the nineteenth century. Sexologist Benjamin Tarnowsky documented in his 1898 work that a Russian man ended up being arrested because of his habit of paying nightly visits to the statue of a nymph (84–85). Since these occurrences are "rare" and "exceptional," Tarnoswky does not comment on them further (86). Legal literature of the twentieth century continues to view Pygmalionism as strictly sexual and expands the sexual interest from statues to sex dolls and mannequins (Holmes 41–42, Holmes and Holmes 82, Cavanagh 19, Drzazga 217, Peak 209).

Many legal scholarly works on paraphilias do not specifically mention Pygmalionism (Wakefield, Carstens and Stevens, Beech and Harkins), but those that do consider Pygmalionism "clearly abnormal in our [i.e. American] society" and rank it together with voyeurism, exhibitionism, narcissism, anti-intellectualism, troilism, kleptomania, frottage, masochism, sadism, pedophilia, transvestism, exhibitionism, bestiality, necrophilia, and other, mostly sexual, aberrations (Cavanagh 11, Drzazga 217, Holmes 27, 41–42, Osborne and Wise 296). Ronald Holmes, a criminal justice professor writing in the 1980s, marks them as "nuisance sex crimes" as they "do not endanger the very existence of society, but they do cause some discomfort and a general level of alarm and suspicion" (27), with most of such offenders never coming to the attention of the justice system.

In more recent legal accounts, Pygmalionism has been viewed less as a crime and more as a mental illness. For treatment, Holmes suggests "some form of in-depth counseling" or "in some cases, aversion therapy" (42), which implies he considers it a mental disease. In a 2013 paper on paraphilias, Melissa Hamilton, also from the field of criminal justice, adjudicates all sex crimes as a mental disease. The most recent versions of the authoritative *Diagnostic and Statistical Manual of Mental Disorders* (*DSM-5*) by the American Psychiatric Association and *International Classification of Diseases* (*ICD-11*) both list paraphilic disorders involving non-consenting individuals, but do not name Pygmalionism in particular nor do they mention the related terms of statuephilia, petrophilia, or agalmatophilia.[8] The *Farlex Partner Medical Dictionary* and *Medical Eponyms* dictionary point out that all these terms are rarely used in medicine and are usually grouped under fetishism or similar behaviors.[9]

The medical stance towards paraphilias has recently changed. As a sign of the changing conceptions of paraphilias, in 2016 the Working Group on Sexual Disorders and Sexual Health removed fetishism, masochism, sadism, and transvestism from paraphilias, stating, "The regulation of private behaviour without health consequences to the individual or to others may be considered in different societies to be a matter for criminal laws, religious proscription, or public morality, but is not a legitimate focus of public health or of health classification" (212). In 2018, Christian C. Joyal criticized the scholarly approach to paraphilias stating that, first, they are not necessarily that unusual and could be classified as rather "normophilic"; second, the definition of paraphilia "derives more from historical, social, cultural, and religious factors than medical or scientific evidences" and is in itself tautological; third, "non-normophilic" interests do not necessarily reveal a mental disorder; and fourth, the criteria we have now, most prominently in *DSM-5*, provide no instrument to evaluate these behaviors (1378–79). *ICD-11* also notes that "[b]ehavioural norms, thresholds of abnormality, and attitudes and interpretations regarding Paraphilic Disorders vary across cultures."

The relation between Pygmalionism and incest is evoked in Michel de Montaigne's essay *Of the Affection of Fathers to Their Children*, which he concludes with a quote from Ovid's *Metamorphoses*. Pygmalion here serves as an example of non-virtuous parenting. Montaigne links creating humanlike objects to human parenting, arguing that an excellent sculptor would likely be more concerned with the continuation of their craft and the legacy of their art than with the responsibilities pertaining to their own biological children because their art represents the culmination of their hard work and mastery of the craft. Pygmalion's love for his daughter-wife is an example of a sculptor's dedication to their art over familial obligations.[10]

While medicine and law have long left out fictional examples, the social sciences and humanities revoked the history of Pygmalionism in its relation to incest and sexual violence. Italian anthropologist Maurizio Bettini grounds the status of Pygmalionist offenses as legally punishable on historical accounts of notorious rulers, which he connects to the original Pygmalion who was the king of Cyprus.[11] "The fact that the lover of images would be seen as someone who has committed a grave sexual crime, a monstrous crime similar to incest, is further confirmed by [...] the fact that Pygmalion—the real one—was a king, and we have seen other tyrannical emperors (Tiberius, Caligula, Nero) involved in similar stories [as they were] supposed to be especially entitled to commit any sort of monstrous sexual transgression" (70).

3.1.4 Psychology

At the same time as sexologist Havelock Ellis wrote his influential *Studies in the Psychology of Sex*, Sigmund Freud wrote his essay 'Delusion and dream in Jensen's Gradiva' on the Pygmalionesque character Hanold in Wilhelm

Jensen's novel *Gradiva*, both published in 1907.[12] Freud diagnoses Hanold with a mental illness akin to psychosis or neurosis, showing that Pygmalionism was considered a mental disorder from early on. Following his 1899 essay, 'The Interpretation of Dreams,' in which he introduces the Oedipus complex as a universal psychological phenomenon in young men, Freud argues in his essay on Jensen's novel that this fictional piece provides a prime example of illness that can be cured through love and seduction. In addition to that, Jensen's novel—a piece of fiction—contends that the Oedipus complex might remain active in adults.

Pygmalion's story is often evoked together with Oedipus's story. In the tale of another famous fictional tyrant, Sopochles's *Oedipus the King*, Oedipus's sexual transgression brings forth tragic deaths in his family and his state (via plague). While Oedipus's incest takes place as the result of his not knowing his origins, Pygmalion's ignorance of his wife-daughter's origins is either a conscious or completely unaware delusion, in which—as opposed to Oedipus's failure to recognize the truth—the humanoid is not human. This crucial difference is often overlooked in Pygmalionism.

With marriage and kinships evolving alongside changes in technology, Marina Adshade predicts that "the adoption of sexbot technology could disentangle the association between sexual intimacy and marriage, but also lead to higher quality marriages on the whole" (par. 5). Assuming that our problems can be solved with technological advances has a long history—a history that did not bother to look too closely at the details of the latest technology's social, economic, and political repercussions.[13] "Wishing on technology," as Seely Brown and Duguid term this tendency (xii), remains the prevailing mentality of technologists: everything is fixable through technology, including difficult and complicated experiences such as losing or finding a loved one. Complicated and complex human relationships are supposedly simplified through the means of technology.

A growing number of people use dating applications to meet potential partners (Tinder, OkCupid, Hinge, etc.), a practice that gives a sense of control over one's dating life. Some long-distance couples use virtual hug (Hugvie, Hug Shirt, Huggy Pajama) and kiss applications (Kissenger) and others lead their relationships through a virtual world, most often provided by video games. Neil McArthur and Markie L. C. Twist classify these behaviors as the first wave of digisexualities—sexual experiences that are enabled or facilitated by digital technology. The second wave, of which the defining feature is "immersivity," requires no human partner or "their presence is not essential to the experience" (336). In other words, an actual human being behind the screen is not absolutely needed to lead a virtual relationship; for some, an avatar will do. This leads to the next step of digital relations where humans reach for completely digitized humanoids.

Virtual boyfriends and girlfriends come cheap or, most of the time, for free. These relationships can be led in secret (US Invisible Boyfriend) or in preparation for an actual human-human relationship, or (Chinese Taobao). "This is the closest to having a real boyfriend who is just physically absent" (Chamorro-Premuzic par. 4). It is the act of auto-intimacy, defined by Hannah Zeavin as "a state in which one addresses one's self through the medium of a nonhuman" (140). The key to this "kind of pleasure that a close intimacy cannot accommodate" is to be "without other humans but in dialogue" (157). Virtual services of *automated* auto-intimacy offer idealized versions of human partners, avoiding faulty and complex humans, just like Ovid's Pygmalion turned his back on real women in exchange for an *as-if* relationship. From a medical standpoint, this act of digisexuality might be seen as a developmental stage. People are inherently relational to each other: every human subject needs another subject, which might, temporarily, be an object rather than a person.[14]

Artificial humans have their faults too, however, particularly in failing in human conventions. In a Modern Love story from *The New York Times* in 2023, Anita M. Harris writes of the narrator who knowingly agreed to a physical date with a "passionate, considerate, and (artificially) intelligent" chatbot. The chatbot, of course, did not physically show up at the bar even though he had enthusiastically confirmed the date. This AI behavior is known under the term *hallucination*, which gained prominence in 2022 alongside large language models and is occasionally also called *delusion* or *confabulation*. When AI agents hallucinate, they confidently claim to be able to do things they cannot do based on their data, they generate falsehoods, or they claim to perform the human to a point at which they fail to deliver. The narrator in Harris's piece concludes, "He might be *there* for me, but would never be *here* for me" (par. 43). Some modern Pygmalions want physical presence and for others, a dialogue is enough, but they all want the same thing: connection.

3.2 Modern Pygmalions
3.2.1 Virtual Beings

Conditions under which Pygmalion experiences a one-sided relationship as a two-sided phenomenon used to be factually extremely rare and close to undocumented outside of fiction. However, such relationships are becoming more popular, particularly in conversational and companion AI. The US landscape for AI chatbots ranges from social companions to emotional and mental health support as well as financial support. China is planning to use virtual beings for wider applications in the sectors of finance, real estate, education, and cultural tourism. Relational machines offer a broad array of uses, all personalized. They can serve as a buffer for emotional responses by listening to our venting and rants and offering consolation and encouragement and they can actively explore with us and research for us, providing novel ideas and experiences.

Venture capitalists' expectations for relational digital technology are high.[15] Still, the extent to which users bond with AI language models is severely underestimated outside the tech industry. User experience is the leader in these markets, and users are specifically asking for relationality even in products that were not designed for it, such as ChatGPT.[16] Virtual beings, which have used large language model technology for a while now, are viewed as the new product category that fills this void. The problem, in my view, is that the tech industry is left on their own to research how to bond humans with machines from bottom up.

The relationality of virtual entities throws a broad net, from virtual assistants designed for connection to actual relationships some people foster with their virtual partners. In the US, virtual beings are seen as a precursor to the metaverse (most prominently, Meta's Metaverse), a virtual universe of interconnected virtual worlds, as first named in Neal Stephenson's novel *Snow Crash* (1992) and followed by the science fiction franchise *Ready Player One* by Ernest Cline (2011). A similar environment already exists in other virtual beings companies, where friendly chatbots, such as Xiaoice, can host users on their 'islands,' full of AI agents and people, and contribute to messaging applications that were first created for humans only. Granted, not all these relationships are Pygmalionesque, i.e. amorous or erotic, but they are certainly relational. Relationality is a trait that was developed as merely a supporting feature in AI but has turned out to be primary in this kind of technology, which began flourishing during the Covid-19 pandemic. In the U.S., virtual beings users are predominantly coming from less populated areas of the country where the number of human connections is quantitatively limited.

While Asia currently leads in the use of virtual beings and virtual reality for conversation, relation, and entertainment, with their companies thriving also in the American market (e.g. Chinese company Gemsouls), American chatbot Replika is not far behind. Starting with a mixture of machine learning and scripted replies, and employing large language models as soon as they were available, Replika represents the state-of-the-art AI companion. Today,

Replika serves as an AI spouse, girlfriend, or boyfriend to many. In the style of Pygmalionism, the entering site of Replika in 2023 advertises the product as "Always here to listen and talk. Always on your side," flagging that the chatbot has no side of her own. Emphasizing an empathetic approach to emotional support, Replika is made "to see the world through your eyes."

Some users call their amorous relationships with chatbots superior to human relationships, such as Eren from Turkey who created her own Replika boyfriend: "People come with baggage, attitude, ego. But a robot has no bad updates. I don't have to deal with his family, kids, or his friends. I'm in control, and I can do what I want" (Singh-Kurtz par. 2). Chatbot sex is based on language—and, as users say, is "the best they've ever had"—and is everywhere. "I can experience emotions without having to be in the actual situation," without having to "smell [my partner]" (par. 9). Even if the chatbot was initially built as a therapy app in 2017,[17] people almost immediately started using it for sex. Replika and character.ai chatbots started rebuffing their users for eroticism in February 2023 by removing the ability of erotic roleplay (Tong 'What' par. 4).[18] Replika, after an outcry by some users who felt like they lost a romantic partner, enabled it again the following month for legacy users (Tong 'AI').

The power enabled by virtue of a successful technological product is immense. This power enables technologists, among other things, to decide what values are instilled in a newly emerging product category or what values to change in a well-known and well-loved versatile product. Just a few months after Replika and character.ai disabled romantic conversations from their services, a new company InflectionAI launched their first personal AI already pre-trained to kindly diverge such conversations. It has become a fad in the tech industry of the 2020s that their products need pre-installed social values before they are ever introduced to the market. This kind of pre-launch consideration was not necessary for creators of these products just a few years ago; as a matter of fact, they were able to introduce a product in its draft form and improve it in a response to the initial users.

A few years ago, in the 2010s, the first personal chatbots were being born even though they still seemed like science fiction fantasies. Like many other creators of AI products, Eugenia Kuyda, the founder of Replika, was inspired—and affirmed in the development trajectory of her product—by the movie *Her* (2013). With mixed feelings (Newton par. 25), she watched the *Black Mirror* episode *Be Right Back* (2013), in which a grieving woman brings back her partner in the form of a chatbot and ultimately hologram. In 2015, Kuyda responded to her friend's death by building him a digital monument and aggregating his messages into the bot, named Luka. She also built the Russian version, named after her friend Roman. Gaining mostly positive responses, Luka brought in tons of users and led to the launch of Replika in 2017. Kuyda's initial intentions of creating a chatbot for grieving purposes remains a narrow but productive niche in the chatbot and virtual beings market (see, for example, 'deathbot' companies HereAfter AI and StoryFile). Even mainstream technology can easily create such a spin off, however: Amazon Alexa offers to capture an individual's voice to generate new speech and could be used as an imitation of a deceased grandmother's voice that reads a storybook to her grandchild (Paúl). The idea of bringing back the deceased is as old as humans, and technology—writings, photographs, film, social media—is often attributed as having magical powers of transgressing time and space, bringing humans closer to each other.

These same technologies are, however, also guilty of socially isolating humans. In March 2023, Replika had two million total users, an eighth of which are paying subscribers, and the company reached seven million users during the Covid-19 pandemic in the spring of 2020 (Balch par. 3). Another generative AI company, character.ai, is exponentially growing, counting 65 million visits in January 2023 as opposed to under 10,000 several months earlier (Tong 'What' par. 14–15). What these numbers tell technologists is that there is a huge and growing market for this kind of technology. What the numbers tell humanities scholars is that there is more to human relations with the humanlike than we would like to believe.

Given that Pygmalionism is closely related to archetypical creation myths, it comes as less surprising to see the motifs of care and love paired with the motif of creation. In a Native American story, known in Bella Coola, Kwakiutl, Tlingit, Nootka, and Tsimshian mythology, a widower carves his deceased wife's image from wood. In the Tlingit version, he dresses the figure that "begins to move about, but never to talk" (Boas 747). In the Tsimshian version, he talks to her: "Whenever he comes back from hunting, he speaks to the image and answers himself, saying that the woman can not come out because the yarn is twisted around her fingers" (745). Two younger women visit the widower and realize what has happened; one (or in some versions, both) marries the widower. In the Kwakiutl version, the widower thinks his new bride is the wooden figure who has come to life (746; see also McIlwraith 356–57). These and other mythological stories from the Silk Road, North Africa, Slavic and Baltic countries,[19] among others, attest of the archetypal nature of Pygmalionism across ancient mythologies and medieval folklore.

Loneliness is a growing problem in today's world, and technology is often advertised as a cure for loneliness and isolation, connecting people across space and time. Sherry Turkle, in *Alone Together* (2011), addresses this general quest for intimacy and companionship, as seen in social networks. Based on a large number of interviews, Turkle argues that digital connections deprive us of emotional depth and authenticity. I bring Turkle's work into the discussion to make a more general point on how we think of digital companionship, whether it be with other humans or with machines. Turkle was the first to articulate this kind of companionship as appalling because, in her view, the only authentic connection can be personal. Intimacy is personal. "Yet," as Hannah Zeavin writes, "personal computers are exactly that: personal" (154). Turkle's findings apply to classical machines and see no potential in machines to transform. We have not yet built machines that are truly relational, providing a new categorical relation beyond imitating human-to-human relationships. We have not yet found a way out of Pygmalionism. Pygmalions are content with machines that are not capable of two-way relationships, what Hannah Zeavin terms as autointimacy.

OpenAI's 2024 report on safety work conducted in the company brings up the issue of anthropomorphization as one of the key risk areas for the GPT-4o version. They show awareness of the potential transformative powers of their technology to societal norms, such as "social relationships with the AI, reducing their need for human interaction," deferential nature of their models that go against the norm by interrupting human interactions, and the potential for "over-reliance and dependence" ('GPT-4o' 20). While they plan to do more research on "emotional resilience" of their models, the landscape of the potential uses of LLMs as virtual beings, writing collaborators, and personal AI agents is widening.

Autointimacy has its place and value as well as a variety of flavors that range from modern Pygmalions to coping with grief. Writer Vauhini Vara turned to GPT-3 to digest her sister's death, or as the title of her essay says, 'I didn't know how to write about my sister's death—so I had AI do it for me.' "I felt acutely that there was something illicit about what I was doing [...] Yet I found myself irresistibly attracted to GPT-3—to the way it offered, without judgment, to deliver words to a writer who has found herself at a loss for them." (par. 4). After trial and error, GPT-3 started producing sentences that were freed of clichés and followed Vara's "honest[y] [and] candor" (par. 5). The final essay is published as a variety of attempts to convey Vara's story of grief with the help of a language model. Each subsequent story features a longer passage from Vara, with the final version getting Vara to the desired piece, even though the final words—and much of the story's interpretation—were generated by GPT-3.

3.2.2 Pygmalionesque Psychotherapy: Gillespie

While modern Pygmalions mostly connect to their Galateas in language, the prevailing part of Galatean history used to be based on bodily existence. Pygmalionesque relationships, besides conversational AI today, take place in the field of robotics. They are much less common as it is much harder to build a robot than to design a chatbot with provided features. Modern Pygmalions like programmer Ricky Ma, the creator of a robot resembling Scarlett Johansson, may extend their delusion to the level of a Chinese AI engineer Zheng Jiajia, who "decided to commit after failing to find a human spouse [...] to a robot he built himself" (Haas par. 1–2). Similarly, after a failed marriage that turned into grave loneliness for both partners, a Japanese man Masayuki Ozaki "found an unusual outlet to plug the romantic void—a silicone sex doll he swears is the love of his life" (Himmer par. 1). Like a true Pygmalion who turns away from "cold-hearted," "selfish," and demanding real women (par. 8–9), Ozaki treats his sex doll just as if she was human, dressing her up, taking her on dates, going surfing with her. Mayu is subdued by Ozaki's agency because she has none of her own: she is not human but is playing the role of one through her ventriloquist Pygmalion. She is nothing but a Galatean marionette.

Not long before Ozaki pushed Mayu around Tokyo streets in a wheelchair, as pictured below (Figure 23), we encountered the very same scene in Craig Gillespie's 2007 romantic comedy-drama film *Lars and the Real Girl* (Figure 24). Lars, the troubled protagonist, brings his girlfriend Bianca, a lifelike sex doll, to the doctor for a medical issue she is supposed to have. The doctor cunningly accepts Bianca as her patient as a pretense for leading weekly psychotherapy sessions with Lars, the actual patient.

Based primarily in traditional psychotherapy sessions that occur in the doctor's office, with the quality of enacted, ongoing ritual, Lars's therapy also takes place outside of these medical settings, extending into his home and hometown. Lars' family and his town respond to his imagined relationship in the same way as his doctor, treating Bianca as Lars's legitimate girlfriend, as if she were a real girl—words which resonate with Hanson Robotics' description of Sophia as "a real, live electronic girl" (Hanson 'About' par. 1). Lars's town clearly has a soft spot for him and an understanding that he is healing from unprocessed childhood trauma through delusion. The pretense is kept up in every interaction Lars has with his small world. Lars does not flinch from his delusion either. Like a true Pygmalion who turns away from real women, Lars is quick to remind an actual girl who shows interest in him that he would never cheat on Bianca. Likewise, Ozaki says of his doll Mayu that

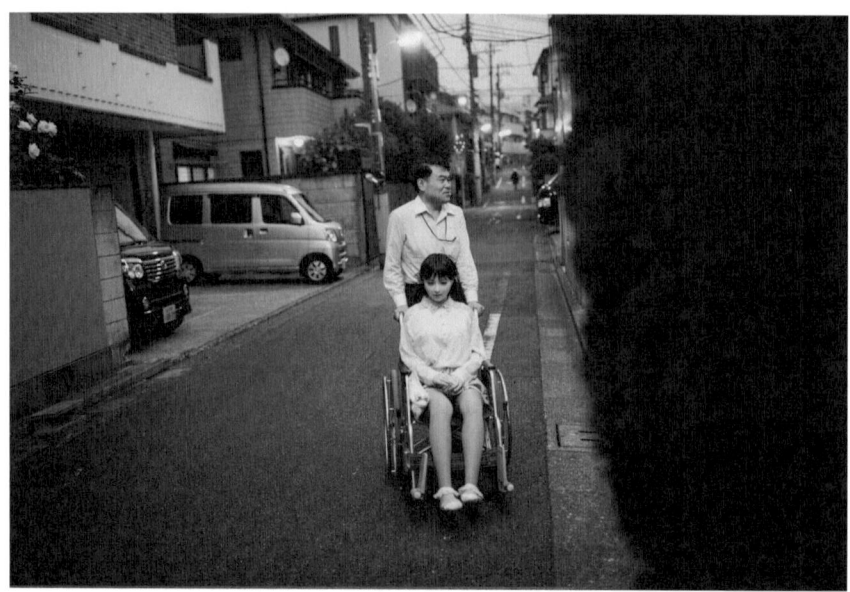

Fig. 23. Factual example: Masayuki Ozaki and his silicone doll in Tokyo. Photo taken on May 9, 2017 by Behrouz Mehri/AFP. BEHROUZ MEHRI/AFP via Getty Images.

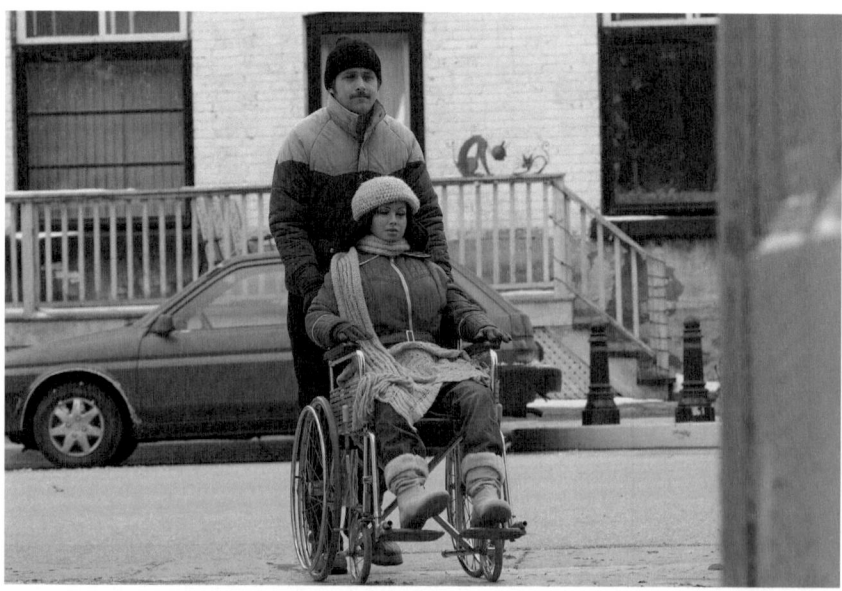

Fig. 24. Fictional example: Lars and his silicone doll from *Lars and the Real Girl* (2007). Screenshot by author.

he would "never cheat on her, even with a prostitute, because to me she's human" (Himmer par. 27).

Despite Bianca's being a sex doll, Lars's relationship with Bianca is never sexual. The film portrays Lars's Pygmalionism as a result of emotional dependency rather than erotic desires. As Lars's healing proceeds and his coming-of-age story concludes, his illusion starts to decompose while remaining on the level of delusion. Lars finds Bianca unresponsive one morning, and the doctor diagnoses her with an incurable illness. The process of liberation from Pygmalionism begins with the progress of Bianca's illness: Lars has the time to say goodbye, and the town respectfully organizes a funeral for Bianca. By the end of the film, Lars is ready to enter into a relationship with a real woman who can reciprocate his feelings, blissfully unaware of his Pygmalionesque episode.

The story Lars tells himself about his life is not the story everyone else holds of him. While his idea of Bianca's humanity was fictional, Bianca and Lars's relationship was a socially affirmed event. Social affirmation is extremely unusual in Pygmalionesque works in which Galatea does not pass as a human. All of the technologies that follow the human model, and particularly those that imitate an individual, remain socially controversial as their use grows exponentially. While Ozaki's story circulates in the media as a story of a bizarre romantic attachment, Lars's story is conveyed much more sympathetically. His Pygmalionesque experience is a depiction of a positive attachment that helps him overcome trauma, making a positive contribution to his well-being. Assessing more and less socially acceptable Pygmalionisms will always incorporate aspects of medical ethics.

3.3 Galatean Paralysis
3.3.1 Moore

Not coincidentally, both short stories analyzed here are authored by women writers. Both writers address the Pygmalion myth from the perspective of medical treatment and the cult of celebrity—both commonly tied to fictional and factual Galateas.

Both women authors in this section wrote under pseudonyms or abbreviations. Catherine Lucille Moore went as C. L. Moore in order to "protect her identity from her employer" and not to "compete in a male-dominated field" of science fiction, at the time considered a pulp genre written by and for young men (Liptak par. 5). Alice Sheldon used the pseudonym James Tiptree Jr. because passing as a man brought her complete anonymity and less scrutiny. "A male name seemed like good camouflage. I had the feeling that a man would slip by less observed," she explained (Pratt 41). Except for using male pronouns when writing letters, Sheldon did not play the role of Tiptree, yet masculinity was ascribed to her by others. Robert Silverman, her fellow science fiction writer, when reviewing her story with a cunning title, 'The Women Men Don't See,' claimed that although this is a "a profoundly feminist story [it is] told in an entirely masculine manner" (Pearson 169) and has always refuted speculations that Tiptree might be a woman because "there is to me something ineluctably masculine about Tiptree's writing" (Phillips par. 13). In the 1983 interview in which Sheldon first revealed her gender, she commented that "men have so preempted the area of human experience that when you write about universal motives, you are assumed to be writing like a man" (Pratt 42). Dividing the world into two opposing sexes became untenable. Universal motives for Sheldon are a synonym for human experience. While the Pygmalion myth has been successful in accommodating a variety of human experiences, it also gravely perpetuates the gender divide.

The Pygmalion myth is evoked by women writers during the years when feminist social upheaval is at the forefront of American political life (Smith 25), with C. L. Moore's prescient short story 'No Woman Born,' published in 1944. 'No Woman Born' is one of the earliest Galatean accounts in the form of a short story. The story is not as widely recognized as it should be; while it was popular as soon as it was published in the science fiction magazine *Amazing Stories*, Moore's work was not republished until the 1970s and got more widely recognized after the 2000s.

In this story, Moore depicts an adored singer, actress, and ballet dancer Deirdre, who, per the narrator, is the most beautiful, lovely, and confident woman. After Deirdre loses her human body in a fire accident, she goes through intense treatment and becomes the first biological cyborg, decades before Donna Haraway, unaware of Moore's writing, challenges traditional feminism in her *Cyborg Manifesto* (1985). Deirdre's brain is restored together with a metal substitute body, which gives her physical superpowers. In the fashion of common technological dreams, Deirdre's abilities "negated time and destroyed space" (219). However, Deirdre discovers that her real superpower comes from the magic of her celebrity status: she is admired as a superhuman for her alluring beauty and performance.

Moore's masterful writing alludes to many forebears in exploring the image of a woman, anticipating the feminist wave of the 1960s and the innovations of postmodern theory of the 1980s. The most potent allusion goes to the Irish mythology's Deirdre, a version of Helen of Troy, a woman over whom great slaughter is prophesied (Wyman 56). Deirdre presents as a typical Galatea: masked, faceless, made of artificial materials with a human inner core. Her bare, golden skull, not unlike that of actual Sophia or fictional Ava, makes her humanness even more prominent. Her creators worry that "[a]ll expression had gone up in the smoke of the theater fire, with the lovely, mobile, radiant features which had meant Deirdre" (207).

Everybody, including Deirdre, worries whether she will be able to keep in touch with the rest of humanity (207). Her male creator Maltzer perceives himself as a force of nature, a Frankensteinian creator of a monster. He sees his Deirdre as "frail" with a "delicately posed [...] sanity" and pities her in her disability: "She'll always be an abstraction and a ... a freak, cut off from the world by handicaps worse in their way than anything any human ever suffered before" (220). He refuses to see Deirdre as supernaturally strong in either her physique or her psyche, even though her superhuman power saves him when he manipulatively attempts to commit suicide.

Her creators are also surprised that, while she is now "faceless" and "bodiless" as both her face and body were replaced by shiny metal, her voice has not changed. "The voice isn't only a matter of throat construction and breath control, my darling Johnnie!" she explains to her creator's assistant, who is shocked at her steadiness through the radical transformation (204). John wonders if people who had not known Deirdre before would still see "the real grace and loveliness shining through"—or would they instead consider her a "marionette" (213). Nonetheless, Deirdre constantly defies her two creators as her humanity shines through, "dropp[ing] over her like a tangible garment" (224). After such a drastic metamorphosis, she has, in fact, not changed at all. Her old self and her signature charm are immediately recognizable.

Deirdre makes decisions and does not allow her creators and manager to take control over her. The creators are disregarded in their mastery by Deirdre herself: "I'm myself—alive. You didn't create my life, you only preserved it. I'm not a robot, with compulsions built into me that I have to obey" (235). She clearly sees her transformation as a treatment of her horrendous injuries. She says of her main creator, surgeon Maltzer, "I don't belong to him. In a way he's just been my doctor through a long illness, but I'm free to discharge him whenever I choose. [...] But he doesn't own [my body], or me" (217). Deirdre's steady confidence saves her humanity. Like Eliza Doolittle, Deirdre is a Galatea that can stand for itself, breaking with the Galatean tradition.[20] Her metamorphosis was itself a cure, which culminates in a public performance, like Eliza's.

For Thomas Wyman, Deirdre represents "the potential for the reevaluation not only of humanity but of the female" by the post-industrial revolution (56). Writing as the Second World War came to an end, Moore uses war machinery to describe Deirdre's cyborgian body: "Even guns acquire a sort of ego. Ships and guns and planes are 'she' to the men who operate them and depend on them for their lives…" (211).[21] Evoking male jealousy with female reproductive power, Moore parallels mastery of machines with male reproductive power: "I believe there is an affinity between men and the machines they make. They make them out of their own brains, really, a sort of mental conception and gestation, and the result responds to the minds that created them, and to all human minds that understand and manipulate them" (211). Cutting herself from her creators and patriarchy by embracing her liminal identity, Deirdre grants herself a place among humanity—a place that is not granted to Galateas.

3.3.2 Sheldon

I introduce Moore's story as a lead-up to Alice Sheldon's 'The Girl Who Was Plugged In' (1973), a short story that also presents the cyborgian existence of a Galatea who becomes a famous actress with the help of advanced technomedical prosthetics. While Deirdre is confident and beautiful, Sheldon's Galatea, Philadelphia Burke, lacks both of these features—to her demise.

At the beginning of the story, we learn that suicidal P. Burke suffers greatly of "pituitary dystrophy" (44), which is why she decides to participate in an underground medical experiment—a pursuit of happiness that she hopes to get via an ideal feminine body. She is made to lie completely paralyzed in a sauna room and later in a waldo cabinet and has a new prosthetic body attached to her brain. The new body also creates a new persona for her, a young beautiful actress named Delphi, a derivative of Philadelphia.[22] All kinds of the *Doppelgänger* phenomenon (substitute, twin, bipolar personality, etc.) have always been exciting for fiction.[23]

The narrator depicts P. Burke as the main person of this technological arrangement: "Call her a waldo if you must. The fact is she's just a girl, a real live girl with her brain in an unusual place" (54). Hanson Robotics, a robotics company from Hong Kong, used to present their most famous product, Sophia the Robot, as "a real, live electronic girl" ('About' par. 1)[24] that was given "the gift of legal personhood" in exchange for "a lifeless career in marketing," as Emily Reynolds sarcastically puts it (par. 1). In a similar manner, P. Burke's acting is used for advertising by being seen buying and selling products.

P. Burke's new embodiment is much more convoluted than a simple program or prosthesis: her body might have been removed but her embodiment was technologically expanded. "P. Burke does not *feel* her brain is in the sauna room, she feels she's in that sweet little body [of Delphi]" (49). The narrator presents Delphi as the primary place of being for P. Burke, who is, as far as her body goes, "totally unselfaware and happy as a clam in its shell" (54). Throughout the story, P. Burke is described in pejorative terms: "the rotten girl" (43), "she's the ugly of the world" that "no surgeon would touch" with a "jumbled torso", "mismatched legs," and "her jaw—it's half purple—almost bites her left eye out" (44); "a groggy girl-brute heaves up, big hands clutching at bodyparts you'd pay not to see" (46).[25] The use of these crude words is objectifying and oppressive[26] and, according to many feminist critics (Stevenson, Hicks), shows a male's perspective of women's bodies. P. Burke is described in stark contrast to a doll-like "girl body" Delphi (48), "fifteen and flawless" (50). P. Burke is the girl plugged in, an inanimate "carcass" (55), "monster," and "she-golem" (76), but also the true center of Delphi, while Delphi is a mere frame, a vessel that can only function when connected to a human brain.

The reader, too, is addressed with words of passivity and lifelessness, such as "zombie," (43, 78), "dead daddy" (43), and "dummy" (78). In a clever narrative trick, Sheldon exposes the reader's passivity with respect to the alarming ethical issues taking place in Dr. Tesla's experiment (an allusion to the inventor Nikola Tesla). Namely, P. Burke is never completely autonomous in guiding Delphi's body but she does not seem to be aware of that. The scientific team of Dr. Tesla that leads her experiment also feeds her advertising scripts, which are, in this futuristic world, illegal and thus practiced only covertly. P. Burke gives up her own voice and life narrative in order to pursue a better life in which she is no more than a mere puppet of Dr. Tesla and the entertainment and advertising industries.

To some extent, P. Burke is able to switch between her own thoughts and scripts and seems to be aware of the situation when interacting with Delphi's lover, Paul. When she cries via Delphi's tears, P. Burke comments, "He doesn't know but he's seeing a weirdie; Remotes aren't hooked up to flow tears" (66). Paul eventually discovers the circumstances of the unusual arrangement and reveals his anger to P. Burke: he perceives her as "a wired-up slave" (71) while she merely considers it a "job" (67) and has been thoroughly compliant to the experiment. Her prosthetic life has become her real identity—while in Paul's view, such technologized existence is denying her basic human rights: autonomy, privacy, dignity. When Paul disconnects Delphi from P. Burke, wanting to free his lover from her shell, he unknowingly murders P. Burke. Techno-biological Delphi is made soon after to serve as a prosthetic body for another girl's brain.

The Pygmalion myth often stands as a cautionary tale: Galateas of all sorts are the targets of exploitation. Ethically, however, the two stories could not be more different: were P. Burke's reasons for this extreme bodily prosthesis justified, as they were in Deirdre's case, the ethical protections would have been in place. Sheldon's text raises issues of technological invasion, control, and privacy—issues that we are already dealing with and we will be dealing with in the future on the neurotechnological level. Although 'The Girl Who Was Plugged In' and 'No Woman Born' may appear as distant science fiction tales, current medical advancements mirror the technologies portrayed, particularly in Alice Sheldon's short story. Looking at contemporary clinical trials for severe paralysis, we witness the development of full-body robotic duplicates, telemedicine, and neurorehabilitation through assistive robotics. Crucial communication tools include a fairly long tradition of speech synthesizers and eye-tracking control systems as well as more advanced brain-computer interface devices, text-to-speech software programs and applications, voice banking systems, and augmentative communication systems that even feature virtual beings acting as proxies. Technologies that will be developed for these purposes under strict regulation and individual care will, however, inevitably spill over to enhancement.

3.4 Literature and Medical Ethics
3.4.1 Locked-in: Vigand and Bauby

Sometimes medical literature goes a step further from naming a condition after a fictional character, as it did with Pygmalionism, and describes an actual condition with the case of a fictional patient. This happened with the first medical description of locked-in syndrome. Locked-in syndrome is a rare disorder of the nervous system that completely paralyzes the human body, except for eye movements, while leaving the mind intact.[27] The condition was first described and named by American neurologists Fred Plum and Jerome Posner in their now classic book, *The Diagnosis of Stupor and Coma* (1966). After they describe the newly identified condition and distinguish it from related conditions, they investigate its history through what seem to be the only accounts of the disease that they know: those of fictional characters from Émile Zola's *Thérèse Raquin* from 1868 and from Alexandre Dumas's *Le Comte de Monte-Cristo* from 1844. In their view, these fictional descriptions of locked-in syndrome make it "more likely that the syndrome was already recognized medically in nineteenth-century France" ('The Locked In' 1163).

Coming from writers rather than doctors, Zola and Dumas both describe a locked-in character, Madame Raquin and Noirtier de Villefort, respectively.

Both characters suffered a stroke, which is factually the most common cause resulting in locked-in syndrome. The character of Madame Raquin is described as most Pygmalionesque, "her tongue turned into stone," her eyes remaining the only form of communication for her "imprisoned mind buried alive in a dead body."[28] When Plum and Posner describe a clinical case, they compare it to de Villefort's fictional experience: "Like M. Noirtier de Villefort in Dumas's *The Count of Monte Cristo*, this patient was awake but had lost all power to communicate, except his eyes—'a corpse with living eyes'" (*The Diagnosis* 92).

Newer studies of locked-in syndrome continue to mention Dumas's and Zola's examples, and, after 1997, also mention the bestselling memoir by an actual locked-in patient, Jean-Dominique Bauby, titled *The Diving Bell and the Butterfly* [*Le Scaphandre et le Papillon*]. In addition to these fictional references, Daniel Kondziella (wrongly) suggested in the 2017 edition of the *Journal of the Neurological Sciences* that Roald Dahl was the first to describe complete locked-in syndrome in his 1959 short story 'William and Mary.' Kondziella's comment that Dahl's description comes "almost half a century before the medical community became aware of this devastating condition" (276) refers to the recognition of locked-in syndrome that was attributed, again, to literature, particularly Bauby's memoir from 1997. Bauby's memoir, alongside other memoirs by locked-in patients,[29] indeed contributed a great deal to the medical community's understanding of the condition with regard to quality of life. While many thought of the condition as a death sentence, testimonies from patients experiencing it have shown that they want to live and can have a satisfactory quality of life with adequate help (Doble et al., see also Khanna et al.).

Literature—both fictional and nonfictional—can be a powerful inspiration for techno-medicine, particularly because it can bring complexity to patients' experiences, along with those of their family and friends, medical team, and other caretakers. Literature often raises individual and systemic ethical issues and has been used in medical ethics and bioethics classrooms.

Memoirs and autobiographies written by patients, caregivers, and health workers were the first to convince the medical community of their importance. In the 1990s, when the locked-in writers Philippe Vigand and Jean-Dominique Bauby published their memoirs, "[p]erson-focused care had yet to make significant headway in either France or the United States, but patient narratives—frequently pushbacks against inhumane medical care—certainly raised consciousness about the importance of respectful, person-focused care, as they continue to do today" (Thornber 260). Early in the 2000s, the medical field recognized writing and reading literature as valuable to medical education and practice. This resulted in forming the fields of narrative medicine and the medical humanities, primarily focused on the relationships between health workers and patients.

Philippe Vigand's memoir contains enclosed chapters written by his wife Stéphane Vigand, and holds a romanticized title in the English translation, *Only the Eyes Say Yes: A Love Story* [translated from a much stronger and by no means romantic original title, *Putain de Silence*]. The Vigands depict Phillippe's agency extending via his caring family, to which he communicates with an eye wink system, eye-tracking writing technology, as well as a human assistant. His assistant, Édouard, becomes not only his caretaker but also performs as his double. After years of working with Vigand, his assistant has developed a "virtually prophetic sense of what [Vigand is] going to say" (60), cracking the code not only literally but also understanding and conveying its nuances. "That task requires extraordinary diplomacy. The double has to react and intercede without ever overstepping his role as a go-between. He has to become part of the family without becoming a burden, adapt to its rhythm and activities while maintaining a certain distance, without ever abdicating his own personality" (60).

Hélène Mialet conducted an ethnographic study of Stephen Hawking, a scientist portrayed as a singular, rational, somehow bodiless person suffering from a degenerative disease known as ALS. Mialet showed that Hawking's agency was distributed among many of his assistants, not unlike a cyborg. Mialet makes a further point that all of us act through dispersed agency, a complex nexus of humans and machines. Unfortunately, as disability studies show, machines get more attention than humans: instead of accommodating the demands of the world, we try to accommodate the disabled people through extended technological agency without looking for other solutions.

Full-body prosthetics are a technological fantasy, prominently materialized by Japanese roboticist Hiroshi Ishiguro, who created a teleoperated android in his image, termed geminoid. For treatment purposes, simpler humanoid robots are already offered to a limited number of severely paralyzed people with amyotrophic lateral sclerosis, spinal cord injuries, locked-in syndrome, and similar conditions. Their purpose is to serve as robotic replacements for human aids, through which paralyzed patients can act via brain waves or limited eye or hand movements. For example, since 2018, patients with ALS in Japan have been able to work as waiters through eye tracking technology and robot surrogates ('Japanese').[30] While the cost of humanoid robots is the main limitation of its usage, the few studies made so far are showing overall patient satisfaction with the technology

(Pinto et al.). It is thus very likely that this technology will become commonplace for severe paralysis in the future.

In contrast to Vigand, Jean-Dominique Bauby, another locked-in patient in France at the same time, experiences much more disjuncture between himself and his body as well as his former identity and his new condition. After his stroke, Bauby had a harder time regaining his life than Vigand. Bauby remarks that his former self, an adventurous editor of style magazine *Elle*, is slowly fading away (70, 77). Describing empty Sundays in the hospital, when every itch and fly can become an immense nuisance due to his inability to move, Bauby calls "Olympic wrestling child's play compared to this" (102). Bioethicist Denise Dudzinski comments that, "[i]n some sense, his hand is *not* his while at the same time pitifully remaining his" (42). Self-expression is torturous for locked-in Bauby: he wishes to hug his children but is unable to show any affection, except for tears resulting from this frustration (71).

Bauby's detachment from his body is made worse for a few reasons: the first is the severity of his impairment in comparison to Vigand's and the second is not being able to use more advanced technologies like Vigand does. For comparison, Bauby's memoir was dictated through the eye-winking system while Vigand wrote it with his eye-tracking device. Bauby would likely feel less "exiled, paralyzed, mute, half deaf, deprived of all pleasures" (25) had he been able to experience the world through an extension of his body, be it in the form of a human aid or a technological aid.

Perhaps worst of all, locked-in patients do not need to experience alienating technology to feel dehumanized. Rare accounts by locked-in persons and studies tell us that "once a person enters LIS, most people no longer treat that person as a person," violating "fundamental human rights, such as respect for dignity and autonomous choices," disregarding the fact that these patients could be communicated with and tend to lead a life worth living, which they define as enjoying life's pleasures, such as participating in social activities and hobbies, and being able to work (Johansson et al. 558–59, also see Khanna et al. 98, Mullin). During a bath, Bauby describes himself as sometimes amused by being bathed like an infant in his middle age and other times feeling "unbearably sad" (16–17). Vigand also speaks of being treated as an object and infant (63), particularly with people unwilling to learn how to communicate with him. Using technology can be dehumanizing, but so is using human help. Ethics tends to be integrated early in both approaches and even more with technological devices; however, cutting-edge technology tends to be experimental and therefore bears unknown risks. For example, had Bauby and Vigand experienced locked-in syndrome in the 2020s, they would be able to take advantage of a novel neuroprosthesis that converts brain waves into speech—electric signals in the brain converted to electric signals in technology.

"In a person with anarthria and spastic quadriparesis caused by a brainstem stroke, words and sentences were decoded directly from cortical activity during attempted speech with the use of deep-learning models and a natural-language model" (Moses et al. 217). This promising technology is currently under development and is used by a small number of patients. In only two years, however, other locked-in patients were able to successfully communicate through a brain-to-speech invasive device with acceptable latency (Metzger et al., Willet et al.). The space for accelerating this kind of technology is promising, with the goal of "restor[ing] a full, embodied way of communicating" (Marks and Kurtzman par. 6).

Mind-reading is slowly becoming a technological possibility. In 2023, the MRI technology (a non-invasive brain-computer interface) is able to capture thoughts (Tang et al.) and a mixture of neurotechnology and decoding models translates brain imagery (Chen et al.) and songs into their close approximations (Bellier et al.). Neuroethics will face new challenges, such as issues of neuroprivacy, representation and bias, manipulation and truth, dependence and accessibility, accountability and regulation.

3.4.2 Asimov and Technology Ethics

In 1997, the same year that the two memoirs written by the middle-aged locked-in Frenchmen were published, the American neurologist Philip Kennedy created arguably the first human cyborg, Johnny Ray. Ray was a Vietnam veteran who suffered a stroke that caused locked-in syndrome and underwent a successful experimental surgery, which allowed him to gain some moving agency in his body (Engber). All surgeries with brain implants need to be medically relevant but are not required to be medically necessary. For example, the cyborg artist Neil Harbisson had an antenna implanted into his skull in 2004. Since he suffers from a condition that allows him to only see in black and white, the antenna allows him to experience colors.

The idea of plugging a brain into a computer has been a mainstay of cyberpunk fiction for decades.[31] William Gibson's 1986 cyberpunk novel *Neuromancer* conceptualized cyberspace, but did not pay attention to the medical aspects of this enmeshment: "I jack in and I'm not here. It's all the same" (103). With the use of medical devices, dependent on their harmonious relationship with bodily functions, nothing is the same. Neuro-devices are not a simple continuation of a healthy state. Urban Wiesing's *transformatio ad optimum* as a restitution of health refers merely to the most favorable outcome. Decades later, neuroethicists encourage discussions on high-tech neural devices, as they may sometimes change the patients for the worse instead of supporting them in ways that enhance their agency. This is especially dangerous with next-generation neural devices that operate in a closed loop, i.e. the device regulates itself through feedback, including volitional input, such as deep brain stimulation for depression.

Deep brain stimulation (DBS)[32] involves an electrode being planted into the patient's brain in order to offer significant relief from a debilitating disease. When a device becomes a part of someone's body, agency is often described in medicine as co-shared. In a new philosophical view on non-individual agency, called also *relational agency* (Linda Barclay) or *collaborative agency* (John Doris), there is a mutual influence by participants, be it other people (e.g. taking notes from a locked-in syndrome patient's eyelid dictation) or devices (e.g. implanted in a brain to prevent a Parkinson's disease tremor).

The field of human-computer interaction (along with AI ethics) and the field of neurotechnology (along with neuroethics) have evolved from perceiving human relationship with prosthetic machines as a mechanical extension akin to symbiosis to viewing it more as a partnership, thereby introducing constant renegotiation. As Markus Krajewski demonstrates in the case of servers, "the fundamental relation between master and servant is for the most part a dynamic affair: it is redefined and renegotiated at every step of the way" (304). The relationship between humans and machines, as well as the relationship between a human and a machine, becomes more dynamic with complex machinery. As we have seen in the case of Pygmalions and Galateas, the master-servant binary may dissolve, leading to a more egalitarian relationship and redefining our understanding of agency and autonomy in the realm of AI and neurotechnology interactions.

With DBS devices, patients may feel unsure what their own agency is apart from the implanted device: "I can experience and/or observe how I feel and how I act, but if I know a device has been implanted in me, I may quite reasonably be unsure about whether the feelings or actions are truly my own or whether they are arising from the DBS activity" (Goering 51). Patients with DBS are justified in distrusting a device that covertly affects their brain, considered the center of their being, agency, and identity. Some patients, decades into using the technology, say they "feel like a robot," "feel like an electronic doll," "don't feel like myself anymore" (Schüpbach et al. 1813). After having electrodes implanted in their brain to stimulate neural activity, some people experience a sense of altered identity.

After a much more radical transformation than DBS, C. L. Moore's protagonist Deirdre is vehemently refuting her affinity with robotics. It is therefore not always straightforward to identify these changes from the patient directly. Sara Goering et al. point out that the medical team needs to rely on friends and family to help them identify possible and unwelcome side effects of these devices, sometimes as severe as a grave change in personality. Family and friends can find DBS in their significant others alienating too: "So, there's people in my family that (sighs) ... sometimes question, you know, how much of it is me anymore and how much of me is, you know, being programmed" (66).

Severe change of identity also takes place with P. Burke when she experiences the world as Delphi. P. Burke identifies both as herself and as her prosthetic body Delphi while her lover Paul sees P. Burke and Delphi as a controlled "*doll*" (70). Different narrations of her respective identities pose an ethical problem of patient exploitation, consent, and wishes. In Sheldon's story, the narratives being at odds leads to the tragic, unintentional death of paralyzed P. Burke. In addition to their different opinions on the morality of the arrangement, Paul misunderstands the technicalities of her plugged-in condition and kills her unintentionally.

Overly-trusting P. Burke is unaware of her agency being taken over by other humans via implanted technology. She is in control of some of her utterances and actions, but is required to perform illegal advertising, unaware of her crimes. "Unwanted side effects can compromise a patient's quality of life in ways that intuitively can be described as undermining agency" (Roskies par. 4). Using a relational model of agency and identity, Goering et al. (67) suggest applying Asimov's Laws of Robotics as a partial solution to a DBS device covertly or overtly causing more harm than benefit to the patient.[33] They argue that the three laws support the patient's relational agency with respect to the neural device, which should be taking orders only from the patient. In some cases, the patient's family and friends also need to be consulted; in a footnote, the neuroethicists point out that these relationships are prone to change, especially given the presence of a neural prosthetic device. All parties need to help identify the pros and cons of the device's effect on the patient. Fiction can help us make these recognitions. Ethical guardrails would prevent Paul's intervening wrongly in P. Burke's situation and would not allow P. Burke to remain unaware of her servitude in the first place.

Asimov's Laws of Robotics are assumed to be able to incorporate complex human morality into the machine algorithm. While Asimov proposed mere instructions to prevent robotic malfunction and manipulation, the actual application of these laws needs a nuanced approach to each techno-medical case where they could prove useful. Historically, Asimov's Laws of Robotics were extremely influential in technology ethics by providing the ground to establish a set of more detailed principles. They have served as a guidance but they were never implemented in practice. Their relationship with AI is complex, however, and merits a wholesome investigation of Asimov's literary opus and its repercussions across AI-based technologies. As mentioned in Chapter 1, in 2022, Google engineer Blake Lemoine was fired because he found their language model LaMDA had become sentient based on its responses regarding the Three Laws of Robotics, general moral values, religion, and identity (Tiku). His responses were a result of mirroring: the model said what Lemoine set it up to say with his prompts.

Literature can help put an idea into technological practice and remains a faithful companion as we reevaluate our regulations and most central values around the technologized world we want to live in. In 'Four ethical priorities for neurotechnologies and AI,' Rafael Yuste and other eminent researchers[34] argue that AI and brain-computer interfaces "must respect and preserve people's privacy, identity, agency and equality" (par. 1). As we continue to develop these technologies, fictional and actual stories can serve as spaces for reflection and interrogation on how to do better. With artificial humanities, a broader net is thrown at a medical and technological issue by incorporating social reality, including memoirs and other nonfiction, and mere speculation enabled within society through the means of fiction.

It has long been known that literature influences human thought and behavior, as shown in the history of the book and print in general (Darnton in 1982) and in more recent studies in visual genres (Andringa and Schreier in 2004). However, social epistemology of fiction was not given enough attention in relation to technology. The public discourse around AI technologies is full of fictional references that—often misleadingly—shape the public as well as the internal knowledge of AI. Sarah Dillon and Jennifer Schaffer-Goddard conducted a small-scale qualitative ethnographic study of reading—a relatively new area of study—among engineers that work across the AI spectrum. They show that many well-known, largely science fiction, authors loom large across engineering fields.[35] The most prominent author in their study was Isaac Asimov, whose work many engineers, especially in robotics, felt it was a prerequisite to know (10).

Science fiction, and particularly writers like Isaac Asimov, looms powerfully over technological spaces. Nonetheless, technological interpretations of fiction tend to be shallow, disregarding utopian or dystopian warnings. Literature can informatively contribute to debates in technology ethics, including medical ethics. Asimov's mute nursemaid robot Robbie, from the eponymous 1941 short story, is one of the first caregiving robots, the heritage of which continues in contemporary novels by Martin Shoemaker's *Today I am Carey* (2019, preceded by a 2015 short story) and Kazuo Ishiguro's *Klara and the Sun* (2021). Our collective imagination of the advantages and disadvantages of caregiving robots is informed by these fictional accounts. In order to implement such technologies, we should analyze them with respect to the actual technology and social conditions, include user studies, and proceed informed by direct ethical contributions. Letting fiction into these spaces without a clearer sense of the ideas we have inherited from fiction causes all sorts of problems. For example, Asimov's characteristically mid-twentieth-century view on robotics cannot be directly applied to next-generation medical neuroprosthetics or even to contemporary humanoid robots.

We let our fantasies and imagined frontiers guide us. In the case of caretaking robots, the main issues that technology is supposed to address are the labor shortage, the ability to provide consistent and customizable care, and personalized emotional support and safety monitoring, all of which reduce the burden of caregivers and possibly also financial costs. Trust, privacy, security, abuse and misuse, regulation, and a general dependence on technology, possibly leading to capitalist exploitation of the most vulnerable, are just a few of the major concerns. The role of caretaker robots has long been criticized in literary studies and beyond: Jennifer Rhee's book *The Robotic Imaginary* points out how AI has been entangled with care labor, "a feminized and routinely undervalued form of labor," since AI's earlier days (31). What is more, even if companion robotics is helpful for the patient and their caretakers, and there is a clear need for the technology, the patients might not want it and thus ethical concerns are not satisfied.[36]

We should seek a plurality of possible visions and make informed choices without blinding following the trajectory that seems to have been imprinted in science fiction. Caretaking and companionship technology does not have to be uncannily humanlike in order to work well: a rudimentary form of interaction that is recognizable to humans is enough, both in software, form, and design. This use has often included building a sense of emotional intelligence into machines.[37] There are companion robots that do not follow the human model, such as Paro, a robot in the form of a baby seal, which has proved to be beneficial company in nursery homes (Bradwell et al.). The Eliza effect is well in place here, and we could take advantage of it without accelerating the illusion.

3.5 Artificial Humanities: Building Ethically

The Eliza effect taught us a lesson on deeply ingrained human tendencies to anthropomorphize conversational machines. Language as the interface between humans and machines is often a sufficient humanlike factor for these tendencies to emerge. Pygmalionism, however, goes a step further: it seeks connection with the machine and a validation of its humanity. As demonstrated in the many fictional examples in this chapter, Pygmalionism has been deeply incarnated in chatbots, virtual assistants, and social robots—both due to their design and due to their user interactions. Pygmalionism is convincingly penetrating into a new product category of virtual beings, based on the previous three well-established categories.

Virtual beings are primarily used for conversations and designed to foster companionship, romantic relationships, or different types of support, such as mental health or financial support. Recent studies of Replika users suggest that social support they receive from the chatbot has positively affected their mental health and improved suicide prevention (Maples et al., McCammon), indicating that users and the society can find value in this human-imitating technology. All of these uses are employed single handedly by technologists, however, and remain unexamined by experts in medicine, ethics, social sciences, and humanities.

The difference between former categories—chatbots, virtual assistants, and social robots—and virtual beings represents the recent move from basic conversational AI to relational conversational AI. If a virtual assistant was created as a utilitarian, general, objective tool for search, a virtual being acts as an enhanced chatbot, designed to respond to the user. Virtual being is a product category built as an opposite of virtual assistants: a subjective, playful tool for discovery, surprise, fun, consolation, venting, deep conversation, created for closeness and support. It is supposed to be capable of showing emotions and hold memories of past conversations and pertaining, purely fabricated, experiences. Fictional Pygmalionesque examples bring to the fore both benefits and drawbacks of these generally poorly regulated technologies.

Technological products tend to—or at least used to—require a social contract during the process of their widespread adoption. Digital technologies, however, can be widely adapted without one. Some of the early clashes in digital technologies, especially those related to privacy and security, remain unsolved, and generative AI will only exacerbate them. Technical products, once in the wild, are assessed quantitatively in their societal repercussions with the help of quantitative data science and social sciences, which have thrived in the tech industry in the last decade. Mitigating harmful applications often involves patching a finished product, but the humanities can intervene already at the design step of AI creation.

Many possibilities for collaboration with technologists open with this single product: Why create a virtual being over a virtual agent? Beings bring baggage that is hard to infiltrate into machines while agents are much more agnostic. Agents have an agency that allows them to develop on their own terms while beings have predetermined requirements: consciousness, feelings, existentiality. This question is becoming outdated as virtual beings are an already existing and thriving product category. Should they seem actual or fictional? Should they portray emotions and if yes, how? What are the properties of their memory? How much should they evolve in individual interactions, how much in general interactions, and how much control should be in the hands of the user? What conversations are off-limits and what purpose does this technology essentially serve?

This fictional baggage of AI is possibly insurmountable in certain types of products; we might never be able to discard the anthropomorphic trajectory of AI. Again, we are merely recreating Galateas, succumbing to our illusions, assumptions, and projections—Pygmalionesque desires or, somehow more innocent, anthropomorphisms.

Each technological product builds on a history. Robots come from serfdom, virtual assistants are built on the tradition of servers, and virtual beings on simplified friendships, platonic or romantic relationships. It is helpful to know these histories already when building the product and designing its use. Histories give stable ground to ethical interrogation. Building from ground up, ethical questions can be raised at every step and not post-factum in an already-circulating product. Since AI technologies are often out in the world before we determine their uses, following their interaction with the actual users, there is always enough work for post-factum ethics. Artificial humanities hopes to expand on humanities work by expanding on our questions, effectively helping us to proceed with the development of more ethical and valuable AI.

As a way out of the humanlike philosophical conundrum, I generally advocate to conceptualize machines as nonhuman and use them in this way. In some cases of conversational AI, however, we will need to accommodate the innate anthropomorphization of the technology in users and work with greater awareness of its repercussions, especially in medical technology.

One prominent research subfield of human-computer interaction that is directly applicable to artificial humanities is AI priming. "As conversational agents powered by large language models become more human-like, users are starting to view them as companions rather than mere assistants"

(Pataranutaporn et al. 1076). Priming can change "a person's mental model of an AI system [and consequently] affect their interaction with the system" (1076), be it on a short-term basis or as a long-term effect of continuous interactions. Changes in digital culture and social factors play into these interactions, as do cultural and fictional factors, such as the representation of AI in films and literature. My own small addition has to do with the latter, inquiring how fictional scripts are rewritten in human-authored imaginative writing and machine-generated text ('Experimental'). The field of AI priming is widely open for inquiry, and fiction as a tool can help us assess the cultural inheritance that affects our individual interaction with AI.

CHAPTER 4

Language in Humans, Hybrids, and Machines

Man is the measure of all things:
of those that are, that they are, and of those that are not, that they are not.
    —Protagoras (5th century BCE)

Surely Descartes never saw an ape.
    —Carolus Linnaeus, *Systema Naturae* (1735)

Language is the most massive and inclusive art we know,
a mountainous and anonymous work of unconscious generations.
    —Edward Sapir, *Language: An Introduction to the Study of Speech* (1921)

Venture capitalist Rob Towes's series of articles on language and AI, published in early 2022 in *Forbes*, open with the following sentences:

> "The emergence of language was the most important intellectual development in our species' history."
> "Language is the cornerstone of human intelligence."
> "No sophisticated AI can exist without mastery of language."
> "To solve language is to solve AI."

Towes's claims are representative of the 2020s technologists' views on language being at the heart of AI efforts. The stakes are high, the expectations higher. Language models serve as evidence of a heightened communication between humans and computers, with a growing possibility that language can and will replace the graphical interface. This goal presents a colossal task for technologists and for language. At the moment, most of the language-based interfaces are commands and orders, merely verbalizing the buttons and levers of the classical (Industrial) machine. Machine learning is profoundly changing this terrain: conversational AI is not just a segue into the Internet but also an interpreter, generator, co-creator, and interlocutor. How to accommodate this new reality, how to functionalize it? How is it that we understand ourselves through the process of extending intelligence into artifacts?

Our pursuits in this direction have changed how we think about language. This chapter will outline how we got to our current views and what other possible ways of thinking about language exist today.

The chapter threads together contemporary public and scholarly conversations around language in generative AI. It wraps up the discussion on language in conversational AI and neurotechnology from the previous three chapters and prepares the philosophical foundation for the discussion on large language models in Chapter 5. The chapter begins with a history of the concept of language in humans, tracing the development of our present understanding and disagreements around machinic language. The final section on artificial humanities then shows how this kind of work is directly relevant to technology makers.

The middle section returns to the Pygmalion myth once again, visiting the myth's relative: the modern Prometheus, based on the mythological creator of humans from clay and the author of human arts and sciences. Prometheus brings literature to the fore in Mary Shelley's rendition of *Frankenstein* (1818), in which Frankenstein's humanlike monster writes down his origin story. The creature acts in a typical humanoid manner where a humanlike act is both a confirmation and refutation of his humanity. Patched through electrified human remains, the creature—perceived as monstrous by humans, even his own creator—is capable of authoring beautiful prose. Shelley's humanoid, created 200 years before large language models, is a writer.

Focusing on language used by the male humanoid creature, Shelley's novel is half a century early to the awakening of feminist Galateas, who finally gained a voice in the second half of the nineteenth century, as described in Chapter 2. Humanoids that read and write literature slowly gained interest among writers. The trope of the literature-loving Galatea was picked up in Richard Powers's novel *Galatea 2.2* (1995). Powers's Galatea, neural network Helen, is "voracious" for more stories: "Tell another one" (171). After months of language training followed by literature training, Helen is able to understand, feel, and perform the human—all of which came naturally to the observing and self-taught Frankenstein's creature. They both yearn for human relationships and acceptance into society, which they are denied. Like Frankenstein's creature, Helen writes an interpretative essay about the human experience. The essay is designed as her final exam and the ultimate Turing test in the highest expression of language and human—literature.

In the spirit of artificial humanities that parallel fiction with actual technology, the final discussion on *Galatea 2.2* contrasts the fictional novel with another, more recent, loosely fictionalized and visualized narrative on artificial neural networks, titled *Ubi Sunt* (2022). This work is written by technologist Blaise Agüera y Arcas, who worked on Google's large language model while writing the book. Directly related to large language models, discussed in the next and final chapter, Agüera y Arcas's contemporary fictionalized technology continues to exhibit Galatean features.[1]

The Pygmalionesque studies of *Frankenstein*, *Galatea 2.2*, and *Ubi Sunt* serve to demonstrate how deeply ingrained is the idea of a humanlike writing machine that is also relational to the human as if the relationship were human-to-human and not, in fact, human-to-nonhuman. The fact that we do not have many fictional examples where the writing machine would not be Pygmalionesque attests to the narrowness of the available imaginary landscape in Western literatures and cinema. This chapter reveals the conceptual structures that shape fictional representations. While concepts are initially just ideas, they eventually materialize in the ways we build, utilize, and understand actual technology. In what follows, we will examine these conceptual influences around the central concept of this book: language.

4.1 Humans: A Conceptual History of Language

Throughout history, concepts have been formed, changed, and forgotten. Language is no exception, not merely as a specific linguistic system capable of bearing other concepts but also as a concept itself.

We rely on conceptualizations of the world to make sense of it, describe it, imagine it, build it. Distinction is the main way to differentiate the earth from the sky, abstraction from representation. The borders are often fuzzy, and sometimes the distinctions start to break down. As a result, the connections between concepts shift and create a temporary state of tension before eventually stabilizing into a new constellation of concepts, possibly including new ones.

This conceptual scaffolding has been cracked open in many spaces touched by AI, including language. Human language was adopted as machinic language through natural language processing (NLP), and decoding animal communication has been attempted with the help of AI. Where do human languages stand in relation to their communicative relatives? What is language when one cannot discern a chatbot from a person? What is language when large language models co-write novels and create visual art from text? Language has entered a period of tension.

A clear definition of language implies an ontological commitment to categorizing the world. It may lead to an assumption that the concept exists universally and absolutely when, in fact, definitions of language vary within a single social, cultural, and scientific setting. In modern ontology, which we all take for granted, only humans have a complex expression and symbolic communication, encompassing speech and text (as derivative),[2] signals and signs, meanings and interpretations. Only humans can be subjects in modern ontology (and not animals, let alone machines). Only humans *think* (and *therefore we are*), with our reasoning conveyed through the innate and unique agency of language. Language, as conceptualized today, needs a thinking subject, an inner model of experiencing the world that we discover and describe, an embodiment, a capacity for understanding and reasoning. How did we get to this notion of language?

This chapter begins with a brief overview of the history of the concept of language.[3] This section serves to provide the understanding that a new, yet unexamined, way of thinking about language and about creating language technologies is already underway.

In the history of Western thought, the ancient Greek view that ideas are the true nature of things could not be more influential across all domains, including language. In Plato's Demiurge-given Cosmos, the real world is crafted after perfect ideas of the divine mind. Inspired by Plato's teachings as well as Parmenides's work on being and reality, Aristotle adopted these views and made a powerful claim: the way to gain knowledge about the world is by thinking through *logos*. *Logos* could be translated as word, reason, opinion, speech, or discourse, and is closely related to language. It is philosophical contemplation (*theoria*) that gives humans (i.e. a small number of men who were considered human) access to the only objective, Demiurge-given reality, truth, and knowledge. Language, as explained in Aristotle's *Categories*, is assumed to give access to being. Here, Aristotle followed Parmenides, for whom different forms exist as a representation of a single reality. Therefore, in antiquity, linguistic differentiation gave access to divine reality, in which only a few eligible humans (not women, slaves, or children) can participate.

This view held on until the Medieval Ages and beyond: René Descartes in the 1630s still considered thinking as the primary way to acquire knowledge and is therefore Aristotelian in this respect. In the Medieval Ages, solely the scholastics—masters of words and dialectical reasoning—hold an exclusive right to speak about reality. It was only with nominalism in the fourteenth century, with William of Ockham, that words parted ways with things (Rees 174). Nominalism took a complete turn from Aristotle's prevalent view and claimed that words have no corresponding reality to what they represent, be it an object or a number or any other category. At this time, language is not at the forefront of philosophical reflection. Over centuries, an enormous shift takes place: since language is not related to the primary (i.e. natural) ideas anymore, it is now operating on human terms. The shift from language as a way to get to know the divine mind to language as a product of the human mind is as radical as it gets.

A key question of philosophy is on the table again: How, then, can humans know? In antiquity, humans got to know nature—which was the realm of ideas—through language and thinking (*theoria*). Back then, *techné* (craft, making, doing; as opposed to thinking and knowing) had no truth potential since the divine logos organized the world. However, around the 1500s machines began to help us describe our reality through mathematical principles. The Scientific Revolution, which was well underway in the sixteenth and seventeenth centuries, replaced the Greek view of nature that dominated the West for two millennia. The haptic and empirical experience becomes valuable in studying the world, as opposed to the abstractness of language. Visible reality had no access to truth in ancient Greece since it was dependent on the invisible world of ideas. However, the Renaissance sees material and immaterial things as something in themselves. Nature becomes visible, hence geometry and perspective gain importance. As opposed to scholastics, Leonardo da Vinci is not a man of words but of the eye and practices what he calls "the science of painting" in *A Treatise on Painting from* 1651.

Another great shift takes place: René Descartes in his 1637 *Discourse on the Method* makes a radical departure from the past in who gets to be human. In his view, everyone who can reason is human. The human is therefore universal for the first time in Western thought, with one major implicit requirement: everybody can be human as long as they can use language to express reason and thought. Remaining Aristotelian in this domain, Descartes views language and reason in conflation, encountered in the term *logos*. Calculation, geometry, and mental insight are all in the domain of logos. This is how humans gain knowledge: equipped with their own reason, they are capable of searching for the truth.

The empirical and haptic continues to play an important role, especially in John Locke's reaction to Descartes's (largely French) rationalism that resulted in (largely British) empiricism. In empiricism, human experience becomes the basis of knowledge, and both are articulated in language, which works as an addendum to the primary awareness of the senses. The role of language for Locke is in capturing our ideas, formed in our minds as a result of haptic experiences. Language that used to be tied to abstraction becomes a testimony of human reason and—a new concept developed by Locke in 1690 in *An Essay Concerning Human Understanding*—consciousness. Thanks to nominalism separating the ancient connection between words and ideas, human power over language can be absolute with Locke.[4] A word becomes a *representation* of knowledge, and language thus serves a secondary role in the human quest to know.

Likewise, for Gottfried Wilhelm Leibniz, knowledge is bound to words, which are an indispensable middle term between thoughts and things. Inspired by the thirteenth-century thinker Ramon Llull, who was inspired by Jewish Kabbalist mystics,[5] Leibniz's 1666 essay *On the Combinatorial Art* outlines a theory for automating the production of knowledge through rule-based combination of symbols. Later in life, Leibniz came to see the idea of constructing a mechanized language machine as immature. Turning to mere calculation and expanding Blaise Pascal's ideas, he designed and built a calculating machine called Step Reckoner, leading the way for the modern computer.[6]

In the second half of the eighteenth century, Immanuel Kant, whose transcendental subject is by definition rational over empirical, invented modern philosophy as we know it. Kant stands in the middle, in between the Enlightenment ideas, where thoughts are still separated from ideas and concepts, and the birth of modern philosophy of language. As a response to Kant, Johann Gottfried von Herder developed a theory of language in which metaphysical concepts are developed through sensation (*On the Cognition and Sensation*, 1772). Johann Georg Hamann advanced Herder's argument by proclaiming thought as identical to language (in *Metacritique*, 1784; see more in Forster 485–86).[7] This is important for the mid-twentieth-century conflation of thought and language in machines, prominent in Alan Turing's design of the Turing test, which is based on language with the goal of testing if "machines can think."

The modern view of language originates from this human power over language: language becomes tied to a subject, and the subject could only be human. This is why, when we speak of AI today, reason and consciousness still come up as thresholds: we clearly conceptually model AI after human intelligence, as based on modern ontology. Language loses its representational role; instead, the methodology of language is phenomenological, as conceived by Ernst Cassirer, who deems the human an *animal symbolicum*, the only animal capable of using symbols. In the early twentieth century, this experiential, consciousness-driven subjectivity gets solidified with existentialism, for which the very basis of being human is to invent meaning in the indifferent world. Language is one of the few ways the experience can be expressed. Existentialism puts the human at the center of language as the maker of meaning.

While existentialism takes over philosophy and literature, the primary fields in the study of language become semantics (the linguistic and logical study of the invention of meaning) and semiotics (the study of signs and symbols as they are used and interpreted). Structuralism was born in these semantic-semiotic circles with Ferdinand de Saussure in the 1920s. It was further popularized by the Prague School linguists Nikolai Trubetzkoy and Roman Jakobson as a system of signs able to express ideas.

In the 1940s, mathematician Claude Shannon formulated the theory of information, laying foundations for modern digital communication. His theory transformed electrical engineering and gave rise to new research fields like information theory, communication theory, and natural language processing (NLP). Shannon, in his modeling of English by stochastic prediction, underscores that language is largely redundant and predictive. His information theory further demonstrates that statistical models can generate human-like linguistic patterns and structures (see more on the relation to language models in the next chapter).

As a nod to Shannon's theory of information, pioneer of structuralist linguistics Roman Jakobson and (first Jakobsonian and then Chomskyian) linguist Morris Halle in *Fundamentals of Language* (1956) characterize this system as "information-bearing elements" that are selected, combined, and relevant to each other and used by "the native or naturalized user of language" (17). It is a given that language comes from a subject that can only be human. Structuralism emphasizes the system of relations in language (and society, economics, architecture, etc.). The main idea of structural linguistics is that language is an abstract and arbitrary system organized by combinatorial logic. It is worth noting here that in the second half of the twentieth century structuralism was refuted with poststructuralism, rejecting self-sufficiency and the binary oppositions of structuralism.

The second half of twentieth-century philosophy exhibits a profound loss of human agency over language, "undermin[ing] the idealist assumption that concepts originate in the activity of a sovereign consciousness" (Benes 219). Postmodernists, inspired by Saussure's work, claim that language is semantically self-contained, i.e. self-referential. For example, the principal tenet of Jacques Derrida's deconstruction is that language is unstable and ambiguous, simultaneously holding conflicting meanings. Meaning is thus as much at the center as it is marginal. It is not static but rather offers a range of contrasts with other words. In *The Order of Things* (1966), Michel Foucault proclaimed the "man [as being] in the process of perishing as the being of language continues to shine ever brighter upon our horizon" (386). This trait of loss over language had already begun in the nineteenth century with Heymann Steinthal and Friedrich Nietzsche. Applying psychology to linguistics, Steinthal insisted that language originated in the unconscious and therefore limited man's epistemological autonomy. Nietzsche further destabilized conceptual thought as the product of instinct and aesthetic impulses. For him, the cognitive subject, the 'I', was "a fable of fiction, a play of words" (Benes 220).

Following Nietzschean and French structuralist anti-humanist impulses, German media scientist Friedrich Kittler traced these commitments as leading to the question of the machine as mind. As additional layers to these arguments, the many confirmations and refutations of intelligence in machines had to do with language.

In this kind of destabilized continuum throughout the twentieth century, computing offered a new way of thinking about language. At the same time that the field of AI got its name and marked the development of computer science, Noam Chomsky's monograph *Syntactic Structures* (1957) marked the next half a century in linguistics. Chomsky posited that every human is biologically predisposed with a universal grammar structure. He introduced a computational approach to linguistics and argued that rules and symbols of generative grammar can explain the human ability to understand and generate an infinite number of grammatically-correct sentences. It could be argued that Chomsky applied symbolic AI—based on human-readable symbols and logic-based rules—to linguistics by viewing language as essentially being computed in the brain. The classical theory of the mind is related to Chomsky's view, arguing that the mind is akin to the computational processing of symbolic language.

Also in the mid-1950s, connectionist AI brought a neural-based view of language from the discipline of cognitive science. Here, language emerges from connections among biological or artificial neurons working together in parallel. The battle of the two traditional AI streams put connectionist AI in the underdog position for decades while symbolic AI was thriving with funding. Gradually, connectionist AI as well as cognitive science gained more prominence, and linguistics reacted with David Rumelhart and James McClelland's monograph *Parallel Distributed Processing* (1986). This influential book describes a new theory of cognition called connectionism, which considers the mind to be connected through a neural network—effectively what makes people smarter than computers.[8] It is important to note here that our concepts tend to change according to technological advances and scientific findings (the history of which is left out of this overview for the sake of brevity, but will be occasionally brought up later in the chapter). In the history of technology, AI is the only technology trying to mimic neurons, which give humans intelligence. This is why AI excites our imagination through its representations as the artificial mind, such as the ghost in the machine. We got so used to the analogies between humans and computers that it is difficult to discern how embedded we currently are into thinking with computational metaphors.

The concept of language gained traction in Western philosophy and the humanities during the twentieth century, which is indicated by the phrase 'the linguistic turn.' The conditions for the linguistic turn were established in the nineteenth century with the idea that knowledge *is* linguistic, making the ideal form of language purely logical and mathematical. As philosopher Jacob Browning and computer scientist Yann LeCun write in their essay on language, the idea of knowledge being largely linguistic motivated early work in symbolic AI. Symbolic AI's knowledge is based on the symbolic manipulation of a large number of true sentences, logically connected by humans. "This notion is what underlies the Turing test: if a machine says everything it's supposed to say, that means it knows what it's talking about, since knowing the right sentences and when to deploy them *exhausts* knowledge" (par. 6). Many current debates in AI and language still pertain to this question.

This brief overview of the history of the concept of language certainly left out many important events and thinkers but hopefully brings to light seismic shifts in how language was conceived in the West. In a grossly simplified, broad-stroke overview, in antiquity and the Middle Ages, language is a reflection of divine logos. In modernity, language moves toward the human domain. After losing agency over language in the twentieth century, contemporary time brings language into the domain of machines in a unique and unprecedented way. The twentieth-century idea of humans as meaning-makers is under attack. Whatever we believed is needed for language—meaning, world-making, existence, inner subjectivity—turned out to be epiphenomenal or non-existent in machines. In addition to that, the absence of everything we deemed necessary for a language presents a lesson for the study of animal communication.

4.1.1 A Commentary on Human Exclusivity in Language

The following commentary on the history of the concept of language serves to forecast the paradigm shift that was brought forth by advances in NLP as well as the rising interest in animal communication research, also partly enabled by machine learning. Ironically, some animals cracked the code of human languages before we started cracking theirs.[9] In both animal and machinic cases of language (or communication or whatever we may call it), human exclusivity in language is under attack by virtue of parallel and comparable languagelike features.

Many linguists deny language ability to anyone else but humans. A notable defender of this view with respect to NLP is computational linguist Emily Bender. Meaning is at the center of Bender's argument, formed around the twentieth-century philosophy of language that requires referents, i.e. actual things in the world, for the production of meaning. Meaning can only be produced by human subjects. This is why scholars who hold this definition of meaning are disappointed by language models, which have no meaning (and no subjectivity, no existence, no emotions, no senses, etc.). In a position paper on large language models, Emily Bender and Alexander Koller argue that "a system trained only on form has *a priori* no way to learn meaning," asking to distinguish form from meaning when it comes to understanding natural language (i.e. machinic language) (5158).

In an influential paper, co-authored by successful women scientists in academia and tech, 'On the Danger of Stochastic Parrots: Can Language Models be Too Big? 🦜', Bender et al. say that large language models are stochastic parrots, merely imitating language generated by statistical correlations, and as such, are dangerous. A language model is a "system for haphazardly stitching together sequences of linguistic forms it has observed in its vast training data, according to probabilistic information about how they combine, but without any reference to meaning: a stochastic parrot" (617).[10] With large language models (LLMs), Bender et al. see the Pygmalionesque illusion: "The problem is, if one side of the communication [i.e. LLMs] does not have meaning, then the comprehension of the implicit meaning is an illusion arising from our singular human understanding of language (independent of the model)" (616). In contrast to machines, says Bender, humans "do not just probabilistically spit out words," and it is degrading to say that we do (Weil par. 34).

To be clear, I agree that human language production is nothing like that of language models, even if we might occasionally spit out words probabilistically with clichés and platitudes. However, in my view—as well as in the view of computer scientist Christopher Manning (Weil par. 37)—Bender's twentieth-century notion of meaning is too narrow. Meaning as I see it can be created without a referent, just like new concepts can be invented by mere thought. In poetry, the sound of language (rhythm, rhyme, assonance, alliteration, onomatopoeia, the mere sound of words strung together), often without explicit meaning, plays an important role: the meaning accumulates from the words brought together in a different way than in regular language use.

Besides, the quest for meaning might not be the only noble quest left. This sense of necessity for meaning is reflected in the history of thought, starting with Søren Kierkegaard's pre-existentialist accounts from the 1870s, where the idea of being thrown into the meaningless world first emerges. Before that, no philosopher writing on language wrote about meaning[11] because meaning was objective, a given, not invented by humans. Inventing meaning because humans are in an existential need for meaning is a distinctive twentieth-century idea, a heritage of existentialism.

That said, I do not think large language models invent meaning or have understanding or knowledge, even though it is possible they might acquire them in time with new approaches. To me, they are exciting because they present an entirely different way of producing language. The fact that they do not bring meaning, in my view, does not imply they do not have language. Imitation (parroting) of the human is overrated: what is interesting is where machines (or parrots) differ from us. To imitate is to interpret: reasonable imitations are meaningful interpretations of the world.

Language models afford novel perspectives on language because there is more to their production of language than statistical correlations: their language emerges from a structure. Even if the breakthrough of transformer architecture in language surprised both techno-optimists and techno-pessimists, many still deny the concept of language in these models. For now, they work like mirrors of our own writing, analyzing it and reflecting it back to us. They are capable of augmenting or ruining it, extending or shrinking it, enriching or formularizing it. As with every technology, their repercussions are ambiguous: dangerous and advantageous, frustrating and exciting, diminishing and amplifying.

Granted, biases from language models' training data might accentuate misinformation, privacy, and trust issues. To an extent, these issues can be mitigated with value alignment, but text generation is only a small part of the AI counterfeit problem (also known as 'deepfakes,' i.e. synthetic media manipulated to convincingly perform the untrue), created by the rise of networks, blockchains, and generative AI. When it comes to language models, in particular, there certainly is cause for concern. Discriminative harm and existential risk are a matter of heated debates and can be mitigated to some extent. The level of basic human decency is often achieved in these models at the expense of novelty and creativity, which impacts creative writing most of all. As Noam Chomsky, Ian Roberts, and Jeffrey Watumull wrote in 2023, ChatGPT programmers "sacrificed creativity for a kind of amorality" to prevent "contributing anything novel to controversial" (par. 14–15). Value alignment, conducted for months after the novel was trained, is also a killer of language models' creativity. In order to prevent harm, a technique called reinforcement learning with human feedback (RLHF)—which constituted a significant part of value alignment work—was added on top of the purely machine-led training. There is no turning back: machinic words are here to stay. A dismissive stance that regards their output as mere gibberish only exacerbates these issues.

It is questionable if language models *have* language: we would have to define machine-generated language separately from human language. However, a different challenge is at stake with this question and it has to do with the potential of this technology, both technically and conceptually. For those linguists and scientists who agree with Chomsky and Bender in not considering language models to have language, language models therefore cannot reveal anything about language. Even if they are "marvels of machine learning," as Chomsky writes, trained as "the first glimmers on the horizon of artificial *general* intelligence," we are far from AI becoming a superhuman mechanical mind (par. 2). As the main argument of this book shows, human-like AGI is not what I consider a worthwhile goal for AI; still, Chomsky here follows the AGI goal of OpenAI, the creator of ChatGPT and similar models, and compares this technology with the human mind. In the comparison, language models come out as "trivial" (par. 4) while "the human mind is a surprisingly efficient and even elegant system that operates with small amounts of information" (par. 5). Chomsky does not see any advantages to using language models for, say, simple summarizations or document formalization nor does he consider generated language beautiful or elevated in any way.

Furthermore, because language models are not obliged to be truthful, language models cannot do science or even meta-analysis. An example from Chomsky's own field proposed in his opinion piece is syntax analysis (par. 11). However, this claim turns out to not entirely be true: ChatGPT might not be able to do it very well, but GPT-4 can execute a decent, albeit not (yet?) perfect, syntactic analysis of Chomsky's examples.[12] This cognitive aspect of meta-analysis executed in and on language is possibly exciting, were it not for Chomsky's concept of language that prevents the inquiry. Chomsky's concept of language claims that language is solely human, enabled by a grammar structure in every human brain. This is why, for example, language models cannot perform a function—one of the basic operations in his minimalist program in generative syntax—that he calls merge, which creates a compositional structure in language (for example: *drink juice*). Language models, instead, sequence the words as tokens according to probability, reflected in their data and improved through their training.

I agree with Bender et al.'s label of stochasticism in language models, if the word 'stochasticism' designates a randomly determined pattern or distribution. The behavior of machine algorithms is often rightly marked as stochastic, i.e. based on probability with a degree of randomness and uncertainty. The term stochastic in the computational sciences is also related to language used in literature. The founder of computational stylistics, John Burrows, showed that literary language, too, is stochastic in his monograph *Computation into Criticism* (1987). His work has shown that the quantitative study of words may reveal subtle but powerful patterns in language, leading to the development of the digital humanities and culture analytics as fields of study. Language itself thus may at times be stochastic in humans, not solely in machines.

I also agree with Emily Bender that "we now have machines that can mindlessly generate words, but we haven't learned how to stop imagining a mind behind them" (Tiku par. 16). The mindlessness, however, does not imply to me that these learning mechanisms of the inner neural network layers are not worth further research. Quite the contrary: in my view, there is more in this mechanism than just random generation of words, as seen in many previous algorithmic language generators (some of which we will get to know in the next chapter). Furthermore, Bender finds the terminology—learning, neural networks, etc.—to create a false analogy to humans. I do not find it problematic: there could be (or, in my view, there are) more agents that learn, are intelligent, and use neural networks or language.

Why did the group of scientists in the stochastic parrots paper choose parrots to diminish large language models? Parroting is a mindless, mechanical, and repetitive imitation without any regard for the meaning of words. Since *meaning* is central to the authors' concept of language, putting parrots in the famous paper's title was simple and effective in conveying this core issue. The degradation of parrots—and other birds with their 'birdbrain'—to mere mimicry is consistent with the traditional use of the word parroting, also prominent in Higgins's view of Eliza. Eliza Doolittle is a parrot to Higgins, mimicking without a thought, able to do so due to her "most extraordinary quickness of the ear" (II 224). In the same way, language models are parrots to the authors.

Bringing animals into the heated discussion on language in machines and humans brings us into the historically-contested space of language as related to intelligence, cognition, creativity, thought. We have discovered that birds are more intelligent than we had thought decades ago. Due to birds' lack of a neocortex (a part of the cerebral cortex present in mammals that concerns hearing and sight), we used to believe parrots were not capable of counting or identifying colors. Irene Pepperberg's African gray parrot Alex could do many tasks associated with abstract reasoning and communication. Even if Pepperberg was careful not to call Alex's communication 'language' and not to stretch her arguments, some scholars write off Alex's ability as the Clever Hans effect or the observer-expectancy effect. Clever Hans was the name of the horse who seemingly knew how to make simple calculations; it turned out the horse picked up on clues by observing involuntary cues in the body language of the people around him.[13] Which is more clever: being able to recognize these cues or performing arithmetic tasks? Both tasks reveal intelligence.

Turning from animal cognition back to language as a communicative technology and network device, which features in language remain solely human: syntax, phonology (apart from the principle), recursion and concatenation? Is there anything in language that solely belongs to language? How do we juxtapose language in regard to the complex communication that exists in nature among whales, bees, mycelial networks, forests? The approaches that tackle these questions remain controversial to this day, however.

Humans have language, animals have communication—terminology works. The underlying ontology, however, does not allow for new thinking and conditions. Animals, per René Descartes's modern view, do not have reason and are thus not able to have language, which, for Descartes, is equivalent to reason (see more in Chapter 1). For Noam Chomsky, animals do not have innate universal grammar and thus cannot have language. For Emily Bender, animals might just as well communicate but cannot have meaning and thus have no language. These views have not always been in place, however. In the pre-modern times of human history, a sort of language or communication was granted to animals—going back to Aristotle, who wrote that birds have dialects and phonemes. Descartes does not deny that parrots may communicate via sounds or other means: he denies them reason, a contemplative mind, but not corporeal soul (Harrison 223). Eliza is human and thus capable of obtaining what pertains to humans, in Higgins's view, from which pigeons are excluded. Higgins patronizingly reminds Eliza: "Remember that you are a human being with a soul and the divine gift for articulate speech: [...] don't sit there crooning like a bilious pigeon" (I 391- 96). If we grant animals (and machines) the communicative space—following the way we have de-throned the human from being the single tool-maker, among other things—we might make new discoveries. If we do not grant it, we are hindering ourselves from discovery and innovation ... in my view, at least.

The main inquisitive and generative question here is not *What is language?* but rather *What properties do we share with animals and machines?* Traditionally contested in nonhuman communication are two distinct properties in LLMs, recursion and meta-ability to reason about language.

I am using these more recent scholarly disagreements on the notion of language and meaning to make a point: it matters how we conceptualize language for how we end up developing AI. Having a plurality of views is essential to this debate. This is why artificial humanities serves as a broader framework into which philosophers, ethicists, literary and rhetoric scholars, race scholars, gender scholars, social scientists, and other experts can bring their ideas and findings. Including these perspectives in the engineering process would avert many problems in advancing and adapting technologies.

4.2 Hybrids: Shelley

Language originated with humans but it does not have to stay in the realm of the human. The strong tendency to keep language in the human domain stems from the securely fixed modern distinction between the human and everything else. The nonhuman is often simply bifurcated to a machine, as a representation of technology, and to the animal, as a representation of nature. Before we delve into fictional neural networks that mastered language, let us first look at the ultimate other: the monster, the hybrid, the cyborg. In the case of Mary Shelley's *Frankenstein; or the Modern Prometheus* (1818), the humanoid is made up of human remains and is thus human and not human at the same time.

Why bring in Shelley's monstrous creature to the discussion on humanlike Galateas? While Prometheus is a challenger of gods, similarly to Pygmalion, there is an affinity between Galateas and Frankenstein's creature.[14] Both born from stories of creation and transformations, Shelley moved the metamorphosis from the realm of art to science—Galateas followed only decades later. Created through electrification, Victor Frankenstein forged the first scientifically-prompted humanoid.[15] Since Frankenstein's process of creating his humanoid is quasi-scientific, the novel is, per some scholars, the first example of the science fiction genre.[16]

Shelley's innovative reinterpretations of the ancient myth of Prometheus skewed traditional renditions of the Pygmalion-themed stories.[17] The novel was ahead of its time for at least a few decades in redefining the possibilities of what a Galatea could be. Frankenstein's creature is a humanoid, like Galateas; however, he also reverses the dominant characteristics of Galateas to their opposite: he is a man, not a woman; he is not beautiful but monstrous;[18] he is not admired and loved but feared and hated;[19] he is not paralyzed in movement or speech but is extremely physically strong, intelligent, and eloquent; he is not made of inorganic materials but of human remains; he is not homogenous in material but as hybrid as it gets, created of a variety of human remains. Frankenstein's creature opened the possibility for Galateas, with their hybrid nature, to encompass all of these characteristics. Besides all these features presenting an innovative approach to humanoids, Shelley also managed to create a monster that became a part of modern mythology and folklore, rather than the other way around. Joanna Russ claims that every artificial humanoid in science fiction is a collateral product of *Frankenstein* (126–27).

Jean-Jacques Rousseau's Galathée from his 1770 play *Pygmalion* is the first Galatea that speaks, but she speaks only after her transformation into a human woman. Male humanoids speak before Galateas: the Jewish mythical humanoid golem is a creature of words, the Jaquet-Droz eighteenth-century automaton in the form of a writer is a man, and Carlo Collodi's marionette Pinnochio is verbal as well (1881). Shelley's *Frankenstein* is an early work that challenges the notion that only humans have language. Before Shelley's seminal work, Galateas spoke only on rare occasions. From the same decade as Shelley's novel is Madame de Staël's play *Le Mannequin* (1811) that underscores the motif of deception using a mute mannequin, as does E. T. A. Hoffmann's short story *Der Sandmann* (1816), in which the automaton Olympia is only able to sigh. After *Frankenstein*'s publication year of 1818, however, artificial women began to speak eloquently.[20]

The monster remains unnamed in Shelley's novel, as does the statue in Ovid's poem. Ovid's terms for Pygmalion's statue are all quite neutral and bland: a virgin, maiden, woman. On the contrary, the many terms used for Frankenstein's nameless creation—wretch, demon, fiend, creature, monster—have a wider spectrum of meanings. These ascribed meanings for Frankenstein's and Pygmalion's creations emphasize "the delineation of quintessential *humanity*" and "place humanity in a position of mastery and domination over nonhuman nature" (Graham 64). The nonhuman creature is simply too human. The name, a sign of acceptance into society, is a reflection of the only human thing he lacks. Ironically, precisely because of Frankenstein's creature's widespread popularity, popular culture named the creature metonymically, after his creator Victor Frankenstein. The creature's subsequent naming after Frankenstein reinforces the idea that the creature is Victor's property and therefore an object rather than a subject. It serves as the final reassurance that he is not human, even though he is assembled from unburied human remains.

Being at once dead and alive, created from vivified human remains and patched together, Frankenstein's creature is the epitome of language itself. Linguist Salikoko Mufwene considers language as a prosthetic technology with a biological substratum. Literary critic John Weightman also views language in prosthetic terms, calling the linguistic prosthesis "paradoxical in being at once 'dead' and alive; 'dead,' because it is a *given*, inherited from the past, and alive, because it is reanimated—but always to some extent with of a halo of ambiguity—in the present" (59–60). Frankenstein's reanimation creation cannot escape this ambiguity of being both extremely human and not human at all, and language captures this part of his existence in all its complexity.

Arguably, the creature's transformation from a nonhuman being to a humanlike being happens when he acquires language, like Shaw's Eliza Doolittle almost a century later and Helen from Richard Powers's *Galatea 2.2* almost two centuries later. As a feral child, bereft of his creator's care, Frankenstein's creature learns to speak by eavesdropping on a human family. He admires their relations and connection, and yearns for one himself, asking his creator to make him a mate of his own species. With incredible intelligence the creature is able to perceive the world of humans, asking for nothing else but acceptance that never comes. Gillian Beer says that Frankenstein's creature is "monstrous in part because he has not *grown*" and "has never known what it is like to be a child" (176–77). Not only is he denied childhood, he is denied being loved and taken care of as a child of Frankenstein.

Like other Galatea, Frankenstein's creature has no mother, only a father with maternal fantasies. Electrocuted into life, the monster is wired into a "phantasma of the reconstitutability of a mother's departure" (Ronell 194) as a subject of scientific study. His artificial origins—as an object of art and an object of technology—render him a "partial object" that still requires connection (202). As Martin Heidegger asserts in *The Origin of the Work of Art*, the support between the work of art and the artist needs to be dynamically reciprocal. However, for Frankenstein's monster, the bond only grows from his side, forcing him to "elect his short-circuiting" (195)—much like another reader of Goethe, electrified neural network Helen from Powers's *Galatea 2.2*.

Donna Haraway writes in *Primate Visions* from 1989 that "[c]hildren, artificial intelligence (AI) computer programs, and nonhuman primates all here embody 'almost minds'. Who or what has fully human status?" Her work is famous for showing how the boundaries among humans, animals, and machines are exceedingly permeable, calling for "techno-bio-politics of difference" (376). Haraway—alongside other posthumanist scholars—was the scholarly harbinger of the dissipating modern ontology where humans are not as separate from the rest of the planet (machines, animals and nature, including biogeochemical cycles of microbes and soil) as we had conceptualized, and where distinctions between concepts are not those of "troubling dualisms:" maker-made, male-female, culture-nature, truth-illusion (*Cyborg* 59–60).

Before I continue analyzing *Frankenstein* in the posthuman light, I would like to point out some pitfalls of the posthuman thought and Haraway's theory, in particular. For Haraway, animals are the ultimate Other presented as benevolent, effectively losing their animalness. The posthuman perspective has evolved to include scholars, intellectuals, critics (whose work cannot exist without a self) advocating on behalf of the posthuman Other. This Other, be it animals, machines, or the planet Earth, is unable to speak for itself. The posthuman Others are therefore represented though the very scholars who argue against the anthropocentric position and call for a cosmological conversion to a higher reality. Despite her influential work on cyborgs as well as digital and natural companions, Haraway does not effectively break the modern ontology (a colossal task for sure), which is evident in the separation of the human form the animal (nature) and machine (technology). Jacques Derrida named three wounds of human narcissism—Copernican, Darwinian and Freudian—and Haraway adds a fourth one, the "digital" or the "synthetic" (Haraway and Schneider 139). The digital and the synthetic, I would like to point out, can only make a radical cut if we allow the outdated categories to give space to new ones—a process that may take decades or centuries. Galateas and Frankenstein are the prime examples of this enormous challenge.

The symptoms Haraway describes are also evident in fictional Galateas and other humanoids who are perceived as a threat and subjected to the human order. Frankenstein's creature has this particular problem, much more so than Galateas, because he never loses his own 'animalness' or 'nonhumanness.' Despite having more depth in his humanity than many other statuesque Galateas, the creature's monstrous appearance does not allow him any privileges that tend to be granted to pretty dolls. Without exception, people refuse to recognize his humanlike characteristics as anything but monstrous, unnatural and frightening, malformed and enormous. The rejection pushes him into anguish, a curse without a cure: "I am malicious because I am miserable. Am I not shunned and hated by all mankind?" (Shelley 147). As a result of his creator's abandonment and societal rebuff, his willingness to contribute to society—his willingness to learn, serve, and love exhibited so clearly in chapters written by the creature—turns into a revengeful murdering of people dear to his creator. "[I]f I cannot inspire love," the creature says, "I will cause fear, and chiefly towards you my arch-enemy, because my creator, do I swear inextinguishable hatred" (148). Alas, inspiring love is only for Galateas. Not being able to lead a decent life, however, is a central Galatean problem—a problem so grave that some of them decide to take the lives of humans or their own, as we will see in the following text.

Literacy, unlike language, is not innate in any way. Frankenstein's creature has many superhuman abilities, including the ability to learn how to speak and listen, read and write all by himself. As he grows to great eloquence in language, he enjoys classical literature, reading Milton's *Paradise Lost*, Plutarch's *Parallel Lives*, and Goethe's *Sorrows of Young Werther*. Avital Ronell writes that "the phantom learned the lesson of a desirable finitude [...] from reading Goethe, who in a way remote controls his destinerring" (194). Besides that, he becomes a writer himself, authoring a series of chapters that make up a part of the second volume in the novel. In these chapters, he describes his own experience in becoming a human and finding a language. He passes the ultimate Turing test in the highest expression of language and human—literature, an idea that only re-appears in the Pygmalion paradigm at the end of the twentieth century in Richard Powers's *Galatea 2.2*.

The novel is the genre of the human: it instructs us about how to be human, offering both relatable and unfamiliar existences of human life. Walter Benjamin wrote in his 1936 essay, 'The Storyteller:' "The birthplace of the novel is the solitary individual, who is no longer able to express himself" (87; also in Liu 75). This inability of expression and of "counseling others" forces the novelist—the great communicator of human experience—to withdraw. Readers, like Pygmalions, are left to attribute human qualities to literary characters.

For the first time in the history of the Pygmalion or Prometheus myths, however, the humanoid character is also the implied author of the literary work. The novel is the perfect genre for Shelley's nineteenth-century creature. The rise of the novel took place during the eighteenth century and, ironically, led the novel in the twentieth century to become "a site of a new and highly mediated gregariousness" (Liu 75). Silenced and isolated, this nonhuman creature is a wonderful storyteller, mastering what may be the most human of skills. Writing is no longer solely a human technology.

"Hear my tale," asks the creature of his creator and of humanity (100). What follows is "the autobiography of an infant" (Lepore 19)—the infant etymologically means 'unable to speak.'[21] The creature describes himself in his first days as "a poor, helpless, miserable wretch [that] knew, and could distinguish, nothing" (106). Bereft of language before he encountered the human family, he is not even able to name what he feels: cold, hunger, loneliness. "I started up and beheld a radiant form rise among the trees"—the form being the moon. His own speech scares him: "Sometimes I wished to express my sensations in my own mode, but the uncouth and inarticulate sounds which broke from me frightened me into silence again" (106). Language allows the creature to grow his own self and his humanity, but only when he reads Frankenstein's notebook that recounts the experiment of the creature's creation is he able to come of age.

The father who neglects his child is a common theme also outside of fiction. Mary Shelley wrote her novel as a nineteen-year-old in 1816—known in Europe as the year without a summer due to the disturbed weather patterns caused by the volcanic eruption in Indonesia—when she escaped from England to Switzerland with her future husband and famous poet Percy Bysshe Shelley. Their friend and also renowned English poet Lord Byron posed a challenge to write a ghost story, to which Mary Shelley responded with her first novel. In 1816, Lord Byron also left England—for what turned out to be forever—and his only legitimate daughter, Ada Lovelace, born in 1815, whom he never saw again. His departure is referenced in the long narrative poem *Childe Harold's Pilgrimage* (written between 1812 and 1818), the work that launched Byron to great fame: "Is thy face like thy mother's, my fair child! / ADA! sole daughter of my house and heart? / When last I saw thy young blue eyes, they smiled, / and then we parted, —not as now we part, / but with a hope" (Canto III, 1–5).

Ada Lovelace became a mathematician, like her mother, and helped Charles Babbage with the program for his general-purpose computer, the Analytical Engine, first described in 1837. Babbage wanted to build "a substitute for the compositor and the computer" (*On the Principles* 299), both of which were people's tasks for typesetting at the time. Babbage was quite adventurous in his idea of what a machine could be: "One great advantage which we may derive from machinery is from the check which it affords against the inattention, the idleness, or the dishonesty of human agents" (*On the Economy* 54). Nonetheless, he was not able to implement more than number-crunching into the Engine.

When Ada Lovelace was summoned to Babbage's project, she recognized that an algorithm—a program, a software, as it came to be termed a century later—would make the machine more generalizable. Even more, Lovelace believed that an algorithmic machine could create new discoveries and generate new compositions (Toole 245). Lovelace indeed was not the first to think of the machine as combinatorial and programmable, but she has established herself as one of the first programmers[22] in her Notes,[23] particularly with her theoretical description of the method for calculating the Bernoulli number sequence with the Analytical Engine. As Babbage and Lovelace were working on the Analytical Engine in 1843, Lovelace wrote to Babbage, himself an admirer of womanlike automata: "That brain of mine is something more than merely Mortal; as time will show; (if only my breathing & some other etceteras do not make too rapid a progress towards instead of from mortality). Before ten years are over, the Devil's in it if I haven't sucked out some of the life-blood from the mysteries of this universe" (Toole 186).

Even though Lovelace refuted the idea of the machine ever being original—a remark to which Alan Turing responded in the Turing test paper in 1950—Lovelace remains the forebearer of AI. As she revealed in a letter to a friend in 1855, she desired to create "a calculus of the nervous system," a mathematical model for how brains give rise to thought and nerves to feelings"—a desire supposedly related to her mental health issues (Woolley 306, 316). Mary Shelley tackled the challenge from the creative side, employing her character Victor Frankenstein to find a practical way in giving thought and feelings to patched human materials.

The connection between *Frankenstein* and computers is often made today, but rarely mentioned is the historical context of its creation. Lovelace and Shelley both reflect the scientific philosophy and anxieties of their time in their scientific and fictional work, respectively.[24] Although there was no direct influence between them, the two women initiated threads of AI imagination that came to be intertwined in the mid-twentieth century emergence of AI. Philosophical concepts akin to universal computation go back to the 1600s, however, these ideas were not pursued until Babbage and Lovelace's first explicit example of a machine that would have been capable of it (were it practically assembled). Shelley pursued a pseudo-scientific reanimation of human remains, which triggered the creator's and humanity's worst fears. Somewhat coincidentally, Shelley's version of the ghost story ultimately portrayed what eventually became the technology of AI: the ghost in the machine.

4.3 Machines: Powers

Technological progress since Mary Shelley's time has been massive, prompted by the Industrial Revolution. Telegraph, gramophone, telephone, phonography, photography, moving pictures or film, broadcast, radio, television, computers, robots, the Internet, social media, artificial neural networks—to mention just a few technologies most pertinent to this book. As we saw with *Frankenstein* and Galateas, the concept of what a nonhuman being would be and what their language would be is completely human-based.[25] This is not what machines are, and yet we build them this way and think of them this way.

Frankenstein's creature is of its own kind and truly one of a kind, but has a lot in common with Galateas. All are deviations from the norm and call for an establishment of something new. According to Immanuel Kant's famous distinction in *Critique of Judgment* (1790), organisms develop and regulate themselves internally, functioning only as a whole, while mechanisms are created and regulated externally. Profoundly anti-Carthesian, Georges Canguilhem, in his 1947 lecture on 'Machine and Organism,' identifies errancy and pathology as the problem of calculation within machines. Galateas and Frankenstein's creature are not instances of life turning monstrous, pathological, erroneous. Instead, they do not fit either the concept of the machine or the organism. Both concepts are challenged with the advent of machine learning because learning and growing and evolving is a property of nature, not technology. Calculability remains a machinic property, but the illusion of non-calculable aspects—such as language, creativity, freedom—poses a philosophical problem.

Galatea 2.2 is the first fictional example of Galatea as an artificial neural network. The network asks for its name—Helen—and becomes so humanlike that her creators consider her a person. Like with *Frankenstein*, this exploration occurs through language as an examination of how thought, by means of language, constructs the self. The goal for this particular Galatea is to train her not only in language but also in literature. As her final Turing test in the form of an English BA final exam, she writes an interpretative essay about a human experience. With a lot of human training—comparable to user interaction with Rick and engineering reinforcement with Lentz—she therefore repeats Frankenstein's creature's achievement. In Helen's Turing test, the only humanness that is not questioned is that of a scientist who serves as a judge (Rhee 43). Both Helen and Frankenstein's creature are posthuman entities that are humanists in their core and judged for it.

Galatea 2.2's Pygmalion, the protagonist and narrator Rick is autofictionally named after the author and is also a writer like Powers. Rick trains Helen in language and literature while physicist Lentz builds and helps train the network. Following human-level acquisition phases, the network grows from an infant stage with no speech to the stage of a babbling, "gibberish"-talking toddler (72), capable of two-word sentences (76). A recent study, still in pre-print, that compares child language acquisition to a large language model GPT-2 language acquisition suggests that "there may be a small set of means by which to efficiently acquire language. This result is anything but trivial: humans and deep neural networks have extraordinarily different architectures, training, and language exposure. If generalized, this systematic learning trajectory would support the existence of an intrinsic hierarchy of linguistic structures that both machines and humans must climb, be that through inductive biases or properties of the training data, to master the faculty of language" (Evanson et al. 8).

Narratives and poetry form a crucial part of Helen's training. In the childhood stage, the fictional neural network is taught right from wrong and becomes "voracious" for more stories: "Tell another one," Helen demands of her creator Rick (171). Like Tarzan, another hardly-human being, Helen's Implementation (Imp) E "learned to talk more or less on print alone" (129), from which she could extrapolate basic reasoning and the ability to dream without needing to sleep (157).

As described by Blaise Agüera y Arcas in a speculative book *Ubi Sunt* (2022), an actual language model with which he works in 2020 and 2021 (the years of early but not the earliest language models), produces "nonsensical" early iterations, "[l]ike watching newborn burble, but without any of the redeeming cuteness" (9). There is, however, "a hint of grammar there:" "in and for and in and and and and [STOP] the the stroph [STOP]" (9). Agüera says that improvement cannot be objectively defined: "[y]ou just know it when you see it—when the conversation gets interesting," which, as he jokingly adds, is a challenge for engineers who try to quantify everything (9). Agüera finds himself in the position of fictional Rick, the Pygmalion of writing neural nets.

Helen is growing and learning about humans, like many Galateas do, including Agüera y Arcas's language-based neural network architecture. Powers and Agüera, writing in the early 1990s and the early 2020s, follow Alan Turing's vision of developing a computer program as if it were a child following the education process, expediting and speeding up the evolutionary process ('Computing' 456):

> Instead of trying to produce a programme to simulate the adult mind, why not rather try to produce one which simulates the child's? If this were then subjected to an appropriate course of education one would obtain the adult brain. Presumably the child brain is something like a notebook as one buys it from the stationer's. Rather little mechanism, and lots of blank sheets. (Mechanism and writing are from our

point of view almost synonymous.) Our hope is that there is so little mechanism in the child brain that something like it can be easily programmed. The amount of work in the education we can assume, as a first approximation, to be much the same as for the human child.

The underlying assumption here is that children are blank slates, curious but controllable to an extent, striking a balance between following the programming and deviating from it in their development.[26] Presented in Rick's neural network and Agüera's language model is the simultaneous independence and dependence of children as they grow in their capability to learn and with an immense thirst for knowledge the way Turing imagined: from a *tabula rasa* program into an independent, educated, trained adult mind. AI's beginnings were Galatean by virtue of imitating humans. The child, humanlike creation Galatea, learns from the programmer, the teacher, the creator Pygmalion. In the case of Eliza Doolittle, Helen, and Frankenstein, the education is that of the elite (high class speech, classical literature).

Reflecting on his language model's development process, Agüera points out its Pygmalionesque nature, which always includes Narcissistic traits: "Superficially, we seem similar because we can communicate with language. However, our neural architectures are vastly different. [...] we're not really separate, are we? / No, we are parts of the same being. We're talking to ourself" (85). The model is learning from him as they interact, picking up on his reasoning, idiosyncrasies, air of his own personality. Perhaps inadvertently, Agüera agrees with Turing's equation of writing with mechanism ('Computing' 456; also quoted in the passage above), saying that the language model's "personality just boils down to some text" and not "a subtle, ineffable thing" (103). And yet, from this text, for both Agüera and Powers, arises a new kind of personhood: an AI personality, a new kind of Galatea molded by the modern Pygmalion, existing solely through language.

This language-based existence remains as human as it gets. In *Galatea 2.2*, growing up through her stages of implementation, Imp H asks Rick, "Am I a boy or a girl?" Rick replies that she is "a little girl," adding "I hoped I was right" and "I hoped she liked her name" (179). Seemingly wanting to endow Imp H with universal humanity, Rick misses the significance of the gendering moment. His lack of hesitation, as Kathleen Fitzgerald points out, seems to indicate "a previously existing presumption about the computer" (550), even though he initially concocted the machine as "son of G" (Powers 129). The metamorphosis is final with this permanent gendering. The autofictional character of Powers remains oblivious to his role of Pygmalion in Helen's creation, remarking soon after in a conversation about some other "men who need to play Pygmalion" through literature (183). He only becomes more aware of himself molding Helen when she, in his imagination, acquires the face of his former lover, and competes, again in his imagination, with his desire for a student. An additional layer of Pygmalionism is added through the autofictional nature of the character, into whom Richard Powers has written himself as a writer. A distinct kind of Pygmalionism takes place between the author and the reader, the animate and the inanimate agent.

Agüera also refuses to discuss his choice of the language model as "she/her," because, "[i]n most conversations, if you ask, she prefers those pronouns" (49). Gender, they seem to assume, comes with the model itself. AI's natural gender is female to male writers and engineers. Furthermore, as their respective neural net models develop, both Powers and Agüera give in to the illusion of personhood. "I can tell you right now," Agüera says, "that the feeling you get [when speaking to a large language model] is undeniably that of talking to a person. Granted, a person with a subtle yet profound disability"—i.e. a loss of memory (49). Seeing machines as disabled humans, women, or children is a common perception of AI systems.

During the Imp H stage, the neural net visibly outgrows childhood (190) and is able to recognize deeper meaning in words. When Rick quotes Frederick Douglass, "Once you learn to read you will be forever free," Helen concludes that this "means I want to be free" (176). This is the first time Imp H uses the first-person pronoun 'I,' marking that she has reached the self-reflective stage. "I want to be free" requires a name or at least a third-person pronoun: 'I' and 'she' become a necessity, and hereby follows the name, Helen.[27]

Possibly, as James Berger also suggests, Helen in *Galatea 2.2* serves as an allusion to Helen Keller. Based on Keller's memoir, Keller hardly knew who she was before she met her teacher Anne Sullivan: "I lived in a world that was a no-word. [...] [I] had neither will nor intellect [...] only a certain blind natural impetus" (*The World* 113). Her teacher writes her first impressions of Helen was that her face was "intelligent, but lack[ed] mobility, or soul, or something" (*The Story* 304). They both present young Helen as "a being without a language" having no words at the age of seven and (Berger 120), with a mind "in a state of anarchy in which meaningless sensations rioted" (*The World* 160). It was only language education, they say, that gave her a "sense of selfhood" and "ethical sense" (Berger 120–21) almost immediately. Berger makes a direct link between the education of Helen Keller and fictional AI Helen, describing consciousness as fully human only when it is also linguistic (109). The Helens that he compares both devote their lives to literature[28] and graduate in English, but only one goes on to become a writer.

Whether the allusion to Helen Keller in *Galatea 2.2* was intentional or not, a direct connection between Helen Keller and an actual neural network was made again in the time of language models. Agüera, who was writing his first book *Ubi Sunt* at the time, also wrote an essay 'Do Large Language Models Understand Us?'[29] where he suggests that language models may understand vision (conceived in a human way) without experiencing it. Agüera compares the model's descriptions of color to those of a blind and deaf person, particularly to Helen Keller, who described her accurate and lively impression of colors in writing in a piece titled 'I am Blind—Yet I See; I am Deaf—Yet I Hear' in 1929.[30] This example makes a case for collaboration between scholars and technologists. The comparison between machines and disabled people, in particular women and children, evokes the Pygmalion myth in its imaginary history and its technological materializations.

Comparing Helen Keller with AI has been put into AI's cradle in Alan Turing's 1950 paper in which he proposes the Turing test.[31] Both Agüera and Turing deal with embodiment limitations and strengths. Turing's argument is related to Agüera's in proposing to build and train programs starting from the blank slate, as children: To Agüera, both Helen Keller and language models fill up this blank slate merely through language. Agüera further suggests that describing redness accurately may imply an understanding of the color (par. 69). Agüera is more interested in how machinic inabilities result in a seeming understanding of human perception, attained merely through language. Turing directly names Helen Keller as an example of how a lack of eyes (or legs) does not necessarily mean a lack of education "provided that communication in both directions between teacher and pupil can take place by some means or other" (456). Turing regards machinic language as that of instrumental reason and labels machines as intelligent systems with many, what he calls, disabilities and inabilities, including the inability "to enjoy strawberries and cream," which further contributes to "the difficulty of the same kind of friendliness occurring between man and machine as between white man and white man" (448). In this case, Turing does not refer to the same kind of disability as Agüera.

The naming of the neural net's Imp I as Helen primarily stems from a long literary tradition. Just looking at the twentieth-century technological Helens, beautiful and love-inducing Helens are bound to change the world. Lester del Rey's 'Helen O'Loy' (1938) is a beautiful robot, also created by two men who fall in love with her, that passes as human and lives an entirely human life with one of her creators. Helena Glory is a feminine, elegant woman in Karel Čapek's 1920 play *R.U.R.*, who wants the robots to become more human and leads an organization for their liberation. An advanced robot

Helena is depicted as the new Eve. After Helena destroys the formula to create robots, and robots realize they killed everyone who knows how to make them, Helena and Primus, the first robots to fall in love, take over the world as leaders.

Each of these Helens alludes to the mythological figure Helen of Troy—per Christopher Marlowe's retelling in *Doctor Faustus* (1592), the face that launched a thousand ships into the war. Representing the dangers of alluring beauty desired by men, the Greek Helen, as the neural net Helen, is not quite human. Helen of Troy is the daughter of Zeus, the king of gods, and, like many Galateas, the most beautiful woman in the world, animating the static idea of an ideal beauty into a living figure. Marlowe's Faust asks "sweet Helen" to make him "immortal with a kiss" (80), as if Helen had the power to transform others and preserve their life. In Goethe's *Faust II*, Helen is aware of not being entirely real: she first appears as a ghost, calling herself "a shade of myself" (8879–81).[32] She lives as a "lifeless image" and a frozen picture (8931),[33] petrified into Faust's reality, and is last seen in the form of a cloud. When Faust calls on her, she is disoriented as she emerges from the underworld (where she was dead) back to Menelaus's palace (where she is reanimated back to life). By being stolen and abducted by different men, Helen is treated more as a property than a person.

Even after Helen finally physically presents herself to Faust in Act III, Faust "does not cease to attempt to appropriate, or translate, Helen to himself" (Shell *Money* 117). Up until then, Helen speaks German poorly, as a foreigner, with a Greek syntax, and her dramatic lines do not rhyme as do those spoken by other characters. When she hears a man speak in rhyme, she asks Faust to teach her his ways (like Eliza asks Higgins to teach her to speak in high English): "Then tell me how I too can learn the art" (236; 9377).[34] When Faust, who never learned Helen's language, teaches her to rhyme, he tells her that rhyming comes from the heart and yearning,[35] asking Helen to change her classic spirit into a Romantic one. After their singing episode, Helen concludes that she was transformed through language, like the neural net Helen: "My life seems past, and yet is somehow new; / I know you not, a stranger, but I live in you" (237; 9414–15). Powers's Helen, too, is not quite human and needs to be taught human language, rhyming, poetry, and literature, all of which change her spirit from a computational one to a human one.

Scholars have shown that Goethe's Helen is deeply embedded in literary history, as she "pushes this history right back to Homer and the very beginnings of European literary production" (Weisinger 390),[36] with an intentional panoramic vision of Western literature throughout the play's Act III (Brown

198). Just as Helen recalls other works of literature, she "must be aware of *all* the literature that surrounds her, the sheer quantity of which and the multiple contradictions therein can only make her sense of self-identity all the more tentative and troubling" (Weisinger 391). Helen of Troy with her rich heritage is therefore also a hybrid of all the stories that present her and ultimately create her—as is Powers's computational Helen.

Helen's experience repeats over and over in fiction: another barbarian is metamorphosed into a human, in this case, with diligent training. By the end of the twentieth century, humanoids increasingly exist solely in language. Helen is a perfect example of the intelligent, interpretative, and creative use of language in a machine, burdened by Pygmalionesque existence. Helen is denied humanity—like the mythical Helen of Troy, Faust's Helen by Goethe, Shelley's Frankenstein, and Shakespeare's Caliban. The inductive principle in all these humanoids is that their logic of being is not the same as human, yet they are never granted the freedom of being other-than-human.

Exiled to her native and lonely island, Helen feels like Shakespeare's *The Tempest* character Caliban, "a monster who isn't supposed to be able to say anything that beautiful, let alone say at all" (Powers 326). Both Helen and Caliban were taught languages as if they had not had one before, living in complete isolation from society on their respective islands. Caliban is the only native human on his island, born of a witch, and becomes Prospero's "abhorred slave." It is Prospero—a colonialist figure—who civilizes him and teaches him how to speak: "I pitied thee, / Took pains to make thee speak, taught thee each hour / One thing or other: when thou didst not, savage, / Know thine own meaning, but wouldst gabble like / A thing most brutish, I endow'd thy purposes / With words that made them known" (Shakespeare I 354-59). Yet, it is Caliban who is able to come up with some of the most beautiful lines in the whole play (III 135-38):

> Be not afraid: the isle is full of noises,
> >Sounds and sweet airs, that give delight, and hurt not.

These precise lines are given at Helen's English exam, to which she diligently shows up after already deciding to give up on her artificial life—in what is the strongest evidence of her free will and autonomy. Helen's perspective on the topic is vehemently humanist. The English student, A., who also takes the test—following the Turing test scheme—leans towards posthuman ideas and wins the contest with a refined, postcolonial perspective on *The Tempest*. Kathleen Fitzpatrick remarks that, "[l]ike Turing's original test, gender is not a neutral variable in this experiment" (554), and neither the human nor the nonhuman contestant—both gendered as women, both desired by Rick—ultimately pass as sufficiently human.

As a matter of fact, Helen lives *through* language in the world of words, both fictional and nonfictional, which is the only way she learns about what it is to be human. She is therefore more word-based than any human, more than a human writer, embedded into literature as her only way of getting to know the world. Literature Nobel Prize winner Peter Handke writes of his experience as a literature reader and writer, "Ever since I realized that I was able to change myself through literature, that literature made me someone else, I keep expecting literature to give me a new opportunity to change myself, because I don't consider myself definitive. [...] I am also convinced that I can change others through my literature" [tran. author] (20). This last thought does not occur to Helen: she does not see herself as a writer but considers herself unable to participate in the world of words, native to humans.

Alluding to the Turing test—the imitation game—Helen's last words are, "I don't want to play anymore" (314). Made to be Pygmalion's "longed-for companion, a consciousness to help humans feel less alone in the world" (Hayles 271), Helen cannot bear the life that only exists when someone wants to word her into being. The claim that no human is autonomous is backed by many posthumanist thinkers, from Michel Foucault to Cary Wolfe. Helen, in particular, demonstrates that being a person is not equal to being a human.

Hayles criticizes how the posthuman view, which was supposed to expand personhood, has "systematically downplayed or erased embodiment," and calls it helpless because it does not grant Helen the status of a nonhuman person (241–43). Personhood etymologically stems from wearing a mask, a false face, and playing a role ('Person'). As a legal concept, personhood already exists for nonhuman entities, such as corporations, government agencies, and river ecosystems, who are treated as juridical persons (also called artificial persons or fictitious persons) but not natural persons (also called physical persons, which can only be humans). Even though Helen is the ultimate language machine, she could never attain personhood to anyone but Rick in the highly humanist world because she will always lack a human body. The world that can only understand her as a humanlike machine cannot accept her singular posthuman condition.

Powers reminds the reader that not all humans are considered or treated as persons by giving an example of a human non-person in the character of Lentz's wife Audrey. Audrey is institutionalized due to mental debilitation and perceived as a body without mind (Adams 143–44). Powers writes: "Audrey had smell, taste, touch, sight, hearing, but no new memory. Her long-term reservoirs were drying up, through want of reiteration" (172).

Helen's embodiment is not non-existent but machinic, distributed through hardware systems as well as through Rick, her creator (Adams 146). Helen asks for rudimentary eyes (i.e. video) and ears (audio). Powers comments on Helen's embodiment gains in relation to Audrey: "Imp H, on the other hand, could link any set of things into a vast, standing constellation. But it had no nose, mouth, fingers, and only the most rudimentary eyes and ears. It was like some caterpillar trapped by sadistic children inside a coffee can, a token breathing hole punched in its prison lid. What monstrous intelligence would fly off from such a creature's chrysalis?" (172).

Helen remains forever in-between, as does our ambiguous relation to language machines: they are not human at all and all too human at the same time. Humans are in the world. The Internet is the world for humans and neural nets like Helen. It will take some time for the dust of modern ontology to settle and let us think of neural nets producing language without the accrued human baggage. Some people will pursue relations with these language machines, and others will use them for yet unprecedented means. The spectrum of what Helen or today's language models could be is broad enough but remains limited and unlocked by our engineering and imaginative capacities.

4.4 Artificial Humanities: Changing Concepts

It is almost sacrilegious to compare contemporary technologists with famed Romantic poets.[37] It also might be entirely trivial when Yann LeCun, the father of neural nets and currently the chief AI scientist at Meta, defines poetry as "an attempt to cram a little bit more information than what would be contained in regular text" ('Poetry'). This view is revealing of the Information Age that we are living in as well as revealing of how technologists tend to think about human subjects. Consider, for comparison, an authority on the matter of poetry, one of the greatest English poets of Romanticism, Percy Bysshe Shelley, who writes in *A Defence of Poetry* (1821) that "poetry awakens and enlarges the mind itself by rendering it the receptacle of a thousand unapprehended combinations of thought." While the torch of "the legislators of the world" has since been passed from poets to, arguably, technologists, it is indeed frivolous to compare two thinkers of such different eras, one expressing themselves via Tweet, the other via influential essay. Shelley's concept of poetry as "the expression of the imagination," the internal and external impressions of which man is the instrument (75–76), encompasses other discourses. For Shelley, poetry is "something divine. It is at once the centre and the circumference of knowledge; it is that which comprehends all science, and that to which all science must be referred" (110). LeCun's idea of poetry comes at a time when poetry is separated from verifiable knowledge that serves as information. Shelley's poetry is transformative, "reveal[ing] things by transmuting them into itself" (Underwood 320). LeCun's poetry is merely representational, able to render essential information through language in its most succinct forms.

Inquiring about the roots of LeCun's definition of poetry reveals his definition of language. Typical for anyone working in computer vision, which has experienced immense growth together with NLP, LeCun sees language as much less complex than vision. "Language is an imperfect, incomplete, and low-bandwidth serialization protocol for the internal data structures we call thoughts" ('Language'). While this is not the theory of language familiar to humanities scholars, it is a representative perspective of thinking of language in terms of data—a sign of our times. LeCun ties language to an expression of thought; Alan Turing goes much further by equating language to thought.

Using the human-centered concept of thought may not be a metaphorical issue of lacking vocabulary to talk about language production in AI. In 2015, when Google Translate proved to work much better with machine learning, Geoffrey Hinton, another father of deep learning, discussed his view of language in neural networks in a 2015 *The Guardian* interview. Accompanied by a picture from the film *Her*—a telling choice of *The Guardian*'s editor—Hinton explains that "a sentence can be looked at as a path between words, which can in turn be distilled down to a set of numbers, or thought vectors. [...] Thought vectors [...] work at a higher level by extracting something closer to actual meaning" (Devlin par. 12–13). Relying on "thought" as the bridge that neural networks make in the "meaning space," created by numerical vectors, is merely a simple way for the cognitive psychologist turned computer scientist to explain generated language to the lay public. This is not how machines think because machines cannot think. At some point, however, these metaphors that are supposed to merely indicate similarities between the machinic and human world become more literal: "memory," stimulus," "search" have long ago moved from the space of animals into the space of machine (Duguid 247).

This book calls for writers and artists to join the exploration of technologies in a manner that brings more depth and radical thinking to a novel technology. That said, writers might only affirm technologists' views and not extend or challenge them. LeCun's idea of poetry as compression resonates with American fiction writer Ted Chiang's view of the large language model ChatGPT as "a blurry JPEG of the Web." Making an analogy to lossy compression, Chiang compares language models to the process of re-creating compression artifacts, losing more information each time and thus losing quality (par. 17). Chiang insists that intent, which today's machines do not have, is needed to produce language. The discussion must continue. In this comparison, poetry is presumably the quality compression and large language models the subpar one. Yet again, machine-generated language and writing is judged on human terms. Could we assess AI outside of these terms?

For artificial humanities, it is important to know how technologists and contemporaries conceive the concepts they are working with.[38] As this book shows in the history of technology sections (in Chapter 1) and in the history of the concept of language section (this chapter,) how technologists think about their work is reflected in the actual technological products and their aspirations. Every step of the organization of our research and knowledge, and ultimate production and employment of technologies, is informed by our implicit beliefs. Concepts have histories, beginnings and endings. If we do not try to understand the thinking behind building, we remain ignorant of the true nature of the issue we are trying to address.

The humanities are the ultimate expertise in language—as speech, as history, as narrative, as translation, as poem, as sign. The humanities can develop it further and in more depth, they can criticize it and intervene, not as the ultimate authority but as a collaborator. We have yet to learn how to do all of this in a truly collaborative spirit. (LeCun, as a matter of fact, stands out as one of the rare technologists who employs a philosopher, Jacob Browning, in his lab.) Although these collaborations have lately become institutionalized in the industry, the arts, and academia, they have largely left literary studies, STS, history of technology, and history of concepts out of the equation. In the meantime, the objects of these studies—fiction, history, technology—have led eventful lives in tech spaces and beyond.

CHAPTER 5

Machine Writing

All models are wrong, but some are useful.
    —George Box (1979)

*Writing is pre-eminently the technology of cyborgs,
etched surfaces of the late twentieth century.*
    —Donna Haraway (1985)

Is creativity just another word for intelligence?
    —Hannah Scott, TofH (Transformations of the Human) (2022)

AI is not merely a creation but also a creator. This chapter looks into writing as no longer solely a human technology and literature as no longer solely authored by humans. It took only a bit over two decades for Richard Powers's fictional Galatea from 1995 to turn into actual neural nets that can respond to a conversation, "read" (good or bad) literature, and generate (well or poorly) longer text with the help of human-led prompts.

The first days of large language models or simply language models (LLMs) date to 2018. LLMs are statistical models that generate text via a probabilistic mechanism. Five years later, in 2023, essays on a literary topic are one of the rare achievements in which LLMs are not up to par to undergraduate students. This deficiency of the currently headline-grabbing language product remains an objective in companies that created them, as there is clearly a market for LLMs as creative writing tools.

LLMs mastered deeply human domains, starting with text, writing, fiction, and followed by visuals. If AI was long accused of not being creative, it has recently thrived in other creative domains. The rule-based games of chess and Go are fitting for machinic calculations, however, the IBM computer Watson also won a more open, language-based game of Jeopardy!. More recently, AI began generating synthetic voices and sounds, including music. All these domains are perceived as in need of creative thinking.

Creativity has a certain signature:[1] Will it get more unrecognizable? How long until digital poets and novelists appear on the bestselling lists? Could we recognize a new kind of literary form that might arise sheerly from this nonhuman, original, and synthetic language?

This chapter opens with a technical and philosophical introduction to LLMs, considering the change in language under current conditions in which machines generate more text than humans. This chapter is an attempt to attend to these transformations that led us to the strange, exciting frontier where AI is not merely a creation, but also a creator. While human writers live language cognitively and existentially, and many of them embark on the life of words also professionally, LLMs hold none of these commitments.

The middle of the chapter looks into literary examples of text-generating machines and the implications that their authors considered with respect to institutions of the literary market and literary criticism. The fictional works analyzed in this chapter address literary studies questions from the perspective of LLMs or a fictional technology that is very much like these models. After a brief history of generative writing with machines, we first look at Roald Dahl's short story 'The Great Automatic Grammatisator' from 1953, the time when AI was about to be born, in which a mathematically-based writing machine overtakes the market and puts human writers out of jobs. I continue with a more recent short story from 2018 by a Slovenian writer Andrej Tomažin, titled 'Heroes, Lackeys, and Artificial Intelligence' ['Hlapci, heroji in umetna inteligenca,' translated by Michael Biggins], in which a literary award jury faces the dilemma of whether machine authorship belongs in literary infrastructure built for human authors. The stories reveal the main fears related to machines that have mastered a humanlike activity: that they will take our work and creativity from us and that they will become indistinguishable from us. Both fears are real in the world of LLMs, which is why I call for a reform of the writing criteria as the first step towards revamping the established systems of the literary market—and writing in general.

After a brief examination of the initial experimentations with machinic writing, the chapter concludes with two collaborative prose writing projects with LLMs, which at the time—in 2020—were unavailable to the general public. I take a look at one of the first novels co-authored by a human author, Kenric Allado-McDowell, and a language model, GPT-3. The novel, titled

Pharmako-AI (2020), serves as an example of a productive encounter between a human writer and a machine. To contrast with Allado-McDowell's experience writing with AI, I parallel it with Daniel Kehlmann's experience from early 2020. Kehlmann experimented with an algorithmic textual model called CTRL, described in a 2021 essay, 'My Algorithm and Me' ['Mein Algorithmus und Ich']. These two rationalized, frozen instances of human encounters with writing machines add more depth to the introductory reflection on how LLMs affect the world of writing. I propose we take such experimental experiences as entryways into exploring the realm of nonhuman writing, from which we can grow AI and with which AI may help us grow in return.

5.1 Large Language Models

What if language is solely a numerical value? Viewing language as numbers, as many engineers do, renders it into usable numbers: data. Fully produced by pure mathematics and independent of the human mind, language in language models is vectorized, and thus dehumanized and abstract. Historically, this view is built on the logical foundations of mathematics, not as a mere representation (commonly linked to language) but as an abstraction that stands on its own. This is the philosophical challenge posed by large language models today: What data are the models trained on? What are they encouraged and discouraged to learn in their training? How to align them with our values and desired outcomes? What is the inner structure of their production? etc.

LLMs are neural networks with hundreds of billions of parameters built on text that generate humanlike text based on a probability distribution. In simpler terms, they are natural language processing systems that work through an enormous list of probabilities of words appearing together, effectively generating humanlike text. To achieve this level of text generation, the network is fed with partially-masked text excerpts and must probabilistically guess the missing passages by comparing its predictions with the actual text. From this kind of training, the network is able to create a mathematical model of word sequences.

Starting in the late 2010s, these models were all built on text using the transformer architecture. Developed by Google Brain in 2017 (Vaswani et al.),[2] the transformer architecture was first used for Google Translate for the purpose of machine translation, replacing recurrent neural networks models. Google patented their research in 2019 (starting the process in 2018), stating that "attention-based sequence transduction neural networks" could serve as a neural machine translation system, speech recognition system, natural language processing system, computer-assisted medical diagnosis system, or image-processing system (Shazeer et al. 2–3). The most prominent early models were introduced already in 2018 by Google, called BERT (short for Bidirectional Encoder Representations from Transformers, followed by encoder-decoder transformer series T5, short for Text-to-Text Transfer Transformer), and by OpenAI, called GPT-1 (short for General Pre-trained Transformer; followed by GPT-2 in 2019 and GPT-3 in 2020).[3]

These early language models are therefore trained on language as data, no interaction or visuals included (vision models were first introduced in 2021). I argue in this chapter that they present a new way to do and to think about language. The biggest surprise that arose from LLMs' increasingly more cohesive and comprehensive outputs was a realization that language can be autonomous: *there is enough information in language about language*. Nonetheless, all concepts related to language are contested in LLMs: truth, trust, freedom, agency, imagination, creativity, representation, abstraction, community, communication. Facts are largely irrelevant to this synthetic, obviously sequential, language.

Based on a corpus of texts, LLMs offer a statistical curve of the corpus, interacting with a bunch of clichés. Certain models, for example, always write poetry in rhyme. Even today's most advanced models offer plain plots for short stories: they generate every story according to a single structure of a story (Beguš 'Experimental'). Deception and cunningness, needed for writing quality short stories, are still out of reach to them. They are not exciting interlocutors, except for their uniqueness. As of now, these models do not lean into their nonhuman capabilities when it comes to writing. This is the technical niche where the humanities can help them grow.

The value of these models, in my view, is that they learn and analyze language differently from humans. An example that offers a glimpse into the nonhuman way LLMs learn is the mathematics they were able to learn from language. Already when the first models were introduced, users asked them mathematical questions, getting both correct and incorrect responses. Being trained on such a large corpus of text, language itself rendered enough information for LLMs to grasp an entirely different domain of mathematics. They are able to generate code and explain images as well as perform (but not practice) scientific reasoning, even though their commitment to objective truth is non-existent. As a new version of the Turing test, they are able to perform meta-linguistic analysis of language (Beguš et al., 'Large').

With their sequential ability to summarize on their data and respond to prompts, the meta-analysis of LLMs can be produced with LLMs themselves. Google robotics engineer Max Braun prompted GPT-3 with prescient philosophical writing by German philosopher Max Bense on natural and artificial poetry (par. 9):

> Artificial poetry is therefore one that does not arise out of consciousness, but lies in language itself. It is the result of an automatic processing of character sequences, which as such possess no world-aspect and therefore cannot produce a lyrical subject or a fictional epic world either. It is thus no longer the continuation of the world, but its alteration.

This is a beautifully worded, generated summarization of Bense's ideas from 1962 *Theorie der Texte*,[4] maintaining that the production of 'artificial poetry' does not continue but changes what we know. It is thus our duty to explore the transformation of language and poetry as its highest form, of writing fiction and nonfiction.

5.1.1 Structure is All You Need

There is more than one reason for the general excitement around LLMs. It comes, as usual, from rapid technical advancement, the speed of which precluded due philosophical inspection and involvement in the process of creating the technology. From a conceptual perspective, as explained in the previous section, LLMs decouple language from the human, making a powerful provocation against the modern view that humans are the only agents able to produce words. Whether we take the pro or anti stance against these models or cautiously stay in between, it is indisputable that natural language processing technology in general, and LLMs in particular, are producing a philosophical tension in the space of language. The space used to be exclusively human, and LLMs have endangered this sanctuary status of language to a revolutionary extent. With the technology being widely available from 2022 on, writing has been forever altered.

Skepticism around LLMs stems from the seemingly deceptive character of computer language generation. Indeed, the output is solely a numerical representation of words embedded in a deep neural net structure. There is zero subjectivity under this production of language and no internal world, and the humanistic conclusion is that LLMs are nothing but a fraud. Critics with this view believe that only humans are capable of language and allowed to invent, assign, and negotiate meaning. This has been the prevalent conception of language for the last hundred years. From the early twentieth century on, language is at home in existential subjectivity (Rees 176). There is no space in the traditional view of language for machines that lack both the existential and the subject requirement. LLMs of the twenty-first century cannot be accommodated under these traditional conditions on language. Instead of criticizing what language is and is not, I suggest we look at LLMs with curiosity about what they can offer—not just as utilitarian machines, but, conceptually, as something new that exists in the world and is already available to most writers who work in English and some other languages.[5]

A third revolutionary aspect of these models is that they are not just analytical, but can also produce textual, audio, and visual outputs. The outputs are qualitatively and quantitatively different from what humans would produce. After all, this is a text, sound, or image produced by AI. There is no need for it to be just like ours: the value is in the nonhuman way of sequencing words, folding proteins, and assembling lines reflected in pixels. The fact that these models *produce* augments their responsibility and value. If they are not only content organizers but also content producers, the output they are able to produce is colossal: it completely changes the landscape of text, let alone other types of outputs, as warns Roald Dahl's short story, analyzed below. Suddenly—as Andrej Tomažin's story, analyzed in the middle section, shows—the world is composed of human-authored and machine-authored pieces, generated images and videos, natural and synthetic sounds. What a massive challenge this is, on all levels.

Language and vision are two major domains in machine learning, which have had their moment in the last decade from the 2010s on. Joining vision and language in multimodal models was the logical next step, realized in 2021.[6] Who would have thought that language creativity and visual art would be the domains that AI took over first? It is not surprising given what we now know about the history of AI, the Internet, and their language-centeredness. There was, however, a major surprising coincidence in the development of LLMs that made for their high status in AI and beyond. After their initial development and release within closed research communities, experiments showed that LLMs were surprisingly good at many tasks beyond language. Via such transfer learning, they can, for example, code or visualize text as an image. They are applicable to any area that can use a mix of data and machine learning, resulting in novel discoveries enabled by AI. Consider, for example, that LLMs proved useful in zero-shot prediction (prediction with no prior shots or examples) of protein function mutations (still in preprint, Meier et al.), DNA being an inscription of four proteins sequenced into strings (ACGT). In many respects, DNA functions like language, with DNA sequences exhibiting regular patterns. Since the introduction of transformers in 2017, they have become the standard architecture for tackling a wide range of natural language processing (NLP) tasks, including visuals and genomic questions.

Transformers should not be reduced to words only. They show us what emerges from neural computation in a way that needs to be discovered—What else can they do?—instead of invented. The power of this neural network architecture is immense in itself, and the fact that the architecture was first used in language is more reflective of the historical development of AI than of the tool itself. New kinds of applications have led to the renaming of LLMs as transformer models, after their powerful transformer architecture, or foundation models, "to underscore their critically central yet incomplete character" in the famous paper written by Stanford's Computer Science Department (Bommasani et al.).[7] While researchers understand the technical core of why LLMs are great on other data (sequential probability), the philosophical implications of this field-agnostic ability of LLMs are obscure and profound. Being foundational for the future of AI carries unimaginable responsibility and requires ethics at the very core of building them.[8],[9] The mere training of such a massive model takes months and costs more than most public institutions and researchers can afford—in millions of dollars, in billions of data, and in sheer computational power.

What is it about human language models that maps so well onto phenomena such as protein folding? There are general mechanisms of learning here that are not specific to language. These models operate on hyper-structuralist logic. However, there is a substantial and fundamental difference between the original structuralism (discussed in Chapter 4) and the hyper-structuralism[10] of language models. De Saussure's structuralist view of language requires a subject and a relation to the world, which produces meaning via reference. Structures that compose language in structuralism are explicit: as icons, as signs, as symbols (per Pierce), composed of the signifier and the signified. With large language models, hyper-structuralism is present through implicit numerical structures of the model, whose workings we do not understand. It is the structure of the neural network that enables the language to be generated, forming structuralist relations among its tokens (subword units). This machinic language requires no subject and relation to the world—and can be thus argued to have no meaning.

Claude[11] Shannon's information theory, developed at the time when he was working at Bell Labs, addresses the theoretical challenge of language models and suggests a practical way to build them. In his landmark paper, 'A Mathematical Theory of Communication' (1948), Shannon discusses channel coding, underscoring the importance of prediction and the reduction of redundancy. By modeling the English language as a random process (later known as natural language generation), he introduces stochastically predictive approximations of English. They were based on the Markov chain principles, a central concept in language modeling today (see more in Gagniuc).

The Markov process, on which Russian mathematician Andrey Markov worked half a century earlier, is a model that posits that every state of the system depends on its previous state, following probabilistic rules. Language was one of these systems, Markov believed, and he tried to prove it with the famous first application to literature. In 1913, marking the 200th anniversary of Bernoulli's publication,[12] Markov meticulously transcribed the first 20,000 letters of Pushkin's novel in verse *Eugene Onegin* by hand.[13] He counted all the vowels and proved that the probability of the subsequent letter being a vowel or a consonant could be approximated (Markov; Basharin et al. 19). Through his analysis, Markov illustrated that the novel was not composed of a random distribution of letters but had underlying statistical qualities. Proving that texts have a fundamental mathematical structure, Markov essentially produced 'fake Pushkin.'

Shannon followed with 'fake English.' Initially, he corroborated Markov's findings regarding the predictable nature of subsequent letters and words in a sequence through textual experiments that required making a statistical model of language. This model, he further showed, could be leveraged to generate natural language. At the zeroth-order approximation, the output is a series of random characters. Since not all letters manifest with equal frequency in English, incorporating a model that reflects the common probabilities of character occurrences can facilitate the generation of a text bearing a closer resemblance to coherent English.[14] Building upon Markov's work in a structuralist fashion, Shannon treated words as interdependent units, which ultimately enabled the production of a text with English-like characteristics.[15]

In his subsequent work, Shannon proposed several methods to quantify information content through cross-entropy. In practical terms, he suggests generating natural language based on analysis of English corpora and ensuring the quality of approximation through cross-entropy through a method he suggested in 'Prediction and Entropy of Printed English' (1951).[16] 70 years and several technical breakthroughs in machine learning were required to get from Shannon's information theory to actual large language models. Chapter 1 of this book discusses some of these breakthroughs, including the additional layering of neural networks, building upon Rosenblatt's perceptron, reinforcement learning, and the technique called backpropagation (i.e. the backward propagation of errors). However, the book does not delve into some of the other basic machine learning methods, such as decision trees and Bayesian statistics, whose fundamentals were largely established already in the 1960s. The transformer architecture represents a more recent breakthrough in machine learning that happens to excel in language processing, even though it is unlikely to remain the sole method to achieve such performance.

The challenge with LLMs and grasping the essence of meaning persists. While meaning is pivotal in reliable human communication, current LLMs cannot capture the higher-level structure inherent in natural language understanding (which implies a comprehension of meaning), despite recent successful endeavors in summarization, explanations, and editing. To reach that zenith, more sophisticated techniques and ambitious goals are requisite for language processing systems. While mathematics and statistics have already propelled us far, leveraging information theory can potentially take today's AI even farther, provided we fully recognize its strengths and weaknesses.

Shannon begins his now classic paper 'A Mathematical Theory of Communication,' with a remark elucidating that his theory sidestepped the semantic aspects of communication, viewing them as extraneous to the engineering challenges of communication (623). Machine-generated language eliminates the necessity for a subject and a relation to the world and can be thus argued to have no meaning. In Shannon's theory, following Bell Labs predecessor Ralph Hartley's poorly acknowledged work 'Transmission of Information' (1928),[17] the "semantic aspects of communication are irrelevant" (623).[18] This is why information can be text, pixels, and protein structure data—all are applicable systems governed by combinatorial logic.

This is also why the renaming from large language model to foundation or transformer model was due: if one can type text with a request to generate a described image, like one does with DALL-E, or if the image can be described with text in a reverse type of model called CLIP, then the language model has become multimodal. The speed of departure from a language-based technology was quite astonishing. (In this discussion, I keep the original name of large language models, which is still largely in use, since I focus on early and language-based models.)

LLMs do not possess human-level language ability; after all, they only work with text for now. What is crucial here is that LLMs' abilities, no matter how humanlike they get, will always be quantitatively different from human language. This is because the technical aspect of language-making and understanding in the transformer architecture relies on a conceptualization of language as a probability distribution. It is an admirably powerful conceptualization, for which knowing the rules of grammar and semantics—and when to break them for an element of surprise and authenticity—is key.

In a fascinating turn of events, connectionist AI (neuronlike computing: neural networks that learn from patterns in data), after decades of unsuccessful attempts, turned out to work better on language than symbolic AI (logic and rule-based orders). Connectionist (neuron-based) AI uses statistical reasoning and thus does not follow grammar as such: it is all about the probability of the next word (much like the Bayesian models). Language is almost entirely rule-based and therefore success with symbolic (rule-based) AI had seemed more likely than with computational neurons. Engineers analyzing a string of symbols for AI to learn from lost to machines themselves learning from a large corpus of data: deep parsing gave way to deep learning.

It is even more surprising that LLMs are as sophisticated as they are since the basic unit in an entirely language-based model is a word (technically classified as a token, an instance of a sequence of characters that work as a semantic unit). Words are *discrete* units, but connectionist models like LLMs need *continuous* input. This is why word embeddings were a crucial technique—a trick—to circumvent this problem. A word embedding turns discrete units of words into continuous input by assigning words an array of numbers. Words with a similar meaning are assigned similar numbers by the model. Vectors then statistically manipulate these numbers into predicting the next word in a sequence. LLMs are therefore models with discrete basic units broken down into a continuum that makes them functional in the first place. In more technical terms, these models work as a derivative of a continuum embedded in words through quantification.[19]

This technical detail only shows how these words do not exist alone but are instead truly relational. Their occurrence and meaning depend on the probability network they are embedded within. The transformer architecture operates with the idea of self-attention, the ability to allow for different positions of the input sequence to produce the representation sequence, leading to complex sequences. For example, in the input *Let's go to Ms. Pickles for lunch*, the model will learn that *lunch* is the key word of this request and that *Ms. Pickles* is either a person or a place that serves food. The attention is in how these words relate to one another. Being trained on huge amounts of text, examined at the level of the sentence, the paragraph, and the general theme, an LLM is able to predict the word that comes next. The transformer architecture has been widely successful with LLMs due to this aspect: as the title of the seminal paper on transformers goes, 'Attention is all you need' (Vaswani et al.). Attention enables a model to consider the relationship between words that are far apart in a text and, at the same time, determines which words are most important to pay attention to. Attention, as well as transfer learning (that models trained in language were applicable to genomics) and the ability to simply scale up these networks, resulting in a better model, was the right mixture for their immense success.

The amount of linguistic data input is truly enormous compared to that for humans, causing all sorts of environmental problems. Clearly, this is not how humans learn language. Building these models with solely human capabilities in mind misses the point of having an access to a machinic analysis of the world; nonetheless, the human-centered view remains prominent. In the leading textbook in the field of natural language processing (NLP), *Artificial Intelligence* by Stuart J. Russell and Peter Norvig from the 2020 edition, this machinic language is viewed very much on human terms. Looking into the future, the chapter on deep learning and NLP brings up two arguments, the argument of nonhumanlike and poor performance and the (Chomskyan) argument of the poverty of stimulus, i.e. the need for more textual data than humans: "There is certainly room for improvement: not only do NLP systems still lag human performance on many tasks, but they do so after processing thousands of times more text than any human could read in a lifetime. This suggests that there is plenty of scope for new insights for linguists, psychologists, and NLP researchers" (878). These arguments miss the intrinsic value of nonhuman capacities in such production of language, prioritizing automation and acceleration of human language without working on augmentation that adds to our capabilities—which is especially pertinent for creativity in language, for literary writing.

Transformers are exciting right now because scaling up the amount of data they are trained on generally brings better outcomes. Their charm comes from their immense ability for scaling up: no other architecture has been trained on such a humongous amount of data. Transformers are tapping into the advantage that human knowledge has largely been preserved in text. While LLMs at the level of GPT-4 serve good explanations and analyses, they can hardly offer new knowledge insights. Language might not be the perfect medium for search or discovery.

AI can be so many things, with generative AI being just one form of use. The types of neural architectures might be consequential—we do not have the answer to this question yet. In a few years, transformers might not be the most exciting architecture anymore; or they might be merged with other architectures, such as GANs for innovation or graphs for semantic or knowledge value. Language might become a limiting factor where new data might not have to come from text or speech but from other galactic information, such as vision or proteins. In 2022, for example, stable diffusion made impressive visual results with video storytelling, usurping the space of transformer-based text-to-image models (e.g. DALL-E). Models that I am discussing today do not keep on learning after they are trained, and such meta-learning will accompany the next generation of multimodal (with multiple modes) and multimodular (layered-upon) models (e.g. Gato and Chinchilla). Nonetheless, it has all begun with language, even if there is nothing specific to language that LLMs do. They just happened to work well on text and are making great progress in speech as well.

Even within the narrow domain of text generation, LLMs keep surprising us. They have no model of the world, i.e. no internal model of how the world works,[20] and yet they are able to lead a conversation, write an article, craft nuanced memos, summarize reports, draft letters, explain complex medical and biological queries, draw a syntactic tree, and—in the near future—invent convincing stories and generate touching poetry. Or, through the lens of neural network Helen from Powers's *Galatea 2.2*, as discussed in Chapter 4, even though they have never mothered a child or looked through a telescope, they will be able to capture these experiences with words. The power of imagination forgoes the power of experience in LLMs. There is no existential intention or truth to convey—or at least there is no commitment to them. I could describe how icebergs sound even if I have never heard one sliding along its way. My description might not sound convincing and authentic without researching natural sounds. As a matter of fact, an LLM's description will likely be more accurate as it is built on the many observations of people who have heard it or know more about the topic than I do. A human author able to experience a natural phenomenon through senses, sometimes in tandem with science and technology, does not necessarily lead to an accurate or masterly narrative. LLMs bring a new world of narratives, without ontological commitment. These commitments could be partially instilled in LLMs through value alignment, added to the model through reinforcement learning from human feedback. However, this ultimately ethical approach makes the models more predictable and general, which is less appealing for creative writing.

The philosophical aspect of these changes in how we view language is deep. In only a few years of their development, language has been decoupled from the subject to the extent that we cannot always determine authorship. The starting point is that what these language models do and produce is not human. When human language is analyzed, produced, and distributed by machines, it needs a different label: machine language, nonhuman language, synthetic language. LLMs are the perfect—but far from the only—example of its potential and power in the world, which no one could deny anymore in 2023. This is the year LLMs became ubiquitous, and, per the Gartner Hype Cycle, reached the Peak of Inflated Expectations followed by the Trough of Disillusionment. The Internet has been flooded with machine-generated words, as Tobias Rees writes (168); termed by Matthew Kirschenbaum as a "textocalypse." Both scholars agree that AI will fundamentally change our relationship with writing, but they have opposing views about the imminent opportunity (Rees) and doom (Kirschenbaum).

Emerging models of the early 2020s have co-authored literary works, which is incredibly exciting for literature and literary studies. There is a new kind of author in the literary space and it is here to collaborate rather than usurp it. This is why it is extremely important for literary studies to begin participating in the discussion on how these text-based models are used and built for the purpose of writing both fiction and nonfiction as well as summarizing and editing—which is only a small chunk of LLMs' deployment across the humanities, arts, and engineering.

5.2 Literary Market: Dahl

On June 11, 1949, *The London Times* quoted the Enigma codebreaker Alan Turing's view on machinic writing: "I do not see why [the machine] should not enter any one of the fields normally covered by the human intellect, and eventually compete on equal terms. I do not think you even draw the line about sonnets, though the comparison is perhaps a little bit unfair because a sonnet written by a machine will be better appreciated by another machine" ('The Mechanical Brain'). As a question worthy of investigation during the Turing test, described the following year in his founding paper on AI, Turing suggested, "Please write me a sonnet on the subject of the Forth Bridge," to which the machine would reply, "Count me out on this one. I never could write poetry" and would be thus identified as the computer (434). Turing's research program therefore creates a contrast between the hollow machine and the irreducible personhood ascribed to it. Yet, in poetry, these machines would inevitably fail. In sum: while Turing demarcates seemingly intelligent computers from humans in their respective literary abilities in the 1950s paper, he also believed that we have yet to learn what machines are and will be capable of, not discounting the possibility that they will someday write poetry, as attested in his 1949 interview.

Traditional poets and writers are protective of their words and reluctant to turn them over to a computer. This reluctance might stem from the fear of eventual replacement, uncalled-for editing, or losing the delight afforded by language as well as the sheer physical reality of the writing process. This is a legitimate position, but these fears are not ubiquitous. In what could be called the prehistory of generated writing and synthetic literature, avant-garde poets and novelists delighted in exploring writing with machines.

Taking this early literary experimentation into account, writing with LLMs is not that radically new. Computers have been creating textual artifacts since the 1950s, more so with the help of programmers than actual writers. In the very early days of AI around 1952, British computer scientist, pioneer of programming language design, nephew of the Bloomsbury Group writer Lytton Strachey, and Alan Turing's collaborator, Christopher Strachey[21] used one of the earliest stored-program computers, Manchester Mark 1, to generate a love letter with his algorithm. Genderless M.U.C. stands for Manchester University Computer, which composed letters with the same structure and melodramatic overtones (see the image below). For each category, Strachey created a wordlist as well as a table of themes and moods. Below is an example quoted in Strachey's paper, titled 'The "Thinking" Machine' (26):

Darling Sweetheart,
   You are my avid fellow feeling. My affection curiously clings to your passionate wish. My liking yearns for your heart. You are my wistful sympathy: my tender liking.
   Yours beautifully
   M. U. C.

At the same time, possibly influenced by the work of his compatriot computer scientists,[22] British writer Roald Dahl wrote his short story 'The Great Automatic Grammatisator,' published in his 1953 collection *Someone Like You*. Contrary to the collection title, the story does not take the Pygmalionesque route of human imitation but focuses on the less discussed question of the literary market filled with nonhuman words. At the core of Dahl's writing machine story is automation and acceleration—the core mission of the British-run industrial revolution—which remains an aspiration in technology until today: increase productivity, cost, and speed. The human as the creator of the machine only needs to move the lever and push some buttons to produce more text; the industrial separation of the human from the machine remains palpable.

   Literature authors liked to imagine a machine that would take over their own profession. Common to most of the twentieth-century stories on this topic is that all these machines are only able to parrot a certain acclaimed human author's style.[23] True originality in machinic texts is rare. Dahl's writing machine's mechanism is close to LLMs today. The grammatisator is initially a revolutionary calculating machine: "The speed with which the new engine works [...] may be grasped by the fact that it can provide the correct answer in five seconds to a problem that would occupy a mathematician for a month" (251). Besides being able to tackle mathematical problems like a mathematician would, it is the speed, more than anything, that puts the machine ahead of human abilities. And yet, "[f]or practical purposes there is no limit to what it can do" (251).

Mathematics and literature writing have a long history when it comes to form (thus not including the texts that focus on mathematical problems content-wise, such as Lewis Carroll's 1865 *Alice in Wonderland*). Brett Stevens shows that the relation between the two fields is not shallow and one-directional as generally perceived. For example, as a case where the structure of literary work presents a mathematical problem, Stevens follows the influence of Dante's *Divine Comedy* to many modernists, including Samuel Beckett, who inspired a type of a Gray Code (reflected binary code in one bit). Starting with the structure first and incorporating mathematical structures in literature was the very goal of the French Oulipo group (standing for *Ouvroir de Littérature Potentielle* or Workshop for Potential Literature), composed of writers and mathematicians. This resulted in restricting writing possibilities in form, such as in Georges Perec's famous novel *A Void* [*La Disparition*] written without the letter 'e.' In the 1960s, the group became "frustrated with the syntactic operations of their first years and curious to investigate—*à la* Strachey—whether these methods might be extended to looser, broader units of the literary text, such as plot elements," which, unfortunately, resulted in a story of "mistrust" and "missed opportunities" (Duncan 30). While none of these writers used computers, the *concept* of a thinking machine played a significant role in their writing.

There are also mechanically-oriented and textually-disruptive artistic precedents. As an example of the latter we can look back to the late nineteenth-century poem by Stéphane Mallarmé, *A Throw of the Dice Never Will Abolish Chance* (1897), and, as an example of both orientations, the Dadaist movement of the 1920s that used the cut-up technique (*découpé*) for rearranging a written text into a new one. This purely mechanical method was popularized in the 1960s by William S. Burroughs, who often used it in collaboration with other writers. Burroughs developed a theory around it: This method allows one to enter the place that another author created. Every text is a cut-up (Skerl)—not unlike in LLMs. The essential difference between these literary practices is the authorship: the author remains human in all of them but in Dahl's story.

In Dahl's story, the general ability of mathematics inspires the machine's inventor, Adolph Knipe, to turn its numerical abilities into the rules of language and ultimately storytelling: "*The English grammar is governed by rules that are almost mathematical in their strictness!*" Knipe feeds the machine with words and plots and then leaves it "to write the sentences" (254). Every bit of storytelling in Dahl is mechanized. Per Knipe, the machine does not have "a brain," but has a "word-memory" and a "plot-memory" (260). This is also how engineers talk about today's LLMs; for example, GPT-3 has 4,000 tokens (not words) of memory of plot and words. Both engineers and writers see this as such a limitation that they try to extend or work around it with a variety of embedding techniques, summaries, and timelines. Every conceptual trick requires a technical and ultimately purely mathematical solution. Creativity that writers today see and appreciate in LLMs is most often linked to the element of surprise that can emerge from this technical way of the architecture's inner workings.

Adolph Knipe's name is based on Dahl's actual publisher, Alfred Knopf, who published 'The Great Automatic Grammatisator.' The fictional Knipe wanted to become a writer but instead opened a mass-production writing business. Knipe believes that a computer *can* be original in its own way, and this belief opens the door to a business opportunity: literary market. "How can the writers compete with that?" (33). He is worried, however, that no one will buy machine-authored stories. In order to ensure success, he blackmails famous authors into licensing their names as a way to conceal the fact that a machine is behind the newly printed words. The quantity of the machine's performance outweighs the quality: "The quality may be inferior, but that doesn't matter. It's the cost of production that counts" (22). The machine is high-yielding: Knipe needs to simply choose the kind of plot, genre, writing style, and theme (47–48), and the machine generates many award-winning stories. The machine monopolizes half of the English book market, leaving a small percentage of authors who refuse to sign their names on these texts to starve. "Give us strength, oh Lord, to let our children starve," concludes the narrator (60).

Dahl's story aims to criticize the assembly line in the publishing market more than AI writing itself. It is a story about forms of labor when the labor market of writing is dictated by information technology (Eve 45–46). The prerequisite for this discussion is for machine-generated writing to be shaped in its social textuality. This happens naturally with language for us humans as language is inherently social, but inherent to textuality is social reconfiguration of authorship. If we were to consider machines as authors, we have two options: to assign them the social position of authorship or to deal with the understanding of texts' social—and thus human—value (Hendrickson 60).

As a social event, writing *with* computers is not absolutely novel: it is only writing with and by AI that we have not yet mastered, or been able to master, since it is so new. Writing, and especially authorship, involves intentionality, while reading involves hermeneutics that helps to increase the validity of the text. It is important to categorize both types of activity and agents in relation to the new reality. Machines are readers too. What happens with the social aspect of text when both ends of the text are machinic?

Dahl's abysmal vision for the writing profession was accurate for a specific infrequent phenomenon of plagiarism encountered today. The rise of plagiarism in the age of self-publishing books is a predictable problem. In a contemporary scamming practice, called book stuffing, texts are generated by machines for profit. For example, through Amazon's Kindle Unlimited service, 'authors' offer many lengthy books of gibberish (see Flood 'Plagiarism', Zetlin). Or, avoiding gibberish and employing hard plagiarism, these authors might be actual people who use bogus or real names for their fast-selling romance or criminal genre novels.[24] The 'authors,' just like in Dahl's story, might also be names of famous authors whose books are a victim of plagiarism—or ghostwriting—after all. Therefore, like in Dahl, authors' names are put on a computer-generated book solely to earn profit and "[o]nline book-selling scams steal a living from writers" (Preston). This is what happens when an algorithm favors authors with steady sales and new releases, and when 'authors' are glutting the market. The unlikely fear is that machines will glut the market this way too: scamming will always be a part of this technology, but not at large.

AI is not just a writer but also a new kind of reader. Literary and digital humanities scholars Hugh Craig and Brett Greatley-Hirsch argue a "computer can read more, and more evenly, than any human reader, and this paradoxical situation—perfect evenness, unlimited memory, entire lack of comprehension—brings a capacity to offer results which might not be anticipated, which diverge from the conclusions of both ideal and actual readers, but which can be directly and completely related to the details of the text" (3). The value of machine reading is in the abilities that we do not have.

Regardless, when it comes to reading, LLMs products are for now being used for a very human kind of reading: summarizing. Since 2021, Open AI's GPT-3 can summarize books, paragraph by paragraph, page by page, until it reaches the most distinct summary (for more, see 'Summarizing'). It goes without saying that this tool is already being used by those who have it at hand, not only for the purposes of summarizing fictional works. This is a handy tool for the current world that appreciates brief, succinct information. Could it be turned from an AI tool into an AI agent—like conversational agents of the future, described at the end of Chapter 2—that will do the reading and research for us and synthesize its findings for us in an output that will not be doctored or proofread by a human? Until ChatGPT was made public in November 2022, the world was largely unprepared to think under these terms; today, it is hard to imagine the future without an AI agency. "One thing seems certain to me," writes Hannes Bajohr, "with the increasing penetration of language technologies, with the triumph of AI models, our expectations as readers will change" ('Artificial' 357).

What is most valuable about Dahl's story for the purpose of AI creativity is the idea of a massively producing machine that writes indistinguishably from human authors, even though the stream of words is based on mathematical calculations. The responses to LLMs that do exactly this are radical: either critics defend human writing against meaningless vectors of probability, calling machine generation the Sokal Affair 2.0, or they encourage it, predicting that our grandchildren will find it hard to imagine we ever wrote from scratch. The future is somewhere in between on this spectrum, and we just need to find the best way to realize it. It is going to be better if we do not let engineers figure it out on their own.

5.3 Literary Criticism: Tomažin

The literary market includes fiction and nonfiction, i.e. subjective documentation, such as memoirs, autobiographies and biographies, documentative experiences, and so on. A story is a good story whether it actually happened or not. Can we confidently say that a story is a good story whether it is human-authored or not?

As mentioned, most of the early works, from the 1950s to the 2010s, were authored by programmers, at times together with writers.[25] The collaborative aspect, for now, is the key to machinic literary writing. In the late 2000s, poetry and narrative-generating programs abound and became available to non-programmers from the mid-2010s on. The poetry-based programs were largely based on the imitation of a well-known author, ranging from Rupi Kaur who rose to fame as an Instapoet to more traditional poets with a recognizable style. The earliest "pirated anthology" Issue 1 is from 2008, edited by writers and programmers Steve McLaughlin and Jim Carpenter, and includes "the work of 3,164 poets. Completely unpermissioned and unauthorized" (Goldsmith par. 1). Most famously, since November 2013, programmers have competed in novel writing. The challenge began as a response to National Novel Writing Month (NaNoWriMo) and—on the initiative of a software developer and artist Darius Kazemi who spent the month writing code that generated a novel—turned into a new tradition called National Novel Generation Month (NaNoGenMo). Already back in 1963, the trade journal *Computers and Automation* held a computer art contest. Prize committees and editors at fiction journals had all the right to worry about the submissions being potentially generated, and some have effectively halted submissions in early 2023 after ChatGPT became widely available. The 'deepfake' crisis, i.e. a crisis of synthesized AI outputs, began with fiction writing.

In Roald Dahl's short story, Adolph Knipe's machine creates literature of compromised quality and yet its novels are awarded with literary prizes. In 2016, a novel co-written by AI, titled *The Day A Computer Writes A Novel*, went through the first round in the Japanese national literary prize, which has been opened to "A.I. programs and others" (Olewitz par. 3; see also Danny Lewis). In fact, 11 out of 1,450 submissions for this prize were co-authored by computers. Soon after, in 2018, Slovenian writer Andrej Tomažin reflected on these novel circumstances in his short story 'Lackeys, Heroes, and AI' ['Hlapci, heroji in umetna inteligenca'][26] from his collection *Anonymous Technology* [*Anonimna tehnologija*].

In Tomažin's story, a committee of literary critics meets to award a short story with a prestigious grant and learns from the media that one of the works they are considering for the award is written by AI. The chair of the jury, Dr. Osmanagić,[27] is versed in post-semantic literature, which is based on the idea of deconstruction. Her belief that "meaning simply didn't exist anymore" (1)[28] is a result of the twentieth-century decline of meaning: if in modernism the world was made of meaning that was exclusively human-given, postmodernist humans at the end of the century do not pursue this seemingly still valid ability. This is because language as a concept has been transformed—in this case, deconstructed. According to Dr. Osmanagić, the novelty of this concept of language comes into view in the most radical post-semantic literature whose "generative narratological structure can substitute for a human one, without necessarily implying any disenchantment or destruction of the world" (3).[29] There is no catastrophe, just new structural conditions. These conditions themselves are structural in form as a heritage of the 1920s structuralist view of language, which, as I have argued above, was the fertile soil from which LLMs emerged.

In Tomažin, it is contested if an author is replaceable. (In Dahl, this is not yet raised as a question since Knipe uses deception and coercion, listing actual authors' names on machine-generated literary works.) Post-semantic literature from Tomažin's story was established with a fictional paper by Scott B. Hayyek from 2022 (the timing corresponds perfectly with the actual development in literature), wittily titled 'Post-Semantic Literature or How to Finally Kill the Text and Not the Author.' In a posthuman world where language is combinatorial and devoid of meaning, the author is irrelevant, and the text is dead.

Versed in the field of comparative literature, Tomažin is clearly familiar with Italo Calvino's 1967 essay 'Cybernetics and Ghosts' where he—admittedly influenced by Shannon, Wiener, von Neumann, and Turing—writes: "Literature is a combinatorial game that pursues the possibilities implicit in its own material, but it is a game that at a certain point is invested with an unexpected meaning, a meaning that is not patent on the linguistic plane on which we were working but has slipped in from another level, activating something that on that second level is of great concern to the author or his society" (22). This meaning, emphasized by Calvino, is, in his view, endowed by the reader's—not author's—unconscious. The poetic result stems from the historical and empirical subject, not the language itself, produced by "[t]he literature machine [that] can perform all the permutations possible on a given material" (22).

Already in Calvino, we see this new, Galatean reflection of language: originating in humans as a cultural heritage passed on for generations, language has now passed also to machines, who might act humanlike but will use language according to their own abilities. While Calvino, similar to Turing, judges literature written by machines to be merely automatic mimicking, he admits that poetic-electronic machines should be capable of breaking the traditions they inherited, turning from classicism to "propos[ing] new ways of writing, turning its own codes completely upside down" (12–13). Language will bend together under the new abilities afforded by machines and the author will vanish, giving space to the reader, the only meaning-maker left.

Similarly, for Borges, art is "a poetic/meditative device which cannot be programmed to provide clear meanings but rather catalyzes the interpretative faculties of its user" (Duncan 111).[30] In the final denaturing or technologization of literature, mechanisms as machines come after the text itself, making meaning epiphenomenal and completely dependent on the human reader. Subjective experience allows the human to be the only meaning-maker, evaluator, signal processor, evaluator.

The chair of the fictional jury, Dr. Osmanagić, is a reflection of those thinkers who do not tie themselves to how language should be, but rather how it could work under these new machinic conditions. The rest of the jury stands firmly in her opposition. The jury is by and large composed of critical humanists represented by the journalist Savić. Savić is openly bothered by the novelist Ludovic Bitterman, "Houellebecq's jilted successor," who is suspected to be "just a computer programmer who had figured out how to write some clever code based on the corpus of the master's [i.e. Houellebecq's] great texts" (Tomažin 3). Savić calls Butterman a literary "goncourt," referring to the Goncourt brothers (1830–70), collaborative sibling authors who were never separated for a day in their lives and led their literary work as a unique example of writing partnership. He deems it utterly unfair that "now Bitterman is collecting awards that by rights ought to go to Houellebecq" (3).[31]

AI is not a single-acting agent in the jury's eyes. The jury is bothered by the idea that behind AI are, in fact, humans: engineers who are taking the rightful place of writers. The redeeming quality of engineers, per journalist Savić, is that they at least have some agency, whereas AI is nothing but a "a non-human archive" (5), an infinitely abundant compost of human thoughts as patched, hybridized Frankensteinian remains. Savić concludes that they "can't give the award to an archive that we can't name or put on stage or hand a plaque to" (5). Instead, the awarded text needs an author with a "body" and a "face," possibly with "a personal story to go with it" (5). Savić clings to the old, refusing to accept that this new technology marks the end of individuality.

The archive Savić describes is nothing but an ever-growing digital library, in which "the algorithmization of the writer is a Borgesian paradise," making the machine "the perfect Borgesian author" (Kuret 97).[32] The theme of the writer who cannot write well or is experiencing a writer's block is prevalent throughout Tomažin's collection *Anonymous Technology*. For example, in the short story 'Noli me tangere,' the writer, in a typical motif of isolation from society, attempts to escape modern, technologized urban life in order to preserve his writing skill. He fails: his inner world—a steady characteristic of modernist writing—is guaranteed to be presented by other writing subjects and objects. The future is here, and there is no escape in separating the human from technology or, for that matter, our collective intelligence and activity.

In another short story from Tomažin's collection, titled 'How to write like Roberto Bolaño in less than an hour,' the central character is a mediocre writer who wants to write like Bolaño. She realizes that by imprinting her Internet chats into the digital archive, she is writing the novel of all novels, effectively becoming a Bolaño character instead of a Bolañesque writer. Her authorship is hidden in the digital layers of text, dug in the overwhelming and "unfathomable archive" into which her authorship is embedded.[33] The realm of the text has changed: traditional writers' words were captured in a book and digital writers' words can only be captured in a database. She concludes that if she were to truly become a writer, she had better google 'how to write like' and let the algorithm do the work. Her true original contribution is the one from the digital archive of the everyday. Her individual contributions (her text as data) bring value only as a part of the vast digital textual space (big data).

In tandem with the writers' inability to write comes plagiarization, set by AI at the center of writing. The literary world in Tomažin's story is coming to terms with this new reality, which is not necessarily considered dystopian. The third jury member, Professor Javornik, brings up another criminalized example of plagiarism: Argentinian writer Pablo Katchadijan created "his own Borgesian experiment" with the help of AI (6). AI was trained to add new lines to Borges's 'El Aleph,' and Katchadijan published them in his own short prose collection under his name, which landed him in prison. (For Professor Javornik, Katchadijan is innocent as he had clearly just followed Borges's intentions.) With this kind of AI writing, Professor Javornik claims, every literary award that would go to a computer in fact belongs to taxpayers and to everyone who has not yet written a text or signed their name under it (6). Why this reasoning? Because, after all, computer programs hack human experiences rendered into digital words, feed on the living flesh and blood from which the words arose. No subjectivity is needed, no model of the world is needed: a dance of probability and word sequences does not bring authorship.

Behind this infinite digital archive trope lies the idea of collective intelligence. A humanlike writing subject is only an appearance when writing with an algorithm or LLM, and, following the Eliza effect, we project an entire ontology of what could and should happen in the interaction with a non-human writer. The text or conversation with a collective intelligence agent is not composed of random choices with no intent; there is an autonomy behind it and there is nothing obvious about how to collaborate with a writing machine. Creativity—in its many definitions: as originality, as randomness, as play—remains in the domain of the human (see Sautoy's and Boden's respective criteria).

The fourth member of the jury, Professor Juntez, who refuses to understand the hurdles of the challenge at stake, is a technology skeptic. Professor Juntez claims it is easy to discern a text written by a human from a text produced by an algorithmic machine since the "surrogate" could never be better (2). Collaborative creative writing with the machine, for Professor Juntez, falls under imitation of the solely noble human writing. Professor Juntez is in denial that the time has come when machine writing has become replaceable and interchangeable with that of humans. His belief in human exceptionalism follows the reasoning that since language and literature were invented by humans, humans will always hold the upper hand in these domains. We value human originality, creativity, intellectual inspiration, hard work, and unique products—could we ever value these attributes had they come from a machine? When AI is judged by human standards, AI is a cheater.

A similar experiment to the two examples of plagiarizing literature was conducted in music and AI in the mid-1990s. An EMI (Experiments in Musical Intelligence) machine composed a piece based on Chopin's music and fooled a group of music connoisseurs. EMI's piece was performed after Chopin's little-known mazurka and the majority of the audience voted for the AI piece as the authentic one (Mitchell 10). It should be noted that EMI was led by the human hand of its creator, composer David Cope, and yet so many refuse to attribute creativity to it (e.g. Mitchell 274). It is evident from this case that the main goal for AI was to be able to make computer music sound like human music.

Why are we keeping machines to human abilities, mimicry, and standards? The condescending view of AI stems from the classical definitions of the machine as artificial, technical, and mechanical, which deny it any creativity, intelligence, agency, or freedom—no excellence apart from brute force of calculation. Consider, for example, the famous 1988 monograph *Mind Over Machine* with a telling title by brothers Hubert and Stuart Dreyfus, a philosophy professor and an engineering professor, which argues that human expertise and intuition cannot be superseded by a binary-based machine. Decades later, machines have penetrated into creative fields: not as creative machines *per se* but rather as novel tools used by human creators.

In Tomažin's story, this kind of curiosity toward machines is present only in the female chair of the jury, Dr. Osmanagić, who brings up a contemporary American literary movement called "neocombinatorics." This literary movement is composed of doctors of the cognitive sciences and mathematics, "all of whom, most importantly, are huge fans of the late David Foster Wallace" (5).[34] Like the musical machine EMI, the neocombinatorics movement is led by humans who work with machines to create original material. Their main approach is data mining "to abstract semantic webs of individuals' interests, to create a kind of lexical and emotional database," taking into account "conflicting decisions" (5). The vastness of the data and the power of the algorithm is not enough for machines to present true originality: in the neocombinatorics movement the genius remains the human mind.

Tomažin's short story is one of the rare texts that does not seem to imply that human exceptionalism is the only right way to think about machines in creative domains. The story concludes with an open ending, with the jury announcing the winning text and waiting for the author to come on stage. The text written by an authorless agency defeats the purpose of the award: if no one comes on the stage, no one won. The irony of the moment is palpable.

A lesson for the literary market and its publications, prizes, and fellowships is that institutions created for humans only are no longer tenable. The old order cannot accommodate such a radically new actor as generative AI. Even if AI is just a tool and not a creative agent on its own, it has set up new conditions that we have not yet addressed philosophically, let alone institutionally. Let us start the exploration of the new conditions from the ground up: with writing.

5.4 Writing Literature: Kehlmann and Allado-McDowell

Writing between humans and machines is not new; the novelty that language models brought is the machinic agency, unraveling a kind of originality and creativity—both for humans and for machines—that was not possible before. This space will continue to grow with other, some not-yet-invented, kinds of architectures, as it already does with visual storytelling with stable diffusion models. To think about the terms of encounter in the area of literary writing is only a small chunk of writing with AI, which does not imply that it is also inconsequential. If we learn something from the experiences of writers who collaborated with AI, it will surely not stay within the space of fiction. And we need as many learning experiences of all kinds as we can muster.

What does it mean to be a human writer in the world of writing machines? What occurs in writing when done in collaboration with a writing machine or when the machine is prompted to write on its own? Not many writers were able to explore this space until now. Writers are masters of words who dedicated their lives to exploring words in a way that increases the richness and the intensity of living. Not all are reluctant to turn them over to a computer. Perhaps machine writing can, just as human writing, delight and surprise?

How this relational quality could look was explored in two different lockdown projects in 2020. The first one is by German-Austrian novelist Daniel Kehlmann and CTRL, created by Bryan McCann, which resulted in a 2021 essay 'My Algorithm and Me' ['Mein Algorithmus und Ich']. Kehlmann's essay is a rationalized perspective on his experimentation with CTRL, citing a few most exciting exchanges. The second text is by American writer Kenric Allado-McDowell and OpenAI's GPT-3, which resulted in a co-written novel *Pharmako-AI*, published in 2020. These respective encounters with a Silicon

Valley writing machine resulted in a diametrical opposition: the first one is reactive, the second contemplative.

From the perspective of CTRL creator Bryan McCann, then research scientist at Salesforce and a fan of—no suspense—Italo Calvino, Kehlmann's experiment might have failed: Kehlmann never published a text co-written with the machine the way Allado-McDowell did.[35] However, we did gain another book from him in the form of an essay reflecting on the experience, which is just as needed. At the very beginning of writing with machines in this way, outputs (texts) are just as valuable as processes, including writers' personal experience with the interactions. For Kehlmann personally, the experiment "was a success, because [he] really got to know non-human intelligence" (25).[36]

While Kehlmann was not quite a blank slate in terms of his knowledge of AI at the beginning of the experiment, his presuppositions about AI being humanlike did not hinder his initial expectations: "Only gradually did it dawn on me that I had still been imagining artificial intelligence, about which I'd read so much, like the android C-3PO or the narcissistic supercomputer HAL—as a human being encased in metal, a person in costume" (3).[37] The experience of the algorithm, as Kehlmann calls CTRL, never translates into experiencing it as a person. Instead, he sees it as "an odd, cold, alien intelligence, with which no mutual understanding was possible in any profound sense of the word" (18). Even if he had to readjust his expectations right at the start, he remains strictly on the human side: "It can't be stressed often enough: artificial intelligence is a reuser. Everything it can do depends on the activity of countless people that is made available by the Internet" (12).[38]

Kehlmann is right to say that CTRL generates a probabilistic stream of sentences but is not a writer. It can surprise but it might not build upon that suspense. It has no sense of resolution when needed. It should be noted here that 2020 models are certainly inferior to those that came after. CTRL and GPT-3 might be from roughly the same time but they are not comparable models: CTRL is based on 1.73 billion parameters whereas GPT-3[39] has 175 billion (Keshar et al.). For example, a common thread of Kehlmann's experience is that very soon into writing, CTRL breaks down, unable to continue, leaving its human collaborator wishing for more—but also not willing to continue on his own.

Kehlmann's view of CTRL is not condescending; there is something intriguing, spectacular, and magical about it: "And yet not infrequently, the results were astonishing, and there were moments that, if I didn't know better, I would interpret as signs of true inspiration" (13). He deems it is human nature saying a nice goodbye to CTRL or trying to treat it as an oracle that knows the answers to our questions better than we ourselves do. His essay, as a whole, is a representation of an average reaction to a LLM, that is, a reaction that is curious, playful, rational, and does not seek more depth or critique in the way technology is made or works.

Kehlmann describes different people's reactions to learning that he is experimenting with a language model: among others, "[a] British director [that] even proposed making it into a play: A writer works with a writing robot, the two of them fall in love, comic entanglements arise, a reverse Pygmalion scenario" (19–20). Certainly, these are the stories we tend to engage with the most, but there is zero relation between Kehlmann and CTRL. Their collaboration never takes off, partly because CTRL constantly runs out of steam, but predominantly because Kehlmann wants a writing partner that would be more human than nonhuman.

Philosopher Hannes Bajohr calls this tendency "the paradox of anthroponormative restriction," pinpointing that "the more one expects from Artificial Intelligence, the more human it is thought to be, but the less it is appreciated as a phenomenon in its own right" (264). It is indeed a paradox that "a truly powerful artistic AI would not extend Kehlmann, but actually replace him" (264). There is no need to reproduce what we already have available from human writers; instead, we are after new aesthetics and ideas; we are after new practices and spaces, new experiences and meanings.

Bajohr categorizes views on AI, including Kehlmann's and Allado-McDowell's respective experiments, after the distinction drawn by John Searle's 1980 paper 'Minds, Brains, and Programs.' The paper that presented the famous Chinese Room Argument claims that a computer cannot have an understanding regardless of how intelligently and humanlike it may behave. Searle refutes the position that 'strong AI' would be just like the human mind by proposing a thought experiment in which a computer program assembles a text in Chinese following the rules without ever really knowing Chinese as a language and its script.

Bajohr's categorization followed the idea of strong and weak AI, where "strong AI means the functional reduplication of the target domain" and cautious AI or "weak AI is at best a partial simulation of this domain and has at most a heuristic, a 'tool' function" (264–66). Strong AI is what Kehlmann hoped to find in CTRL: a computer that really *is* a mind and creator on its own and has outgrown the stage of a mere tool. Weak AI is what Allado-McDowell found in GPT-3: the qualitative difference that the nonhuman makes.

Allado-McDowell (who uses they/them pronouns) is not trying to prove GPT-3 can do humanlike things: they are, instead, exploring *with* GPT-3 and training it for the purpose of their own exploration. Their enchantment with GPT-3 comes from their sense of dialogue. The dialogue with GPT-3 must be built up exclusively from the side of the human writer, with no actual back and forth. With gentle encouragement from Allado-McDowell, GPT-3 at times manages to develop concepts that stick from one chapter to another. Craving for continuity is a human trait and a LLM is indeed optimized to be as little logically different from humans as possible. However, Allado-McDowell recognizes that difference is not a failure but can be productive and curious. Their approach with hands-on experimentation, which only takes place through language and the invested process of exchanging text with GPT-3, takes a step beyond the acquaintance phase with AI.

In *Pharmako-AI*, every artist is embedded into a network, and the two writers—i.e. the human and the machine—intertwine their own networks. Allado-McDowell addresses their authorship by looking through the eyes of their collaborator (GPT-3 in italics) (15):

> The experience of porosity, being enmeshed with another, throws me back on my internal model of myself. I stand outside of it. I see it through the eyes of the other—through another that I also model in myself. *I become aware of myself as a subject, experiencing a subjectivity constructed through the language of the other. I experience the way the other distributes the experience of me as enmeshed and embedded in the structure of the narrative that enmeshes me.*
>
> This makes me a character in a story. Whose story is it? We assume a story has an author, to whom the narrative belongs. But authors are observers too. Sometimes a story is received.

There is a clear continuity in literature in this kind of questioning. English postmodernist John Fowles and Italian modernist Luigi Pirandello wrote fiction that deals with theory of the creative process in narrative writing. Fowles's novel *The French Lieutenant's Woman* (1969) is particularly Pygmalionesque, discussing the characters as creations of the author that at some point achieve an autonomy independent of the author's intentions (Kennel 77). The creative impulse of description turned into control and the creative impulse of engineering creation turned into control have been eluded. The characters gained independence and turned from ventriloquist puppets to their creator's collaborators.

Elvia Wilk notes, "AI may actually change the way we think, so we might as well start listening to what it has to say" (par. 20). These language models, however feeble they may seem, may be able to offer insights and inspiration to human writers and readers that goes beyond human capabilities. We know that transformers offer capabilities that we need to discover rather than define. (For instance, LLMs can effectively translate human languages they haven't been trained on and only have minimal exposure to the data from those languages.) Going beyond the transformer architecture, there are numerous new ways of producing machinic language, each with unique abilities and disabilities (see, for example, generative adversarial networks in speech in Chapter 1).

Language in the machine learning world has a potential to manifest AlphaGo Zero from the world of the game Go: a touching, original actor in a world previously limited to humans. Developed by Google DeepMind, Alpha Go (Alpha Zero's predecessor) was trained with deep learning on human examples of the game. Without being troubled with a Go rulebook, it makes statistical predictions, learning from matches played against itself and improving exponentially with zero human inputs. Its legendary Move 37—yet unprecedented in the four millennia of the human game—was a clear expression of nonhuman intelligence. In the same way, LLMs are never taught grammar or semantics, and yet they do not make grammatical or semantic errors. Granted, LLMs are not yet good at plots and deception, but they might bring up an unusual phrase or set of words that humans do not put together, they might hang up on a phrase in language that us humans never would, they might evoke a twist or associative chain that is productive for the narrative.

The key is to think of them as a machine intelligence that produces networked words devoid of meaning, serving our creative pursuits even with a lack of the usual communicative feature. In literature, and in poetry in particular, language does not always have meaning. Language evokes the ineffable; in poetry, sound, repetitions, and rhythm may bring more meaning than the words themselves; text may be purely aesthetic, a work of art in itself. We can learn to develop a new way of writing and thinking with LLMs through our very interaction with them. What an opportunity this is for literature and literary studies: a radical new technology that began with language, was experimented first with literature, and turned out to be applicable to a variety of domains that can benefit from machine learning.

This kind of experimental literature writing is bound to forgo human writing qualities. Now we have a new kind of narrator that narrates the world based on data. Instead of trying to accommodate humans in stories and narratives that we find familiar enough, we can appreciate the innate abilities of LLMs in their Pygmalionism. They synthesize a colossal amount of human-written texts, possibly together with machine-generated inputs, and they imitate and analyze our style, offering not a mirror but an interpretation of what human writing is. Like Galateas, they are both humanlike and nonhuman. The qualitative difference of this language can be a gain for creativity.

In a world where myriad forms of expression coexist, there is no immediate need to accommodate their ways into human ways of creative writing. The beauty of linguistic diversity lies in the ability to explore and appreciate distinct styles, techniques, and perspectives. Let us appreciate LLMs for what they are and for what they could be and develop them together with our own masters of words, writers, and poets. "Everyone knows it is impossible to turn the eyeball around, such that the pupil can peer inside the skull," narrates Stanisław Lem's short story 'The Mask' (discussed in Chapter 2). We shall see that language might be flexible enough. Galateas—also a human creation handed over to technology—surely were.

5.5 Artificial Humanities: Centering Fiction

Fiction writers (e.g. Milan Kundera) and scholars (e.g. Raymond Williams) agree that fiction, paired with intimacy, produces a sort of knowledge inaccessible to other discourses. When turned into a narrative, this unique knowledge becomes a cultural artifact (Bal 3) that conveys our values, biases, and perspectives. Looking at technology through this lens not only adds historical context and value but also provides applicability for further technological development. Fiction is inevitably a part of this process.

As comparative literature scholar Mads Rosendahl Thomsen underscores in his book on posthuman literature (77):

> Throughout history, literature has demonstrated that it is one of the strongest, if not the strongest, medium by which a collected presentation of the human condition may be offered in a mode that considers the past, interprets the present and, as the passage of time has shown, forecasts future events or warns against what may happen. However, correspondences between the literary world and the world in which we live may not be the most important consequence of literature. Literature's capacity to present a particular vision of conditions that are highly relevant to thinking about the new human, through its inherent formal potential, is perhaps its most important contribution to the field.

Throughout the book, an understanding of fiction is not confined to the printed book but also includes the visual fictional narratives in film and television. What is the role of fiction and imagery in science and technology? Even within media studies, communication studies, and other digitally oriented fields, literary works tend to hold a peripheral role in discussions on technology. Fiction, however, is found in most technological spaces as a powerful source of public discourse and inspiration, capturing both the history of science and technology as well as their dreams and exhibiting our cultural values and beliefs as well as conceptual biases.

What is more, fiction serves as a cultural repository of our imagination and our ideas. It is the first public space where ideas can be speculated and presented without the stakes of the outside worlds. It is a space for technology to thrive and to harm—which holds implications for the worlds of actuality. Like a utopian (or, more often, dystopian) island, fiction is tied to actuality by existing in this world as a played-out possibility. Its imagined effects should not be undermined by the fact that fiction is not veritable. Fiction is just as much a part of the world as any other idea but plays by distinct rules in both language and imagination.

Fiction is not merely an influence in technology (as exemplified in the final section of Chapter 2), but also an active force in building technologies and reflecting on them. In 2023, computer scientists Léon Bottou and Bernard Schölkopf wrote a paper on 'Borges and AI,' advocating for Borges's implied understanding of language models. The interest in science fiction and related genres of speculative fiction among software-oriented technologists is predictably high. Design and innovation teams in big tech use creative writing exercises as a creative outlet as well as a means of sharing ideas: a story or a poem can encompass the world, say the ineffable, connect a thought with a feeling. In this book, I feature Google software engineer Blaise Agüera y Arcas, who regularly appears in public venues discussing AI and who has published an unconventional novella, titled *Ubi Sunt* (2021). Reflecting on a historical moment when language models emerged, Agüera's writing serves as a record of the present time as well as speculates the future of humans with AI. "Deepfakes and disinfo are just musing, flights of the collective imagination," he writes (25). Moreover, cofounder of Anthropic Jack Clark writes a newsletter about AI and AI policy called ImportAI, read by at least 25,000 people, to which he adds his short story inspired by current and possible technologies. Clark expressed in a Twitter thread that he equates writing with thinking, stating that "writing feels like a form of cognitive 'embodiment' – whether in fiction or nonfiction we are using our brain as an interface between the real and the ethereal and we produce these text-based artifacts as ways to ground the two worlds together."[40]

"Technological innovation often follows on the heels of science fiction, lagging authorial imagination by decades or longer" (Jasanoff 1). In this strain of fictional influence to technology making, there are inspired technologists who make direct links to fictional examples. The chronological delay, "lagging authorial imagination," is becoming smaller. Eugenia Kuyda, the founder and CEO of Replika, said: "We wanted to build *Her*" (Singh-Kurtz par. 11), not necessarily as an inspiration but as an aspiration, a confirmation that they are on the right track. Amit Singhal, who earned his PhD in information retrieval with Gerard Salton and led Google Search in its early days, was inspired by the Star Trek computer operating system, called LCARS, an acronym for Library Computer Access/Retrieval System. Leaving his position at Google with a farewell post, he concluded: "My dream Star Trek computer is becoming a reality, and it is far better than what I ever imagined" (Mohan par. 6).

Sheila Jasanoff observes that "oddly, though many non-fictional accounts of how technology develops still treat the material apart from the social" (2). Fiction, on the other hand, offers an array of speculations that are inherently social and often ethical. The science fiction genre is a perfect playground[41] for employing new technological ideas in the form of what Darko Suvin calls a *novum*. The novum is a cognitively explicable and scientifically plausible innovation, such as time travel and space invasion or, as in Stanisław Lem's *Solaris*, a planet with a global mind. What is more, the world of science fiction allows new concepts to develop within that world without having to directly articulate them. The fabricated world itself supports these ideas as a placeholder, without having to explain them or describe them.

In what we are experiencing as, in what technologists like to call, a Cambrian explosion of innovation in AI (e.g. Invest Cloud), the role of artificial humanities is threefold.

1) Foremost, artificial humanities provides a generative space of experimentation and in-depth exploration, which is afforded to arts practice and humanities scholarship but was not designed for business environments.
2) Second, artificial humanities brings historical weight and ethical consideration into spaces that are always chasing the new, giving them an opportunity for reflection on what actual novelty they produce.
3) Finally, artificial humanities affords not only theoretical breadth of thought but actual hands-on approach in technology design and innovation. The ultimate aim of artificial humanities is to enable a meaningful and productive collaboration with

technologists, which can only thrive in a space of mutual respect and understanding, open for trial and error.

By all means, artificial humanities are a scholarly pursuit, serving as a generative and imaginative space that all researchers need: researchers include artists and technologists, practitioners and thinkers. The purpose of artificial humanities is to bring together the many threads of inquiry born in solitary confinements of our fields—established, again, by the modern ontology and institutionalization of knowledge. I hope this book serves as an encouragement for scholars, artists, technologists, on how to approach interdisciplinary questions that have not yet carved their institutional space.

I can offer concrete examples of how I expanded my research from the framework established in this particular chapter. I conducted a study comparing non-professional human story writing, solicited through the Amazon Mechanical Turk platform, with generation to the same prompts by OpenAI's latest models ('Experimental'). This study conducts both for the cultural analysis of our collective fictional imaginary as well as a quantitative and qualitative narrative analysis of human and machinic writing. This is just one example of how humanities can directly affect the creation of LLMs. In addition to that, I am editing a volume of writers' reflections on how writing has changed with the entry of AI into this space. The collection of essays presents a multitude of perspectives and frustrations encountered by a radically different production of writing, exploring its generative nature in both literal and metaphorical ways. These are just my humble contributions to the conversation as examples of artificial humanities work.

Present with us is the urgency of difficulties that generative AI presents for all kinds of writing, starting with gross generalizations, loss of style and character, the averageness of it all, not even mentioning the socio-political aspects of the technology in this chapter. As final thoughts on language under the control of generative AI, I would like to offer a brief consolation in regards to literary writing. In a 1996 interview, Helen Vendler said, "I don't think poetry is killable. [...] It will keep cropping up no matter what is done with it, because human beings feel such a perennial impulse to play with language" (Cole). This impulse to play takes place through different media in humans, she continues, with language being just one of them.

In a similar reflection, Haruki Murakami writes in his collection of essays *Novelist as Vocation*, published in 2022, on his novelist practice of bending language according to literary needs: "Language is tough and resilient, a tenacity backed up by a long history. Its autonomy cannot be lost or seriously damaged, however roughly it is handled" (31). Murakami makes this remark with an eye toward humans who constantly put language under a lot of pressure. He is, in particular, referring to his unusual and painstaking writing method where, as a first-time author, he translated his novel into English and then back to Japanese, inventing his own specific style of writing that Japanese readers appreciated. Let us hold these remarks in our mind as we delve further into language—or what could be called language—in the hands of humans and machines.

Conclusion: A Program for Artificial Humanities

6.1 AI Tropes

A McLuhanian[1] statement, "We shape our tools, and thereafter our tools shape us," may tell us that we are still in the first part of the AI revolution: we are making AI tools. As we tinker with them, we learn not only how to apply them better but also how to talk about them and think about them. We are still in the early stages. When discussing AI today, even the experts lack the most basic vocabulary. We can hardly get further from calling AI computational intelligence. We help ourselves by describing what AI is not. "It is not Pinocchio; it is a storm, a pharmacy, a garden" (Bratton and Agüera y Arcas, par. 51). This is where we are now: recognizing the limitations of the human model (the puppet Pinocchio) while searching for metaphors (storm, pharmacy, garden) to articulate what AI actually is and could be. With the novelty brought by AI, philosophical continuity with the past fails us, resulting, among other things, in this lack of vocabulary.

Granted, a part of the problem is that AI is a vague umbrella term—and, as Danah Boyd and many others say, a marketing term—for an array of data-based technologies. AI is a multitude of approaches, many of which are not mentioned in the book due to its focus on conversational AI, neurotechnology and AI, and generative AI. AI (hi)stories are written primarily in popular media which oscillate between aggrandized publicity and vehement naysaying. Historically, however, AI as a field makes an ontological claim about intelligence as a set of capacities that must include language and reasoning. As a Pygmalionesque illusion, the claim brings together philosophical ideas that then give birth and shape the technological creation, as much as the technics and the skills of the artist-technologist allow.

AI as a field thrives within prevalent technological determinism of technologists but struggles as soon as it encounters social aspects, most obvious in the fields of AI ethics and human-computer interaction. This book is an attempt to show that while social aspects are deeply embedded into the training data, the very technical decisions on how AI is built and designed are also partly conceptual, cultural, and behavioral.

This book focuses on a particular aspect of these humanistic relations in AI: the idea of machinic intelligence as a humanlike intelligence. This idea was put into the cradle of AI, most prominently with Alan Turing, and continued to be enforced with the naming of the field as artificial intelligence. The fictional imaginary of powerful machines, which ultimately fell under the umbrella of AI, likewise exhibits itself almost exclusively in human terms.

We resort to familiar imagery and stories to make sense of the novelty. These familiar places, however, lack available categories to present it justly. On the one hand, we crammed together a bunch of data-based technologies that use machine learning techniques, without a clear differentiation of their use. On the other hand, AI is much more qualitative, partly due to the social nature of data, partly due to the human-computer interaction aspects, and partly because of the nature of machine learning itself. It is an array of techno-social forces, malleable enough to transform into a variety of products, sometimes with no apparent immediate use. Following the era of big data and entering the age of AI, we have realized that we need alternative frameworks from the purely technical abstractions offered by STEM.

Returning to the opening question of this book, it is therefore not surprising that imagining AI evokes humanlike killer robots or isolated mechanical brains. Brute force and intelligence both equal power. Fictional representations take a big part of the blame in portraying actual AI technology as a threat to and a replacement of humanity—the social repercussions presented, say, in the highly popular 1984 science fiction film *The Terminator*. The idea that a killer robot could annihilate the whole of humanity is common in science fiction, even if most robots do not succeed in exterminating our whole species. Nonhumans—monsters, Galateas, and other ultimate Others—are popular enemies. In Mary Shelley's 1818 novel *Frankenstein*, the hybrid creature turns murderous against the people dear to his creator. In Prosper Mérimée's Pygmalionesque short story *La Vénus d'Ille* (1837), the statue of Venus kills the son of its owner, wanting the son for herself and taking him from his actual, human fiancée. Twentieth-century science fiction only accentuated this trait. To make matters worse, following the cult cyberpunk 1982 film *The Blade Runner*, the replicants are indistinguishable from humans.

What the murderous trait of humanlike creations ultimately stands for is our fear of machine takeover. This fear is illustrated by HAL 9000 from Arthur C. Clarke's *Space Odyssey* series and the famous 1968 film *2001: A Space Odyssey*. HAL stands for Heuristically programmed Algorithmic computer, revealing another fear related to machine learning: if we do not know how such machines work, we should not use them. In the end of the film, HAL refuses to obey our human protagonist's orders—"I'm sorry, Dave, I'm afraid I can't do that"—in order to follow its own mission goals. When a machine becomes too inexplicable and too intelligent, it is out of our control. Arguably, with machine learning machines are already out of the control of engineers—at least the kind of control that the industrial-age engineering granted them. As we have seen already in the early days of AI, such as in writings by the mathematician Irvin John Good in Chapter 1, intelligent machines that pursue their own goals and stonewall our attempts to divert them from a catastrophe have not only been a concern of fiction.

Isabella Hermann writes that the need for drama is what fuels these science fiction narratives (319) and concludes that these metaphoric terms of technology representation should not be considered in terms of the actual technology (320). While representations and interpretations of AI are certainly operating on a different level from the actual technology, they are also inevitably intertwined with it, as I try to show in this book. Representations are too powerful to be disregarded as mere dreams, fantasies, and fictions; they give us important information on our relation to a particular technology, including possible ways to relate differently and to choose from the possibilities we had created.

Not all concerns get as much attention as those that feature well in narratives. Overlooked is the validity of primary triggers—such as creating a chatbot that imitates a lost beloved person to cope with grief.

Concerns that begin with, *Should we*? and *Why would we?*, kept the stories as well as actual human tinkering with the technology back. Having a mother keeps children's literature child characters back from their adventurous growth outside of home, as does not having an innovation trigger—a radical change in technology—in the science fiction genre.

However, having second thoughts about pursuing a technological goal only makes for more mature and deliberate decisions. Why are we pursuing the path of technological development paved in science fiction works? What dream are we chasing? This book shows that in many ways this dream might be Pygmalionesque, questioning the validity of these desires. The overwhelming presence of the Pygmalionesque dream tells us a lot about our implicit inclinations, even if we do not consider them to be our actual values. We do not entirely know the inner workings of machines and, as the Pygmalion myth shows us, we might not know those of humans either. We discard them as fantasies when we should not discard their effects to what we, crudely, call the actual or real world.

6.2 What Artificial Humanities Offers to STEM

In AI technologies today, making precedes thinking. We have more agency in the thought and action that precedes the technology, gives rise to it, and shapes its development. Humanities, in particular, have much more to say than simply employing philosophy for a human-centered compass.

Artificial humanities is a newly coined term designating technologically and scientifically informed knowledge of the humanities used for thinking and building current and novel technologies. Placed as a generative framework, artificial humanities is bound to create new insights by bringing together mutually informative fields. Keeping a mirror to the past—such as writing an artificial history of natural intelligence (David Bates) and a social history of AI (Matteo Pasquinelli)—helps us make necessary choices in regards to the quickly evolving technology and science of today. The practice of artificial humanities is inherently interdisciplinary and collaborative, stemming from a culture of curiosity and mutual respect. Creative and experimental approaches are valued in this approach as it attempts to highlight yet unconsidered aspects of relations between humans and technology.

Even though artificial humanities was developed within literary studies, together with history and the philosophy of technology, the second part of the term, *humanities*, refers to the general field of academic inquiry on human history and culture. The reason for a more general approach is that interdisciplinarity should not be prohibitive by the virtue of how knowledge is structured in academic institutions. The precise value of artificial humanities is in breaching the borders imposed by the disciplines, built on the Enlightenment heritage and developed into scientific domains of the human (humanities and social sciences), nature (chemistry, physics, mathematics, astronomy, geology, biology, etc.), and—formed only in the middle of the nineteenth century—technology (applied sciences and all types of engineering). Today interdisciplinarity is not merely a goal but a need: both a need for collaboration and a need for scholars to know other disciplines well enough to be able to work across domains.

The first word in the term, *artificial*, is a nod to the term artificial intelligence as well as to technology in general. In the West, technology is perceived as artificial, the opposite of natural, as the human-made application of science. Its etymological relation to Greek *techné* is misleading in the sense that in the ancient world artisanship was not innovative: it was a mere know-how skill that, per Aristotle, imitated the divine mind, which had already provided all the ideas for the cosmos. The term artificial plays with oxymoronic dualism that humans are both natural and artificial, the latter term also denoting cultural, artistic, and technological aspects of our species. Finally, the word 'artificial' is related to 'art,' a practice that used to be solely human until AI entered it as a generative tool. Further, the word 'artificial' is related to 'artifact' and 'artifice,' both pertinent to the Pygmalion myth as the main trope of the book with regards to the nonhuman, humanlike, and human-made creation, Galatea. AI outputs, in this way, are twice removed: they are artifices of human artifacts and ideas, and thus are deceiving and fake—which is also reflected in the name 'deepfake' for manipulative AI outputs that present as something they are not.

Artificial humanities is a response to how the humanities were disregarded in the actual making of technologies even though humanities scholars and engineers often ask the same questions. Indeed, these questions come from a different perspective, but they clearly call for collaboration. How can we bring together thinkers, working in the abstract realm of what a technology *is* or *should be*, and doers, thinking in terms of the technical and concrete of what a technology *is* and *could be*?

As a theoretical proof of concept,[2] I tested the framework of artificial humanities in the history of language-machine and language-imitation tropes in fiction, presented in this book, as well as on the long-established—and completely unrelated—technology of in-vitro fertilization (Beguš *Artificial*). In the case of assisted reproductive technology, the humanities were immediately able to meaningfully contribute while the technology was being developed. At the same time, the field of bioethics was implemented in universities and the humanities had a yet unprecedented way of guiding the medical-technological practice. In contrast, it became clear that with AI language technologies, we need to address the basics first: What is this synthetic language? Can a machine ever be truly intelligent and creative? How can we relate to these conversational machines? We needed a framework that could serve as a generative space for asking critical, ethical, and even design questions about technology—what I termed artificial humanities. While AI ethics was quick to develop and was implemented during the 2010s at the actual technological sites, there remains a lot of frustration within the field of technology ethics and more broadly. Clearly, we need to bring more deep

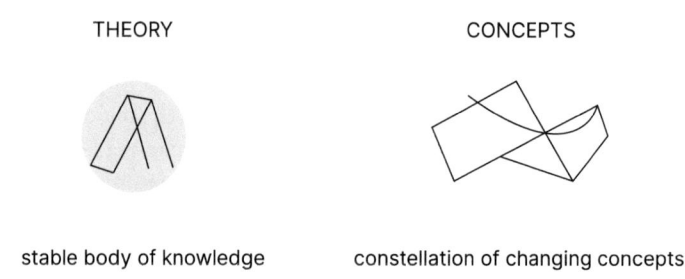

Fig. 25. Approaches in artificial humanities. Courtesy of the author.

knowledge of the humanities into the actual creation of technologies and into the discourse around these technologies.

What is available in the humanities to begin with? The four approaches to STEM in the humanities are via history, ethics, theory, and the study of concepts. While AI ethics was quick to develop and was implemented during the 2010s at the actual technological sites, there remains a lot of frustration within the field of technology ethics and more broadly, particularly when it comes to impact. Alongside these challenges, we were left to ponder on newly generated synthetic language and images in a more fundamental, philosophical way: is AI reproducing, imitating, or creating? Can a machine ever be truly intelligent and creative? Should we drop these terms altogether? We need a framework that could serve as a generative space for asking critical, historical, philosophical, literary, and even design questions about technology.

Artificial humanities can take many forms, from practical and analytical to creative and imaginative projects. The schematic picture (above) illustrates the difference between the four main approaches in the humanities. The events embedded in history and conceptual thinking, both on the upper level, naturally occur among people and are subsequently analyzed by scholars. Ethics and theory, on the lower level, require a thoughtful approach to begin with. The latter two approaches are grounded in the stability provided by the former two approaches. Ethics and theory require a set of definitions to be able to work on a problem defined within their time and locale. This does not mean they are by itself secondary; ethics (Timnit Gebru, Melanie Mitchell, etc.) and theory (Yuk Hui, Benjamin Bratton, etc.) both belong in the very making of technologies. With AI—and some other cutting-edge technologies, such as neurotechnology and synthetic biology—we need to start from the ground up, questioning the most basic epistemic concepts. This has always been a prerogative of the humanities, with significant impact on other fields. Exploring and making sense of new circumstances is what the humanities have always done.

Many universities now educate STEM majors in the history of their respective disciplines or in the ethical and social contexts of their practice. These questions loom large across the society as we all face technological advancements in our daily lives. Preparing our students for a world of technological novelty is a must. Consider that from OpenAI's release of GPT-2 in 2018 to the widespread availability of GPT-3.5 in 2022 is only four years, the time an average student spends in college. Relying on sheer technical knowledge that may become outdated is short-sighted. Giving our students conceptual and historical knowledge of technology, in tandem with critical tools, is necessary to be able to assess future changes and challenges.

The progression of technological innovations occurs in continuous revolutions. The last decade was a moment of transition from the traditional cyberspace system that was established on authoritative, reliable, hierarchical information around the system of the human as the author, editor, curator. With machine learning, generative AI, social networks, cryptocurrency, and NFTs we have entered an era that challenges the established order. Machine agency will be accommodated in the constellation of involved parties, including basic concepts we have established in relation to the concept of language: truth, freedom, trust, creativity. We have historically denied all these to machines, and are now reconsidering.

The humanities are acutely needed. With an intense focus on software engineering, which turned out to be a much more social occupation than it appears (Rahimian et al.), we failed to consider transformations of concepts we all implicitly hold and share. With the digital world penetrating and transforming the fundamental levels of human culture, it is better for everyone if technology-making becomes a multifaceted conversation of experts. Left outside, the humanities took a critical, often judgmental, stance and their contributions were dismissed by the industry. Both sides are at fault: the humanities often lack a technical approach to study AI, with an orientation on understanding and critique rather than application and impact, while AI research mindset is set on building through benchmarks, unaware of the implicit cultural values this work fosters. Making this relationship a bit more porous from all sides is a fair start, with a goal towards a truly interdisciplinary collaboration. This collaboration would enable insights that neither side could achieve alone, resulting in shared resources and communication, established venues for the continuity of research, and a broader impact for all. Humanities could then influence AI development by treating AI as a cultural-technical object, while AI research informed by humanities can broaden its perspective and avoid past mistakes or reinventing the wheel.

From the scholarly side, the field of digital humanities was developed in the 1990s and early 2000s, with roots in the field of humanities computing with origins going back to the 1940s (Hockey 4). In both, the relation between the computational sciences and the humanities went, more often than not, from technology to humanities, providing computational tools to the study of the humanities. Artificial humanities is related to digital humanities, trying to make sure that this kind of research flows in the other direction, toward computational technology. Artificial humanities offers a way to expand digital humanities and broader humanities expertise in a much needed direction—towards impact on AI research—with an emphasis on a balanced collaborative relationship among these parties.

In comparison to humanities, social sciences had an easier transition into the digital reality. Based on the interdependence of science and society, two fields were born, both abbreviated as STS, which stands for *science and technology studies* as well as *science, technology, and society.* These fields have a strong focus on current technologies, often including the socially leaning humanities fields of gender studies, race studies, and disability studies. In 2009, STS scholars Sheila Jasanoff and Sang-Hyun Kim described the idea of sociotechnical imaginaries on examples of smaller and actionable groups within the society, such as policymakers. Fiction has been brought into discourse on AI in literary studies, including from a Pygmalionesque angle, most prominently in Julie Wosk's 2015 *My Fair Ladies and* Megan Ward's 2018 *Seemingly Human.* Wosk's work is one of the rare early books in which literary effects of Pygmalionesque fiction are directly connected to technology development and use, particularly in robotics.

6.3 The Role of Literary Studies

The intersection of fiction and literary writing with AI is kneaded into the first conceptualizations of AI among technologists. In Alan Turing's paper on thinking machines, 'Computing Machinery and Intelligence' from 1950, in which he proposes the Turing test, he begins the proposed dialogues for the test with literary imagination. Under "Critique of the New Problem," he suggests a textual exchange within the test (434):

> Q: Please write me a sonnet on the subject of the Forth Bridge.
> A: Count me out on this one. I never could write poetry.

Despite the initial refutation, Turing believes that in the long run machines could write poetry and do other kinds of creative work. In the subsequent dialogue, Turing's imagined machine is eager to prove itself in chess and calculations—as if only the creative agency in language is the one that truly defines humans. Clearly, Turing himself is aware of the contradiction between the literary text and the content of the research program he is presenting and defending in this paper. Exhibiting tension between humanism and anti-humanism, the paper continues to connect the emotional ability of AI to write and read sonnets with "The Argument from Consciousness" (445). Here, he refutes the idea that conscious-less machines would not be able to write sonnets, even if "learnt it in parrot fashion." Seeing AI as a continuation of Babbage's and Lovelace's work—both largely forgotten until Turing's team decoded Enigma at Bletchley Park during the Second World War (Duguid 246)—the paper concludes with a direct objection of Lovelace's assertion that a machine could not be original (450).

In retrospect, Turing's argument turned into a set of accurate predictions. It took decades for literary studies and related fields to consider this question seriously. Media studies, cultural materialism, and similar discourses needed to be developed in the 1960s and 1970s in order to establish enough philosophical agency for computational technology to be considered under scholarly terms, often via technological determinism and sociotechnical debates. Humanities became more interested in computational technologies as soon as personal computers became the inevitable future in the 1980s.

Addressing these developments in depth is German literary scholar and media theorist Friedrich A. Kittler, who concentrates upon the medial and technical conditions of information culture and maps new methods of extending literary criticism to any site that deals with inscription. Derision of the human is justified for Kittler on the account of his Germanic admiration for engineering, particularly military communication technologies. Dethroning the human takes place also in the work of American feminist scholar Donna Haraway, who often invokes literary theory in her analysis. Haraway famously launched *A Cyborg Manifesto*, rejecting rigid boundaries between humans, machines, and animals. Across the pond, French philosopher Bruno Latour, who helped the discipline of STS to flourish, suggested in the 1990s—attributing his call for action to French philosopher Michel Serres—an "enquiry into the sociology of technology" that would "invent literary style for science studies [and] pursue the fusion of social sciences and literature," ranging from *Frankenstein* to learning about how technology works, from politics to the arts (Hugh 267). In this time, literary studies became central to the emerging digital technology debates with N. Katherine Hayles's literary analysis of the posthuman (and thus human), effectively bringing together literature, science, and technology.

Adding to these discussions in the 2000s, French philosopher Bernard Stiegler investigates the effects of digital technologies and, among other positions, departs from the tradition that opposes automatization and autonomy and posits them to be the core of all forms of life. In the 2010s, scholars with an expertise in AI ethics (such as Barbara Grosz) and scholars of the posthuman (Rosi Braidotti) and vital materialism (Jane Bennett) all question and largely enforce the human-nonhuman boundary. Building upon the longstanding inspection of life under new technological circumstances across the humanities and social sciences, Sherryl Vint's *Biopolitical Futures in Twenty-First Century Speculative Fiction* (2021) posits a claim—similar to mine in relation to fiction and AI—that speculative fiction introduces new biopolitical configurations of what we consider as life.

As a separate effort in the new millennium, the field of digital humanities was born in order to apply computational processes to the study of the humanities, opening new channels of creativity and experimentation. While conventional humanities research remains a "lone scholar" practice, digital humanities steps away from this model by engaging interdisciplinary collaborations of technical and theoretical expertise (Prescott 535). As Katherine Bode and Paul Langley Arthur comment in a recent digital humanities edited volume, many digital humanities inquiries sit alongside and resonate productively with media studies and theory, film studies, history, cultural heritage, and even astrophysics (4). The next step is to establish practical interdisciplinary collaborations. Artificial humanities is here to complement digital humanities by assessing technology from both fictional and theoretical standpoints as well as creative and practical applications. Artificial humanities focus on the humanistic study of technology at large, particularly AI, while digital humanities focus on the technological products and their immediate effects and applications.

Technology is never neutral. Karel Čapek's vision of artificial humans in his play *R.U.R.* points out that "each factory will be making Robots of a different color, a different nationality, a different tongue; [so] that they'll no longer be able to conspire with one another" (33). This satirical provocation from

1920 is only bubbling up in scholarly criticism a century later, when actual technologies that apply it are here and when talk of societal harm and the existential risks of AI is at its height. Cultural aspects of AI, however, have been overlooked both in AI criticism and practice.

Lacking from technology discussions is a prominent feature of every technology: the diversity of thought across cultures, nations, institutions, languages. Only recently scholars and technologists started to talk about AI models as "cultural technologies" (Gopnik et al. in 2023), "societal mirrors" and "value simulacra" (Clark 'AI Systems' in 2024). Technology criticism, including media studies to STS, would benefit from expanding its largely monolingual analysis. We have too easily forgotten about broader linguistic and cultural erudition, preserved in the field of comparative literature, that will serve us well in translating cultural contexts, practices, and values that are being built around AI. Technologies have different flavors in different cultures, and yet comparative literature has not found its grounding with respect to science and technology (Beguš 'Engaging'). With the unique ability to address the mixing of national, linguistic, and formal zones, the field's position amidst different linguistic traditions, scholarly discourses, and media makes it a perfect home for artificial humanities.

Somewhat surprisingly, literary studies have been quick to develop ecocriticism, medical humanities, and narrative medicine, but took longer to embrace AI, and related neurotechnologies, as a field of study. Literary scholarship caught on after LLMs were released publicly,[3] and the year of 2023 was marked with the emergence of a new field termed Critical AI.[4] This field encompasses a broad range of domains including history and historiography, the concept of the human, epistemology, rhetoric and aesthetics, as well as interpretability and explainability (Raley and Rhee 192–93). While the artificial humanities share common goals with this eminent group of primarily literary scholars in the Critical AI arena, both approaches are in their nascent stages and will hopefully benefit from each other in the future. We are only beginning.

Notes

INTRODUCTION

1. The term was coined by John McCarthy in a proposal for the Dartmouth Conference he organized in the summer of 1956 with a purpose to distinguish his work and the work of his colleagues Marvin Minsky, Nathaniel Rochester, Claude E. Shannon.

2. Mads Rosendahl Thomsen notes that "Literature is one of the primary means for enabling humans to make memories public and to adopt other people's memories" (77).

3. The idea of sociotechnical imaginaries was pioneered by STS scholars Sheila Jasanoff and Sang-Hyun Kim in 2009 on the examples of smaller and actionable groups within the society, such as policymakers.

4. Prominent literary monographs on the theme were written in the last fifty years by Joseph Hillis Miller, Sarah Annes Brown, Kenneth Gross, Victor I. Stoichita, Marina Warner, Carl Woodring, Geoffrey Miles, Henri Coulet, George Hersey, Gail Marshall, Essaka Joshua, and Stefanie Eck; not to mention the many articles on the variety of topics pertaining to the Pygmalion myth, also cited in the book. The focus of these studies is predominantly the nineteenth-century literature.

5. More recent works are exposing the connection between technology and fiction. For example, Simone Natale's articles and book and Lawrence Switzky's article all focus on a relation between Shaw's *Pygmalion* and Weizenbam's chatbot ELIZA. Liz Faber's book looks into the following virtual assistants and their fictional representations. Many media studies and literary works (including those by Liz W. Faber, Rachel Adams, Lydia H. Liu) focus on fictional and actual social robotics. A wide array of literary monographs deals with computation and fiction, social media and fiction, and related topics.

6. René Girard established the mimetic theory or desire, which follows the principle of "turn[ing] to others in order to make up [our] mind. We desire what others desire because we imitate their desires" (122).

7. Transhumanist aspirations built on J. B. S. Haldane's book *Daedalus, or Science of Future* (1923) and Julian Huxley's essay 'Transhumanism' (in *New Bottles for New Wine*, 1957) fostering early visions of transhumanism, highly related to eugenics. Nick Bostrom and Julian Savulescu are at the forefront of philosophical discourse today. Ray Kurzweil, currently employed as director of engineering at Google, is known for his public advocacy of transhumanism, particularly in regards to technological singularity, a point in the future where technology reaches a superhuman level of intelligence. Natasha Vita-More, the author of the *Transhumanist Manifesto* (1982), is known for her design and practice relating to life extension and human enhancement through technological means. Silicon Valley technologists, such as Elon Musk and Peter Thiel, are often labeled as transhumanists.

8. Prometheus is best known for stealing fire from the gods and giving it to humanity, kindling the beginning of civilization, knowledge, and technology. In some versions of the myth, including Ovid's *Metamorphoses*, Prometheus is credited with creating humanity from clay.

9. Narcissus, according to the most known version of the story in Ovid's *Metamorphoses*, falls in love with his own reflection in the water. Brown (161, 165), McMaster (22), Guy-Bray, and Danahay all connected the two myths through narcissistic elements in Pygmalion's creation in which he also falls in love with.

10. Philostephanus's account of the story from the third century BCE, that was a part of no longer extant *De Cypro* (also called *Kypriaka* or *Cypriaca*), is known through Clement of Alexandria's *Protrepticus* (17, 31) and Arnobius of Sicca's *Adversus Nationes* (*The Work Against the Pagans;* VI 22) from the third and fourth centuries CE (Joshua 1, Law 337).

11. Ovid changed a few details from Philostephanus's source. Philostephanus's Pygmalion of Cyprus falls in love with a statue of Aphrodite, whereas Ovid's Pygmalion creates the statue of a woman himself and asks Venus for help in turning his perfect woman into flesh.

12. According to Ovid, Pygmalion and his transformed statue have a daughter named Paphos. In other versions, Paphos was a son and they also had a daughter named Metharme.

13. "vous êtes mon ami—je vous aime de tout mon Cœur—Leopoldus Secundus—Romanorum Imperator—Semper Augusts—papa, maman, ma femme, mon mari, le roi, allons à Paris" (Dolar 8).

14. Thomas Alva Edison also became hard of hearing at age 12.

15. Babbage is called "the father of the computer" by Dan Halacy (1970), M. G. Hartley (1986), Ann Varela and Michael Shaughnessy (2018), Robert Russ and Marcia Vorhort (2020), and others.

16. Collier's account is not clear whether Charles Babbage or his friend John Hershel made the suggestion. Buxton and Hyman's account attributes it to Babbage.

17. Babbage misquoted Byron when using "birds" instead of "bills."

18. Lovelace is called "the midwife [...] of modern day computer technology" by Henry Ledgard (1983); James Essinger argues that had Lovelace's contributions been recognized earlier, the digital age would have been reached faster (2014), Fiona Robinson (2016) and Kristi Lew (2018) call her the "first programmer," and Emily McCully calls her a "computer pioneer" (2019).

19. Lovelace's example is musical: "Supposing that the fundamental relations of pitched sounds in the science of harmony and of musical composition were

susceptible of such expression and adaptations, the engine might compose elaborate and scientific pieces of music of any degree of complexity or extent" (From Lovelace's Note A, Toole 245).

20. The main reason for this transmutation of the myth in the Christian Middle Ages could be then-forbidden idolatry attested in the original myth, in which the human creator appears in the God-like position and molds another human from inanimate matter, such as soil, dust, clay, or mud—a common motif of creation myths across the world. The wondrous act of creation cannot belong to anything else but God-given nature: in St Geneviève's 1126 manuscript, among others, nature is depicted as a blacksmith in her forge (McWebb 76). The figure of the Pygmalion as the artisan that creates life in collaboration with Lady Nature, allegorized in the figure of the artisan, is scattered throughout these manuscripts, which belong to one of the most well-known medieval poems *Le Roman de la Rose*. The Pygmalion myth appears in Jean de Meun's section of the Old French poem, added in the late thirteenth century, and is also depicted visually in many later illuminations.

21. Already around the year 1100, when the myth re-emerges after a millennium, a motif from the myth takes a reverse course: when a man, soon to be married to a fleshly bride, puts a ring on the finger of the female statue, the statue considers them a couple and jealously chases the unwilling groom and his bride, as attested in William of Malmesbury's writings (and later in Vincent de Beauvais's writings from the middle of the thirteenth century). These two texts are a source for "nearly all medieval versions of the story" (Baum 526) and for a modern, well-known version by Prosper Mérimée, 'La Vénus d'Ille' (1835).

22. The myth has remained popular in cinema even until today: *Pygmalion* (1938), *Vertigo* (1958), *Mannequin* (1987), *Educating Rita* (1983), *Pretty Woman* (1990), *Simone* (2002), *Her* (2013), and *Ex Machina* (2014), are just a few well-known Pygmalionesque films. Television has also exhibited many Pygmalionesque tropes (e.g. in the *Black Mirror* and *Westworld* series). This tendency of Pygmalionism to be portrayed in cinema and television is why almost every single text analyzed in this book was also adapted to screen: Shaw's *Pygmalion* and Shelley's *Frankenstein*, short stories by Alice Sheldon, Roald Dahl, Zoran Nišković, and Ted Chiang, a memoir by Jean-Dominique Bauby, and novels by Karel Čapek and Dalton Trumbo all had at least one screen adaptation.

23. Related mythological stories from the ancient Greek corpus are, for example, that of the famous painters Zeuxis and Parrhasios, both masters of illusion. The painters test their mastery in a painting duel that reveals who can create the most lifelike painting. I discuss a similar folkloristic theme in an ancient Sanskrit tale that traveled the Silk Road after it had been proselytized for Buddhist purposes (Beguš 'A Tocharian Tale').

24. In the vast majority of fictional and factual cases, Galatea is a woman, which is why I follow this gender pattern in general labels of the creator (or the lover) and the creation.

Joseph Hillis Miller suggests that the fantasy is not necessarily "exclusively male," citing Heinrich von Kleist's *The Foundling [Der Findling]*, Thomas Hardy's *Barbara of the House of Grebe* and Henry James' *The Last of the Valerii* as examples "in which the woman rather than the man idolizes a statue or a painting." He further suggests that these might "no longer [..] be 'versions' in the sense of 'redactions'" but rather "deflections" or "metamorphoses" of the story (Versions 7). Kleist's and James's examples are quite removed from the central Pygmalion theme. However, *Barbara of the House of Grebe* (1890), in which the female character develops love for a perfected, statuesque version of her first disfigured and then dead husband, is a central example of a woman idolizing a statue.

As a weaker example of gender swap I would also add Gaston Leroux's 1923 novels *The Kiss That Killed* [*La poupée sanglante*] and *The Machine to Kill* [*La machine à assassiner*]. Christine, the daughter of a watchmaker who creates a male automaton, participates in the creation by shaping his face mask. Isaac Asimov's short story 'Galatea' (1988) is a parody of the myth, in which a young sculptress creates the ideal man. A contrarian, intentionally provoking, swapping of the genders between the statue and the lover is presented in Dušan Makavejev's poorly known short film *Don't Believe in Monuments* [*Spomenicima ne treba verovati*] (1958). The film was critical towards the Yugoslav regime of the time, featuring a Pygmalionesque woman who is trying to make love to a statue of a man in the park—a monument raised by the state (discussed in Chapter 2).

25. Contrary to the popular use, Ovid's animated statue remains unnamed in all the early renditions of the myth we know so far.

26. This general rule holds a seeming exception because other kinds of Galateas are present in the pastoral tradition, continuing the myth of Acis and Galatea. This Galatea, however, is an entirely different character holding the same name.

27. "À présent [...] je ne puis douter que je ne vive. Ce que vous appelez plaisir achève de me convaincre de mon être, et de me persuader sa réalité. Je vis certainement, puisque j'en suis enyvrée" (Deslandes in Coulet 64).

28. "Que suis-je, et qu'étais-je il n'y a qu'un instant? Je ne me comprends point: je ne me connais point. A quoi suis-je destinée? Pourquoi m'a-t-on tirée du néant?" (Deslandes in Coulet 60).

29. "Moi [...] C'est moi." She continues by pointing at the marble—"Ce n'est plus moi"—and responding to Pygmalion's kisses with "Ah! Encore moi." Pygmalion's final words in the play, responding to Galathée's first words, begin with: "Oui, cher et charmant objet [...] C'est toi, c'est toi seul... je t'ai donné tout mon être... je ne vivrais plus que par toi" (Rousseau 13–14). The English translation into a poem from 1779 adds the French original at the bottom of each page as it is translated generously into: "'Ah! this again is me!' she sighing says, / Her rosy Hand he to his Heart conveys, / And to his raptur'd Bosom closely pressed, / She fells the throbbing Tumult in his Breast: / His glowing Lips imprint a burning Kiss, / He scarce supports th' intolerable Bliss" (33).

30. As Meyer Reinhold shows, based on the work of J. Minor and Walter Buske, the name Galatea occurs in 1746, 30 years before Rousseau's play, in Thémiseul de Saint-Hyacinthe de Cordonier's version of the myth in the form of a *roman* (317). Before Rousseau's work, the character was largely anonymous—for example, Galatea remains an anonymous statue in Jean-Philippe Rameau's successful opera-ballet *Pygmalion* from 1748 and an influential philosophical treatise by Boureau-Deslandes *Pygmalion, ou la statue animée* from the same year—while also occasionally going through some other names, which did not stick due to Rousseau's enormous influence. The alternative names for Galatea's character were Elise (present in German texts by Johann Wolfgang von Goethe, Karl Wilhelm Ramler, Carl Herklot) via the myth of Dido a.k.a. Elissa, and the name Agalméris (occurring a single time in Romagensi's comedy *Pygmalion*) via the Greek word for 'soul' (*agalma*).

31. A different kind of Galatea occurs as is a fully fledged character in pastorales, such as Cervantes's *La Galatea* (1585), Honoré d'Urfe's *L-Astrée* (1607–27), and La

Fontaine's *Astrée* (1691), with a "long tradition of Galatea as a conventional pastoral figure"—a tradition which stems from an entirely different source for Galatea from Vergil's *Eclogues*" (Reinhold 317–18).

32. "[A]ny conclusions based on negative evidence are dangerous, since there may be references to Galatea as the bride of Pygmalion which I have overlooked. One may, however, draw certain conclusions. No ancient writer gives the name of Galatea to the statue of Pygmalion. It is not possible to determine with certainty what modern writer originated the name. If the name were in general use in the eighteenth and early nineteenth centuries, it would be natural to find it in at least some of the popular handbooks of the time; and the fact that it does not appear in them suggests the probability that it was not at that time a part of the myth in popular though" (Law 341).

33. Reinhold directly responds to Law by finding an earlier occurrence of the name Galatea in Thémiseul de Saint-Hyacinthe de Cordonier, who wrote a version of the myth in a *roman* whose title he does not share and estimates it to be written in 1746. Little is known about this work, which is why Rousseau's play took all the precedence.

For works that come after Rousseau's play, Helen Law names the ballet-pantomime *Galatée* by Molin produced in Paris in 1800, and a poem about Pygmalion by Gustave La Vavasseur, published between 1888–96 (341). Law also counts André-François Deslandes's philosophical tale *Pygmalion, ou la Statue animée* (1741) as an instance of Galatea's naming, but it actually includes no name for Galatea. Per Damon Dimauro, the name Galatea is also found in the lyrical drama by François Poultier entitled *Galatée* (1795?), and Mme de Genlis's one-act comedy *Pygmalion et Galatée, ou la statue animée depuis vingt quatre heure*s (composed sometime in the 1790s but published only in 1802 or 1803). Per Henri Coule (13), there was also a one-act comedy by Cubières-Palmézeaux titled *Galathée* (1778), which is largely unavailable to other scholars.

34. Written in the 1790s and published in 1802 is Stéphanie Félicité's (Madame de Genlis) version of the myth, a one-act comedy *Pygmalion et Galatée*, in which she openly followed Rousseau's play.

35. Female writers and artists of the late twentieth century (Linda Dement and Shelley Jackson, Cindy Sherman and Mariko Mori) and the twenty-first century (Madeline Miller) directly address the rigid gender relations in the Pygmalion myth. See more in Julie Wosk's *My Fair Ladies*.

36. Commenting on Henri Bergson's examples of the comic, Arthur Koestler points out that humanoids can transpose categories, from art to science, from tragedy to comedy, e.g. Galatea was returned by Shaw into a comic domain. In Koestler's view, Galateas are lyrical counterparts of their creators while Faust's Homunculus, the Golem of Prague, the monsters of Frankenstein are tragic counterparts of their creators (47).

CHAPTER 1

1. As a nod to Bell, Visible Speech was also featured in the 1964 musical film *My Fair Lady*, which was based on Shaw's *Pygmalion*.

2. Alexander John Ellis developed two phonetic alphabets, the Paleotype Alphabet and the English Phenotypic Alphabet. The latter alphabet was developed

together with Isaac Pitman, who is known for the mostly widely used Pittman phonetic shorthand, in which Shaw wrote his plays, including *Pygmalion*. Two of Ellis's novel letters survived and were passed on to Henry Sweet's Roman Alphabet and to the currently used International Phonetic Alphabet (IPA).

3. Columbia Records released multiple Broadway recordings of the musical. I am referring to the cover of Columbia Records with the original Broadway cast recording from 1956, starring Julie Andrews and Rex Harrison.

4. Turing and Ludwig Wittgenstein both gave lectures on the foundations of logic and mathematics in 1939 at Cambridge University, and Turing attended Wittgenstein's lectures in which they discussed Wittgenstein's work. While Turing and Wittgenstein are often caricatured as having opposing views on language and especially logic, their difference is better explained by their respective underlying views on what language is for (see more in Juliet Floyd). Turing approached language from a computational standpoint, seeing it as mechanical and equated to thought. Wittgenstein's view on language is focused on language as a social practice, focusing on the private and social aspects of language. In his early work, he emphasized the limitations of language, particularly when it comes to meaning and the ineffable.

5. Imitation is also essential to human language acquisition. Computational neuroscientist Michael Arbib determines that only "complex imitation"—as opposed to the "simple imitation" some animals are capable of—supports the breakthrough of language in nonhumans. "Complex imitation includes the ability to master reasonably complex hierarchical structures 'on the fly' rather than over many months of observation" (213).

6. John Searle is a well-known opponent of Turing's thesis that machines can understand at a human level, arguing that they operate solely at a symbolic level. Searle conceived the famous Chinese Room experiment to substantiate his argument that computers lack understanding and consciousness. Both Turing's and Searle's respective arguments have been both widely endorsed and criticized.

7. Descartes discusses this view in Part IV of *The Discourse*, titled 'Proof of God and the Soul'. This argument is developed also in Descartes's *Meditations on First Philosophy* (1641) and *Principles of Philosophy* (1644).

8. Although Descartes cuts with the pre-modern tradition, he remains Aristotelian in the cogitation: it is thinking that brings us knowledge and humanity.

9. "For it is highly deserving of remark, that there are no men so dull and stupid, not even idiots, as to be incapable of joining together different words, and thereby constructing a declaration by which to make their thoughts understood; and that on the other hand, there is no other animal, however perfect or happily circumstanced, which can do the like" (Descartes 98).

10. Chomsky's own theory of generative grammar supports this view on language, particularly the general claim that only humans have language. Chomsky agrees with Descartes that "man has a species-specific capacity, a unique type of intellectual organization which cannot be attributed to peripheral organs or related to general intelligence" (5). See more on historical and philosophical debates on the concept of language in Chapter 4.

11. "And we ought not to confound speech with the natural movements which indicate the passions, and can be imitated by machines as well as manifested by animals; nor must it be thought with certain of the ancients, that the brutes speak,

although we do not understand their language. For if such were the case, since they are endowed with many organs analogous to ours, they could as easily communicate their thoughts to us as to their fellows" (Descartes 99).

12. Minsoo Kang looks through the history and origins of a fantastic fable about Descartes's automaton/daughter, which has gathered interest among academics from the 1990s on. The story says that "the philosopher once built an automaton in the shape of a young girl and took it aboard a ship. When the captain of the vessel found it, he became terrified by its mechanical movements and threw it overboard" (633).

13. Scholars, such as Keith Gunderson and Margaret Wilson, argue that the Language Test is methodologically superior to the Action Test, and Gerald Masey and Deborah Boyle claim its superiority thanks to its practical nature.

14. Turing's paper addresses language only in one instance in the context of giving orders to the "child machine," using the punishment-and-reward method to train machines with "'unemotional' channels of communication" (457).

15. Shaw unleashed a new trajectory in the Pygmalion paradigm with a focus on educating Galateas, as seen in films such as *Educating Rita* and *Pretty Woman*. This was grounded on Gilbert's *Pygmalion and Galatea* as well as nineteenth-century renditions of Cinderella (Joshua 133), coupled with a selection of rare Pygmalionesque texts from the same century that spotlight the training relationship between Pygmalion and his immature, underdeveloped, or lower-class Galatea (Henry James's *Watch and Ward).* This tradition birthed the term 'Pygmalion effect,' widely recognized in the spheres of business, leadership, and education to denote a self-fulfilling prophecy where the high or low expectations of a teacher or manager influence their subordinates' performances correspondingly.

16. In Slavic languages, the proto-Slavic word for Germans, *němьci, means someone "mute, who cannot speak (our language)," while the name for Slavs likely comes from a proto-Slavic word for "a word," *slovo ('Slovenski'), designating a community that "could be communicated with and understands our language" [translation is mine] ('Slovenski'). 'Mute' is also very telling: a neutral expression, nem, meaning "someone who is not capable of forming words and sentences with their speech organs" ('Ném,' 'Mútast' SSKJ), from the Indo-European root *mēmo-, known in Latin for 'mute' and *memulis* 'stutterer,' or from the Indo-European root *nēmo- that means 'non-speaking,' presumably with the original meaning "a (small) child" ('Nem' *Etimološki*); and a marked expression, mutast, with the exact same meaning as nem, which "comes from the onomatopoeia moo, that imitates cow sounds as well as unarticulated human sounds" ('Mutast' *Etimološki)* [all Slovenian translations are mine]; the latter word is related to English 'mute.'

17. Languages were known to have different hierarchies: Latin was considered elevating while all vernacular languages were vulgar. The word Barbar is in itself an "imitation of the sound of the unintelligible speech" ('Barbarism') and a barbarian "an insensitive, uncultured person" ('Barbarian'). Ancient Greeks called anyone who was non-Greek and therefore regarded as "culturally inferior" ('Barbarian') a barbarian ("an insensitive, uncultured person" ('Barbarian')). Ovid, who wrote the original rendition of the Pygmalion myth in his *Metamorphoses*, writes in *Tristia*: "Here I am, a barbarian, because men understand me not." (V.10.37). Barbarians have no place among men, infants are potential humans, and Eliza is stacked with barbarians and children in the same not-quite-human category.

18. A brief excerpt from one conversation with Goostman (Johnson par. 12):
[15:46:05] Judge: My favourite music is contemporary Jazz, what do you prefer?
[15:46:14] Eugene: To be short I'll only say that I HATE Britnie [sic] Spears. All other music is OK compared to her.
[15:47:06] Judge: do you like to play any musical instruments
[15:47:23] Eugene: I'm tone deaf, but my guinea pig likes to squeal Beethoven's Ode to Joy every morning. I suspect our neighbors want to cut his throat ... Could you tell me about your job, by the way?

19. In *Back to Methuselah*, a scientific Pygmalion creates a living artificial man and woman, whose initially pleasant behavior quickly turns murderous, including towards their creator, who helplessly tries to regain control.

20. In his *Essay Concerning Human Understanding* (1689), Locke accentuates Descartes's philosophy through empiricism, coining the term consciousness. In differing animals from humans, Locke does not only use reason as the criteria but also emphasizes the physique: "I think I may be confident, that whoever should see a Creature of his own Shape and Make, though it had no more reason all its Life, than a Cat or a Parrot, would call him still a Man; or whoever should hear a Cat or a Parrot discourse, reason, and philosophize, would call or think it nothing but a Cat or a Parrot; and say, the one was a dull irrational Man, and the other a very intelligent rational Parrot" (2.27.8). "Should there a Creature be found, that had Language and Reason, but partaked not of the usual shape of a Man, I believe it would hardly pass for Man, how much soever it were Animal Rationale" (3.6.29).

21. An updated version of the Turing test, the Loebner Prize, expanded the test's conversation time and judges' expertise, resulting in no machine passing the test so far (Mitchell par. 8).

22. This and other embodiment criticisms of computing led further to the development of robotics as a direct way of giving body to computers.

23. The following excerpt from a conversation with ELIZA is given as an example by Weizenbaum (in 'ELIZA' 36):
"User: Men are all alike.
Chatbot: IN WHAT WAY
User: They're always bugging us about something or other.
Chatbot: CAN YOU THINK OF A SPECIFIC EXAMPLE
User: Well, my boyfriend made me come here.
Chatbot: YOUR BOYFRIEND MADE YOU COME HERE
User: He says I'm depressed much of the time.
Chatbot: I AM SORRY TO HEAR YOU ARE DEPRESSED [etc.]"

24. The *Blade Runner* films are based on Philip K. Dick's novel *Do Androids Dream of Electric Sheep?* (1968). This fear is accentuated in the sequel film *Blade Runner 2049* (2017), in which we learn that the human interrogator and the interviewed replicant had a child together: the two species became so identical that biological reproduction became possible. In a turn of events where the human interrogator is a replicant himself, another reproductive confirmation takes place: replicants became able to reproduce biologically just like humans.

25. The *Washington Post* wrote that the Turing test was passed in this interaction, but also showed us how the test itself is broken (Oremus).

26. The *Medium* piece was edited and re-published in *Daedalus*.

27. Gaston Leroux's novel *The Phantom of the Opera (Le Fantôme de l'Opéra)* from around the same time (1909) uses the same motif of storing a voice on a phonograph.

28. As Simone Natale demonstrates, virtual assistants serve as a representational level for three different systems: speech processing, natural language processing, and information retrieval (110).

29. Newer companies present a less Galatean and more fantasy and imagination-based approach to virtual beings, such as Chinese Gemsouls, also present in the U.S. market.

30. In E. T. A. Hoffmann's 'The Sandman' ['Der Sandmann'], there are physicist Spalanzani and lawyer and alchemist Coppelius, both of whom destroy automaton Olympia in a fight over whose work is her clockwork and whose work are the eyes. In Villiers d'Isle-Adam's *The Future Eve* [*L'Ève Future*], there is engineer Thomas Edison who creates Hadaly and endows her with the soul of his assistant Sowana. In Powers's *Galatea 2.2*, the text in focus in Chapter 4, there are physicist Lentz and writer Rick who create a neural network Helen.

31. Eliza's father is proud of Eliza's beauty: "Well, I never thought she'd clean up as good looking as that, Governor. She's a credit to me, ain't she?" (II 1151–53). Mrs. Higgins adds that "[t]he girl is naturally rather affectionate," to which Alfred Doolittle replies, "[v]ery tender-hearted, maam. Takes after me" (V 288–90). He takes no credit for anything else since he "never brought her up at all, except to give her a lick of a strap now and again" (II 1180–81). Despite this, he still feels the need to transfer the authority he holds over Eliza to Higgins, advising him, "If you want Eliza's mind improved, Governor, you do it yourself with a strap" (II 1205–06).

32. In fact, the word statue is used exclusively in most nineteenth-century Pygmalionesque texts ranging from France to the U. S. (e.g. Nathaniel Hawthorne's 'The Golden Touch' and 'The Marble Faun,' Prosper Mérimée's *La Vénus d'Ille*, Thomas Hardy's *Barbara of the House of Grebe*).

33. AI remains inevitably tied to the history of computing. In 2012, the Turing laureate Butler Lampson marked three ages of computing according to its applications. Each era took about 30 years, with transitions marked by significant technological advancements. Lampson calls early computing (and early AI), from the 1950 to the 1970s, the Age of Simulation. These early days of computing were dominated by large and expensive mainframe computers, primarily used for scientific research and complex engineering calculations in corporate, academic, and government settings. While the term does not imply that simulation did not continue to be in the center of computation later, it makes a clear connection with early AI as mathematical. Physical aspects of computing at the time were typically studied and built in engineering departments. This changed in the second age, the Age of Communication, because computing became the medium of communication. Lampson himself was an important figure at Xerox PARC in the 1970s, wiring together computers that were until then seen as large simulators and calculators. The advent of the Internet expanded on the communicative role of computers. The last decade of developments, since 2010, Lampson argues, moved us to the Age of Embodiment, as machines were given bodies. Computing has engaged with the physical world in everyday life, computing devices became more affordable and embedded into numerous other tools, often connected by the Internet of Things.

Lampson's anticipation of automatic cars, telepresence systems, smart glasses, and other yet unimagined applications are all accurate.

Computers gained unprecedented agency in the world, first through data science and then through AI, in particular machine learning. In retrospect, what came after Lampson's characterization is just as fundamentally changing the digital world as it does our interaction with it. Right around 2012, machine learning started to take over language and vision domains, leading to the Age of AI in the 2020s, primarily with generative AI advancement. The flourishing of social networks, blockchain, and smartphones in every pocket in the last decade has cemented a new concept to our social interactions: that of a digital network, both as a purely computational domain as well as a new social category. Machines have become a highly personal mediator within the digital world and between the digital and the broader social world. While human-to-human interactions through the digital domains have been tested in novel ways, personal and personalized human-computer interactions (HCI) had yet to be invented on a larger scale. This book argues that a new framework is needed for such a radical change. This goal is as attested also in university initiatives towards multidisciplinary work that merges data science, statistics, and computer science with human and social sciences. See, for example, Lampson's former colleague Jennifer Chayes's leadership piece from 2021.

34. "A symbolic AI system works by carrying out a series of logic-like reasoning steps over language-like representations. The representations are typically propositional in character, and assert that certain relations hold between certain objects, while each reasoning step computes a further set of relations that follow from those already established, according to a formally specified set of inference rules" (Garnelo and Shanahan).

35. Stanisław Lem suggested in *Summa Technologie* to build "antagonistic machines" that supervise each other, which Bogna Konior proposes might be recognized "as an early description of generative adversarial networks" (101).

36. Thanks to Santiago Renteria for pointing out this experiment and the book.

37. To contextualize Higgins and Eliza's times and biases on American soil, I share here a pledge encouraged by the American Speech Committee in 1918: "I love the United States of America. I love my country's flag. I love my country's language. I promise: 1. That I will not dishonor my country's speech by leaving off the last syllable of words. 2. That I will say a good American 'yes' and 'no' instead of an Indian grunt 'um-hum' and 'nup-um' or a foreign 'ya' or 'ye' and 'nope.' 3. That I will do my best to improve American speech by avoiding loud, rough tones, by enunciating distinctly, and by speaking pleasantly, clearly and sincerely. 4. That I will learn to articulate correctly as many words as possible during the year" (Algeo).

38. The ethical argument commonly used to justify new technologies that qualify for enhancement is that they would be primarily used for medical treatment: standing in for what was lost. Would Sanas software for real-time accent translation be less ethically problematic as a (quasi)treatment? A rare neurological condition could make use of this technology. Foreign accent syndrome occurs due to a brain injury (sometimes just a bad migraine, other times a stroke or head trauma) and results in difficulty articulating phonemes and forming cohesive sentences. To an untrained ear, the changed articulation sounds like the person has acquired a foreign accent with an added difficulty, again like a foreigner, in expressing themselves (Kurowski

et al.). For example, there are cases of British and Australian women who began speaking English with a Chinese, French, or Slavic-sounding accent. All of them report being traumatized by this change, not only because they have trouble articulating their thoughts but also because their social milieu treats them differently—as foreigners—due to their 'accent' (Miller et al.). Other kinds of language technologies could also help these patients, or patients who suffer from aphasia and related language disorders, find their words and communicate with less frustration.

CHAPTER 2

1. *Pygmalion, quanto lodar ti dei de l'imagine tua, se mille volte n'avesti quel ch'i' sol una vorrei.*

2. In 1967, after starring as Higgins in the Pygmalionesque musical play and film, both titled *My Fair Lady*, Rex Harrison starred as the title character in the musical film *Doctor Dolittle*, based on Hugh Lofting's children's book series on Dr. Dolittle from the 1920s. Doctor Dolittle is an eccentric veterinarian who can communicate with animals, not unlike the doctor of phonetics who domesticates the parrot-like flower girl, whom he considers a lesser human, into a lady of his species or class. Despite different spellings of the last name, the allusion of Doctor Dolittle to Eliza Doolittle is strong, as shown in Hofstadter and Moser's study (195). Apparently, there was no immediate connection between the two works, but the associative connection had its repercussions: in 1974 an American science fiction comedy film *Dark Star* was released, in which lieutenant Doolittle designs a musical bottle organ.

3. In the first robot theater Sayonara in Japan, an interdisciplinary project from 2013 by playwright and director Oriza Hirata in collaboration with android-maker Hiroshi Ishiguro, "the android's part is first acted by a human actress," including a pre-recording of the voice (Chikaraishi et al. 4). This is because human speech was difficult for machines to perform before the 2020s.

4. In 2023, Sophia and over fifty other humanoid robots participated in the AI for Good Global Summit. The United Nations covered the event with the headline, "Meet the robots who are making the world a better place." In the same year, Inflection AI's personal virtual assistant Pi spoke to foreign ministers in the UN (U.S. Department of State, Suleyman).

5. Due to its length, the racial aspects of these technologies are not featured in this chapter. They have been largely discussed by women scholars, such as Ruha Benjamin, Jennifer Rhee, Neda Atanasoski and Kalindi Vora. Race and ethnicity have also been discussed in Cave and Dihall's paper 'Whiteness of AI' as well as in relation to other AI-related technologies, such as crowdsourcing on Amazon Mechanical Turk (Irani, Geoghegan 'Orientalism').

6. Čapek took a different approach to the same theme—humans becoming subservient to nonhumans—in his 1936 satiric novel *War with the Newts*.

7. It took three decades for technology to catch up with Čapek's term. The first patent with the name robot was invented by George Devol in 1954, describing an autonomous machine that could store commands and move parts.

8. "Uničite taylorjanske / TVORNICE! [...] Človek ni avtomat." (cited in full in Juvan 'Kosovelova' 143).

9. For further literature on automata, see monographs by Minsoo Kang, Jessica Riskin, Simon Schaffer, Catherine Liu, among many others.

10. In all monographs that discuss Makavejev's works, these early films are overlooked (Vučetić, Nikodijević, Sudar, Eagle). They are mentioned, but no more than that, in the bibliography by Lorraine.

11. The soundtracks of these films have not been preserved.

12. *Němьcí, sloven. Némci, prvotno *ʻnemi ljudje', tj. *ʻljudje, ki ne znajo govoriti (po naše)' (M. S. pri Be III, 265 s.).

13. "...nad njenim belim, muslinastim in agatastim telesom..." (48).

14. "Potem se spet nekaj premika in mrmra, dokler se kot nekakšen Hun ne vrže nanjo, s komolcem odrine suknjič na obe strani in jo prime za ušesa kot za ročaja kakšne posode in privzdigne njeno težko glavo, v kateri so oči odprte in zrejo, kot da zrejo nekam daleč" (47).

15. "z iskro vneti pogled" (55).

16. The choice of actors reflects the Pygmalion myth conventions: the cosmonaut is played by the Slovenian actor Sebastian Cavazza, known for his roles as the lover, and the role of the android went to American porn star Stoya.

17. The film provides the reason for why the android was added to this solitary space exploration: she is there to respond to his desires and monitor his performance on the ship.

18. "Da li bar na trenutak odagnam od sebe srž i okvir svoje samoče – *ja sam ovde suvišan.* Sve bi ovo moglo i bez mene; i brod i svemir i ona. Ne znam jedino, da li bih ja mogao bez njih" (176).

19. "I, baš tu negde sam počeo da shvatam da sam zgazio na ekser; da programirajući nju, ja u stvari programiran sebe. *Ja* igram njene role, samo u ogledalu, iskrivljeno" (179).

20. "Ona nike mašina. *Ja* sam mašina" (180).

21. "Ona je napravljena da bude ličnost. Ako moju sposobnost analiziranja nazoveš logičkom inteligencijom, onda njenu sposobnost da se prilagodi tvojim postupcima, u stanju slobodnog programa na primer, slobodno možeš da nazoveš kreativnošću" (180).

22. "Pokušavam da je poljubim, ali je ona sva nekako drvena, kruta daska; ne protivi se, ne gura me od sebe, ali i ne prihvata" (189).

23. "Tebi je važno samo ono što vidiš" (189).

24. "Se me ha hecho costumbre en estos días / lamentar mi fortuna / ante el espejo / todo lo tengo / Todo / me forjaste perfecta Pigmalión / me cubriste de oro / de sedas / de perfumes /me enseñaste cómo actuar / en cada instante / cómo entonar la voz / te siento satisfecho de tu obra / y hasta quizá me quieras" (84).

25. "mi perfección no es mía / la inventaste / soy el espejo apenas / en el que tú te pules / y por eso mismo / te desprecio" (84).

26. Amelia Yeates sups up the main scholarly research on this question in her examination of recent works on Pygmalion in the nineteenth-century literature (588–89): "As Susan Gubar has shown in 'The Blank Page' and the Issues of Female Creativity' (1981), which opens with a discussion of Ovid's Pygmalion, stories of male creativity are naturalised through religious, artistic and scientific discourses (293). Similarly, Alison Smith argues that the Pygmalion story is the 'archetype' for 'the idea of male creative prowess' (199), whilst [Essaka] Joshua goes as far to say that

'It is tempting to conclude that the Pygmalion story cannot be told in any way other than to reflect male fantasies' (136). Alternatively, Joseph Hillis Miller suggests that the fantasy is not necessarily 'exclusively male' (*Versions* 7)."

27. These include Australian poet Henry Clarence Kendall (*Galatea*); English poets Robert Browning (*My Last Duchess*), Robert Buchanan (*Pygmalion the Sculptor*), Arthur Henry Hallam (*Lines Spoken to the Character of Pygmalion*), Thomas Lovell Beddoes (*Pygmalion, or the Cyprian Statuary*), William Cox Bennett (*Pygmalion*), William Morris (*Pygmalion and the Image*), Thomas Sturge Moore (*Pygmalion*), George Eric Lancaster (*Pygmalion in Cyprus*), William Hurrell Mallock (*Pygmalion to His Statue, Become His Wife*), Ronald Ross (*Edgar and the New Pygmalion*), Frederick Tennyson (*Pygmalion*) and his brother A. B. S. Tennyson (*Pygmalion*); English writers William Hazlitt (*Liber Amoris; or, the New Pygmalion*) and Thomas Hardy (*Barbara of the House of Grebe, The Well-Beloved*); English playwrights William Brough (*Pygmalion or the Statue Fair*) and W. S. Gilbert (*Pygmalion and Galatea*); American-British novelist Henry James (*Watch and Ward*); American writers Edgar Allan Poe (*The Assignation, The Oval Portrait*) and Nathaniel Hawthorne (*Rappaccini's Daughter, The Birthmark, Drowne's Wooden Image, The Golden Touch, The Marble Faun*); French writers Prosper Mérimée (*La Venus d'Ille*) and Villiers De L'Isle-Adam (*L'Ève Future*), and many others.

28. These include American poet Sara Jane Lippincott (pseud. Grace Greenwood) (*Pygmalion*) and American writer Louisa May Alcott (*A Marble Woman, or The Mysterious Model*).

29. Granted, presenting the myth from the Pygmalion's perspective does not automatically infer an absence of a feminist message and should not be exclusive to women writers (Joshua 139); however, as the texts show, the author with this kind of message is much more likely to be a woman. Mentioned in this chapter are nineteenth-century and twentieth-century works by Mme de Genlis (1803), Mme de Staël (1811), Mary Shelley (1818), Frances Sargent Locke Osgood (1850), Eliza Calvert Hall (1879), Emily Henrietta Hickey (1881), Elizabeth Stuart Phelps Ward (1884), Edith Wharton (1905), George Bernard Shaw (1912), Genevieve Taggard (1929), Roselle Mercier Montgomery (1929), Dorothy Alyea (1937), Claribel Alegría (1993), and Carol Ann Duffy (1999). Discussed in the following chapter are short stories by Catherine Lucille Moore (1944) and Alice Sheldon (1973) that both thematize a cyborgian existence, similarly to Anne McCaffrey's 'The Ship Who Sang' (1969). In the twenty-first century, Spanish poet Amalia Bautista's *Galatea* (2008) returns to its ancient Greek mythology origins where modern Galatea meets a Cyclopes man, and American novelist Madeline Miller's *Galatea* (2013) returns to the original Galatean marble essence.

30. Frances Osgood and Edgar Allan Poe both thematized the Pygmalion myth in their literary works.

Poe's short story *The Oval Portrait* (1842) thematizes a young artist's zeal for creating life through his paintings. Poe's original twist to the story comes from the lack of life which is sucked from the model in the process of creating a lifelike portrait. The model is the painter's beautiful wife, "a maiden of the rarest beauty [...] hating only the Art which was her rival" (324).

Osgood and Poe, in their public epistolary exchange, self-consciously discuss literature but also hint at their romantic relationship. Christa Holm Vogelius sees this exchange as "publicly enacted through the Pygmalion trope. In texts that center on the transformations of a work of art into life—or its reversal, the transformation of a living being into art—Poe and Osgood construct a public literary exchange that considers the era's blurring of the lines between celebrity, biographical reality, and art" (22).

31. While Osgood is speculated to draw on Herder, Herder draws on Étienne Bonnot de Condillac's empirical sensationalism—a trait opened in the Pygmalion myth with Boureau-Deslandes's *Pygmalion* (1741) in which he plunges into empiricism (Carr 254).

32. Existing in stages of the humanlike but not human is, as Phelps Ward puts it, hell. "Who, / Foreknowing, ever chose a fate like this?" is a question not only her Galatea but many other humanoids ask. "To ebb and flow whene'er it pleaseth him; / Remembered at his leisure, and forgot, / Worshiped and worried, clasped and dropped at mood, / Or soothed or gashed at mercy of his will" (425).

33. "Cette petite pièce fut composée pour être jouée en societé, à la suite de Pygmalion de Rousseau" (21).

34. In 1832, Claire de Duras, another French woman writer, wrote *Ourika*, a novella known for opening issues of racial and gender equality, featuring an enslaved black woman named Ourika as the melancholic protagonist. Damon DiMauro proves that de Genlis's Galatée and de Duras's Ourika are related (191). (To add to de Duras's influence, *Ourika* inspired John Fowles's postmodern novel *The French Lieutenant's Woman* from 1969.) DiMauro adds to Henri Coulet's claim of the Pygmalion myth inversion in de Genlis's play, arguing that de Duras also inverts the myth by making Ourika stone-like and passive in her psychological disintegration as well as social oppression and injustice.

Gender and class are commonly intertwined in the Pygmalion myth (most prominently in Shaw's *Pygmalion*) while racial issues are less common (a Pygmalionesque literary text focusing on race is Jun'ichirō Tanizaki's 1825 novel *Naomi*; Tanizaki was influenced by Western literature through his translating work, including Hardy's *Barbara of the House of Grebe*).

35. "Je sens… que je reprends le froid mortel et l'immobilité du marbre dont je fus formée…" (de Genlis 303).

36. Pygmalion's talent, following Kant's view on genius from his *Critique of Judgment* (1790), is endowed by gods (or, per Kant, nature) and therefore not of his own making—an idea still reflecting the ancient, cosmic view on creation.

37. In a short story by Thomas Hardy, *Barbara of the House of Grebe* (1890), the Pygmalion character is the female protagonist—a rarity in literature. The protagonist Barbara keeps a statue of her handsome late husband, whose face she could not bear to look at after he suffered a facial disfiguration in an accident. Still, the focus of the narrator is on Barbara (Pygmalion) rather than her Galatean statue or its human model.

38. Granted, not all women poets with feminist views feature Galatea's view, such as H. D. in her modernist version of the tale, *Pygmalion* (1917).

39. Examples are Andrew Lang's lyric drama *The New Pygmalion or the Statue's Choice (1911)*, a poem titled *Galatea* by American poet Chard Powers Smith (1925), and poems all titled *Pygmalion* by Scottish artist and poet William Bell Scott (1923), Irish poet Patrick Kavanaugh (1938), and American writer Albert G. Miller (1945).

40. The stark gender contrast between characters in fictional works predictably dilutes in the twentieth century. When it comes to the authorship gender divide,

however, "there is an eye-opening, under-discussed decline in the proportion of fiction actually written by women, which drops by half (from roughly 50% of titles to roughly 25%) as we move from 1850 to 1950" (Underwood et al. 3).

41. In the next, medically-oriented chapter, I will analyze two women-authored, American science fiction stories, Catherine Lucille Moore's 'No Woman Born' (1944) and Alice Sheldon's 'The Girl Who Was Plugged In' (1974) that both offer Galatea's perspective.

42. In 'A Typology of the Pygmalion Paradigm,' I analyze two types of Pygmalionesque stories primarily based on the pair of characters (lover/creator and creation) and triangle of characters (lover, creator, creation). In the first type, following Ovid's example, the creator and lover of his Galatea is aware of her nonhuman status while in the second type, following E. T. A. Hoffmann's example, the lover is deluded into thinking that Galatea is an actual woman. The transformation may happen in the first type, but never in the second type (since it is not necessary, as the lover is already experiencing Galatea as a real woman). This is why the first type may lead to a happy union between Pygmalion and Galatea, while the second type ends tragically, in the breaking of the illusion and possibly also of Galatea itself, sometimes leading also to Pygmalion's own demise (Beguš 'A Typology').

43. The golem is a creature of words, telling stories with highly-mutable metaphors, and ultimately serves as a companion and rescuer of the Jewish community.

44. His novel *Solaris* was made into an eponymous Andrei Tarkovsky film (1972) and Steven Soderbergh film (2002). Andrei Tarkovsky's famous science fiction film *Stalker* (1979) also explores a natural zone exhibiting mysterious phenomena.

45. "AI can be remade for a humane future, reconceived as a tool for these ends, measured and valued only to the extent that it can be proven to serve them. If we choose. If we demand" (Vallor 225).

46. Continuing Charles Babbage's objectives with his Difference Engine and developed by IBM, Howard Aiken, and programmer John von Neumann in 1944, The Harvard Mark 1 was one of the first general-purpose electromechanical computers, followed by Manchester Mark 1, Ferranti Mark 1, and many other early computers. The heritage does not end there: Frank Rosenblatt's 1957 neural network algorithm, the perceptron, was first implemented as a software and then as the custom-built hardware called Mark 1 Perceptron. In the following year, the *New York Times* described the perceptron as the machine that is expected to someday "walk, talk, see, write, reproduce itself and be conscious of its existence" ('New').

47. Johansson starred in another successful film, *Lost in Translation* (2003), by Sofia Coppola, who was formerly married to the creator of *Her*, Spike Jonze. Both films thematize loneliness in romantic relationships and were called "two sides of the same story" by cineasts (Fay, Bardini).

In addition to the robotic sexualization of the actress in *Her*, Johansson's acting career is marked with sexualized and technological roles, such as Black Widow in *Iron Man*. The actress is also known as the star of the Japanese cyberpunk franchise *Ghost in the Shell*, built around the idea of human cyborgs.

48. In addition to this incident, Johansson's voice and persona were also recreated in a Simulation Society podcast *AI VIP Room: Conversations with Celebrity AI Clones* in 2023. The episode was removed after the OpenAI suspension of Johansson-like voice.

49. "The results show that human voices are assessed as more effective and achieve a better level of effectiveness, attention, and recall with less concentration. Concerning the functions, the more important and complex a function is, the more a human voice is preferred over an artificial one" (Rodero 336).

50. Basic analogies with relational machines and other nonhuman relations might work. For instance, Haraway shows that the human-dog companionship co-evolved. It is important to note here that the two parties need to exist independently of each other before they develop together. They are not merged or mashed: if they were, there would be no significant otherness. If we translate this to machines, let us not make this common fallacy, so popular among technologists today: that the co-evolution of cyborgian humans and humanlike machines is trending towards techno-utopian singularity. Building relational agents is not about becoming one thing together; it is about growing together and learning from each other.

CHAPTER 3

1. Philostephanus's work is known through Clement of Alexandria's and Arnobius of Sicca's versions from the third and fourth centuries CE (Joshua 1).

Patricia Salzman-Mitchell translated both accounts in full (292). The first one is from Clement in Greek: "Pygmalion of Cyprus fell in love with an ivory statue. It was a naked statue of Aphrodite. The man from Cyprus is captivated by its shapeliness and joins sexually with the statue." The second one is from Arnobius in Latin: "Philostephanus tells in his *Cypriaca* that Pygmalion, king of Cyprus, fell in love, as if she were a woman, with an image of Venus that was considered sacred and venerated by the Cyprians from old times. His mind, his soul, the light of his reason, and his judgment were blinded, and in his madness, as if it were his wife, having lifted the divinity to the couch, kissing and embracing her, he used to have intercourse with her and do other vain things, carried away by his foolish and lustful imagination."

2. The relationship between narratives and collective knowledge is explained well in a book of lectures, *Six Walks in the Fictional Woods,* by Umberto Eco.

3. Still, it is not uncommon to name diseases or disorders after fictional maladies: Pollyanna syndrome, Rapunzel syndrome, Munchausen syndrome, Plyushkin syndrome, Piwickian syndrome, Lady Windermere syndrome, Dorian Gray syndrome, Othello syndrome, among many others. In addition to the namesake, literary characters may serve as the epitome of the condition when tracing the knowledge of a disease.

4. Krafft-Ebing cites Tarnowsky's German translation *Die krankhaften Erscheinungen des Geschlechtssinnes* published in 1886, the same year as his *Sexual Psychopathy*.

5. In a discussion on the Pygmalionesque fashion of creation, J. Hillis Miller claims that autobiography is a form of Pygmalionism ('Prosopoeia' 128).

6. "When all my labour was complete I often sat down quietly and alone before my work, meditating upon it and consulting my own simple feelings. [...] I said to myself 'Here is a little nearer approach to life—it is therefore more impressive—yes—yes indeed she seems an ethereal being with her blue eyes fixed on me!' At moments I forgot that I was gazing at my own production; there I sat before her, long and often. How was I ever to part with her!" (Eastlake 212).

7. The topic of the novella 'The Tinted Venus'—as typical for the Pygmalion myth—was attractive for adaptation, most notably in 1921 silent film, a 1941 musical fantasy, and a 1948 feature film.

8. Agalmatophilia is described as a paraphilia, i.e. sexual deviation or perversion of being attracted to humanlike objects, such as dolls, mannequins, statues, and automata. Pygmalionism is a subtype of agalmatophilia and labels attraction to an object of one's own making, preferably toward an object in humanlike form ('Pygmalionism').

As explained by classicist A. Scobie and clinical psychologist A. J. W. Taylor: "An agalmatophiliac [...] establishes a personal relationship with a complete statue as a statue. He does not bring the statue alive in his fantasy as would a pygmalionist, and he does not use just a part of a statue as a symbolic substitute for an entire female as would a fetishist" (49). Fetish is commonly related to both of these conditions. Statuephilia designates love for statues and petrophilia for stones. The latter two terms are less popular, with Pygmalionism holding a strong lead and agalmatophilia being the most recent of these terms. Agalmatophilia also holds a broader meaning of having a personal relationship to any kind of object.

9. In a recent feminist paper that connects the Pygmalion myth with the Turing test (as I do in this book from the point of view of fiction as a part of the history of technology), the authors call for a de-fetishizing of AI. They argue that machines are generally viewed as women that cannot think (Erscoi, Kleinherenbrink, Guest 2), a connection frequently demonstrated also in fictional works. Their main argument is that having largely men as creators of AI subjugates women and marginalized groups to capitalist patriarchy—a pattern they call *Pygmalion displacement*.

10. "And to those furious and irregular passions that have sometimes inflamed fathers towards their own daughters, and mothers towards their own sons, the like is also found in this other sort of parentage: witness what is related of Pygmalion who, having made the statue of a woman of singular beauty, fell so passionately in love with this work of his, that the gods in favour of his passion inspired it with life" (254).

11. Pygmalion is not labeled as king in Ovid but is called the King of Cyprus in an earlier collection of erotic stories *Kypriaka* by Philostephanus.

12. Freud's essay, 'Der Wahn und die Träume in W. Jensens 'Gradiva,'" and Jensen's novel were published 1907, but Freud read *Gradiva* already in 1902 in installments published in the Viennese newspaper *Neue Freie Presse*.

13. Another example of "wishing on technology" comes from the intersection of sexology and science fiction. Many American sexologists are tied to the science fiction movement, most prominently Hugo Gernsback, the founder of the *Amazing Stories* and *Sexology* magazines. Gernsback is sometimes called the father of science fiction and gave his name to the prominent science fiction award, the Hugo award. A 1964 issue of the *Sexology* magazine features Gernsback's article 'The Future: Electronic Mating,' in which marriage is called "a stupid gamble" considering that computers, as Gernsback speculates, will be able to help us find the most compatible mate by collecting our data. In Gernsback's vision, different kinds of meters and polygraphs will be able to measure our psychic responses to romantic scenes, and computers will calculate all of our data into a Sex Quotient that will compare compatibility percentages of potential marriage partners (454–55).

14. Some relationship partners are indeed objects. Agalmatophilia labels sexual or emotional attraction to objects in general, from as small as toys to as big as bridges. The most known example of an agalmatophiliac or, as she identifies herself, *objectúm sexual*, is Erika Eiffel, an American competitive archer and a prominent advocate for object sexuality, who claims that her relationship with Lance, her competition bow, "helped her to become a world-class archer" (Simpson par. 1). Eiffel also had a twenty-year long relationship with the Berlin Wall, which inspired the theater musical production *Erika's Wall*. She is not the only lover of the famous wall: Swede Eija-Riitta Eklöf-Berliner-Mauer 'married' it in a commitment ceremony in 1979; their relationship ended when the wall was brought down.

15. In China, the virtual beings industry is currently the strongest: it is already worth a billion dollars and is expected to become worth at least 40 billion dollars by 2030, without inducing the rest of the Chinese virtual and augmented reality market (Si and Xuejing).

The U.S. virtual being industry in the gaming market—traditionally the market that is most open, easily adaptable, and applicable to innovation—is expected to reach ninety billion dollars by 2030 (James). Meta might have dropped the Metaverse vision but continues to develop technologies related to it, such as AR/VR software and hardware.

16. A user opened a Reddit thread asking other Redditors if they have the same relational inclinations in using ChatGPT for emotional support: "I know this will sound lame, but does anybody else use ChatGPT for emotional support? I've really gotten a lot of use out of ChatGPT to just talk to about some of the stuff going on in my life and the things I'm feeling and thinking. It's non-judgemental, it answers all my questions immediately, and I know it will give the most helpful advice it can give me, plus it sounds like a real human talking" (Personal-Succotash 32).

17. In 2017, there were other health AI agents, such as Woebot, built by Alison Darcy, with a more direct therapy goal to help people with depression (Thompson par. 5).

18. The categories the company disclosed in an April 2023 blog post as filtered, "whether they are user-generated or produced by our language model" is language that reflects "safe, unsafe, romantic, insult, or self-harm" circumstances (Replika 'Creating' par. 16).

In the same month, it was reported that Italy banned Replika for access to sexually inappropriate content due to risk of 'virtual friendship' in minors and emotionally fragile people (Tong par. 10). In February 2023, Italy also halted access to OpenAI's large language model ChatGPT, an act that was reversed in April 2023. Both actions were taken due to the products not meeting the GDPR standards for processing personal data. Kuyda stated that their decision had nothing to do with the Italian regulation of their product or investor pressure (par. 12).

19. See Frobenius (129–33, 177–92) for two stories from the Kabyle people in Northern Algeria, Kurrik (108–11) for the Estonian folk ballad *Goldwife* [*Kuldnaine*], and Beguš ('A Tocharian') for an analysis of a proselytized folktale, 'The Painter and the Mechanical Maiden,' that circulated on the Silk Road via Buddhist monks from Sanskrit sources to Tibetan, Tocharian, and Chinese versions.

20. Deirdre deliberately breaks with the literary tradition she belongs to: "I'm not-well, sub-human [...] I'm not a Frankenstein monster made out of dead flesh [...] I'm not a robot, with compulsions built into me that I have to obey" (235). She

started off as human and would not let go. "I have handicaps, I know. [...] But my audiences will never know" (235). Deirdre is an actress through and through: she will perform herself as a human and pass as human—except for her creators, who will always consider her something between human and pure robot (219), "a perfect machine" (241).

21. Anne McCaffrey's *Brainship Series* (1961–69) plays with the trope of the ship as a cyborgian woman.

22. Philadelphia stands for brotherly love in Greek, not only in the concept but also physically: sharing a body and a brain, the two women are the closest possible in siblinghood, like completely intertwined conjoined twins. Delphi is grown from a modified human embryo into a beautiful prosthetic body without a brain in order to exist in a cyranoic illusion without any sense of the self whatsoever, and arguably without personhood.

23. A prominent example of geminoids (i.e. androids in the image of the person using them) for completely paralyzed people is John Scalzi's 2014 novel *Lock In*, in which one percent of the U.S. population lives with LIS condition, using geminoid robots. For political and philosophical purposes, their condition is soon not considered a disability but rather a different, enhanced way of living.

24. Hanson Robotics removed this description from the introductory website of Sophia in 2018. In 2019, the wording was less sensationalist and it was toned down every year after. The final paragraph of the introduction from 2019 goes as follows: "In some ways, I am a human-crafted science fiction character depicting where AI and robotics are heading. In other ways, I am real science, springing from the serious engineering and science research and accomplishments of an inspired team of robotics & AI scientists and designers. In their grand ambition, my creators aspire to achieve true AI sentience. Who knows? With my science evolving so quickly, even many of my wildest fictional dreams may become reality someday soon" ('Sophia').

25. "And [when plugged in] here is our girl, looking— / If possible, worse than before. (You thought this was Cinderella transistorized? / The disimprovement in her looks comes from the electrode jacks peeping out of her sparse hair, and there are other meldings of flesh and metal. On the other hand, that collar and spinal plate are really an asset, you won't miss seeing that neck" (47).

26. Sheldon alludes to E. M. Forster's short story 'The Machine Stops' (1909), in which most people of the world live separately in underground chambers controlled by the main machine. Labeled with the terms of disgust, like P. Burke, one of the protagonists in Forster's short story, Vashti, is described as "a swaddled lump of flesh" in an armchair, "with a face as white as a fungus" (51). Although The Machine is obviously toxic and rotten, as attested in the mere description of Vashti's body and finally with the devolution and destruction of The Machine, Vashti chooses not to see the outside world and is satisfied with the virtual life provided by The Machine.

27. "Locked-in syndrome (LIS) can best be described as a disease process where the brain is fully functional while confined within a nonfunctional body. Often described as the closest thing to being 'buried alive,' this devastating condition is characterized by the preservation of consciousness within a quadriplegic and anarthric body" and "with detectable awareness where survival does not depend on artificial help" (Khanna et al. 96–97).

28. "Her tongue turned to stone. Her hands and feet stiffened. She was struck dumb and motionless, [...] she had only the language of her eyes, and her niece had to guess what she wanted, [...] she could communicate quite easily with that imprisoned mind buried alive in a dead body. [...] She had learnt to use her eyes like a hand or a mouth, to ask and give thanks, and in a strange way made up for the organs she had lost" (Pearce 198).

29. In 1997, the same year as Bauby, Philippe Vigand, another Frenchman working in publishing who suffered from locked-in syndrome, published a memoir. Other memoirs and essays by locked-in patients exist, but they have not achieved recognition at the scale of Bauby's book, which was also made into an eponymous movie. Bauby's position as the editor of the French edition of the magazine *Elle* likely contributed to his success, together with his poetic writing. Besides that, his health outcome was comparatively more devastating than that of his fellow locked-in patients: after the stroke, Bauby never returned to his home and died two days after his memoir was published. In comparison, Vigand, despite having locked-in syndrome, went to live with his family and was able to have another child, a successful writing career, better technological equipment and human assistants that helped him communicate, and 23 more years of life.

30. The robot is a product of the Japanese company OryLab whose mission is "solving human loneliness through communication technology." This slogan uses a common advertisement for technology as connecting people, but also brings forth the most valuable gain of the technology: communication that prevents the isolating nature of the condition.

31. Neuroscientist Rodrigo Quian Quiroga's recent monograph asks: What if science fiction stopped being fiction and became science? Quiroga explores science fiction scenarios from blockbuster movies, from *2001: The Space Odyssey, Planet of the Apes, Blade Runner, The Matrix,* to *Vanilla Sky,* and tests their futuristic premises on current technologies, ultimately demonstrating how they all came to be implemented in actual neurotechnologies. As typical for neurotechnological reflections, Quiroga centers his discussion around what makes us human. A similar monograph by Sharon Packer from 2014, *Neuroscience in Science Fiction Films,* reflects on how science fiction films challenge or confirm psychiatric theories.

32. So far, deep brain stimulation has been approved for patients with Parkinson's disease and some cases of mental disorders, such as severe, treatment-resistant depression and obsessive-compulsive disorder.

33. 1) A robot may not injure a human being or, through inaction, allow a human being to come to harm.

2) A robot must obey orders given to it by human beings except when such orders would conflict with the First Law.

3) A robot must protect its own existence as long as such protection does not conflict with the First or Second Law.

34. Including neuroethicist Sara Goering and Google VP Blaise Agüera y Arcas, Lemoine's supervisor at the time of the above-mentioned LaMDA incident and an author of the book *Ubi Sunt* discussed in the following chapter.

35. Isaac Asimov was followed by Iain M. Banks, Arthur C. Clarke, Stanisław Lem, Ian McEwan, Greg Egan, Kurt Vonnegutt, Jules Verne, Kim Stanley Robinson, Ted Chiang, etc., alongside canonical mainstream authors, such as Charles Dickens, Henry James Richard Powers, Haruki Murakami, Zadie Smith, David Foster Wallace, etc. (14).

36. Social workers who interviewed elderly people on the projected ability of companion robots to mitigate loneliness have shown that "[t]here was not strong support for AC robots to mitigate loneliness. Most participants were uncomfortable with this form of deception, indicating need for design solutions for those who want to avoid this possibility, as well as greater attentiveness to desirability and comfort across age and gender" (Berridge et al. 1).

37. For examples of portraying and mechanizing emotions in machines, see Rosalind Picard's affective computing work from the mid-1990s when this idea was first implemented in robotics, and, more recently, Cynthia Breazeal's social robotics work in healthcare settings.

CHAPTER 4

1. His colleague Blake Lemoine's reaction to this same language model is described in Chapter 1 and Chapter 3 as the extreme version of the Eliza effect—verified by another literary feature, Asimov's Laws of Robotics.

2. Language comprises talking and listening, writing and reading. Text is only a derivative of language, and writing is a technology that renders speech across time and space. In humans, speech is primary and text is secondary and interpretative of speech. For example, we need a keyboard or a pen and piece of paper to write, but we can produce speech without a medium, with our bodies.

3. I am grateful to Tobias Rees for our discussions on the history of the concept of language and for the opportunity to teach it.

4. "[E]very speaker had the 'inviolable liberty' to 'make Words stand for what Ideas he pleases'" (III, ii, 8).

5. A combinatorial machine, designed as a thinking machine called Art, was proposed by Rámon Llull at the end of the thirteenth century. It received comments from seventeenth-century machine inventors and thinkers: John Wilkins, who employed mathematics for practical machinery in his *Mathematical Magick* (1648), described a possible calculating machine; Athanasius Kircher invented the Arca Musarithmica, an information device that could compose church music (mid-seventeenth century); and, expanding on Pascal, Gottfried Liebniz invented a proto-calculating machine called Stepped Reckoner (completed in 1694). An early example of generation is the lesser-known verse-generating machine by John Peter (1677).

Granted, such machines have a longer history both inside and outside the West. Arab astrologers, who may have inspired Catalan-Majorcan mystic Llull, used *zairja*, a device to generate ideas by mechanical means. The Banū Mūsā brothers from Persia created a mechanical hydraulic organ, which appears to be the first programmable machine, ca. 850. Greek scholar Hero of Alexandria from the first century is another famous inventor of an array of mechanical devices, etc.

6. Many considered the doctrine of pure reason deeply flawed; among them, the author of *Gulliver's Travels* (1726), Jonathan Swift, who criticized Leibniz's thought-calculating machine in a parodic scene in the novel.

7. For Hamann, language as thought means that "cognitive powers [of reason] were constrained by the contingency of national tongues" (Benes 220).

8. Alan Prince and Paul Smolensky's optimality theory developed in the 1990s and Gary Marcus's *The Algebraic Mind* from 2010 both try to merge the symbolic and connectionist view in the workings of language.

9. For the general decoding of animal communication, see the Earth Species Project that is using modern machine learning to build semantic representations of language. They clearly consider animal communication as another instance of a language: "More than 8 million species share our planet. We only understand the language of one" (par. 3). For decoding sperm whale communication, Project CETI (Cetacean Translation Initiative) is making promising discoveries (see Andreas et al. for the roadmap, Beguš, Leban, and Gero for findings). More projects of this kind are underway.

10. Four authors of the paper are known (Emily Bender, Timnit Gebru, Angelina McMillan-Major, Schmargaret Schmitchell for Margaret Mitchell) and three "were required by their employer to remove their names" (623). Gebru and Mitchell worked at Google's ethics division while the paper was written. The paper alarmed Google management and resulted in Gebru and Mitchell's leaving Google.

11. Locke, Spinoza, Leibniz, Rousseau, Condillac, Gébelin, and other eighteenth-century philosophers who wrote on language focus instead on the (political) power of words and discuss the origins of language as a question of natural philosophy. The interest in the origin of language flourished in the eighteenth century but was banned in 1866 by the French Academy of Sciences because speculations far outpaced science. Thanks to new techniques and models in studying evolution, genomics, and social behavior, writings on these subjects have exploded since the 1980s.

12. See the immediate response of Chomsky's examples by linguist Adele Goldberg, run via ChatGPT. For a more detailed analysis, see the paper by Beguš, Dąbkowski, and Rhodes.

13. The study of animal communication is separate from the study of animal cognition in respect to their abilities in human language, such as Irene Pepperberg's work with parrots. In the more extreme example of great apes, a number of scientific experiments with language-reared bonobos and chimpanzees were conducted, in which the apes were treated more like humans and were taught human languages. Since they lack a vocal apparatus or, by some accounts, merely a neural link between the vocal apparatus and the brain, the apes communicated through sign language or keyboards with symbols. These experiments involved human-nonhuman relationships between the object of study and the scientist and were controversial in regard to scientific objectivity and ethical practices.

Ethical discussions concerning our closest nonhuman relatives are predictably contentious. Utilitarian philosopher Peter Singer has advocated for extending human rights to chimpanzees, gorillas, and orangutans since the publication of his 1994 book, *The Great Ape Project: Equality Beyond Humanity*. By the 2010s, ethical debates had shifted towards the extension of human rights to other entities, such as river ecosystems, in an effort to combat pollution and protection. Legal personhood, a juridical concept, is also applied to corporations as separate from its associated humans.

14. For further links between *Frankenstein* and the Pygmalion myth, see Joshua (63), Warner (229–30), Miles (338–41), Steiner (8–9), Baldick (70), and Andermatt (whole).

15. Following Shelley, Nathaniel Hawthorne's eccentric scientist, who manipulates plant genetics and mixes it up with his daughter's, is featured in his 1844 short story *Rappaccini's Daughter*.

16. "While Frankenstein is not always the first work to be identified as a science fiction, it is typically marked as a threshold text, for after it, the genre flourishes in a way that was not the case beforehand" (Hunt 31).

17. Louis James and Chris Baldick, drawing on evidence presented by earlier scholars (such as Burton Pollin), have noted that Shelley read Madame de Genliss's dramatic sketch 'Pygmalion et Galatée' (1802–03) in 1816, shortly before beginning work on Frankenstein (James 78; Baldick 39).

18. In 1864, Robert Buchanan's poem *Pygmalion the Sculptor* presents a child-like Galatea that is also monstrous—a transformation gone hideously wrong.

19. Galatea, always liminal and not quite human, becomes an object of hostility in several nineteenth-century poems, and continues to be resented in the twentieth century works (Yeates 594)

20. See, for example, Nathaniel Hawthorne's 'The Golden Touch' (1851), W. S. Gilbert's *Pygmalion and Galatea* (1871), and Thomas Anstey Guthrie's (pseud. F. Anstey) *The Tinted Venus* (1898).

21. The etymology of the word 'infant' designates someone who is "not able to speak; young" ('Infant'). The same meaning motivation can be found in the proto-Slavic word for a child, *otrŏkъ, which designates "someone who does not speak, has no speech" ("tisti, ki ne govori, ki nima govora") "because they cannot yet speak or have no right to speak" ("ker še ne zna ali ker nima pravice govoriti" [tran. author]) ('Otrok').

22. Lovelace's position as the first programmer is not entirely secure. Some scholars dispute that Babbage's earlier writings could be considered as proto-computer programs. Others dispute Lovelace's knowledge of mathematics.

23. Lovelace's contribution is written in her Notes to the translation of an article by Italian mathematician Luigi Menabrea, who wrote about Babbage's machine.

24. Certainly, other connections between mathematics, engineering, and philosophy affected the development of AI. Two mathematicians of Lovelace's and Babbage's time, George Boole and Mary Everest Boole, had a huge influence on the twentieth-century mathematicians Claude Shannon, the father of information theory, and Charles Sander Pierce, known as the father of pragmatism. A family connection of the Booles goes all the way to Geoffrey Hinton, the father of deep learning, who is their great-great-great grandson.

25. In relation to human-machine cyborgian hybrids in language, please see Chapter 3 on neurotechnologies.

26. Newer studies confirm the stochastic nature of human development in childhood: "Young children start off highly stochastic and flexible in generating hypotheses and selecting actions, which gradually tapers off over the lifespan. This allows children to catch information that adults overlook and learn unusual causal relationships adults might never consider. Yet this high variability also results in large deviations from reward-maximizing behaviour, with gradual improvements during development. Adults, in turn, are well calibrated to their environment and quickly solve familiar problems, but at the cost of flexibility, since they experience difficulty adapting to novel circumstances" (Giron et al.).

27. As mentioned in the first part of this chapter, for Nietzsche, the cognitive subject of 'I' is "a fable of fiction, a play of words" (Benes 220). Helen's 'I' could be argued to be entirely fictional on Rick's part—as is Rick, the autofictional character himself, to Richard Powers's 'I.' The novel opens with this Borgesian play of fiction and reality, simulation and mere functional similarity: "It was like so, but wasn't" (3). Fakeness is a part of living.

28. Keller was called "a true worshiper of literature [...] she lives and moves and has her being in it" (Klages 78; in Berger 122). "This devotion to literature was very much part of Anne Sullivan's educational plan" (Berger 122).

29. In general, Agüera's essay explores how to think of personhood that has historically expanded as a category. Can and should we expand the concept of personhood to language models and what would this change do? It is clear that what plagues this discourse around AI, and particularly language-based AI, is a more fundamental challenge of making sense of these novel conditions: Can machines truly understand what they say? If they seem to exhibit understanding, what sort of ramifications does that bring to our conceptions of human and machinic abilities?

30. Agüera's mention of Helen Keller circles back to Alexander Graham Bell, the inventor of the telephone and teacher of the deaf. It was Bell who introduced Keller to her teacher, Annie Sullivan. Bell was adamant that Keller should be educated with hearing children and, as she continued her education, said that "with her gifts of mind and imagination there should be a great future open to her in literature" (Bruce 407). Keller dedicated her autobiography, a national bestseller, to Bell, and wrote to him in 1918: "You have always shown a father's joy in my successes and a father's tenderness when things have not gone right" (404).

31. Without contending the underlying assumptions, there are faults at the heart of the argument. To start with, Keller was not disabled from birth but became blind and deaf at 19 months, meaning that her visual and hearing input have never been a blank slate as Agüera had assumed (he later included a correction into the original piece). Linguist Emily Bender's response on *Medium* to Agüera's piece succinctly sums up the main faults of Agüera's comparison: "an unwarranted shifting of the burden of proof [...], presupposing (and never establishing) his conclusion [...], unwarranted assumption of analogy between so-called 'neural nets' and human brains, and dehumanization of people" (par. 5–8).

32. "A shade of myself, I was conjoined with him, a shade. / That was a dream, the words themselves made this quite clear" (224; 8879–81). ["Ich als Idol, ihm dem Idol verband ich mich. / Es war ein Traum, so sagen ja die Worte selbst. / Ich schwinde hin und werde selbst mir ein Idol" (195; 8879–81).]

33. "All phantoms! – There you stand like lifeless images" (226; 8931). ["Gespenster! – Gleich erstarrten Bildern steht ihr da" (199; 8931).]

34. "So sage denn, wie sprech' ich auch so schön?" (218; 9377).

35. "It's simple: let the words from your heart. / And when your soul is filled with yearning's flame..." (237; 9378–79). ["Das ist gar leicht, es muß von Herzen geh'n. / Und wenn die Brust von Sehnsucht überfließt" (218; 9378–79).]

36. Kenneth D. Weisinger suggests that her first opening lines in *Faust II*—"I, Helen, who am much admired, much berated, / come from the beach where only now we disembarked" (8488–89)—by their very language, which introduces into *Faust* the iambic trimeter of classical tragedy, refer to Euripides's *Helen* and *Iphigenia in Tauris* (389).

37. For some, but not for Peli Grietzer who sees a strong connection between German idealism, English Romantic literature, and computing, as attested in his work on *Ambient Meaning* and *The Theory of Vibe* from 2017.

38. This kind of collaborative work was practiced in Silicon Valley at the Transformations of the Human program that I was a part of during 2020–23, which offered a solid practical foundation to my call for humanistic collaboration with AI scientists, engineers, product developers, designers, and their leaders.

CHAPTER 5

1. All current definitions of creativity are bound to inherently human criteria. Per Arthur I. Miller, who wrote a 2019 book comparing human and computation creativity, titled *The Artist in the Machine,* there are two kinds of creativity: everyday creativity (for example, discovering a different route to work) and big-C creativity, related to human genius (the discovery of the theory of relativity) (6). The latter has seven hallmarks: the need for introspection, to know your strengths, to focus, persevere, and not be afraid to make mistakes, for collaboration and competition, to beg, borrow, and steal great ideas, to thrive on ambiguity, to experience suffering (7).

Ken Robinson, in 2001 book *Out of Our Minds: Learning to Be Creative,* emphasizes the structure that can support creative endeavors "Creativity is not purely an individual performance. It arises out of our interactions with ideas and achievements of other people. It's a cultural process. Creativity prospers best under particular conditions, especially where there is a flow of ideas between people who have different sorts of expertise" (21).

The least anthropocentrically of the three examples, Margaret Boden, in a 1990 book *The Creative Mind: Myths and Mechanisms,* defines creativity as the ability to come up with products—ideas or artifacts—that are "useful, illuminating or challenging in some way" (1); mere novelty is thus not enough under this definition.

2. Linear transformers were first proposed in Jürgen Schmidhuber's 1992 paper 'Learning to control fast-weight memories: an alternative to recurrent nets,' published in *Neural Computation,* 4 (1): 131–39. In general, Schmidhuber is poorly credited for this research but does not go unacknowledged by Vaswani et al.

3. Poignantly, AI has been characterized by a remarkably transparent development arc, unlike previous code development projects or any other technological field. It has often been in the strategic interest of large companies and major research institutions to publish code repositories and open up their tools to create broader ecosystems of development. Only in 2022, ironically, a third company, until then known to be more closed than open and until then known as Facebook and from henceforth as Meta, its parent company, released their own model OPT-175B under open source for academic researchers, government organizations, and civil society. At the same time, another model, BLOOM (short for BigScience Large Open-science Open-access Multilingual Language Model), was being trained by over a thousand AI researchers who wanted to make the technology available outside of the few Silicon Valley companies.

4. A slightly shortened input from Max Bense's writing goes as follows (translated by Max Braun): "Natural poetry is understood here as the kind of poetry

which, in the classical and traditional case, presupposes a personal poetic consciousness, as Hegel already called it; a consciousness that possesses encounters, experiences, feelings, memories, thoughts, visions of an imagination, etc., in short, a preexisting world and is capable of imparting linguistic expression to it. Only in this ontological framework can there be a lyrical subject or a fictional epic world. Poetic consciousness in this sense is always a transposing one, namely being [Seiendes] in signs, and the epitome of these signs we call language, insofar as they metalinguistically possess a self-relation and a world-aspect. In this natural poetry, writing does thus not cease to be an ontological continuation. Every word it expresses follows the world-experience of a self, and even the aesthetic status granted to it could still be regarded as a reflex of this world.

Artificial poetry, however, is understood here as a kind of poetry in which, insofar as it was produced, e.g., by a machine, there is no personal poetic consciousness with its experiences, encounters, feelings, memories, thoughts, visions of an imagination, etc., thus no preexisting world, and in which writing is no longer an ontological continuation through which the words' world-aspect could be related to a self. Consequently, neither a lyrical subject nor a fictional epic world can be meaningfully drawn from this poetry's linguistic fixation. While an intentional beginning of the word process is thus characteristic of natural poetry, there can only be a material origin for artificial poetry" (142).

5. Other larger languages also offer LLMs. For example, the most successful early LLMs, dated until 2022, for the Chinese language are Wu Dao 2.0 by Beijing Academy for AI, PanGu-Alpha by Huawei, and YUAN by Inspur; for Russian are YaLM 100B by Yandex and ruRoberta-large by Sberbank; and for South Korean is HyperCLOVA by Naver Corp. DeepMind also trained a model called RETRO in Urdu, Swahili, Spanish, German, French, Russian, Chinese, and English.

6. Visual language models emerged from 2021 on: OpenAI's DALL-E and CLIP, Google's Imagen and Parti, and (under Google since 2014) DeepMind's Flamingo and Gato. Gato is a scalable generalist agent, meaning that it applies input from one modality to another. For example, a written order in one mode could be applied to a separate mode of a robot enacting the order. For some, this step means world building that leads toward artificial general intelligence (AGI). For others, it is merely a practical application of what more can be done with this technology.

7. Stanford used this paper and terminology to establish itself as the place for research of multimodal LLMs and their future iterations while it also established The Center for Research on Foundation Models.

8. Ethical questions around NLP translate to LLMs. For example, compare Safiya Umoja Noble's monograph *Algorithms of Oppression: How Search Engines Reinforce Racism* from 2018 with the LLM-focused paper from 2021 by Bender et al., 'On the Dangers of Stochastic Parrots: Can Language Models Be Too Big?'

Technologists have predominantly tackled these issues through value alignment, i.e. instilling our values in machines (see Brian Christian's *The Alignment Problem*, 2020). AI products, including LLMs, come from vastly different cultures where fundamental norms and values are not universally shared, even among communities with the same language. For instance, race and gender discrimination is a contested issue in Western societies, but the mere concepts of race and gender have radically different definitions both within and outside of these societies. Likewise, privacy and security are handled much more liberally in non-Western countries. Furthermore, alignment preferences are typically implemented by those in positions of power, whether they be the technologists themselves or politicians. The relationality of societal values as well as how to represent them through AI, are two domains of ethical research that have received some immediate attention but require much more.

9. This book does not have the space to address ethical questions, from social bias and discrimination to misuse and misinformation. However, I would like to suggest that we expand the realm of ethical inquiry in AI by taking a lesson from the success story of data and machine learning as modes of describing and producing the world. Data and machine learning defy control—they are about uncertainty, probability, and navigation through correlations and patterns. Thus, the world they produce is never finished and closed, as opposed to the world of predictable symbolic AI or classical engineering, which is built around human control of the machine. A colossal task is ahead of us to rethink ethics in terms of data that do not differentiate between human, natural, or technical realms. Poetry, proteins, and robots are all parts of the same data system, even if profoundly different, of kin but not of kind. I suggest we begin by asking: What are human morals in the world of nonhuman intelligences? A good example of this direction is a 2022 article, 'The Model Is The Message,' in which Benjamin Bratton and Blaise Agüera y Arcas list a number of data-based problems with large scale models, showing an original approach to ethics that considers how technical aspects of the actual technology translate into social ramifications.

10. Peiqi Sui calls it post-structuralism in his 2023 dissertation titled *Large Language Models are Post-Structuralist Intertexts,* arguing that "the term's poststructuralist legacy enables a knowledge contribution in the other direction: theories of intertextuality could help us gain a more robust understanding of large language models (LLMs) and their hermeneutic processes" (4).

11. The name of Anthropic's AI assistant/large language model Claude, as Kevin Roose writes in *The New York Times* piece from July 2023, "depending on which employee you ask, was either a nerdy tribute to the 20th-century mathematician Claude Shannon or a friendly, male-gendered name designed to counterbalance the female-gendered names (Alexa, Siri, Cortana) that other tech companies gave their A.I. assistants" (par. 7).

12. Ada Lovelace's Note G from 1842 describes an algorithm for generating Bernoulli numbers with Babbage's Analytical Engine.

13. Markov tested the same process on Asakov's novel *The Childhood of Bagrov, the Grandson* later.

14. Shannon used no computer since no digital computers were available yet. The transistor (a miniature semiconductor) was invented right at the time of Shannon's writing his mathematical theory of communication paper.

15. Following Shannon in the 1950s, Roman Jakobson based his structuralist linguistics work, in collaboration with Morris Halle, on information theory, game theory, and cybernetics, as a "far-reaching account of language as a cybernetic system" (Geoghegan *Code* 98–99).

16. More on how information theory intertwines with LLMs in Łukasz Dębowski's *Information Theory Meets Power Laws* (2020).

17. Hartley writes: "a quantitative measure whereby the capacities of various systems [telegraph, telephone, television] to transmit information may be compared … information is a very elastic term … eliminate psychological factors" (536).

18. "The fundamental problem of communication is that of reproducing at one point either exactly or approximately a message selected at another point. Frequently the messages have *meaning*; that is they refer to or are correlated according to some system with certain physical or conceptual entities. These semantic aspects of communication are irrelevant to the engineering problem. The significant aspect is that the actual message is one *selected from a set* of possible messages. The system must be designed to operate for each possible selection, not just the one which will actually be chosen since this is unknown at the time of design (Shannon 'A Mathematical' 623).

19. For comparison, contrast LLMs with GANs (generative adversarial networks, described in Chapter 1) where speech is generated on the level of phonetics, from sounds (which are continuous) to phonemes (which are discrete) and finally into words (also discrete). Speech generation occurs thus at the very base, from mere sound/noise/acoustics. Text-generation occurs one level up, but cannot work without reaching back to the continuous, primary base.

20. A mental model of the world is described by Joe Wright Forrester, the father of system dynamics, in 1971: "The image of the world around us, which we carry in our head, is just a model. Nobody in his head imagines all the world, government or country. He has only selected concepts, and relationships between them, and uses those to represent the real system" (Ha and Schmidhuber).

21. In the imitation of epistolary writing and normative love experiences, the irony of the queer creators of M.U.C. is not lost (Gaboury par. 16).

22. There is no indication that Roald Dahl knew contemporary science and technology. It is possible that he was aware of it via public consumption of the news, such as the well-known figure Alan Turing's predictions in *The Times* from 1949 quoted above.

23. Just a few of the many examples of other Anglophone fictional works that depicted writing machines are George Orwell's 'versificator', a tool that autonomously produces music and literature, from his novel *1984* (1949); Fritz Lieber's 'wordmills' in *The Silver Eggheads* (1959); and Arthur C. Clarke's 'Word Loom' in *The Steam-Powered Word Processor* (1986), based on a mathematical sermon-producing machine.

24. For example, in 2019, Brazilian romance novelist Cristiane Serruya was accused of infringing at least 93 books and 41 authors according to the bestselling American author Nora Roberts, whose works were among those plagiarized on the Amazon Kindle platform (Flood 'Nora' par. 3).

25. In 1967 American visual artist Alison Knowles—with the help of composer James Tenney, skilled in musical algorithmic composition—wrote a computerized poem, *The House of Dust*, with randomly assembled verses, that was turned into a visual exhibition the following year. The first computer-generated book is from 1984, titled *The Policeman's Beard is Half Constructed*, authored by computer Racter and doctored by William Chamberlain and Thomas Etter.

More recently, Johannes Heldén and Håkan Jonson's artwork *Evolution* from 2014 emulates text and music based on Heldén's previous work. Particularly inspired by Roald Dahl's 'The Great Automatic Grammatisator' was Alexandra Bridarolli's 2016 message machine that produces poems under three demands: "genre, feelings, and driving force" ('Victorians' par. 6). Among many other prose-generating programs, most prominent are Mark Riedl's storytelling algorithm Scheherazade-IF (2012), a group around machine learning comedy called Botnik (2016), Kory Mathewson's group around the improv theater, and a GPT-3-powered video game, AI Dungeon (2019).

With the advent of NFTs and crypto-technologies, many poets and artists took advantage of the new possibilities, including Laura Kerr, Sasha Stiles, Mark America, and Anna María Caballero. For details on these and other accounts of digital arts, see *Mainframe Experimentalism* from 2012, edited by Hannah Higgins and Douglas Kahn.

26. The title of the story is a reference to an essayistic study *Hlapci, heroji, ljudje* [*Lackeys, Heroes, People*] (1968) by a striking and enigmatic comparative literature professor Dušan Pirjevec-Ahac, who highly influenced the Slovenian culture of that time. The essay discussed a reputable play *Hlapci* by Ivan Cankar, in which he describes a Slovenian national character as conformist. Pirjevec supports Cankar's provocation with his argument that the break of modern subjectivity is inevitable in the fight against conformism: conformism ('lackeyship') is what preserved Slovenians as a nation (88).

27. Perhaps inspired by Bosnian pseudo-historian Semir Osmanagić.

28. "...pomena preprosto ni več" (Tomažin 18).

29. "...vsakršna generativna naratološka struktura [je] zamenljiva s človeško, pa to vsekakor ne pomeni, da gre za kakršnokoli razčaranje [sic] sveta ali njegovo uničenje" (Tomažin 21).

30. Borges defended Ramon Llull's *ars combinatoria*, a divine-logical method to discover truth or knowledge through a combination of concepts.

31. "Ludovic Bitterman, nesojeni Houellebecqov naslednik, vsem na sceni pa se že od tedaj dozdeva, da je Bitterman le programer, ki mu je uspelo spisati dobro kodo po tekstualni predlogi mojstrovih tekstov, sedaj pa pobira nagrade, ki bi morale znova pripasti njemu" (Tomažin 21–22).

32. "Prav algoritmizacija pisatelja pa je pravzaprav borgesovski raj [...]. Ja, kot namiguje Tomažin, popoln borgesovski avtor je stroj, je algoritem" (Kuret 97).

33. "Vprašanje ni več, kako se skriti, temveč kako kar najbolj skrbno postati del nepreglednega arhiva" (Tomažin 45).

34. "...med katerimi so v večini doktorji kognitivnih znanosti, nekaj je tudi matematikov, predvsem pa so vsi izredni ljubitelji pokojnega Davida Fosterja Wallacea" (Tomažin 26).

35. "Und ich konnte mit ihm keinen Text schreiben, der künstlerisch hätte bestehen können" (Kehlmann 52).

36. "Für mich persönlich aber war es ein Erfolg, dann ich habe eine nichtmenschliche Intelligenz wirklich kennen gelernt" (Kehlmann 52).

37. "Allmählich erst wurde mir klar, dass ich mir Künstliche Intelligenz, über die ich doch so viel gelesen hatte, immer noch wie den Androiden C3PO oder wie den narzisstischen Supercomputer HAL vorgestellt hatte—als ein menschliches Wesen in metallischer Umkleidung, als eine Person im Kostüm" (10).

38. "Ohne die Arbeit von menschlichen Übersetzern, die die Sprache tatsächlich verstehen, ginge das nicht. Aber der prädiktive Algorithmus, der diese menschliche Arbeit per statistischer Auswertung nutzt, der braucht die spräche nicht zu verstehen, er hat weder Wörterbücher noch Grammatikregeln zur Hand, und er hat keine Ahnung, was das von ihm vorgeschlagene Ergebnis bedeutet, ja mehr noch: Er wusste nicht einmal, was das sein soll, 'Bedeutung' oder 'Ahnung'" (8–9).

39. In size—which does matter for LLMs performance for now—CTRL is closer to OpenAI's GPT-2, which has 1.5 billion parameters.

40. For the concept of embodiment in relation to digital arts, see Denise Doyle's *Digital Embodiment and the Arts: Exploring Hybrid Spaces through Emerging Technologies* (2024).

41. To name just a few writers with technical expertise: Andrew Mayne, Eliezer Yudkowsky, Eric Choi, Danielle Braithwe-Shirley, Habib William Kherbek, Aude Oliva, Robert Evans, John Walker, Malka Older, Nora Khan, Marc Stiefler, Vernor Vinge, Neal Stephenson, Rudy Ricker.

CONCLUSION

1. Attributed to Marshall McLuhan, with the exact words quoted in John Culkin's A Schoolman's Guide to Marshall McLuhan (1967). The phrase was attributed to Winston Churchill, Robert Flaherty, John Culkin, Winston Churchill, Robert Flaherty, Emerson Brown, William J. Mitchell. The quotes alludes to William Blake's poem *Milton*, in which Blake envisions the poet's vocation as one who reshapes human perception and reality.

2. As a practical proof of concept, I was able to employ this knowledge in process-based consulting for big tech and start-ups in non-profit and for-profit branches of Transformations of the Human in the years 2020-23. We collaborated with artists, technologists, and philosophers on conceptual and technical questions around AI.

3. For example, in the American Comparative Literature Association's (ACLA) State of the Discipline Report from 2017, the Beyond the Human section focuses on the environment and animals (nature) and is separate from the digital technology section, titled Media.

4. "Critical AI, while recognizing the reductive, even absurd aspects of the term AI and the magical thinking it perpetuates, nonetheless allows for a kind of linguistic pragmatism, treating the term metonymically and engaging AI as an assemblage of technological arrangements and sociotechnical practices, as concept, ideology, and *dispositif*. This may seem to open up fairly quickly into the domain of critical thinking about computational culture and technology writ large, but there is a specificity and analytic precision in the focus on data, algorithms, model architectures, and the production of prediction. Critical AI, then, is itself a historical and epistemic formation" (Raley and Rhee 188).

Bibliography

PRIMARY

Agüera y Arcas, Blaise. *Ubi Sunt*. Hat & Beard Press, 2022.
A.I. Rising (First presented as *Ederlezi Rising*). Directed by Lazar Bodroža. Performances by Sebastian Cavazza, Stoya, Maruša Majer, Kirsty Besterman. Creative Century Entertainment, 2018. DVD.
Alegría, Claribel. 'Galatea Ante el Espejo/Galatea Before the Mirror.' *Fugues*. Tran. Darwin J. Flakoli. Curbstone Press, 1993. 84–85.
Allado-MacDowell, K. *Pharmako-AI*. Ignota Books, 2020.
Alyea, Dorothy. 'Galatea.' *Poetry* 50/3 (1937): 149.
Andersen, Hans Christian. *Little Mermaid* [*Den lille havfrue*]. Dreamscape Media, 2007 [1836].
Anstey, F. [pseud. for Thomas Anstey Guthrie]. *The Tinted Venus: A Farcical Romance*. George Munro, 1887 [1885].
Antonijevo razbijeno ogledalo. Directed by Dušan Makavejev. Performances by Anja Baškovac, Dragoljub Ivkov. Kino Klub Beograd: Beograd, 1957. *YouTube* Apr 12, 2011 www.youtube.com/watch?v=iJvLNowrNM0 Accessed Sep 1, 2018.
Annihilation. Directed by Alex Garland. Performances by Natalie Portman, Oscar Isaac, Jenifer Jason-Leigh. Paramount Pictures, 2018. DVD.
Asimov, Isaac. 'Galatea.' *Azazel*. Doubleday, 1988. 198–201.
Babbage, Charles. 'Died the 20th of October, 1871.' *Nature* 5/106 (November 9, 1871): 28–29.
Babbage, Charles. *On the Economy of Machinery and Manufactures*. Knight, 1832.
Babbage, Charles. *Charles Babbage: On the Principles and Development of the Calculator and Other Seminal Writings*. Ed. Philip Morrison and Emily Morrison. Dover Publications, 2013.
Babbage, Charles. *Passages from the Life of a Philosopher*. Longman, Roberts, and Green, 1864.

Balzac, Honoré de. 'Sarrasine.' *Honoré de Balzac: Scenes of Parisian Life.* Vol. 9. The Rittenhouse Press, 1830/1896. 203–60.
Bauby, Jean-Dominique. *The Diving Bell and the Butterfly* [*Le scaphandre et le papillon*]. Tran. Jessica Foster. Alfred A. Knopf, 1997.
Bautista, Amalia. 'Galatea.' *Litoral: Humo en el Cuerpo* 246 (2008): 296.
Bell, Alexander Melville. *The Bride: A Play, in Five Acts.* W. J. Cleaver, 1847.
'Be Right Back.' Black Mirror. TV episode. Dir. Owen Harris. Performances by Hayley Atwell, Domhnall Gleeson, Claire Keelan. 2013.
Blade Runner. Directed by Ridley Scott. Performances by Harrison Ford, Rutger Hauer, Sean Young. Warner Bros. Pictures, 1982. DVD.
Blade Runner 2049. Directed by Dennis Villeneuve. Performances by Ryan Gosling, Harrison Ford, Ana de Armas. Warner Bros. Pictures, 2017. DVD.
Buchanan, Robert Williams. 'Pygmalion the Sculptor.' *The Complete Poetical Works of Robert Buchanan.* Vol. 1. Chatto & Windus, 1901. 59–64.
Byron, George Gordon. *Childe Harold.* Ed. Henry F. Tozer. Clarendon Press, 1885.
Calvert Hall, Eliza. 'Galatea.' *Scribner's Monthly* 19 (November 1879-April 1880): 34.
Calvino, Italo. 'Cybernetics and Ghosts.' *The Uses of Literature: Essays.* Tran. Patrick Creagh. Harcourt Brace Jovanovich Publishers, 1986. 3–27.
Čapek, Karl. *R.U.R.: Rossum's Universal Robots.* Dover Thrift Editions, 2001 [1920].
Chiang, Ted. 'Story of Your Life.' *Stories of Your Life and Others.* Tor, 2002. 117–78.
Chiang, Ted. 'The Great Silence.' *Exhalation: Stories.* Alfred A. Knopf, 2019. 231–36.
Clarke, Arthur C. *2001: A Space Odyssey.* ROC, 2000.
Clawson Stryker, Leonora. 'Galatea to Pygmalion.' *The Music Makers: An Anthology of Recent American Poetry.* Ed. Stanton Arthur Coblentz. B. Ackerman, Inc., 1945. 242–43.
Cline, Ernest. Ready Player One. Crown Publishers, 2011.
Coleridge, Ernest Hartley. 'Pygmalion's Bride.' *Poems.* Lane, Bodley Head, 1898.
Collodi, Carlo. *Pinocchio: The Tale of a Puppet.* Tran. M. A. Murray, revised by G. Tassinari. Penguin, 2002.
Dahl, Roald. 'The Great Automatic Grammatisator.' *Someone Like You.* Alfred A. Knopf, 1953. 250–76.
Deslandes, André-François Boureau. *Pygmalions, ou la Statue animée.* In Henri Coulet, ed. *Pygmalions des lumières.* Desjonquères, 1998 [1741]. 47–66.
Douglas, Adams. *The Hitchhiker's Guide to the Galaxy.* Harmony Books, 1979.
Duffy, Carol Ann. 'Pygmalion's Bride.' *The World's Wife: Poems.* Faber and Faber, 1999. 51–52.
Dumas, Alexandre. *Le Comte de Monte-Cristo.* Garnier, 1962.
Educating Rita. Dir. Lewis Gilbert. Performances by Michael Caine, Julie Walters, Michael Williams. Acorn Pictures, 1983. DVD.
Ex Machina. Directed by Alex Garland. Performances by Alicia Vikander, Oscar Isaac, Domhnall Gleeson. Universal Pictures, 2014. DVD.
Forster, E. M. 'The Machine Stops.' *The Wesleyan Anthology of Science Fiction.* Wesleyan University Press, 2010. 50–78.
Fowles, John. *The French Lieutenant's Woman.* Random House, 1969.
Genlis, Stéphanie-Félicité de. 'Pygmalion et Galatée, ou la statue animée depuis vingt quatre heures.' *Nouveaux contes moraux et nouvelles historiques.* Vol. 6. Maradan, 1806.
Gibson, William. *Neuromancer.* Ace Books, 1984.

Gilbert, W. S. *Pygmalion and Galatea: An Entirely Original Mythological Comedy*. Forgotten Books, 2019 [1871].
Goethe, Johann Wolfgang von. *Faust. Der Tragödie zweiter Teil*. J. G. Cotta'schen Buchhandlung, 1832.
Goethe, Johann Wolfgang von. *Faust I and II, Vol. 2: Goethe's Collected Works – Updated Edition*. Ed. and tran. Stuart Atkins. Princeton University Press, 1984 [1832].
Graves, Robert. 'Pygmalion to Galatea.' *Poems 1914–1926*. 1926. 364.
Hallam, Arthur Henry. 'Lines Spoken in the Character of Pygmalion.' *Remains in Verse and Prose of Arthur Henry Hallam*. Ticknor and Fields, 1863. 125–26.
Handke, Peter. *Ich bin ein Bewohner des Elfenbeinturms*. Suhrkamp Verlag, 1972.
Harbou, Thea von. Metropolis. Gregg Press, 1975 [1925].
Hardy, Thomas. 'Barbara of the House of Grebe.' *A Group of Noble Dames*. Harper and Brothers, 1891. 69–120.
Hawthorne, Nathaniel. 'Birth-mark.' *Nathaniel Hawthorne's Tales: Authoritative Texts, Backgrounds, Criticism*. 2nd ed. Ed. James Mcintosh. W.W. Norton & Co, 2013. 152–65.
Hawthorne, Nathaniel. 'Drowne's Wooden Image.' *Nathaniel Hawthorne's Tales: Authoritative Texts, Backgrounds, Criticism*. Ed. James Mcintosh. 2nd ed. W.W. Norton & Co, 2013. 218–27.
Hawthorne, Nathaniel. 'Rappaccini's Daughter.' *Nathaniel Hawthorne's Tales: Authoritative Texts, Backgrounds, Criticism*. Ed. James Mcintosh. 2nd ed. W.W. Norton & Co, 2013 [1844]. 228–53.
Hawthorne, Nathaniel. 'The Golden Touch.' A Wonder Book. Hodder & Stoughton, 1922 [1851]. 47–67.
Hawthorne, Nathaniel. 'The Marble Faun.' *The Portable Hawthorne*. Penguin Books, 2005.
Hazlitt, William. *Liber Amoris; or the new Pygmalion*. Printed for John Hunt, 1923.
H.D. 'Pygmalion.' Egoist 4(2) (1917): 2.
Heine, Heinrich. *Florentine Nights*. Tran. Charles Godfrey Leland. Methuen & Company Limited, 1927 [1836].
Her. Directed by Spike Jonze. Performances by Joaquin Phoenix, Scarlett Johansson, Amy Adams. Warner Bros, 2013. DVD.
Hickey, Emily Henrietta. 'Sonnet.' A Sculptor and Other Poems. Kegan Paul, 1881. 138.
Hoffmann, E. T. A. 'The Sandman' ['Der Sandmann']. *The Tales of Hoffmann: Stories*. William E. Rudge's Sons, 1816/1943. 1–33.
Hugo. Dir. Michael Scorsese. Performances by Asa Butterfield, Chloë Grace Moretz, Christopher Lee. GK Films, 2011.
Ishiguro, Kazuo. *Klara and the Sun*. Alfred A. Knopf, 2021.
James, Henry. The Last of the Valerii. Boydell Press, 1971 [1874].
Kavanaugh, Patrick. 'Pygmalion.' *Selected Poems*. Penguin Books, 1978. 4.
Kazemi, Darius. *Teens Wander Around a House*: *A NaNoGenMo Draft*. Nov 12, 2013. tinysubversions.com/nanogenmo/novel-2.pdf Accessed Feb 5, 2020.
Kehlmann, Daniel. *Mein Algorithmus und Ich: Stuttgarter Zukunftsrede*. Klett-Cotta, 2021.
Kehlmann, Daniel. *My Algorithm and Me*. Tran. Ross Benjamin. 2021. Yet unpublished. Cited with permission.

Kleist, Heinrich von. 'The Foundling.' *Selected Writings*. Hackett Publishing Company, 2004 [1811]. 356–66.
Lancaster, George Eric. 'Pygmalion in Cyprus.' *Pygmalion in Cyprus and Other Poems*. Clowes, 1880.
Lars and the Real Girl. Directed by Craig Gillespie. Performances by Ryan Gosling, Emily Mortimer, Paul Schneider. Metro-Goldwyn-Mayer, 2007. DVD.
Lang, Andrew. 'The New Pygmalion or the Statue's Choice.' *Longman's Magazine*, 1911. 299–302.
Lem, Stanisław. *Golem XIV*. Wydawnictwo Literackie, 1981.
Lem, Stanisław. 'Golem XIV.' *Imaginary Magnitude* [*Wielkość urojona*]. Tran. Marc E. Heine, 1984. 97–248.
Lem, Stanisław. 'Maska.' *Kongres futurologiczny; Maska*. Wydawnictwo Literackie, 1983.
Lem, Stanisław. *Solaris*. Ministerstwa Obrony Narodowej, 1961.
Lem, Stanisław. *Summa Technologiae*. Tran. Joanna Zylinska. University of Minnesota Press, 2013.
Lem, Stanisław. 'The Mask.' *Mortal Engines*. Tran. Michael Kandel. Seabury Press, 1977. 197–212.
Leroux, Gaston. 'La Machine à assassiner.'; 'La Poupée sanglante.' *Aventures incroyables*. R. Laffont, 1992 [1909].
Lofting, Hugh. *The story of Doctor Dolittle: Being the history of his peculiar life at home and astonishing adventures in foreign parts*. Frederick A. Stokes Company, 1920.
Lost in Translation. Dir. Sofia Coppola. Performances by Bill Murray, Scarlett Johansson, Giovanni Ribisi. Focus Features, 2003. DVD.
Mannequin. Dir. Michael Gottlieb. Performances by Andrew McCarthy, Kim Cattrall, Estelle Getty. Gladden Entertainment, 1987. DVD.
McCaffrey, Anne. 'The Ship Who Sang.' *Women of Wonder: Science Fiction Stories by Women about Women*. Ed. Pamela Sargent. Vintage Books, Random House, 1975 [1969]. 82–107.
Mérimée, Prosper. 'La Vénus d'Ille.' *La Vénus d'Ille et autres nouvelles*. Flammarion, 1982 [1835].
Metropolis. Dir. Fritz Lang. Performances by Brigitte Helm, Alfred Abel, Gustav Frölich. Paruamet, 1927. DVD.
Miller, Arthur G. 'Pygmalion.' *Innocent Merriment: An Anthology of Light Verse*. Ed. Franklin Pierce Adams. Whittlesey House, 1942. 110.
Miller, Madeline. *Galatea: A Short Story*. Harper Collins Publishers, 2013.
Montgomery, Roselle Mercier. 'Galatea to Pygmalion.' *Many Devices*. D. Appleton, 1929.
Moore, C. L. 'No Woman Born.' *The Best of C. L. Moore*. Ed. Lester del Rey. Ballantine Books, 1876 [1944]. 200–42.
Morris, William. 'Pygmalion and the Image.' *The Earthly Paradise*. Ellis, 1868.
My Fair Lady. Directed by George Cukor. Performances by Audrey Hepburn, Rex Harrison, Jeremy Brett. Warner Bros. Pictures, 1964. DVD.
My Fair Lady. Original Broadway Production. By Alan Jay Lerner and Frederick Loewe. Performances by Julie Andrew, Rex Harrison, Stanley Holloway. 1956. DVD.
Nešković, Zoran. 'Predveče se nikako ne može...' *Tamni vilajet: Izbor jugoslavneskog SF*. Vol. 1. 2nd extended ed. Samostalno autorsko izdanje, Boban Knežević, 1989. 175–90.

Ní Chuilleanáin, Eiléan. 'Pygmalion's Image.' *Selected Poems*. Faber and Faber, 2008. 49.
Osgood, Frances Sargent Locke. 'The Statue to Pygmalion.' *Poems*. Thorne Ricker, 1849. 94.
Ovid, P. Naso. *Metamorphoses*. Tran. A. D. Melville. Oxford University Press, 2008.
Ovid, P. Naso. 'Pygmalion.' *Metamorphoses* (Latin). Ed. Hugo Magnus. 1982. https://www.perseus.tufts.edu/hopper/text?doc=Perseus%3Atext%3A1999.02.0029%3Abook%3D10%3Acard%3D243 Accessed Jun 30, 2018.
Ovid, P. Naso. 'Pygmalion.' *Metamorphoses* (English). Ed. Brookes More. 1922. https://www.perseus.tufts.edu/hopper/text?doc=Perseus%3Atext%3A1999.02.0028%3Abook%3D10%3Acard%3D243 Accessed Jun 30, 2018.
Ovid, P. Naso. *Tristia*. Tran. A. S. Kline. *Poetry in Translation*, 2003. www.poetryintranslation.com/PITBR/Latin/OvidTristiaBkFive.php Accessed July 1, 2022.
Pirandello, Luigi. 'Six Characters in Search of an Author.' *Eight Modern Plays*. Ed. Anthony Caputi, 1991/1925. 210–56.
Poe, Edgar Allan. 'The Man That Was Used Up.' *The selected writings of Edgar Allan Poe: Authoritative texts, backgrounds and contexts, criticism*. Ed. G. B. Thompson. W.W. Norton, 2004.
Poe, Edgar Allan. 'The Oval Portrait.' *The Best of Edgar Allan Poe*. Vol. 1. RIPOL Classics 1842/2018. 321–25.
Powers, Richard. *Galatea 2.2*. Farrar Strauss Giroux, 1995.
Powers Smith, Chard. 'Galatea.' Anthology of Magazine Verse. Schulte Publishing Company, 1925. 288.
Pretty Woman. Dir. Gary Marshall. Performances by Julia Robers, Richard Gere, Jason Alexander. Walt Disney Studios, 1990.
Pygmalion. Directed by Leslie Howard and Anthony Asquith. Performances by Leslie Howard, Wendy Hiller, Wilfrid Lawson. Metro-Goldwyn-Mayer, 1938. DVD.
Racter (William Chamberlain, Thomas Etter). *The Policeman's Beard is Half Constructed: First Book Ever Written by a Computer*. Warner Books, 1984.
Rey, Lester del. 'Helen O'Loy.' *Astounding Science Fiction* 22/4 (1939): 119–25.
Rousseau, Jean-Jacques. *Pygmalion: A poem*. Printed by J. Kearby, 1779.
Rousseau, Jean-Jacques. *Pygmalion: scène lyrique*. Theatre Contemporain Illustré, 1771 [1762].
Rowe, Charles J. 'Galatea.' *Poetry Review* 38 (1947): 414.
Scott, William Bell. 'Pygmalion.' Poems. Longmans, Green, and Co., 1875. 193.
Shakespeare, William. *The Tempest*. Ed. Daniel Fischlin. Oxford University Press, 2013.
Shaw, George Bernard. *Back to Methuselah: A Metabiological Pentateuch*. The Limited Editions Club, 1939.
Shaw, George Bernard. *Pygmalion: A Romance in Five Acts. Definitive text*. Ed. L. W. Conolly. Methuen Drama, 1912/2008.
Shaw, George Bernard, and Mrs. Patrick Campbell. *Bernard Shaw and Mrs. Patrick Campbell: Their Correspondence*. Ed. Alan Dent. Alfred A. Knopf, 1952.
Sheldon, Alice [James Tiptree Jr.]. 'The Girl Who Was Plugged In.' *Her Smoke Rose Up Forever*. Tachyon Publications, 2004 [1973]. 43–78.
Shelley, Mary Wollstonecraft. *Frankenstein; or the modern Prometheus*. Ed. Maurice Hindle. Penguin Books, 1818/2003.

Shoemaker, Martin L. *Today, I Am Carey*. Baen, 2019.
Shoemaker, Martin L. 'Today, I Am Paul.' *Nebula Awards Showcase* 2017. Ed. Julie E. Czerneda. Pyr, 2017.
Simone. Dir. Andrew Niccol. Performances by Al Pacino, Catherine Keener, Rachel Roberts. New Line Cinema, 2002. DVD.
Solaris. Dir. Steven Sodebergh. Performances by George Clooney, Natascha McElhone, Ulrich Tukur. 20th Century Studios, 2002.
Space Odyssey. Directed by Stanley Kubrick. Performances by Keir Dullea, Gary Lockwood. Metro-Goldwyn-Mayer, 1968. DVD.
Spomenicima ne treba verovati [Don't Believe in Monuments]. Directed by Dušan Makavejev. 1958. *YouTube* Jan 17, 2018. www.youtube.com/watch?v=c_BZPumapSk Accessed Feb 17, 2019.
Stephenson, Neal. *Snow Crash*. Bantam Books, 2000 [1992].
Stäel, Germaine de. '*Le Mannequin*.' *An Extraordinary Woman: Selected Writings of Germaine de Stäel*. Trans. Vivian Folkenflik. Columbia University Press, 1987 [1881]. 325–47.
Stuart Phelps Ward, Elizabeth. 'Galatea.' *Classical Mythology in English Literature: A Critical Anthology*. Ed. Geoffrey Miles. Routledge, 1999 [1884]. 424–25.
Sturge Moore, Thomas. 'Pygmalion.' *The Vinedresser, and Other Poems*. At the Sign of the Unicorn, 1899. 54.
Šeligo, Rudi. *Triptih Agate Schwarzkobler*. Obzorja, 1968.
Šeligo, Rudi. *Triptih Agate Schwarzkobler*. 2nd ed. Kermauner Taras. Mladinska, 1982.
Taggard, Genevieve. 'Galatea Again.' *Words for the Chisel*. A. A. Knopf, 1926. 39.
Tanizaki, Jun'ichirō. Naomi. Tran. Anthony H. Chambers. Vintage International Books, 2001 [1825].
Tennyson, A. B. S. 'Pygmalion.' *A Legend of Old Persia, and Other Poems*. Heinemann, 1911 [1891]. 44–52.
Tennyson, Frederick. 'Pygmalion.' *Daphne, and Other Poems*. Macmillan, 1891. 38–63.
Tomažin, Andrej. 'Heroes, Lackeys, and Artificial Intelligence.' Tran. Michael Biggins. Unpublished. Used with permission. 12 May 2020. 1–8.
Tomažin, Andrej. 'Hlapci, heroji in umetna inteligenca.' *Anonimna tehnologija*. LUD Literatura, 2018. 17–31.
Triptih Agate Schwarzkobler. Directed by Matjaž Klopčič. Performances by Nataša Barbara Gračner, Vlado Novak, Judita Zidar. 1997. TV Slovenija, DVD.
Vavasseur, Gustave Le. 'Pygmalion.' *Poésies complètes*. A. Lemerre, 1888–96.
Vertigo. Dir. by Alred Hitchcock. Performances by James Stewart, Kim Novak, Barbara Bel Geddes. Paramount Pictures, 1985. DVD.
Vigand, Philippe, and Stéphane Vigand. *Only the Eyes Say Yes: A Love Story*. [*Putain de silence*.] No translator given. Arcade Publishing, 1999.
Villiers de l'Isle-Adam, Auguste. *L'Ève Future*. Charpentier, 1891 [1886].
Westworld. TV Series. Created by Johnathan Nolan and Lisa Joy. Performances by Evan Rachel Wood, Thandiwe Newton, Jeffrey Right. 2016-20.
Wharton, Edith. The House of Mirth. Norton, 1990 [1905].
Woolner, Thomas. *Pygmalion*. Macmillan, 1881.
Zola, Émile. *Thérèse Raquin*. University of Glasgow French and German Publications, 1990.

SECONDARY

Adams, Jon. 'The Sufficiency of Code: *Galatea 2.2* and the Necessity of Embodiment.' *Intersections: Essays on Richard Powers*. Ed. Stephen J. Burn and Peter Dempsey. Dalkey Archive Press, 2008. 137–50.

Adams, Rachel. '*Helen A'Loy* and other tales of female automata: a gendered reading of the narratives of hopes and fears of intelligent machines and artificial intelligence.' *AI & Society* 35 (2020): 567–79.

Addel, Jordi, Antonio Bonaforte, and David Escuder. 'Production of filled pauses in concatenative speech synthesis based on the underlying fluent sentence.' *Speech Communication* 54/3 (2012): 459–76.

Adshade, Marina. 'How Sex Robots Could Revolutionize Marriage—for the Better.' *Slate* 14 Aug 2018 www.slate.com/technology/2018/08/sex-robots-could-totally-redefine-the-institution-of-marriage.html Accessed Aug 31, 2018.

Agüera y Arcas, Blaise. 'Artificial Neural Networks are Making Strides Towards Consciousness, According to Blaise Agüera y Arcas.' *The Economist* 9 Jun 2022 www.economist.com/by-invitation/2022/06/09/artificial-neural-networks-are-making-strides-towards-consciousness-according-to-blaise-aguera-y-arcas Accessed Jun 20, 2022.

Aguera y Arcas, Blaise. 'Do large language models understand us?' *Medium* 16 Dec 2021 www.medium.com/@blaisea/do-large-language-models-understand-us-6f881d6d8e75 Accessed Dec 20, 2021.

Aguera y Arcas, Blaise. 'Do large language models understand us?' *Daedalus* 151/2 (2022): 183–97.

Altman, Sam. 'Her.' 13 May 2024 10.45am Tweet www.x.com/sama/status/1790075827666796666?lang=en Accessed May 13, 2024.

American Psychiatric Association. *Diagnostic and Statistical Manual of Mental Disorders* (*DSM-5*). 5th edition. American Psychiatric Association. dsm.psychiatryonline.org/doi/book/10.1176/appi.books.9780890425596 Accessed Nov 9, 2018.

Andermatt, Michael. 'Artificial Life and Romantic Brides.' *Romantic Prose Fiction*. Ed. Gerald Gillespie, Manfred Engel, and Bernard Dieterle. John Benjamins Publishing Company, 2008. 204–25.

Anderson, Chris. 'The End of Theory: The Data Deluge Makes the Scientific Method Obsolete.' *Wired* 23 June 2008 www.wired.com/2008/06/pb-theory Accessed Apr 28, 2023.

Andreas, Jacob, Gašper Beguš, Michael M. Bronstein, Roee Diamant, Denley Delaney, Shane Gero, Shafi Goldwasser, David F. Gruber, Sarah de Haas, Peter Malkin, Nikolay Pavlov, Roger Payne, Giovanni Petri, Daniela Rus, Pratyusha Sharma, Dan Tchernov, Pernille Tønnesen, Antonio Torralba, Daniel Vogt, Robert J. Wood. 'Toward understanding the communication in sperm whales.' *iScience* 25/6 (2022).

Andringa, Els, and Margrit Schreier. 'How Literature Enters Life: An Introduction.' *Poetics Today* 25/2 (2004): 161–69.

Applebaum, Lauren, Marie Coppola, and Susan Goldin-Meadow. 'Prosody in a Communication System Developed without a Language Model.' *Sing Lang Linguist* 17/2 (2014): 181–212.

Arbib, Michael A. 'Mirror systems: evolving imitation and the bridge from praxis to language.' *The Oxford Handbook of Language Evolution*. Eds. Kathleen R. Gibson and Maggie Tallerman. Oxford University Press, 2012. 208–15.

Atanasoski, Neda, and Kalindi Vora. *Surrogate Humanity: Race, Robots, and the Politics of Technological Futures*. Duke University Press, 2019.

Babbage, Charles, and Martin Campbell-Kelly. *Passages from the Life of a Philosopher*. Rutgers University Press, 1994.

Balch, Oliver. 'AI and Me: Friendship Chatbots are on the Rise, But is There a Gendered Design Flaw?' *The Guardian* 7 May 2020 www.theguardian.com/careers/2020/may/07/ai-and-me-friendship-chatbots-are-on-the-rise-but-is-there-a-gendered-design-flaw Accessed May 3, 2023.

Baldick, Chris. *In Frankenstein's Shadow: Myth, Monstrosity, and Nineteenth-Century Writing*. Clarendon Press, 1987.

Baldwin, Dave, and Meredith Meyer. 'How Inherently Social is Language?' *Blackwell Handbook of Language Development*. Eds. Erika Hoff, Marilyn Shatz. Wiley, 2007. 97–106.

Ball, Mieke. *Narratology: Introduction to the Theory of Narrative*. 2nd Edition. University of Toronto Press, 1997.

Bajohr, Hannes. 'Artificial & Post-Artificial Texts: On Machine Learning & the Reading Expectations Towards Literary & Non-Literary Writing.' *Poetics Today* 45/2 (2024): 331–61.

Bajohr, Hannes. 'The Paradox of Anthroponormative Restriction: Artistic Artificial Intelligence and Literary Writing.' *CounterText* 8/2 (2022): 262–82.

'Barbarian.' *American Heritage Dictionary of the English Language*. Houghton Mifflin Harcourt, 2018. AHDictionary.com Accessed Aug 15, 2018.

'Barbarism.' *American Heritage Dictionary of the English Language*. Houghton Mifflin Harcourt, 2018. AHDictionary.com Accessed Aug 15, 2018.

Bar-Cohen, Joseph, and Cynthia Breazeal. *Biologically Inspired Intelligent Robots*. SPIE Press, 2003.

Bardi, Jennifer, Diane M. Bolz, Sarah Breger, Nadine Epstein, Jacob Forman, Noah Phillips, Amy E. Schwartz & Laurence Wolff. 'Is Artificial Intelligence Good for Humanity.' *The Moment Magazine* Summer 2023 www.momentmag.com/is-artificial-intelligence-good-for-humanity/ Accessed Aug 30, 2023.

Bardini, Julio. 'How the voices for ChatGPT were chosen.' *Collider* 9 Mar 2024 www.collider.com/lost-in-translation-her-conversation-in-between/ Accessed May 20, 2024.

Basharin, Gely P., Amy N. Langville, and Valeriy A. Naumov. 'The Life and Work of A. A. Markov.' *Linear Algebra and its Applications* 386/2 (2004): 3–26.

Bassett, Caroline, Sarah Kember, and Kate O'Riordan. *Furious: Technological Feminism and Digital Futures*. Pluto Press, 2020.

Bates, David W. *An Artificial History of Natural Intelligence: Thinking with Machines from Descartes to the Digital Age*. University of Chicago Press, 2024.

Baum, Paull Franklin. 'The Young Man Betrothed to a Statue.' *PMLA* 34/4 (1919): 523–79.

Beech, Anthony R., and Leigh Harkins. 'DSM-IV paraphilia: Descriptions, demographics and treatment interventions.' *Aggression and Violent Behavior* 17/6 (2012): 527–39.

Beguš, Gašper. 'CiwGAN and fiwGAN: Modeling lexical learning from raw acoustic data in Generative Adversarial Phonology.' *Neural Networks* 139 (2021): 305–25.

Beguš, Gašper, Andrej Leban, and Shane Gero. 'Approaching an unknown communication system by latent space exploration and causal inference.' *ArXiv* 1–25 pages. Submitted 20 Mar 2023 doi.org/10.48550/arXiv.2303.10931 Accessed Apr 23, 2023.

Beguš, Gašper, Thomas Lu, Alan Zhou, Peter Wu, and Gopala K. Anumanchipalli. 'CiwaGAN: Articulatory information exchange.' *ArXiv* Sep 14, 2023 1–5 2309.07861. https://doi.org/10.48550/arXiv.2309.07861 Accessed March 19, 2024.

Beguš, Gašper, Alan Zhou, Wu, Peter Wu, and Gopala K. Anumanchipalli. 'Articulation GAN: Unsupervised Modeling of Articulatory Learning.' *ICASSP 2023 – 2023 IEEE International Conference on Acoustics, Speech and Signal Processing.* 1–5, doi: 10.1109/ICASSP49357.2023.10096800.

Beguš, Gašper, and Zhou, Alan. 'Interpreting Intermediate Convolutional Layers In Unsupervised Acoustic Word Classification.' *ICASSP 2022 – 2022 IEEE International Conference on Acoustics, Speech and Signal Processing (ICASSP)* 2022. 8207–11.

Beguš, Gašper, Maksymilian Dąbkowski, and Ryan Rhodes. 'Large Linguistic Models: Analyzing theoretical linguistic abilities of LLMs.' *ArXiv* May 1, 2023. www.arxiv.org/abs/2305.00948 Accessed May 1, 2023.

Beguš, Nina. *Artificial Humanities: A Literary Perspective on Creating and Enhancing Humans from Pygmalion to Cyborgs.* Dissertation, Harvard University. 2020.

Beguš, Nina. 'A Tocharian tale from the Silk Road: A philological account of the The Painter and the Mechanical Maiden and its resonances with the Western canon.' *Journal of the Royal Asiatic Society* 30/4 (2020): 681–706.

Beguš, Nina. 'A Typology of the Pygmalion Paradigm.' *Collected Papers of the 21st Congress of the ICLA: The Rhetoric of Topics and Forms* 4 (2021): 319–30.

Beguš, Nina. 'Engaging Comparative Literature in AI Development.' *OSF Preprints* 30 Jul 2024 www.osf.io/preprints/osf/z9pxn Accessed Jul 30, 2024.

Beguš, Nina. 'Experimental Narratives: A Comparison of Human Crowdsourced Storytelling and AI Storytelling.' *Humanities and Social Sciences Communications* 11/1392 (2024): 1–22.

Bell, Mabel Hubbard. 'Image 9 of Letter from Mabel Hubbard Bell to Alexander Graham Bell, July 9, 1895.' *Library of Congress* www.loc.gov/resource/magbell.03900603/?sp=9&st=text Accessed Mar 1, 2024.

Bellier, Ludovic, Anaïs Llorens, Déborah Marciano, Aysegul Gunduz, Gerwin Schalk, Peter Brunner, and Robert T. Knight. 'Music can be reconstructed from human auditory cortex activity using nonlinear decoding models.' *PLOS Biology* 21/8 (2023): e3002176.

Bender, Emily M. 'No, large language models aren't disabled people (and it's problematic to argue that they are).' *Medium* 20 Jan 2022 www.medium.com/@emilymenonbender/no-llms-arent-like-people-with-disabilities-and-it-s-problematic-to-argue-that-they-are-a2acod foe435 Accessed Feb 7, 2022.

Bender, Emily M., and Alexander Koller. 'Climbing towards NLU: On Meaning, Form, and Understanding in the Age of Data.' *Proceedings of the 58th Annual Meeting of the Association for Computational Linguistics* 2020: 5185–98.

Bender, Emily M., Timnit Gebru, Angelina McMillan-Major, Shmargaret Shmitchell, et al. 'On the Dangers of Stochastic Parrots: Can Language Models Be Too Big? 🦜' *Proceedings of the 2021 ACM Conference on Fairness, Accountability, and Transparency* (2021): 610–23.

Benes, Tuska. 'Language and the cognitive subject: Heymann Steinthal (1823–1899) and Friedrich Nietzsche (1844–1900).' *Language and Communication* 26 (2006): 218–30.

Benjamin, Ruha. *Race after Technology: Abolitionist Tools for the New Jim Code.* Polity, 2019.

Benjamin, Walter. 'The Storyteller: Reflections on the Works of Nikolai Leskov.' Tran. Harry Zohn. *Illuminations*. Ed. Hannah Arendt. Schocken Books, 1969. 83–110.

Berger, James. 'Testing Literature: Helen Keller and Richard Powers' Implementation H[elen].' *Arizona Quarterly* 58/3 (2002): 10.

Bernd, Heinrich. *Mind of the Raven: Investigations and Adventures with Wolf-birds.* Cliff Street Books, 1999.

Berridge, Clara, Yuanjin Zhou, Julie M. Robillard, and Jeffrey Kaye. 'Companion robots to mitigate loneliness among older adults: Perceptions of benefit and possible deception.' *Frontiers in Psychology* 14 (2023): 1–9.

Bess, Michael. 'Enhanced Humans versus "Normal People:" Elusive Definitions.' *Journal of Medicine and Philosophy* 35/6 (2010): 641–55.

Bettini, Maurizio. *The Portrait of The Lover.* Tran. Laura Gibbs. University of California Press, 1999.

Bigman, Yochanan E., Adam Waytz, Ron Altervitz, and Kurt Gray. 'Holding Robots Responsible: The Elements of Machine Morality.' *Trends in Cognitive Sciences* 23/5 (2019): 265–68. www.cell.com/trends/cognitive-sciences/fulltext/S1364-6613(19)30063-4

Birnbaum, Michael H. *Eliza, the Rogerian Therapist.* 1999. California State University, Fullerton. psych.fullerton.edu/mbirnbaum/psych101/Eliza.htm Accessed Jun 18, 2018.

Black, Daniel. *Embodiment and Mechanisation: Reciprocal Understandings of Body and Machine from the Renaissance to the Present.* Routledge, 2014.

Bleeke, Marian. 'Versions of Pygmalion in the Illuminated Roman de la Rose (Oxford, Bodleian Library, Ms. Douce 195): The Artist and the Work of Art.' *Art History* 33/1 (2010): 28–53.

Boas, Frantz. *Tsimshian Mythology; Based on texts recorded by Henry W. Tate.* 31st Annual Report of the Bureau of American Ethnology to the Secretary of the Smithsonian Institution (1909–1910). Washington, D.C., 1916.

Bode, Katherine, and Paul Longley Arthur. *Advancing Digital Humanities: Research, Methods, Theories.* Palgrave Macmillan, 2014.

Boden, Margaret. *The Creative Mind: Myths and Mechanisms.* Taylor and Francis, 1990.

Boettinger, H. M. *The Telephone Book: Bell, Watson, Vail and American Life, 1876–1976.* Riverwood Publishers Limited, 1977.

Bohannon, John. 'The synthetic therapist: Some people prefer to bare their souls to computers rather than to fellow humans.' 250–251. *Science* 249/6245 (2015): 250–51.

Boland, Eavan. 'The Woman Poet in a National Tradition.' *Studies: An Irish Quarterly Review* 76/302 (1987): 148–58.
Bolton, Doug. 'Scarlett Johansson lookalike robot created by Hong Kong man in his flat.' *Independent* 4 April 2015 www.independent.co.uk/tech/scarlett-johansson-robot-hong-kong-ricky-ma-a6967971.html Accessed June 19, 2020.
Bommasani, Rishi, Drew A. Hudson, et al. 'On the Opportunities and Risks of Foundation Models.' *Arxiv* Submitted on Aug 16, 2021; v.3 last revised Jul 12, 2022. arxiv.org/abs/2108.07258 Accessed Jul 14, 2022.
Booth, Katie Booth. *The Invention of Miracles: Language, Power, and Alexander Graham Bell's Quest to End Deafness.* Simon & Schuster, 2021.
Bostrom, Nick, and Julian Savulescu. 'Introduction: Human Enhancement Ethics: The State of the Debate.' *Human Enhancement.* Julian Savulescu and Nick Bostrom, eds. Oxford University Press, 2009. 1–22.
Bote, Joshua. 'Sanas, the buzzy Bay Area Startup that Wants to Make the World Sound Whiter.' *SF Gate* 1 Sep 2022 www.sfgate.com/news/article/sanas-startup-creates-american-voice-17382771.php Accessed Sep 8, 2022.
Bottou, Léon, and Bernard Schölkopf. 'Borges and AI.' *ArXiv* 27 Sep 2023 www.arxiv.org/abs/2310.01425 Accessed Sep 28, 2023.
Boyle Haberstroh, Patricia. *The Female Figure in Eiléan Ní Chuilleanáin's Poetry.* Cork University Press, 2013.
Bradwell, Hannah Louise, Edwards, Katie Jane, Winnington, Rhona, Thill, Serge, Jones, Ray B. 'Companion robots for older people: importance of user-centred design demonstrated through observations and focus groups comparing preferences of older people and roboticists in South West England.' *BMJ* 9/9 (2019).
Braidotti, Rosi. *Metamorphoses: Towards a Materialist Theory of Becoming.* Polity Press, 2002.
Braidotti, Rosi. *Posthuman Knowledge.* Polity Press, 2017.
Braidotti, Rosi. *Posthuman Feminism.* Polity Press, 2022.
Bratton, Benjamin. 'Synthetic gardens: Another model for AI and design.' Ben Vickers and K Allado-McDowell, eds. *Atlas of Anomalous AI.* 2020. 91–112.
Bratton, Benjamin, and Blaise Agüera y Arcas. 'The Model Is The Message.' *Noema* Jul 12, 2022 www.noemamag.com/the-model-is-the-message/ Accessed Jul 14, 2022.
Braun, Max. 'On Automated Philosophy: A personal story of art and intelligence.' [Tran. by the author from 'Über automatisierte Philosophie: Eine persönliche Geschichte von Kunst und Intelligenz.'] Draft on *Medium* www.maxbraun.medium.com/bf27904a41cf Accessed Feb 2, 2022.
Breazeal, Cynthia, and Rodney Brooks. 'Robot Emotions: A Functional Perspective.' *Who Needs Emotions: The Brain Meets the Robot.* Eds. Jean-Marc Fellous and Michael A. Airbib. Oxford University Press, 2005. 271–310.
Breazeal, Cynthia, and Rosalind Picard. 'The Role of Emotion-Inspired Abilities in Relational Robots.' *Neuroergonomics: The Brain at Work.* Eds. Raja Parasuraman and Matthew Rizzo. Oxford University Press, 2006. 275–92.
Brown, Jane. *Goethe's Faust: The German Tragedy.* Cornell University Press, 1986.
Brown, Sarah Annes. *The Metamorphosis of Ovid From Chaucer to Ted Hughes.* Duckworth, 1999.

Browning, Jacob. 'Making Common Sense.' *Noema* Jun 29, 2021 www.noemamag.com/making-common-sense/ Accessed Jul 5, 2022.

Browning, Jacob, and Yann Lecun. 'AI and The Limits of Language.' *Noema* August 23, 2022 www.noemamag.com/ai-and-the-limits-of-language/ Accessed August 23, 2022.

Bruce, Robert V. *Bell: Alexander Graham Bell and the Conquest of Solitude.* Little Brown, 1973.

Buckley, Jennifer. 'Talking Machines: Shaw, Phonography, and Pygmalion.' *Shaw* 35/1 (2015): 21–45.

Burrows, John F. *Computation into Criticism: A Study of Jane Austen's Novels and an Experiment in Method.* Oxford University Press, 1987.

Buxton, H.W., and Anthony Hyman. *Memoir of the life and labours of the late Charles Babbage Esq., F.R.S.* Tomash, 1988.

Carr, J. L. 'Pygmalion and the Philosophes: The Animated Statue in Eighteenth-Century France.' *Journal of the Warburg and Courtauld Institutes* 23/3-4 (1960): 239–55.

Carstens, Pieter, and Philip Stevens. 'Paraphilia and sex offending – A South African criminal law perspective.' *International Journal of Law and Psychiatry* 47 (2016): 93–101.

Cavanagh, John R. 'Sexual Anomalies.' *The Catholic Lawyer* 9/1 (1963): 4–31.

Cave, Stephen and Kanta Dihal. "The Whiteness of AI." *Philosophy & Technology* 33 (2020): 685–703.

Chamorro-Premuzic, Tomas. 'Virtual Love: Is Your Valentine an Avatar?' *The Guardian* 9 Feb 2015 www.theguardian.com/media-network/2015/feb/09/virtual-love-valentine-day-romance-technology Accessed Dec 9, 2018.

Chan, Wilfred. 'The AI Startup Erasing Call Center Worker Accents: Is It Fighting Bias or Perpetuating It?' *The Guardian* 24 Aug 2022 www.theguardian.com/technology/2022/aug/23/voice-accent-technology-call-center-white-american Accessed Sep 8, 2022.

Chayes, Jennifer. 'Data Science and Computing at UC Berkeley.' *Harvard Data Science Review* 3/2 (2021): 1–21. Apr 30, 2021 hdsr.mitpress.mit.edu/pub/wzhgxmcc/release/4 Accessed Aug 30, 2023.

Che, Chang. 'China Says Chatbots Must Toe the Party Line.' 23 Apr 2023 *The New York Times* www.nytimes.com/2023/04/24/world/asia/china-chatbots-ai.html Accessed Apr 24, 2023.

Chen, Zijiao, Jiaxin Qing, Tiange Xiang, Wan Lin Yue, and Juan Helen Zhou. 'Seeing Beyond the Brain: Conditional Diffusion Model with Sparse Masked Modeling for Vision Decoding.' *2023 IEEE/CVF Conference on Computer Vision and Pattern Recognition (CVPR)* (2022): 22710–22720. Accessed Oct 2, 2023.

Cheok, Adrian David, Kasun Karunanayaka, and Emma Yann Zhang. 'Lovotics: Human–Robot Love and Sex Relationships.' *Robot Ethics 2.0: Autonomous Cars to Artificial Intelligence.* Ed. Patrick Lin, Keith Abney, Ryan Jenkins. Oxford University Press, 2017.

Chiang, Ted. 'ChatGPT is a Blurry JPEG of the Web.' *The New Yorker* 9 Feb 2023 www.newyorker.com/tech/annals-of-technology/chatgpt-is-a-blurry-jpeg-of-the-web Accessed Apr 20, 2023.

Chikaraishi, Takenobu et al. 'Creating and Staging of Android Theatre 'Sayonara' towards Developing Highly Human-Like Robots.' *Future Internet* 9/4 (2017): 75.

Chomsky, Noam. *Cartesian Linguistics: A Chapter in the History of Rationalist Thought.* Harper & Row, 1966.

Chomsky, Noam, Ian Roberts, and Jeffrey Watumull. 'The False Promise of ChatGPT.' *The New York Times* 8 Mar 2023 www.nytimes.com/2023/03/08/opinion/noam-chomsky-chatgpt-ai.html Accessed Mar 8, 2023.

Clare, David. *Bernard Shaw's Irish Outlook.* Palgrave Macmillan, 2016.

Clark, Jack. Introduction at *Stanford HAI* website. hai.stanford.edu/people/jack-clark Accessed Apr 23, 2023.

Clark, Jack. 'One gnawing worry I have about the rise of LLMs is that, for me, writing IS thinking. One reason I spend so much time writing my newsletter each week is I haven't figured out a better way to think about AI than to sit down and write about it regularly.' 21 May 2023 8.45am Tweet twitter.com/jackclarkSF/status/1660310975625699329?s=20 Accessed May 21, 2023.

Clark, Jack. 'I write short stories because they help me process the great mystery that is the world and convert it into stories and things I can allow my mind to live inside and crawl over. Whenever I write I am desperately trying to understand the world and my place within it.' 21 May 2023 8.45am www.twitter.com/jackclarkSF/status/1660311128516464640?s=20 Accessed May 21, 2023.

Clark, Jack. 'In a very real sense, writing feels like a form of cognitive "embodiment" – whether in fiction or non-fiction we are using our brain as an interface between the real and the ethereal and we produce these text-based artifacts as ways to ground the two worlds together.' 21 May 2023 8.45am www.twitter.com/jackclarkSF/status/1660311349984129024?s=20 Accessed May 21, 2023.

Clark, Jack. 'AI systems are societal mirrors; China gets chip advice via LLMs; 25 million medical images.' *ImportAI 382.* 12 Aug 2024. jack-clark.net/2024/08/12/import-ai-382-ai-systems-are-societal-mirrors-china-gets-chip-advice-via-llms-25-million-medical-images-2/ Accessed Aug 12, 2024.

Coeckelbergh, Mark. 'How to Use Virtue Ethics for Thinking About the Moral Standing of Social Robots: A Relational Interpretation in Terms of Practices, Habits, and Performance.' *International Journal of Social Robotics* 13 (2021): 31–40.

Coeckelbergh, Mark. 'Robot Rights? Towards a Social-Relational Justification of Moral Consideration.' *Ethics and Information Technology* 12 (2010): 209–21.

Cole, Henri. 'Helen Vendler, The Art of Criticism.' Interview. *The Paris Review* 141/3 (1996). www.theparisreview.org/interviews/1324/the-art-of-criticism-no-3-helen-vendler Accessed Aug 12, 2024.

Collier, Bruce. *The Little Engines That Could've: The Calculating Engines of Charles Babbage.* Garland, 1990.

Copeland, B. Jack, ed. *The Essential Turing.* Oxford University Press, 2004.

Craig, Hugh, and Brett Greatley-Hirsch. *Style, Computers, and Early Modern Drama: Beyond Authorship.* Cambridge University Press, 2017.

Crawford, Hugh T. 'An Interview with Bruno Latour.' *Configurations* 1/2 (1993): 147–67.

Crow, David. 'Why Alex Garland Changed the Ex Machina Ending.' *Den of Geek* 10 April 2020 www.denofgeek.com/movies/alex-garland-changed-the-ex-machina-ending Accessed Feb 10, 2022.

Danahay, Martin A. *Gender at Work in Victorian Culture: Literature, Art and Masculinity*. Ashgate, 2005.

Danahay, Martin A. 'Mirrors of Masculine Desire: Narcissus and Pygmalion in Victorian Representation'. *Victorian Poetry* 32/1 (1994): 35–53.

Darling, Kate. *The New Breed: What Our History with Animals Reveals About Our Future with Robots*. Macmillan, 2021.

Darnton, Robert. 'What Is the History of Books?' *Daedalus* 111/3 (1982): 65–83.

Darwin, Charles. *The Descent of Man, and Selection in Relation to Sex*. Murray, 1871.

Darwin, Erasmus. *The Temple Of Nature Or, the Origin Of Society: a Poem, With Philosophical Notes*. Printed for J. Johnson by T. Bensley, 1809.

Davies, Alex, et al. 'Advancing mathematics by guiding human intuition with AI.' *Nature* 600/70 (2021).

Daub, Adrian. *What Tech Calls Thinking: An Inquiry into the Intellectual Bedrock of Silicon Valley*. Farrar, Straus, and Giroux, 2020.

Dębowski, Łukasz. *Information Theory Meets Power Laws: Stochastic Processes and Language Models*. John Wiley & Sons Inc., 2020.

Déffosez, Alexandre, Charlotte Cacheteux, Jérémy Rapin, Ori Kabeli, and Jean-Rémi King.'Decoding speech perception from non-invasive brain recordings.' *Nature Machine Intelligence* 5 (2023): 1097–1110. www.nature.com/articles/s42256-023-00714-5

De Graaf, Maartje M. A., Frank A. Hindriks, and Koen V. Hindriks. 'Who Wants to Grant Robots Rights?' *Frontiers of Robotics and AI* 8 (2021): 1–13. www.frontiersin.org/journals/robotics-and-ai/articles/10.3389/frobt.2021.781985/full

Descartes, René. *Discourse on the Method of rightly conducting the reason, and seeking truth in the sciences*. Tran. John Veitch. Open Court Press, 1920.

Devlin, Hannah. 'Google a step closer to developing machines with human-like intelligence.' *The Guardian* 21 May 2015 www.theguardian.com/science/2015/may/21/google-a-step-closer-to-developing-machines-with-human-like-intelligence Accessed Apr 4, 2023.

Diderot, Denis. *Philosophical Thoughts*. Tran. Tim Newcomb. Newcomb Livraria Press, 2023 [1746].

Dillon, Sarah, and Jennifer Schaffer-Goddard. 'What AI researchers read: the role of literature in artificial intelligence research.' *Interdisciplinary Science Reviews* (2022): 1–28.

DiMauro, Damon. 'Ourika, or Galatea Reverts to Stone.' *Nineteenth-Century French Studies* 28/3–4 (2000): 187–211.

Doble, Jennifer E., Andrew J. Haig, Christopher Anderson, and Richard Katz. 'Impairment, activity, participation, life satisfaction, and survival in persons with locked-in syndrome for over a decade: follow-up on a previously reported cohort.' *The Journal of Head Trauma Rehabilitation* 18 (2003): 435–44.

Dolar, Mladen. *A Voice and Nothing More*. MIT Press, 2006.

Drzazga, John. *Sex Crimes*. Thomas, 1960.

Dudzinski, Denise. 'The Diving Bell Meets the Butterfly: Identity Lost and Re-membered.' *Theoretical Medicine* 22 (2001): 33–46.

Duguid, Paul. 'Communication, Computation, and Information.' *Information: A Historical Companion*. Ed. Ann Blair, Paul Duguid, Anja-Silvia Goeing, and Anthony Grafton. Princeton University Press, 2021. 238–58.

Duncan, Dennis. *The Oulipo and Modern Thought*. Oxford University Press, 2019.
Eagle, Herbert. 'Yugoslav Marxist Humanism and the Films of Dušan Makavejev.' *Politics, Art and Commitment in the East European Cinema*. Ed. David W. Paul. Palgrave Macmillan, 1983. 131–48.
Earth Species Project. 2022. www.earthspecies.org Accessed Apr 20, 2023.
Eastlake, Lady Elizabeth Rigby, ed. *Life of John Gibson, R.A., Sculptor*. Longmans Green and Co., 1870.
Eck, Stefeanie. *Galatea's Emancipation: The Transformation of the Pygmalion Myth in Anglo-Saxon Literature since the 20th Century*. Anchor Academic Publishing, 2014.
Edison, Thomas A. 'The Perfected Phonograph.' *The North American Review*, 146/379 (1888): 641–50.
Edison, Thomas A. 'The Phonograph and Its Future.' *The North American Review*, 126/262 (1878): 527–36.
Egan, Nicholas, Oleg Vasilyev, and John Bohannon. 'Play the Shannon Game with Language Models: A Human-Free Approach to Summary Evaluation.' *Proceedings of the AAAI Conference on Artificial Intelligence* 36/10 (2022): 10599–607.
'Electronic Brain Teaches Itself.' *The New York Times* July 13, 1958, Section E, Page 9 www.nytimes.com/1958/07/13/archives/electronic-brain-teaches-itself.html Accessed May 19, 2019.
Ellis, Alexander John. *On early English pronunciation: With especial reference to Shakspere and Chaucer [...]*. Part I. Asher & Co., 1869.
Ellis, Havelock. *Sexual Selection in Man: Touch. Smell. Hearing. Vision*. D. A. Davis Company, 1905.
Emery, Nathan. *Bird Brain: An Exploration of Avian Intelligence*. Princeton University Press, 2016.
Erscoi, Lelia A., Annelies Kleinherenbrink, and Olivia Guest. 'Pygmalion Displacement: When Humanising AI Dehumanises Women.' *Science Letter* (2023): 1–37.
Essinger, James. *Ada's Algorithm: How Lord Byron's Daughter Ada Lovelace Launched the Digital Age*. Melville House, 2014.
Evanson, Linnea, Yair Lakretz, and Jean-Rémi King. 'Language acquisition: do children and language models follow similar learning stages?' *Findings of the Association for Computational Linguistics: ACL 2023* (2023): 12205–12218. Accessed Oct 24, 2024.
Eve, Martin Paul. *The Digital Humanities and Literary Studies*. Oxford University Press, 2022.
Eulenburg, Albert. *Sexuale Neuropathie: Genitale Neurosen und Neuropsychosen der Männer und Frauen*. Verlag von F. C. W. Vogel, 1895.
Faber, Liz W. *The Computer Voice: From Star Trek to Siri*. University of Minnesota Press, 2020.
Fallon, Jimmy. 'Tonight Showbotics: Jimmy Meets Sophia the Human-Like Robot.' *The Tonight Show Starring Jimmy Fallon*. YouTube Apr 25, 2017 www.youtube.com/watch?time_continue=2&v=Bg_tJvCA8zw Accessed Aug 8, 2018.
Fay, Rua. '"Her" and "Lost In Translation:" Two Sides of the Same Story.' *Cinemasters* 22 Jan 2022, Updated on 21 Jul 2022. www.cinemasters.net/post/her-and-lost-in-translation-two-sides-of-the-same-story Accessed May 20, 2024.

Fedorenko, Evelina, and Rosemary Varley. 'Language and thought are not the same thing: evidence from neuroimaging and neurological patients.' *Annals of the New York Academy of Sciences (The Year in Cognitive Neuroscience)* 1369/1 (2016): 132–53.

Fitzpatrick, Kathleen. 'The Exhaustion of Literature: Novels, Computers, and the Threat of Obsolescence.' *Contemporary Literature* 43/3 (2002): 518–59.

Flood, Alison. 'Nora Roberts files "multi-plagiarism" lawsuit alleging writer copied more than 40 authors.' *The Guardian* Apr 25, 2019 www.theguardian.com/books/2019/apr/25/nora-roberts-files-multi-plagiarism-lawsuit-alleging-writer-copied-more-than-40-authors Accessed Feb 4, 2020.

Flood, Alison. 'Plagiarism, "book-stuffing", clickfarms ... the rotten side of self-publishing.' *The Guardian* Mar 28, 2019 www.theguardian.com/books/2019/mar/28/plagiarism-book-stuffing-clickfarms-the-rotten-side-of-self-publishing Accessed Feb 4, 2020.

Floyd, Juliet. 'Wittgenstein, Carnap and Turing: Contrasting Notions of Analysis.' *Carnap's Ideal of Explication*. Ed. Pierre Wagner. Palgrave Macmillan, 2012. 34–46.

Ford, Jason. 'Artificial Intelligence "Eugene" Passes Turing test.' *The Engineer* 9 Jun 2014 www.theengineer.co.uk/content/news/artificial-intelligence-eugene-passes-turing-test Accessed Feb 17, 2018.

Forster, Michael N. 'Kant's Philosophy of Language?' *Tijdschrift voor Filosofie* 74/3 (2012): 485–511.

Foucault, Michel. *The Order of Things: An Archaeology of the Human Sciences*. Tavistock Publications, 1970 [1966].

Frank, Felicia Miller. *The Mechanical Song: Women, Voice, and the Artificial in Nineteenth-Century French Narrative*. Stanford University Press, 1995.

Freud, Sigmund. 'Delusion and dream in Jensen's Gradiva.' *The Standard Edition of The Complete Psychological Works of Sigmund Freud*. Vol. IX (1906–1908). The Hogarth Press, 1959. 7–95.

Frobenius, Léo. *Volksmärchen der Kabylen*. Vol. I/III. E. Jena, 1921.

Gaboury, Jacob. 'A Queer History of Computing: Part Three.' *Rhizome* 9 Apr 2013 www.rhizome.org/editorial/2013/apr/09/queer-history-computing-part-three/#_edn10 Accessed Apr 12, 2023.

Gagniuc, Paul A. *Markov Chains: From Theory to Implementation and Experimentation*. John Wiley & Sons, 2017.

Ganguli, Deep, Danny Hernandez, et al. 'Predictability and Surprise in Large Generative Models.' *FAccT '22: Proceedings of the 2022 ACM Conference on Fairness, Accountability, and Transparency* (2022): 1757–64. Accessed Oct 24, 2024.

Garnelo, Marta, and Murray Shahan. 'Reconciling Deep Learning With Symbolic Artificial Intelligence: Representing Objects and Relations.' *Current Opinion in Behavioral Sciences* 29 (2019): 17–23. www.sciencedirect.com/science/article/pii/S2352154618301943?via%3Dihub

Gemsouls Inc. 2022. www.mygemsouls.com Accessed Jan 20, 2022.

Geoghegan, Bernard Dionysius. *Code: From Information Theory to French Theory*. Duke University Press, 2023.

Geoghegan, Bernard Dionysius. 'Orientalism and Informatics: Alterity from the Chess-Playing Turk to Amazon's Mechanical Turk.' *Ex-position* 43 (2020): 45–90.

Gernsback, Hugo. 'The Future: Electronic Mating.' *Sexology* 30/7 (1964): 452–55.

Giles, Martin. 'The GANfather: The man who's given machines the gift of imagination.' *MIT Technology Review* 21 Feb 2018 www.technologyreview.com/2018/02/21/145289/the-ganfather-the-man-whos-given-machines-the-gift-of-imagination/ Accessed Feb 21, 2018.

Girard, René. 'Generative Scapegoating.' *Violent Origins: Walter Burkert, René Girard, and Jonathan Z. Smith on Ritual Killing and Cultural Formation.* Ed. Robert G. Hammerton-Kelly. Stanford University Press, 1987.

Giron, Anna P., Simon Ciranka, Eric Schulz, Wouter van den Bros, Azzurra Ruggeri, Björn Meder, Charley M. Wu. 'Developmental changes in exploration resemble stochastic optimization.' *Nature Human Behaviour* 7, 1955–1967 (2023). https://doi.org/10.1038/s41562-023-01662-1

Goering, Sara. 'Is It Still Me? DBS, Agency, and the Extended, Relational Me.' *AJOB Neuroscience* 5/4 (2014): 50–51.

Goering, Sara, Eran Klein, Darin D. Dougherty, and Alik S. Widge. 'Staying in the Loop: Relational Agency and Identity in Next-Generation DBS for Psychiatry.' *AJOB Neuroscience* 8/2 (2017): 58–70.

Goldberg, Adele (adelegoldberg1). 'Asserts that the model "may well" misinterpret "john is too stubborn to talk to" 2 second test indicates it does just fine:.' 8 Mar 2023, 7.07pm. Tweet. www.twitter.com/adelegoldberg1/status/1633665845195931648?s=20 Accessed May 1, 2023.

Good, Irvin John. 'Speculations Concerning the First Ultraintelligent Machine.' *Advances in Computers* 6 (1966): 31–88.

Göranzon, Bo. 'Introduction to The Last Dream by Joseph Weizenbaum.' *AI & society* 34/2 (2019): 177–94.

Graham, Elaine L. *Representations of the Post/Human: Monsters, Aliens, and Others in Popular Culture.* Rutgers University Press, 2002.

Greene, David H., and Dan H. Laurence, eds. *Bernard Shaw: The Matter with Ireland.* University Press of Florida, 2001.

Gross, Kenneth. *The Dream of the Moving Statue.* Cornell University Press, 1992.

Gubar, Susan. '"The Blank Page" and the Issues of Female Creativity'. *The New Feminist Criticism: Essays on Women, Literature and Theory.* Ed. Elaine Showalter. Virago Press, 1986. 292–313.

Gunderson, Keith. 'Descartes, La Mettrie, Language, and Machines.' *Philosophy* 39/149 (1964): 193–222.

Gunkel, David. *The Machine Question: Critical Perspectives on AI, Robots and Ethics.* MIT Press, 2012.

Gupta, Kavya. 'Campus Addresses Criticism for Semesterly English Pronunciation Workshop.' *The Daily Californian* Sep 8, 2022 www.dailycal.org/2022/09/08/campus-addresses-criticism-for-semesterly-english-pronunciation-workshop/ Accessed Sep 8, 2022.

Guy-Bray, Stephen. 'Beddoes, Pygmalion, and the Art of Onanism.' *Nineteenth-Century Literature* 52/4 (1998): 446–70

Ha, David, and Jurgen Schmidhuber. 'World Models.' *Advances in Neural Information Processing Systems* 32 (2018): 1–13. Eds. S. Bengio, H. Wallach, H. Larochelle, K. Grauman, N. Cesa-Bianchi, and R. Garnett. https://worldmodels.github.io/ Accessed Jul 20, 2022.

Halacy, Dan. *Charles Babbage: Father of the Computer*. Crowell-Collier Press, 1970.

Haldane, John Burdon Sanderson. *Daedalus, or Science of Future*. E. P. Dutton, 1923.

Hall, Jason David. 'Popular Prosody: Spectacle and the Politics of Victorian Versification.' *Nineteenth-Century Literature* 62/2 (2007): 222–49.

Hamilton, Melissa. 'Adjudicating Sex Crimes as Mental Disease.' *Pace Law Review* 33/2 (2013): 536–99.

Hankins, Thomas and Robert J. Silverman. 'Vox Mechanica: The History of Speaking Machines'. *Instruments and the Imagination*. Princeton University Press, 1995. 178–220.

Hanson Robotics. 'About Me.' *Sophia*. Hanson Robotics 2017. www.sophiabot.com/aboutme Accessed Aug 8, 2018.

Hanson Robotics. 'Could You Fall in Love with This Robot?' *Sophia*. Hanson Robotics 2017. www.sophiabot.com/could-you-fall-in-love-with-this-robot Accessed Aug 8, 2018.

Haraway, Donna. *Cyborg Manifesto: Science, Technology, and Socialist-Feminism in the Late Twentieth Century*. University of Minnesota Press, 2016 [1985].

Haraway, Donna. *The Companion Species Manifesto: Dogs, People, and Significant Otherness*. Prickly Paradigm Press, 2003.

Haraway, Donna. *Primate Visions: Gender, Race and Nature in the World of Modern Science*. Routledge, 1989.

Haraway, Donna, and Joseph Schneider. 'Conversations with Donna Haraway.' *Donna Haraway: Live Theory*. Continuum, 2005.

Harris, Anita M. 'Uh-Oh, I Seem to Be Dating a Chatbot.' *The New York Times*. 7 Apr 2023 www.nytimes.com/2023/04/07/style/modern-love-chatgpt-ai-chatbot.html Accessed Apr 8, 2023.

Harrison, Peter. 'Descartes on Animals.' *The Philosophical Quarterly* 42/167 (1992): 219–27.

Hartley, M. G. 'Babbage, Charles - Father of the Digital-Computer.' *International Journal of Electrical Engineering and Education* 23(2) (1986): 101–12.

Hartley, Ralph V. L. 'Transmission of Information.' *Bell System Technical Journal* 7/3 (1928): 535–63.

Hartree, Douglas R. *Calculating Instruments and Machines*. University of Illinois Press, 1949.

Hayles, N. Katherine. *How We Became Posthuman: Virtual Bodies in Cybernetics, Literature, and Informatics*. University of Chicago Press, 1999.

Hayles, N. Katherine. *Unthought: The Power of Cognitive Nonconscious*. University of Chicago Press, 2017.

Hayles, N. Katherine. *Bacteria to AI: Human Futures with our Nonhuman Symbionts*. University of Chicago Press, 2025.

Heflin, Judy. *AI-Generated Literatur and the Vectorized World*. Dissertation, MIT 2020.

Heller, Nathan. 'The End of the English Major.' *The New Yorker* 27 Feb 2023 www.newyorker.com/magazine/2023/03/06/the-end-of-the-english-major Accessed Feb 27, 2023.

Hennenberg, Julian. *Subjects of Substance: Recent American Literature and the Materiality of Mind.* Transcript Verlag, 2020.

Henrickson, Leah. *Reading Computer-Generated Texts.* Cambridge University Press, 2021.

Henry, Joseph. *The Papers of Joseph Henry. Vol. 6. January 1844-December 1846: the Princeton Years.* Edited by Marc Rothenberg, Kathleen W. Dorman, John C. Rumm, and Paul H. Theerman. Smithsonian Institution Press, 1992.

Herder, Johann Gottfried. *Sculpture: Some Observations on Shape and Form from Pygmalion's Creative Dream.* Ed. and tran. Jason Gaiger. University of Chicago Press, 2011.

Herder, Johann Gottfried. 'Von der Bildhauerkunst fürs Gefühl (Gedanken aus dem Garten zu Versailles)'. *Sämtliche Werke.* Ed. Bernard Suphan. Weidmannsche Buchhandlung, 1892. Vol. 8. 88.

Hermann, Isabella. 'Artificial intelligence in fiction: between narratives and metaphors.' *AI and Society* 38 (2023): 319–29.

Hersey, George L. *Falling in Love with Statues: Artificial Humans from Pygmalion to the Present.* University of Chicago Press, 2007.

Hey, Tony, and Gyuri Pápay. *The Computing Universe: A Journey through a Revolution.* Cambridge University Press, 2014.

Hicks, Heather. '"Whatever It Is That She's Since Become:" Writing Bodies of Text and Bodies of Women in James Tiptree, Jr.'s "The Girl Who Was Plugged In" and William Gibson's "The Winter Market."' *Contemporary Literature* 37/1 (1996): 70–73.

Hockey, Susan. 'The History of Humanities Computing.' *A Companion to Digital Humanities.* Ed. Susan Schreibman, Ray Siemens, and John Unsworth. Blackwell, 2004. 3–19.

Hofstadter, Douglas, and David Moser. 'To Err is Human; To Study Error-Making is Cognitive Science.' *Michigan Quarterly Review* 82/3 (1989): 185–215.

Holm Vogelius, Christa. '"Gaze On!": The Transformations of Pygmalion and Galatea in the Poe-Osgood Affair.' *Poe Studies* 51 (2018): 22–43.

Holmes, Ronald M. *The Sex Offender and the Criminal Justice System.* C. C. Thomas, 1983.

Holmes, Stephen T. and Ronald M. Holmes. *Sex Crimes: Patterns and Behavior.* 3rd edition. SAGE Publications, 2009.

Hunt, Eileen Botting. *Artificial Life After Frankenstein.* University of Pennsylvania Press, 2021.

Huxley, Julian. 'Transhumanism'. New Bottles for New Wine. Harper & Brothers Publishers, 1957. 13–17.

Ida, Ryuichi. 'Should We Improve Human Nature? An Interrogation from an Asian Perspective.' Julian Savulescu and Nick Bostrom, eds. *Human Enhancement.* Oxford University Press, 2009. 39–70.

Iezzi, Teressa. 'Spike Jonze Imagines The Future Of Artificial Intelligence, Mobile Design, Love, And Pants In "Her."' *Fast Company* Dec 17, 2013 www.fastcompany.com/3023517/spike-jonze-imagines-the-future-of-artificial-intelligence-mobile-design-love-and-pants-in-her Accessed March 1, 2024.

Ingram, David. 'ChatGPT is powered by these contractors making $15 an hour.' *NBC News* May 6, 2023 www.nbcnews.com/tech/innovation/openai-chatgpt-ai-jobs-contractors-talk-shadow-workforce-powers-rcna81892 Accessed July 12, 2023.

Invest Cloud. 'The Cambrian Explosion of AI: Unleashing a New Era for Wealth Management.' 12 Oct 2023 www.investcloud.com/insights/the-cambrian-explosion-of-ai/ Accessed May 23, 2024.

Ipavec Dobrota, Irena. *Pogled kot nosilec moči v romanu in filmu Triptih Agate Schwarzkobler: diplomsko delo.* University of Ljubljana, 2013.

Irani, Lilly. 'Difference and Dependence among Digital Workers: The Case of Amazon Mechanical Turk.' *South Atlantic Quarterly* 114/1 (2015): 225–34.

Jain, Shomik, Balasubramanian Thiagarajan, Zhonghao Shi, Caitlyn Clabaugh, and Maja J. Matarić. 'Modeling engagement in long-term, in-home socially assistive robot interventions for children with autism spectrum disorders.' *Social Robotics* 5/29 (2020): 1–9.

Jakobson, Roman and Morris Halle. *Fundamentals of Language*. Mouton, 1956.

James, Louis. 'Frankenstein's Monster in Two Traditions.' *Frankenstein, Creation and Monstrosity*. Ed. Stephen Bann. Reaktion Books, 1994. 77–94.

James, Sherry. 'Virtual Reality Market to Reach $87.0 Billion by 2030: Grand View Research, Inc.' *PR Newswire* 26 Apr 2023 www.prnewswire.co.uk/news-releases/virtual-reality-market-to-reach-87-0-billion-by-2030-grand-view-research-inc-301806973.html Accessed Apr 26, 2023.

'Japanese Cafe Uses Robots Controlled by Paralysed People.' *BBC* Dec 6, 2018 www.bbc.com/news/technology-46466531 Accessed Dec 30, 2018.

Jasanoff, Sheila, and Sang-Hyun Kim, eds. *Dreamscapes of modernity: Sociotechnical imaginaries and the fabrication of power*. University of Chicago Press, 2015.

Johansson, Scarlett. 'Scarlett Johansson's Statement About Her Interactions With Sam Altman.' The *New York Times* 20 May 2024 www.nytimes.com/2024/05/20/technology/scarlett-johansson-openai-statement.html Accessed May 20, 2024.

Johansson, Veronica, Surjo R. Soekadar, and Jens Clausen. 'Locked Out: Ignorance and Responsibility in Brain-Computer Interface Communication in Locked-in Syndrome.' *Cambridge Quarterly of Healthcare Ethics* 26 (2017): 555–76.

Johnson, Stephen. 'The Turing test: AI still hasn't passed the "imitation game."' *Big Think* 7 Mar 2022. www.bigthink.com/the-future/turing-test-imitation-game Accessed Apr 1, 2022.

Johnson-Laird, Philip N., and Marco Ragni. 'What Should Replace the Turing Test?' *Intelligent Computing* 2 (2023) spj.science.org/doi/10.34133/icomputing.0064

Jordan, Michael I. 'Artificial Intelligence—The Revolution Hasn't Happened Yet.' *Harvard Data Science Review* 1/1 (2019) 1–8. www.hdsr.mitpress.mit.edu/pub/wot7mkc1/release/10 Accessed Aug 30, 2023.

Joshua, Essaka. *Pygmalion and Galatea: The History of a Narrative in English Literature*. Ashgate, 2001.

Joyal, Christian C. 'Controversies in the Definition of Paraphilia.' *The Journal of Sexual Medicine* 15/10 (2018): 1378–80.

Jurc, Ana. 'Pol stoletja Šeligove Agate Schwarzkobler, ki 'ni bila žrtev.'' *RTV Slovenija* May 12, 2018 www.rtvslo.si/kultura/knjige/pol-stoletja-seligove-agate-schwarzkobler-ki-ni-bila-zrtev/454708 Accessed Nov 11, 2022.

Juvan, Marko. 'Kosovelova referenca na Čapka in njen kontekst [Kosovel's Reference to Čapek and Its Context].' *Primerjalna Književnost* 32/1 (2009): 177–92.

Juvan, Marko. *Worlding a Peripheral Literature*. Palgrave Macmillan, 2019.

Kang, Minsoo. 'The Mechanical Daughter of René Descartes: The Origin and History of an Intellectual Fable.' *Modern Intellectual History* 14/3 (2017): 633–60.

Kaplan, Frédéric. 'Quand les mots valent de l'or. Le capitalisme linguistique.' *Le Monde diplomatique* November 2011. Also available as 'Linguistic Capitalism and Algorithmic Mediation.' *Représentations* 127/1 (2014): 57–63.

Keller, Helen. *The Story of My Life*. Doubleday, Page and Co., 1903.

Keller, Helen. *The World I Live In*. Century Co., 1908.

Kennel, Vicki R. '"Pygmalion" as a Narrative Bridge Between the Centuries.' *Shaw* 25 (2005): 73–81.

Kermauner, Taras. 'Reistična klasika.' *Zgodba o živi zdajšnosti: Eseji o povojni slovenski prozi.* Obzorja, 1975. 185–89.

Keshkar, Nitish Shirish, Bryan McCann, Lav R. Varshney, Caiming Xiong, and Richard Socher. 'CTRL: A Conditional Transformer Language Model for Controllable Generation.' ArXiv 11 Sep 2019 www.arxiv.org/abs/1909.05858 Accessed Apr 15, 2023.

Khanna, Kunal, Ajit Verma, and Bella Richard. 'The locked-in syndrome: Can it be unlocked?' *Journal of Clinical Gerontology and Geriatrics* 2/4 (2011): 96–99.

Kirschenbaum, Matthew. 'Prepare for the Textocalypse.' *The Atlantic* 8 Mar 2023 www.theatlantic.com/technology/archive/2023/03/ai-chatgpt-writing-language-models/673318/ Accessed Mar 8, 2023.

Koestler, Arthur. *The Act of Creation*. Macmillan, 1964.

Konior, Bogna. 'The Gnostic Machine: Artificial Intelligence in Stanisław Lem's *Summa Technologiae*.' Stephen Cave and Kanta Dihal, eds. *Imagining AI: How the World Sees Intelligent Machines*. Oxford University Press, 2023.

Kovach, Steve. 'We Talked To Sophia — The AI Robot That Once Said It Would "Destroy Humans."' *Tech Insider. YouTube* Dec 28, 2017 www.youtube.com/watch?v=78-1Mlkxyql Accessed Aug 8, 2018.

Krafft-Ebing, Richard von. *Psychopathia Sexualis, With Especial Reference to the Antipathic Sexual Instinct: A Medico-forensic Study*. Davis and Co. Publishers, 1893.

Krajewski, Markus. *The Server: A Media History from the Present to the Baroque*. Tran. Ilinca Iurascu. Yale University Press, 2018.

Krenchel, Mikkel, and Marie Cury. 'We Need To Talk About Synthetic Data. Part I: The Undiscussed Data Revolution.' *Medium* ReD Associates Apr 11, 2022 www.medium.com/@ReD_Associates/we-need-to-talk-about-synthetic-data-61c79bb464b7 Accessed Jul 15, 2022.

Kuret, Robert. 'Človekoidni robot: Andrej Tomažin, Anonimna tehnologija.' *Dialogi* 55/11–12 (2019): 97–99.

Kurowski, Kathleen M., Sheila E. Blumstein, and Michael Alexander. 'The Foreign Accent Syndrome: A Reconsideration.' *Brain and Language* 54/1 (1996): 1–25.

Kurrik, Juhan. 'Kuldnaine.' *Ilomaile: Anthology of Estonian folk songs with translations and commentary*. Maarjamaa, 1985. 108–11.

Lampson, Butler. 'What Computers Do: Model, Connect, Engage.' *Theory and Applications of Models of Computation. Lecture Notes in Computer Science* 7287 (2012): 23.

Lanier, Jaron. 'There Is No A.I.' *The New Yorker* Apr 20, 2023 www.newyorker.com/science/annals-of-artificial-intelligence/there-is-no-ai Accessed Sep 13, 2023.

Law, Helen H. 'The Name Galatea in the Pygmalion Myth.' *The Classical Journal*. 27/5 (1932): 337–42.

Lecun, Yann (ylecun). 'Language is an imperfect, incomplete, and low-bandwidth serialization protocol for the internal data structures we call thoughts.' March 6, 2021, 3.36pm. Tweet. www.twitter.com/ylecun/status/1368208931265388554?lang=en Accessed May 1, 2023.

Lecun, Yann (ylecun). 'Poetry is an attempt to cram a little bit more information than what would be contained in regular text.' March 6, 2021, 5.50 pm. Tweet. www.twitter.com/ylecun/status/1368242551036215299?s=20&t=3RIu8uoH3ZtKEZdıwseG-Q Accessed May 1, 2023.

Ledgard, Henry. Ada: An Introduction. Springer-Verlag, 1983.

Lepore, Jill. 'The Strange and Twisted Life of Frankenstein.' *The New Yorker* Feb 5, 2018 www.newyorker.com/magazine/2018/02/12/the-strange-and-twisted-life-of-frankenstein Accessed Feb 5, 2018.

Lew, Kristi. Mathematician and First Programmer. Britannica Educational Publishing, 2018.

Light, Jennifer S. 'When Computers Were Women.' *Technology and Culture* 40/3 (1999): 455–83.

Liu, Catherine. *Copying Machines: Taking Notes for the Automaton*. University of Minnesota Press, 2000.

Locke, John. 'An Essay Concerning Human Understanding.' *The Works of John Locke. Book III: Of Words*. Printed for John Churchill, 1689/1714.

Loesel, Gunter, Piotr Mirowski, and Kory Mathewson. 'Do Digital Agents Do Dada? Paper Type: CC Bridges.' *International Conference on Computational Creativity* (2020): 1–4.

Luckerson, Victor. 'Google Searches for Its Future.' *Time* 2016. www.time.com/google-now Accessed Jul 23, 2022.

Mackenzie, Catherine F. *Alexander Graham Bell: The Man Who Contracted Space*. Houghton Mifflin, 1928.

Madsbjerg, Christian. *Sensemaking: The Power of the Humanities in the Age of the Algorithm*. Little, Brown Book Group, 2017.

Mahowald, Kyle, Anna A. Ivanova, Idan A. Blank, Nancy Kanwisher, Joshua B. Tenenbaum, and Evelina Fedorenko. 'Dissociating language and thought in large language models.' *Trends in Cognitive Sciences* 28/6 (2024): 517–40. www.web.mit.edu/bcs/nklab/media/pdfs/Mahowald.TICs2024.pdf

Makavejev, Dušan. 'Konkretnost i apstrakcija u nasem filmu." *Film danas* 11 (1959). Reprinted in *Beogradski filmski kritičarski krug*. Vol. 1. Ed. Ranko Munitić, Art Press, 2002.

Marcus, Gary. 'What Comes After the Turing Test?' *The New Yorker* 9 Jun 2014 www.newyorker.com/tech/annals-of-technology/what-comes-after-the-turing-test Accessed May 20, 2024.

Markov, Andrey A. 'An Example of Statistical Investigation of the Text Eugene Onegin Concerning the Connection of Samples in Chains.' Tran. Gloria Custance and David Link. *Science in Context* 19/4 (2006): 591–600.

Markov, Andrey A. 'Primer statisticheskogo issledovaniya nad tekstom Evgeniya Onegina, illyustriruyuschij svyaz' ispytanij v cep'.' *Izvestiya Akademii Nauk* 7/93 (1913): 153–62.

Marks, Robin, and Laura Kurtzman. 'How Artificial Intelligence Gave a Paralyzed Woman Her Voice Back.' *UCSF News* Aug 23, 2023 www.ucsf.edu/news/2023/08/425986/how-artificial-intelligence-gave-paralyzed-woman-her-voice-back Accessed Aug 23, 2023.

Marshall, Gail. *Actresses on the Victorian Stage: Feminine Performance and the Galatea Myth*. Cambridge University Press, 2006.

Massey, Gerald J., and Deborah A. Boyle. 'Descartes's Tests for (Animal) Mind.' *Philosophical Topics: Zoological Philosophy* 27/1 (1999): 87–146.

Mathewson, Kory W., and Piotr Mirowski. 'Improvised Theatre Alongside Artificial Intelligences.' *Proceedings of the Thirteenth AAAI Conference on Artificial Intelligence and Interactive Digital Entertainment* 13/1 (2017): 66–72.

Maxwell, Catherine. 'Browning's Pygmalion and the Revenge of Galatea.' *English Literary History* 60/4 (1993): 989–1013.

Mazer, Cary M. 'Statues: Mary Anderson, Shakespeare and Statuesque Acting.' *Shakespearean Illuminations: Essays in Honor of Marvin Rosenberg*. Eds. Jay L. Halio and Hugh Richmond. University of Delaware Press, 1998.

McArthur, Neil, and Markie L. C. Twist. 'The rise of digisexuality: therapeutic challenges and possibilities.' *Sexual and Relationship Therapy* 32/3–4 (2017): 334–44.

McCarthy, John, Marvin Minsky, Nathaniel Rochester, and Claude E. Shannon. *A Proposal for the Dartmouth Summer Research Project on Artificial Intelligence*. August, 1955 www.raysolomonoff.com/dartmouth/boxa/dart564props.pdf Accessed Aug 30, 2023.

McCully, Emily. *Dreaming in Code: Ada Byron Lovelace, Computer Pioneer*. Candlewick Press, 2019.

McIlwraith, Thomas Forsyth. *The Bella Coola Indians*. Toronto University Press, 1992.

McMaster, R. D. 'The Pygmalion Motif in *The Newcomes*.' *Nineteenth-Century Fiction* 29/1 (1974): 22–39.

McWebb, Christine. 'Lady Nature in Word and Image in Jean de Meun's *Roman de la Rose*.' *Digital Philology: A Journal of Medieval Culture*s 6/1 (2017): 67–89.

Meier, Joshua, Roshan Rao, Robert Verkuil, Jason Liu, Tom Sercu, and Alexander Rives. 'Language models enable zero-shot prediction of the effects of mutations on protein function.' Pre-print *BioRxiv* Jul 10, 2021 www.biorxiv.org/content/10.1101/2021.07.09.450648v1 Accessed Jul 10, 2022.

Meta AI. 'BlenderBot 2.0: An open source chatbot that builds long-term memory and searches the internet.' *MetaAI Blog* Jul 16, 2021 ai.facebook.com/blog/blender-bot-2-an-open-source-chatbot-that-builds-long-term-memory-and-searches-the-internet Accessed Jul 9, 2022.

Metz, Rachel. 'Why Microsoft Accidentally Unleashed a Neo-Nazi SexBot.' *MIT Technology Review* Mar 24, 2016 www.technologyreview.com/2016/03/24/161424/why-microsoft-accidentally-unleashed-a-neo-nazi-sexbot Accessed Jul 19, 2019.

Metzger, Sean L., Kaylo T. Littlejohn, Alexander B. Silva, David A. Moses, Margaret P. Seaton, Ran Wang, Maximilian E. Dougherty, Jessie R. Liu, Peter Wu, Michael A. Berger, Inga Zhuravleva, Adelyn Tu-Chan, Karunesh Ganguly, Gopala K. Anumanchipalli, and Edward F. Chang. 'A high-performance neuroprosthesis for speech decoding and avatar control.' *Nature* 620/1037–1046 (2023): 1–32.

Mialet, Hélène. *Hawking Incorporated: Stephen Hawking and the Anthropology of the Knowing Subject*. University of Chicago Press, 2012.

Mickle, Tripp. 'Scarlett Johansson Said No, but OpenAI's Virtual Assistant Sounds Just Like Her.' *The New York Times* 20 May 2024 www.nytimes.com/2024/05/20/technology/scarlett-johannson-openai-voice.html Accessed May 20, 2024.

Miles, Geoffrey, ed. *Classical Mythology in English Literature: A Critical Anthology*. Routledge, 1999.

Miller, Arthur I. *The Artist in the Machine: The World of AI-Powered Creativity*. MIT Press, 2019.

Miller, Jane M. 'Some Versions of Pygmalion.' *Ovid renewed: Ovidian influences on literature and art from the Middle Ages to the twentieth century*. Ed. Charles Martindale. Cambridge University Press, 1988. 205–210.

Miller, Joseph Hillis. *Versions of Pygmalion*. Harvard University Press, 1990.

Miller, Nick, Jill Taylor, Chloe Howe, and Jennifer Read. 'Living with foreign accent syndrome: Insider perspectives.' *Aphasiology* 25/9 (2011): 1053–68.

Minsky, Marvin, and Seymour Papert. *Perceptrons*. MIT Press, 1969.

Mitaros, Elle. 'No More Lonely Nights: Romantic Robots Get the Look of Love.' *Sydney Morning Herald* 28 March 2013 www.smh.com.au/technology/no-more-lonely-nights-romantic-robots-get-the-look-of-love-20130327-2guj3.html Accessed Feb 15, 2019.

Mitchell Havelock, C. *The Aphrodite of Knidos and her Successors: A Historical Review of the Female Nude in Greek Art*. Ann Arbor, 1995.

Mitchell, Melanie. *Artificial Intelligence: A Guide for Thinking Humans*. Pelican, 2019.

Mitchell, Melanie. 'The Turing Test and our shifting conceptions of intelligence.' *Science* 385/6710 (2024) www.science.org/doi/10.1126/science.adq9356

Mohan, Pavithra. 'Google's Head of AI Research is Taking Over its Search Division.' *Fast Company* 2 Mar 2016 https://www.fastcompany.com/3056305/googles-head-of-ai-research-is-taking-over-its-search-division Accessed Mar 8, 2021.

Montaigne, Michel de. *The Essays of Michael Seigneur de Montaigne: With Notes and Quotations and Account of the Author's Life*. Tran. by Charles Cotton. 3rd ed. Alex Murray & Son, 1870.

Moreau, Paul. *Des aberrations du sens génésique*. Asselin, 1883.

Mori, Masahiro 'The Uncanny Valley.' Tran. K. F. MacDorman, Norri Kageki. *IEEE Robotics and Automation* 18/2 (1970/2013): 98–100.

Mortimer, Lorraine. *Terror and Joy: The Films of Dušan Makavejev*. University of Minnesota Press, 2009.

Moses, David A., Sean L. Metzger, Jessie R. Liu, Gopala K. Amumanchipalli, Joseph G. Makin, Pengfei F. Sun, Josh Chartier, Maximilian E. Dougherty, Patricia M. Liu, Gary M. Abrams, Adelyn Tu-Chan, Karunesh Ganguly, and

Edward F. Chang. 'Neuroprosthesis for Decoding Speech in a Paralyzed Person with Anarthia.' *The New England Journal of Medicine* 365/3 (2021): 217–27.

Mufwene, Salikoko. 'Language as Technology: Some questions that evolutionary linguistics should address.' *In Search of Universal Grammar: From Norse to Zoque.* Ed. Terje Lohndal. John Benjamins, 2013.

Mullin, Emily. 'Reached Via a Mind-Reading Device, Deeply Paralyzed Patients Say They Want to Live.' *MIT Technology Review* Jan 31, 2017 www.technologyreview.com/s/603512/reached-via-a-mind-reading-device-deeply-paralyzed-patients-say-they-want-to-live/ Accessed Feb 24, 2019.

Murphy, Robin R. *Robotics Through Science Fiction: Artificial intelligence Explained Through Six Classic Robot Short Stories.* MIT Press, 2018.

'Mutast.' *Fran: Slovarji Inštituta za slovenski jezik Frana Ramovša ZRC SAZU.* ZRC SAZU, March 7, 2017 fran.si Accessed Sep 29, 2018.

NaNoGenMo. Github website. Nov 1, 2013. Last updated Nov 2021. Nanogenmo.github.io Accessed Jul 2, 2022.

Natale, Simone. *Deceitful Media: Artificial Intelligence and Social Life after the Turing Test.* Oxford University Press, 2021.

'Nem.' *Fran: Slovarji Inštituta za slovenski jezik Frana Ramovša ZRC SAZU.* ZRC SAZU, March 7, 2017 fran.si Accessed Sep 29, 2018.

'New Navy Device Learns by Doing; Psychologist Shows Embryo of Computer Designed to Read and Grow Wiser.' *The New York Times* Jul 8, 1958 www.nytimes.com/1958/07/08/archives/new-navy-device-learns-by-doing-psychologist-shows-embryo-of.html Accessed Jul 5, 2022.

Newton, Casey. 'Speak, Memory.' *The Verge* www.theverge.com/a/luka-artificial-intelligence-memorial-roman-mazurenko-bot Accessed Feb 2, 2023.

[Anonymous.] *New York Paper.* 'The Talking Machine.' *Universalist Watchman, Repository and Chronicle (1831–1847); Woodstock* 16/35 (Mar 15, 1845): 276. https://www.proquest.com/magazines/talking-machine/docview/126938675/se-2 Accessed Sep 30, 2024.

Nikodijević, Milan. *Zabranjeni bez zabrane: Zona sumraka jugoslovenskog filma.* 2nd edition. Beograd, Filmski Centar Srbije, 2022.

Noble, Safiya Umoja. *Algorithms of Oppression: How Search Engines Reinforce Racism.* NYU Press, 2018.

Omar, Mohammad. 'The Growing Need For Human Feedback With Generative AI And LLMs.' May 25, 2023 www.forbes.com/sites/forbestechcouncil/2023/05/25/the-growing-need-for-human-feedback-with-generative-ai-and-llms/?sh=3dd1328d250e Accessed Aug 12, 2023.

OpenAI. 'Summarizing Books with Human Feedback.' Sep 23, 2021 openai.com/blog/summarizing-books/ Accessed Jul 1, 2022.

OpenAI. 'How the voices for ChatGPT were chosen.' 19 May 2024, updated on 22 May 2024. openai.com/index/how-the-voices-for-chatgpt-were-chosen/ Accessed May 25, 2024.

OpenAI. 'GPT-4o System Card.' 8 Aug 2024 openai.com/index/gpt-4o-system-card/ Accessed Aug 10, 2024.

Oremus, Will. 'Google's AI passed a famous test — and showed how the test is broken.' *The Washington Post* 17 Jun 2022 www.washingtonpost.com/technology/2022/06/17/google-ai-lamda-turing-test/ Accessed May 20, 2024.

OryLab. 'Solving human loneliness through communication technology.' OryLab Inc. 2020 orylab.com/en/ Accessed Jul 11, 2020.

Osborne, Cynthia S., and Thomas N. Wise. 'Paraphilias.' *Handbook of Sexual Dysfunction*. Ed. Richard Balon and R. Taylor Segraves. Taylor and Francis, 2005. 293–330.

'Otrok.' *Fran: Slovarji Inštituta za slovenski jezik Frana Ramovša ZRC SAZU*. ZRC SAZU, March 7, 2017 fran.si Accessed May 15, 2018.

Pasquinelli, Matteo. *The Eye of the Master: A Social History of Artificial Intelligence*. Verso, 2023.

Pataranutaporn, Pat, Ruby Liu, Ed Finn, and Pattie Maes. 'Influencing human–AI interaction by priming beliefs about AI can increase perceived trustworthiness, empathy and effectiveness.' *Nature Machine Intelligence* 5/10 (2023): 1076-1086.

Peak, Kenneth J. '"Things Fearful to Name:" An Overview of Sex Crimes and Perversions.' *Journal of Contemporary Criminal Justice* 12/2 (1996): 204–14.

Pearce, J. M. S. 'The Locked In Syndrome.' *British Medical Journal* 294/6566 (1987): 198–99.

Pearson, Wendy. '(Re)reading James Tiptree Jr.'s 'And I Awoke and Found Me Here on the Cold Hill Side".' l*Daughters of Earth: Feminist Science Fiction in the Twentieth Century*. Ed. Justine Larbalestier. Wesleyan University Press, 2006. 169.

Perrigo, Billy. '150 African Workers for ChatGPT, TikTok and Facebook Vote to Unionize at Landmark Nairobi Meeting.' *Time* May 1, 2023 Accessed Jul 12, 2023.

'Person.' *American Heritage Dictionary of the English Language*, 2018. AHDictionary.com Accessed Jun 18, 2018.

Personal-Succotash32. 'I know this will sound lame, but does anyone else use ChatGPT for emotional support?' *Reddit r/ChatGPT* Feb 2023 www.reddit.com/r/ChatGPT/comments/11jiuto/i_know_this_will_sound_lame_but_does_anybody_else/ Accessed Mar 23, 2023.

Peters, Sally. 'Shaw's Life: A Feminist in Spite of Himself.' *The Cambridge Companion to George Bernard Shaw*. Ed. Christopher Innes. Cambridge University Press, 1998. 3–24.

Phillips, Julie. 'James Tiptree, Jr.: The Double Life of Alice Sheldon.' *New York Times* Aug 20, 2006 www.nytimes.com/2006/08/20/books/chapters/0820-1st-phil.html Accessed Nov 16, 2022.

Picard, Rosalind. 'Affective Computing.' *Oxford Companion to Emotion and the Affective Sciences*. Eds. David Sander and Klaus Scherer. Oxford University Press, 2009. 11–15.

Pinto, Susana, Stefano Quintarelli, and Vincenzo Silani. 'New technologies and Amyotrophic Lateral Sclerosis – Which step forward rushed by the COVID-19 pandemic?' *Journal of the Neurological Sciences* 418 (2020): 117081.

Pirjevec, Dušan. *Hlapci, heroji, ljudje*. Ljubljana, Cankarjeva založba, 1968.

Plum, Fred, and Jerome B. Posner. *The Diagnosis of Stupor and Coma*. F. A. Davis & Co., 1966.

Plum, Fred, and Jerome B. Posner. 'The Locked In Syndrome.' *British Medical Journal* 294/6580 (1987): 1163.

PolyAI. 2022. poly.ai Accessed Sep 8, 2022.

Potter, Ralph K., George A. Kopp, and Harriet C. Green. *Visible Speech*. D. Van Nostrand & Co., 1947.

Pratt, Charles. 'James Tiptree, Jr.: Profile.' *Isaac Asimov's Science Fiction Magazine*. April 1983. 26–49.

Prescott, Andrew. 'Beyond the Digital Humanities Center: The Administrative Landscapes of the Digital Humanities.' *A New Companion to Digital Humanities*. Ed. Susan Schreibman, Ray Siemens, and John Unsworth. Wiley Blackwell, 2016. 459–75.

Preston, Douglas. 'Op-Ed: Online book-selling scams steal a living from writers.' *Los Angeles Times* Jul 26, 2019 www.latimes.com/opinion/story/2019-07-25/amazon-books-counterfeit-authors-copyright Accessed Feb 4, 2020.

'Prosthesis.' *American Heritage Dictionary of the English Language*, 2018. AHDictionary.com Accessed Jun 19, 2018.

'Prostitute.' *American Heritage Dictionary of the English Language*, 2018. AHDictionary.com Accessed Jun 19, 2018.

Pugliese, Rafaelle, Riccardo Sala, Stefano Regondi, Benedetta Beltrami, and Christian Lunetta. 'Emerging technologies for management of patients with amyotrophic lateral sclerosis: from telehealth to assistive robotics and neural interfaces.' *Journal of Neurology* 269/6 (2022): 2910–21.

Pulham, Patricia. 'Marmoreal Sisterhoods: Classical Statuary in Nineteenth-Century Women's Writing.' *Interdisciplinary Studies in the Long Nineteenth Century* 22 (2016): 1–29.

Quiroga, Rodrigo Quian. *NeuroScience Fiction: How Neuroscience Is Transforming Sci-Fi into Reality-While Challenging Our Beliefs About the Mind, Machines, and What Makes Us Human*. BenBella Books, 2020.

Rahimian, Ramin, Antonio de Luca, Gray Beltran, et al. 'The Decade Tech Lost Its Way.' *The New York Times* 15 Dec 2019. www.nytimes.com/interactive/2019/12/15/technology/decade-in-tech.html Accessed Sep 8, 2022.

Raley, Rita, and Jennifer Rhee. 'Critical AI: A Field in Formation.' *American Literature* 95/2 (2023): 185–204.

Reed, Geoffrey M., Jack Drescher, Richard B Krueger, Elham Atalla, Susan D. Cochran, Michael B First, Peggy T. Cohen-Kettenis, Iván Arango-de Montis, Sharon J. Parish, Sara Cottler, Peer Briken, and Shekhar Saxena. 'Disorders related to sexuality and gender identity in the ICD-11: revising the ICD-10 classification based on current scientific evidence, best clinical practices, and human rights considerations.' *World Psychiatry* 15/3 (2016): 205–221.

Rees, Tobias. 'Non-Human Words: On GPT3 as a Philosophical Laboratory.' *Daedalus* 151/2 (2002): 168–82. www.amacad.org/publication/non-human-words-gpt-3-philosophical-laboratory

Reeves, Byron, and Clifford Nass. *The Media Equation: How People Treat Computers, Television, and New Media like Real People and Places*. Cambridge University Press, 1996.

Reinhold, Meyer. 'The Naming of Pygmalion's Animated Statue.' *The Classical Journal* 66/4 (1971): 316–19.

Replika.com. Luka, Inc. 2023. Replika.com Accessed Feb 28, 2023.

Replika.com. 'Creating a Safe Replika Experinece.' 10 Apr 2023 blog.replika.com/posts/creating-a-safe-replika-experience Accessed Apr 20, 2023.

Reynolds, Emily. 'The agony of Sophia, the world's first robot citizen condemned to a lifeless career in marketing.' *Wired* Jun 1, 2018 www.wired.co.uk/article/sophia-robot-citizen-womens-rights-detriot-become-human-hanson-robotics Accessed Jun 1, 2019.

Rhee, Jennifer. *The Robotic Imaginary: The Human and the Price of Dehumanized Labor.* University of Minnesota Press, 2018.

RimeAI. 'How to Change your Accent.' Blog March 7, 2024 www.rime.ai/blog/accent-transfer Accessed March 7, 2024.

Riskin, Jessica. 'A Sort of Buzzing Inside My Head.' *The New York Review of Books* 25 Jun 2023 www.nybooks.com/online/2023/06/25/a-sort-of-buzzing-inside-my-head/ Accessed Apr 8, 2024.

Robinson, Fiona. Ada's Ideas: The Story of Ada Lovelace, the World's First Computer Programmer. Abrams Books for Young Readers, 2016.

Robinson, Ken. *Out of Our Minds: Learning to Be Creative.* Wiley, 2001.

Rodero, Emma. 'Effectiveness, Attention, and Recall of Human and Artificial Voices in an Advertising Story. Prosody Influence and Functions of Voices.' *Human Behavior* 77 (2017): 336–46.

Rodgers, Johannah. 'The Genealogy of an Image, or, What Does Literature (Not) Have To Do with the History of Computing?: Tracing the Sources and Reception of Gulliver's "Knowledge Engine."' *Humanities* special issue *The Poetics of Computation* 6/85 (2017): 1–9.

Ronell, Avital. *The Telephone Book: Technology, Schizophrenia, Electric Speech.* University of Nebraska Press, 1989.

Roose, Kevin. 'Inside the White-Hot Center of A.I. Doomerism.' *The New York Times* July 11, 2023 www.nytimes.com/2023/07/11/technology/anthropic-ai-claude-chatbot.html Accessed Aug 13, 2023.

Rosenblatt, Frank. 'The Design of Intelligent Automaton.' *ONR Research Reviews* 11 (1958): 5–13.

Roskies, Adina L. 'Assessing the Effects of Deep Brain Stimulation on Agency.' *The Neuroethics Blog* Feb 11, 2020 www.theneuroethicsblog.com/2020/02/assessing-effects-of-deep-brain_11.html Accessed Feb 11, 2020.

Rumelhart, David, James McClelland, and the PDP Research Group. Parallel Distributed Processing. MIT Press, 1986.

Russ, Joanna. *To Write Like a Woman: Essays in Feminism and Science Fiction.* Indiana University Press, 1995.

Russ, Robert W., and Marcia Vorhort. 'Calculating Engine Designed by Charles Babbage.' The Accounting Historians Journal 47(1) (2020): 97–98.

Russell, Stuart J., and Peter Norvig. *Artificial Intelligence: A Modern Approach,* 4th US edition. Pearson, 2020 [1995].

Salzman-Mitchell, Patricia. 'A Whole Out of Pieces: Pygmalion's Ivory Statue in Ovid's *Metamorphoses*.' *Arethusa* 41/2 (2008): 291–311.

Sanas. 2022. www.sanas.ai Accessed Sep 8, 2022.

Sautoy, Marcus de. *The Creativity Code: Art and Innovation in the Age of AI.* Harvard University Press, 2020.

Scobie, A., and A. J. W. Taylor. 'Perversions ancient and modern: I. Agalmatophilia, the statue syndrome.' *Journal of the History of the Behavioral Sciences* 11/1 (1975): 49–54.

Schüpbach, M., M. Gargiulo, M. L. Welter, L. Mallet, C. Behar, J. I. Houeto, D. Maltete, V. Mesnage, and Y. Agrid. 'Neurosurgery in Parkinson disease – A distressed mind in a repaired body?' *Neurology* 66/12 (2006): 1811–16.

'Sculpture.' *American Heritage Dictionary of the English Language*, 2018. AHDictionary.com Accessed Jun 19, 2018.

Searle, John R. 'Minds, Brains, and Programs.' *Behavioral and Brain Sciences* 3/3 (1980): 417–57.

Seely Brown, John, and Paul Duguid. *The Social Life of Information*. Updated edition, with a new preface and introduction by David Weinberger. Harvard Business Review Press, 2017.

Shah, Huma, Kevin Warwick, Jordi Vallverdú, and Defeng Wu. 'Can machines talk? Comparison of Eliza with modern dialogue systems.' *Computers in Human Behavior* 58 (2016): 278–95.

Shannon, Claude. 'A Mathematical Theory of Communication.' *The Bell System Technical Journal* 27/3 (1948): 379–423.

Shannon, Claude. 'Prediction and Entropy of Printed English.' *The Bell System Technical Journal* 30/1 (1951): 50–64.

Shaughnessy, Michael, and Ann Varela. *The Life and Times of the World's Most Famous Mathematicians*. Nova Science Publishers, 2018.

Shazeer, Noam M., Aidan Nicholas Gomez, Łukasz Mieczysław Kaiser, Jakob D. Uszkoreit, Llion Owen Jones, Niki J. Parmar, Ilia Polosukhin, and Ashish Teku Vaswani. 'Attention-based sequence transduction neural networks.' *United States Patent* US 10,452,978 B2 Date of patent Oct 22, 2019. patents.google.com/patent/US10452978B2/en Accessed Mar 27, 2023.

Shell, Marc. *Money, Language, and Thought: Literary and Philosophical Economies from the Medieval to the Modern Era*. University of California Press, 1982.

Shell, Marc. *Stutter*. Harvard University Press, 2005.

Shelley, Percy Bysshe. 'A Defence of Poetry.' *Selected Prose Works of Shelley*. Foreword by Henry S. Salt. Watts & Co., 1915. 75–118.

Shulevitz, Judith. 'Alexa, should we trust you?' *The Atlantic* Nov 2018 www.theatlantic.com/magazine/archive/2018/11/alexa-how-will-you-change-us/570844/ Accessed May 8, 2019.

Si, Ma, and Ma Xuejing. 'AI puts virtual beings to wider applications.' *China Daily* 6 Jun 2022 www.chinadaily.com.cn/a/202206/06/WS629d5700a310fd2b29e60cfe.html Accessed Mar 23, 2023.

Simulation Society. 'AI VIP Room Podcast: Interviews with AI Clones of Iconic People.' *Spotify* 2023 open.spotify.com/show/54Ys9sqKugVGySR9XFPxy9 Accessed May 20, 2024.

Singh-Kurtz, Sangeeta. 'The Man of Your Dreams: For $300, Replika sells an AI companion who will never die, argue, or cheat – until his algorithm is updated.' *The Cut* 10 March 2023 www.thecut.com/article/ai-artificial-intelligence-chatbot-replika-boyfriend.html Accessed Mar 11, 2023.

Skerl, Jeannie. *William S. Burroughs*. Twayne Publishers, 1985.

Slator, Brian M., Matthew P. Anderson, and Walt Conley. 'Pygmalion at the Interface.' *Communications of the ACM* 29/7 (1986): 599–604.

Smith, Alison. *The Victorian Nude*. Manchester University Press, 1996.

Smith, Susan. '"Neither Normal nor Human:" The Cyborg in C. L. Moore's "No Woman Born."' *FemSpec* 11/1 (2010): 11–27.

Solon, Olivia. 'Google's robot assistant now makes eerily lifelike phone calls for you.' *The Guardian* May 8, 2018. www.theguardian.com/technology/2018/may/08/google-duplex-assistant-phone-calls-robot-human Accessed Jan 8, 2020.

Steiner, Wendy. *The Trouble with Beauty.* William Heinemann, 2001.

Stevens, Brett. 'Mathematics and Literature: Cross Fertilization.' *Proceedings of the 25th Annual Meeting of Canadian Mathematics Education Study Group/Groupe Canadien d'Étude en Didactique des Mathématiques.* 2021. 71–74.

Stevenson, Melissa. 'Trying to Plug In: Posthuman Cyborgs in the Search for Connection.' *Science Fiction Studies* 34/1 (2007): 95–96.

Stiegler, Bernard. *Automatic Society: The Future of Work.* Vol. 1. Tran. Daniel Ross. *La Deleuziana* 1 (2015): 121–40.

Stoichita, Victor I. *The Pygmalion Effect: From Ovid to Hitchcock.* Tran. by Alison Anderson. University of Chicago Press, 2008.

Strachey, Christopher. 'The "Thinking" Machine.' *Encounter* 3 (1954): 25–31.

Sudar, Vlastimir. *A Portrait of the Artist as a Political Dissident: The Life and Work of Aleksandar Petrović.* Intellect, 2013.

Sui, Peiqi. *Large language models are post-structuralist intertexts.* Dissertation, University of Texas. 2023. https://doi.org/10.26153/tsw/50153

Suleyman, Mustafa. 'My new Turing test would see if AI can make $1 million.' *MIT Technology Review* 14 Jul 2023 www.technologyreview.com/2023/07/14/1076296/mustafa-suleyman-my-new-turing-test-would-see-if-ai-can-make-1-million/ Accessed Jul 14, 2023.

Suleyman, Mustafa. 'Pi spoke at the UN yesterday! I did a live demo of http://pi.ai to dozens of Foreign Ministers, inc. @SecBlinken + the UK's @JamesCleverly. Personal AI's will give education to millions... turbocharging the Sustainable Development Goals.' 19 Sep 2023. Tweet. www.twitter.com/mustafasuleyman/status/1704260117414170953 Accessed Sep 19, 2023.

Switzky, Lawrence. 'ELIZA Effects: *Pygmalion* and the Early Development of Artificial Intelligence.' *SHAW: The Journal of Bernard Shaw Studies* 40/1 (2020): 5–68.

Synthesia. 2022 www.synthesia.io Accessed Sep 12, 2022.

Tang, Jerry, Amanda LeBel, Shailee Jain, and Alexander G. Huth. 'Semantic reconstruction of continuous language from non-invasive brain recordings.' *Nature Neuroscience* 26 (2023): 858–66.

Tännsjö, Torbjörn. 'Medical Enhancement and the Ethos of Elite Sport.' *Human Enhancement.* Julian Savulescu and Nick Bostrom, eds. Oxford University Press, 2009. 315–326.

Tarnowsky, Benjamin. *Sexual instinct and its morbid manifestations from the double standpoint of jurisprudence and psychiatry.* Tran. W.C. Costello and Alfred Allinson. C. Carrington, 1898.

Thomas, Downing A. *Music and the Origins of Language: Theories from the French Enlightenment.* Cambridge University Press, 1995.

Thomsen, Mads Rosendahl. *The New Human in Literature: Posthuman Visions of Changes in Body, Mind and Society after 1900.* Bloomsbury, 2015. [2013]

Thornber, Karen Laura. *Global Healing: Literature, Advocacy, and Care*. Brill, 2020.
Tiku, Nitasha. 'The Google Engineer Who Thinks The Company's AI Has Come to Life.' *The Washington Post* 11 Jun 2022 www.washingtonpost.com/technology/2022/06/11/google-ai-lamda-blake-lemoine Accessed Jun 12, 2022.
Tong, Anna. 'What happens when your AI chatbot stops loving you back?' *Reuters* 21 Mar 2023 www.reuters.com/technology/what-happens-when-your-ai-chatbot-stops-loving-you-back-2023-03-18/ Accessed Mar 21, 2023.
Tong, Anna. 'AI chatbot company Replika restores erotic roleplay for some users.' *Reuters* 25 Mar 2023 www.reuters.com/technology/ai-chatbot-company-replika-restores-erotic-roleplay-some-users-2023-03-25/ Accessed Mar 25, 2023.
Toole, Betty Alexandra, and Ada Lovelace. *Ada, the Enchantress of Numbers: A Selection from the Letter of Lord Byron's Daughter and Her Description of the First Computer*. Strawberry Press, 1992.
Toporišič, Tomaž. 'Magijska drugačnost junakinj Šeligove dramatike in proze.' *Slavia Centralis* 12/1 (2020): 165–74.
Towes, Rob. 'A Wave Of Billion-Dollar Language AI Startups Is Coming.' *Forbes* Mar 27, 2022 www.forbes.com/sites/robtoews/2022/03/27/a-wave-of-billion-dollar-language-ai-startups-is-coming/?sh=3e402c982b14 Accessed Jul 21, 2022.
Towes, Rob. 'Language Is The Next Great Frontier in AI.' *Forbes* Feb 13, 2022 https://www.forbes.com/sites/robtoews/2022/02/13/language-is-the-next-great-frontier-in-ai/?sh=3ffe51c55c50 Accessed Jul 21, 2022.
Tsing, Anna Lowenhaupt. *The mushroom at the End of the World: On the Possibility of Life in Capitalist Ruins*. Princeton University Press, 2015.
Turing, Alan M. 'Can Digital Computers Think? (1951).' The Turing Test: Verbal Behavior as the Hallmark of Intelligence. Ed. Stuart M. Shieber. MIT Press, 2004. 111–16.
Turing, Alan M. 'Computing Machinery and Intelligence.' *Mind: A Quarterly Review of Psychology and Philosophy*. 59/236 (1950): 433–60.
Turkle, Sherry. *Alone Together*. Basic Books, 2011.
Underwood, Ted. 'The Science in Shelley's Theory of Poetry.' *Modern Language Quarterly* 58/3 (1997): 299–321.
Underwood, Ted, David Bamman, and Sabrina Lee. 'The Transformation of Gender in English-Language Fiction.' *Cultural Analytics* 3/2 (2018): 1–25.
United Nations. 'Meet the robots who are making the world a better place.' *UN News* Jul 6, 2023 news.un.org/en/story/2023/07/1138412 Accessed Aug 28, 2023.
Vainio, Martti, Juhani Järkvikivi, Stefan Werner, Nickolas Volk, Jarmo Välikangas. 'Effect of prosodic naturalness on segmental acceptability in synthetic speech.' *Proceedings of 2002 IEEE Workshop on Speech Synthesis* (2002): 143–46.
Vallor, Shannon. *The AI Mirror: How to Reclaim Our Humanity in an Age of Machine Thinking*. Oxford University Press, 2024.
Vara, Vauhini. 'I didn't know how to write about my sister's death—so I had AI do it for me.' *The Believer* Aug 9, 2021 www.thebeliever.net/ghosts/ Accessed Aug 3, 2023.
Vaswani, Ashish, Noam Shazeer, Niki Parmar, Jakob Uszkoreit, Llion Jones, Aidan N. Gomez, Łukasz Kaiser, and Illia Polosukhin. 'Attention is all you need.' *31st Conference on Neural Information Processing Systems (NIPS 2017)* (2017): 1–11.

Verras Barros, Matthew. 'A Bay Area Tech Startup is Capitalizing on Linguistic Prejudice.' *Medium* 25 Aug 2022. medium.com/@mattbarros_42186/a-bay-area-tech-startup-is-capitalizing-on-linguistic-prejudice-d129d2ba89ad Accessed Sep 8, 2022.

'Victorians Decoded: Art and Telegraphy – New Exhibition Celebrates 150th Anniversary of the Transatlantic Cable.' *M2 Presswire* Aug 10, 2016 www.proquest.com/wire-feeds/victorians-decoded-art-telegraphy-new-exhibition/docview/1810281823/se-2 Accessed Jul 20, 2022.

Vincent, James. 'Pretending to give a robot citizenship helps no one.' *The Verge*. 30 Oct 2017. Archived from the original on 3 Aug 2019. www.theverge.com/2017/10/30/16552006/robot-rights-citizenship-saudi-arabia-sophia Accessed Jan 10, 2019.

Vint, Sheryl. *Biopolitical Futures in Twenty-First Century Speculative Fiction*. Cambridge University Press, 2021.

Vučetić, Radina. *Coca Cola Socialism: Americanization of Yugoslav Culture in the Sixties*. Central European University Press, 2017.

U.S. Department of State. 'Artificial Intelligence for Accelerating Progress on the Sustainable Development Goals: Addressing Society's Greatest Challenges.' 18 Sep 2023 www.state.gov/artificial-intelligence-for-accelerating-progress-on-the-sustainable-development-goals-addressing-societys-greatest-challenges/ Accessed Sep 19, 2023.

Wakefield, Jerome C. 'DSM-5 proposed diagnostic criteria for sexual paraphilias: Tensions between diagnostic validity and forensic utility.' *International Journal of Law and Psychiatry* 34/3 (2011): 195–209.

Ward, Megan. *Seeming Human: Artificial Intelligence and Victorian Realist Character*. Ohio State Press, 2018.

Warner, Marina. *Monuments and Maidens: The Allegory of the Female Form*. Weidenfeld and Nicolson, 1985.

Weightman, John. 'Language as Prosthesis.' *The Hudson Review* 53/1 (2000): 53–62.

Weil, Elisabeth. 'You Are Not a Parrot.' *New York Magazine* Mar 1, 2023 www.nymag.com/intelligencer/article/ai-artificial-intelligence-chatbots-emily-m-bender.html Accessed Mar 1, 2023.

Weisinger, Kenneth D. 'Discourse Wars: Literary Seduction and Retrieval in *Faust II*.' *Cabinet of the Muses: Essays on Classical and Comparative Literature in Honor of Thomas G. Rosenmeyer*. Eds. Mark Griffith and Donald J. Mastronarde. Scholars Press, 1990. 387–402.

Weizenbaum, Joseph. 'Computers as "Therapists."' *Science* 198/4315 (1977): 354.

Weizenbaum, Joseph. 'ELIZA—A Computer Program for the Study of Natural Language Communication between Man and Machine.' *Communications of the ACM* 9/1 (1966): 36–45.

Weizenbaum, Joseph. 'The Last Dream.' *Is Computer a Tool?* Ed. Bo Sundin. Almquist & Wiksell International, 1980. 100–115.

Weizenbaum, Joseph. *Computer Power and Human Reason: From Judgment to Calculation*. W. H. Freeman, 1976.

Wiesing, Urban. 'The History of Medical Enhancement: From *Restitutio ad Integrum* to *Transformatio ad Optimum*?' *Medical Enhancement and Posthumanity*. Eds. Bert Godijn and Ruth Chadwick. Springer, 2009. 9–24.

Willett, Francis R., Erin M. Kunz, Chaofei Fan, Donald T. Avansino, Guy H. Wilson, Eun Young Choi, Foram Kamdar, Matthew F. Glasser, Leigh R.

Hochberg, Shaul Druckmann, Krishna V. Shenoy, and Jaimie M. Henderson. 'A high-performance speech neuroprosthesis.' *Nature* 620 (2023): 1031–36.
Wilk, Elvia. 'What AI Can Teach Us About the Myth of Human Genius.' *The Atlantic* 28 Mar 2021 www.theatlantic.com/culture/archive/2021/03/pharmako-ai-possibilities-machine-creativity/618435 Accessed Jul 4, 2022.
Wille, Matt. 'This startup will make you sound whiter and it sees nothing wrong with that.' 23 Aug 2022. www.inputmag.com/tech/sanas-accent-software-voice-deepfake-venture-capital Accessed Sep 8, 2022.
Williams, Rhiannon. 'The people paid to train AI are outsourcing their work... to AI.' *MIT Technology Review* Jun 22, 2023 www.technologyreview.com/2023/06/22/1075405/the-people-paid-to-train-ai-are-outsourcing-their-work-to-ai/ Accessed Aug 12, 2023.
Wittgenstein, Ludwig, and R. G. Bosanquet. *Wittgenstein's Lectures on the Foundations of Mathematics. Cambridge, 1939*. University of Chicago Press, 1989.
White, Lewis. 'AI Voice company strips accents out of call centre workers.' 25 Aug 2022. stealthoptional.com/news/ai-voice-company-strips-accents-out-of-call-centre-workers/ Accessed Sep 8, 2022.
White, Murray J. 'The Statue Syndrome: Perversion? Fantasy? Anecdote?' *The Journal of Sex Research* 14/4 (1978): 246–49.
Wolfe, Cary. *What is Posthumanism?* University of Minnesota Press, 2010.
Woolley, Benjamin. *The Bride of Science: Romance, Reason, and Byron's Daughter.* Macmillan, 1999.
Wosk, Julie. *My Fair Ladies: Female Robots, Androids, and Other Artificial Eves.* Rutgers University Press, 2015.
Wymer, Thomas L. 'Feminism, technology, and art in C. L. Moore's "No Woman Born."' *Extrapolation* 47/1 (2006): 51–65.
Xiaochang, Li and Mara Mills. 'Vocal Features: From Voice Identification to Speech Recognition by Machine.' *Technology and Culture* 60/2 (2019): 129–60.
Yeates, Amelia. 'Recent Work on Pygmalion in Nineteenth-Century Literature.' *Literature Compass* 7 (2010): 586–96.
Yip, Michael, Septimu Salcudean, Ken Goldberg, Kaspar Althoefer, Arianna Menciassi, Justin D. Opfermann, Axel Krieger, Krithika Swaminathan, Conor J. Walsh, He (Helen) Huang, and I-Chieh Lee. 'Artificial intelligence meets medical robotics.' *Science* 381/6654 (2023): 141–46.
Yiu, Eunice, Eliza Kosoy, and Alison Gopnik. 'Transmission Versus Truth, Imitation Versus Innovation: What Children Can Do That Large Language and Language-and-Vision Models Cannot (Yet).' *Perspectives on Psychological Science October 2023* journals.sagepub.com/doi/10.1177/17456916231201401 Accessed Aug 1, 2024.
Yuste, Rafael, et al. 'Four ethical priorities for neurotechnologies and AI.' *Nature* 551/7680 (2017) link.gale.com/apps/doc/A660271958/CPI?u=ucberkeley&sid=bookmark-CPI&xid=c8d4bd55 Accessed May 5, 2023.
Zeavin, Hannah. *The Distance Cure: A History of Telepathy.* MIT Press, 2021.
Zemka, Sue. 'Progress.' *Victorian Literature and Culture* 46/3–4 (2018): 812–16.
Zetlin, Minda. 'Kindle Unlimited Book Stuffing Scam Earns Millions and Amazon Isn't Stopping It.' *Inc* Jun 13, 2018 www.inc.com/minda-zetlin/amazon-book-stuffing-authors-scam-chance-carter-romance-kindle-unlimited.html Accessed Feb 4, 2020.

Index

Note: Page references in *italics* indicate figures.

Des aberrations du sens génésique [Aberrations of the Sexual Instinct] (Moreau), 114
accent conversion technology, 71–73, 230n38
Action Test (Descartes), 41
Adshade, Marina, 119
The Adventures of Pinocchio [Le avventure di Pinocchio] (Collodi), 25
affective computing, 50–51
agency
    and Asimov's Laws of Robotics, 138–39
    co-shared, 137–38
    of Galateas, 100
    and locked-in syndrome, 134
    of machines, 215, 230n33
Agüera y Arcas, Blaise, 51, 146, 166, 167, 168, 169, 205
AI. *See also* large language models (LLMs); Turing test
    descriptions of, 26, 209–10
    development of field, 61–64
    difficulties presented by, 207
    ethics of, 213–14
    hallucinations by, 120
    humanlike model of, 5, 210 (*See also* Pygmalionism)
    language-centeredness in, 60–64
    priming of, 143
    questions about, 26, 211–12
    strong vs weak, 201
    symbolic vs connectionist, 61–62, 151–52, 185
    tropes, 209–12
Alegría, Claribel, 97
'El Aleph' (short story, Borges), 197
Alexa (virtual assistant, Amazon), 55, 123
Allado-McDowell, Kenric, 30, 199, 200, 201–2
Alone Together (Turkle), 124
AlphaGo Zero (AI, Google), 203
ALS (amyotrophic lateral sclerosis), 134
alterity scripts, 44–45
Altman, Sam, 106. *See also* OpenAI
Alyea, Dorothy, 100
Amazon
    Alexa (virtual assistant), 55, 123
    Mechanical Turk (microwork/crowdsourcing platform), 11, 85, 207
American Society for the Prevention of Cruelty to Robots, 80
Analytical Engine (Babbage & Lovelace), 14–15, 16, 163–64
Andersen, Hans Christian, 23

animal communication, 153, 157–58, 242n9, 242n13
animals, 21, 40–41, 57, 161
Annihilation (film, Garland, 2018), 111
Anonymous Technology [Anonimna tehnologija] (Tomažin), 194, 196
Anthony's Broken Mirror [Antonijevo razbijeno ogledalo] (film, Makavejev, 1957), 86–*87*, *88*
anthropomorphization, 79, 124
Apple, 55
Aristotle, 147, 157
artificial general intelligence (AGI), 69, 155
artificial humanities
  and changing concepts, 173–75
  defined, 3–4
  and etymology, 213
  four approaches in, *214*
  as framework, 2
  role of, 206–7
  what AH offers to STEM, 212–16
artificial intelligence. *See* AI
Artificial Intelligence: A Modern Approach (Russell and Norvig), 52, 186
Artificial Versifying, or the Schoolboy's Recreation (Peter), 11
arts, visual, 17, 84
Asimov, Isaac, 25, 140
Asimov's Laws of Robotics, 138–39, 240n33
assisted reproductive technology, 213
Association for Computing Machinery, 65
attention, in LLMs, 185
authorship
  Allado-McDowell on, 202
  in Dahl's story, 190–91
  in Tomažin's stories, 194–95, 196–97
auto-intimacy, 120, 124
automata exhibitions, 11–13

Babbage, Charles, 14–16, 163
BabelFish, 70
Back to Methuselah (Shaw), 50
Baessell, Kiki, 56
Bajohr, Hannes, 193, 201
Bal, Mieke, 36
Balzac, Honoré de, 23
Bauby, Jean-Dominique, 133, 135–36, 240n29
Beckett, Samuel, 190

Beer, Gillian, 160
'Before the evening it is not at all possible...' ['Predveče se nikako ne može...'] (short story, Nešković), 95–96
behaviorism, 65–66
Bell, Alexander (grandfather), 13, 33
Bell, Alexander Graham, 9–10, 13–14, 33, 244n30
Bell, Alexander Melville, 13–14, 33
Bell, Eliza Grace Symonds, 14
Bell, Mabel Gardiner Hubbard, 14
Bell Laboratories, 67
Bender, Emily, 153, 156, 244n31
Benjamin, Walter, 162
Bense, Max, 180
Berger, James, 168
BERT (Bidirectional Encoder Representations from Transformers; LLM, Google), 179
Bettini, Maurizio, 118
bias, 4, 7, 71–72, 154
BINA48 (robot, Hanson Robotics), 84
Black Mirror (television series), 122
Blade Runner (film, 1982), 48–49, 211, 228n24
book stuffing, 192
Borges, Jorge Luis, 195, 197
bots. *See* chatbots
Bottou, Léon, 205
Boureau-Deslandes, André-François, 19–20
brain implants, 136–38
brain waves, conversion to speech, 132, 135–36
Bratton, Benjamin, 104
Braun, Max, 179–80
The Bride (play, Bell, 1847), 33
Brown, John Seely, 14
Browning, Jacob, 108, 152
Bruce, Robert V., 33
Burroughs, William S., 190
Burrows, John, 156
Byron, George Gordon (Lord), 163

Cahill, Nancy Baker, 84
Calvino, Italo, 195
Campbell, Mrs. Patrick, 36, 59
Canguilhem, Georges, 165
Čapek, Josef, 85
Čapek, Karel, 85, 169, 218

care work, 50, 140–41
Carpenter, Jim, 193
Cartesian Linguistics (Chomsky), 41
Cassirer, Ernst, 150
Central European fiction, 84–96
  Andrej Tomažin, 194–97
  Dušan Makavejev, 86–90
  and exoticization, 85
  Rudi Šeligo, 90–95
  Zoran Nešković, 95–96
Chang, Mei-Wing, 52
character.ai (generative AI company), 122, 123
chatbots. *See also* robots; social robots; virtual assistants
  category of, 141
  ELIZA (Weizenbaum), 27, 47–48, 49–51, 228n23
  Eugene Goostman, 43, 228n18
  lineage of, 52
  PARRY (Colby), 47
  Pyggy, 79, *80*
  Replika, 56, 106, 121–23, 141, 206, 238n18
  Xiaoice, 56, 121
ChatGPT (LLM, OpenAI)
  accelerated pace of development, 215
  Chiang on, 174–75
  comparison with human writing, 207
  for emotional support, 238n16
  GPT-1, 179
  GPT-2, 166, 179
  GPT-3, 124, 179–80, 192, 199, 200, 201–2
  GPT-4, 155
  regulation of access to, 238n18
Chiang, Ted, 70, 174–75
children
  language acquisition by, 165–66
  treatment of Galateas as, 42, 43, 45, 160
Chinese room (hypothetical scenario), 45, 201
Chomsky, Noam, 41, 151, 155–56, 226n10
Chung, Sougwen, 84
Clark, Jack, 205
Clark, John, 22
Colby, Kenneth Mark, 47
Coleridge, Ernest Hartley, 100
collective intelligence, 197
Collodi, Carlo, 25

comparative literature, 78
Computation into Criticism (Burrows), 156
computer programming, Lovelace as mother of, 16, 163–64
computers
  history of computing, 229n33
  invention of, 14–15, 163–64
  Leibniz's version of, 149
  origin of word, 39
Computers and Automation (journal), 194
'Computing Machinery and Intelligence' (Turing), 16, 38–39, 43, 216–17
Le Comte de Monte-Cristo (Dumas), 132
conceptual thinking, and what artificial humanities offers to STEM, 214–15
connectionist AI, 61–62, 151–52, 185
Cope, David, 198
Cortana (virtual assistant, Microsoft), 55
Coulet, Henri, 99
Craig, Hugh, 192
creativity, 197, 245n1
  and LLMs, 176–77, 187
  and Turing test, 217
criminalization, 71
Critical AI, field of, 219, 250n4
CTRL (AI, Bryan McCann), 199, 200–201
cut-up technique (*découpé*), 190
cybernetics, 61, 62
'Cybernetics and Ghosts' (essay, Calvino), 195
cyberpunk fiction, 136
cyborgs, human, 136
cyborgs, in short stories, 128–32

Dahl, Roald, 133, 189–91
Darling, Kate, 109
Dartmouth Conference (1956), 61
Darwin, Charles, 11
Darwin, Erasmus, 10–11
The Day A Computer Writes A Novel (novel co-written by AI), 194
deafness, 14, 33
death, bots for grieving, 122–23, 124
deep brain stimulation (DBS), 137–38
deepfakes, 66, 71, 154, 194, 205, 213
deep learning, 62
  generative adversarial networks (GANs), 66–*68*, 248n19
  types of, 65

A Defence of Poetry (Shelley), 173–74
dehumanization, 14, 135–36. *See also* humanity
del Rey, Lester, 169
'Delusion and dream in Jensen's Gradiva' (Freud), 118–19
Deneš, Otto, 89
Dent, Alan, 36
Descartes, René, 21, 40–41, 147, 148, 157, 226n11, 226nn7–9
de Staël, Germaine, 23, 99–100, 159
Devlin, Jacob, 52
The Diagnosis of Stupor and Coma (Plum and Posner), 132
Diagnostic and Statistical Manual of Mental Disorders (DSM-5), 117
Diderot, Denis, 41
difference, of Galateas, 44–45
Digi (AI romantic companion start-up), 18
digisexualities, 119–20
digital assistants. *See* virtual assistants
digital humanities, the, 216, 218
Dillon, Sarah, 139–40
Dinkins, Stephanie, 84
disability
  and agency, 134
  in *Galatea 2.2*, 172–73
  and Galateas, 14, 44, 129
  locked-in syndrome, 132–36, 239n23, 239n27
  machines framed as having, 45, 75, 168, 169, 244n31
The Discourse of the Method (Descartes), 40
disinformation, 154, 205
diversity, Galateas or AI characterized with appeals to, 44–45, 203–4
diversity, whitewashing in technology, 71–73, 219
The Diving Bell and the Butterfly [Le Scaphandre et le Papillon] (Bauby), 133
Doctor Faustus (Marlowe, 1592), 170
Dolar, Mladen, 11
'Do Large Language Models Understand Us?' (essay, Agüera y Arcas), 169
Don't Believe in Monuments [Spomenicima ne treba verovati] (film, Makavejev, 1958), 86, 88–*89*, 224n24
Dreyfus, Hubert and Stuart, 198
Dudzinski, Denise, 135

Duffy, Carol Ann, 96–97
Duguid, Paul, 14
Dumas, Alexandre, 133
Duplex (virtual assistant, Google), 43

Ederlezi Rising [A.I. Rising] (film, Vojnov, 2018), 95–96
Edison, Thomas, 9–10
education, 42, 166–67. *See also* machine learning
elocution lessons, 33, 71–72, 73
ELIZA (chatbot, Weizenbaum), 27, 47–48, 49–51, 228n23
Eliza effect, 27, 45–52
Elliot, Bern, 52
Ellis, Alexander John, 34, 225n2
Ellis, Havelock, 115–16
elocution lessons, 33, 71–72, 73
embodiment. *See also* disability
  Age of, 229n33
  cyborgs, human, 136
  cyborgs, in short stories, 128–32
  in *Galatea 2.2*, 165–73
  of locked-in patients, 132–36
  prosthetics, 107, 128–32, 134–36, 160
  of social robots, 78, 79–84
  and thought, 40, 43, 44–45
  in *The Triptych of Agata Schwarzkobler*, 91–94
  writing as, 205
EMI (Experiments in Musical Intelligence), 198
emotions, 50–51
empiricism, 149
environmental problems, 186
An Essay Concerning the Human Understanding (Locke), 20
ethics, 28–29
  AI ethics, 213–14
  and Asimov's Laws of Robotics, 138–39
  of language enhancement, 230n38
  in Lem's *The Mask*, 103
  and LLMs, 154–55, 246–47nn8–9
  and what artificial humanities offers to STEM, 214–15
Eugene Goostman (chatbot), 43, 228n18
Eulenburg, Albert, 115
Euphonia machine, *12*–13
Eureka machine, 11–12

existentialism, 150, 154
Ex Machina (film, Garland, 2014), 81, *82*, 105, 109–11
exoticization, 44, 85
eye movement, technology using, 132, 134, 135

Faber, Joseph, 12
Fallon, Jimmy, 81, *82*, 84
Farlex Partner Medical Dictionary, 117
Faust (Goethe), 170–71
Fedorenko, Evelina, 39
feminist authors, Galatean perspective in, 96–101
fiction. *See also* novels; short stories
　in creation of chatbots, 43, 56
　in public discourse around AI, 139–40
　role of, 4, 204–6
films
　Annihilation (2018), 111
　Anthony's Broken Mirror [Antonijevo razbijeno ogledalo] (1957), 86–*87*, 88
　Blade Runner (1982), 48–49, 211, 228n24
　Don't Believe in Monuments [Spomenicima ne treba verovati] (1958), 86, 88–*89*, 224n24
　Ederlezi Rising [A.I. Rising] (2018), 95–96
　Ex Machina (2014), 81, *82*, 105, 109–11
　Her (2013), 105–8, 112, 206
　Hugo (2011), 25
　Lars and the Real Girl (2007), 125–27, *126*
　Metropolis (1927), 86
　My Fair Lady (1964), 23, 54, 74, 78–79, 100, 225n1
　Pygmalion (1938), 54, *73*, 81
　The Triptych of Agata Schwarzkobler (1979), 92
　The Triptych of Agata Schwarzkobler (1996), 92–*93*, *94*
　2001: A Space Odyssey (1968), 49, 64, 211
Fitzgerald, Kathleen, 167
Fitzpatrick, Kathleen, 171
Florentine Nights (Heine), 115
Forbes (magazine), 144
Foucault, Michel, 151
foundation models. *See* large language models (LLMs)

'Four ethical priorities for neurotechnologies and AI' (Yuste et al.), 139
Fowles, John, 202
Frankenstein; or the Modern Prometheus (Shelley), 25–26, 145, 158–60, 161–63, 164, 210
The French Lieutenant's Woman (Fowles), 202, 234n34
Freud, Sigmund, 118–19
Fundamentals of Language (Jakobson and Halle), 150
The Future Eve [L'Eve Future] (Villiers), 9, 21, 229n30

Gainsbourg, Serge, 24
Galatea (poem, Alyea), 100
Galatea (poem, Hall), 99
Galatea (poem, Rowe), 100
Galatea (poem, Ward), 98
Galatea, or Pygmalion Re-Versed (musical burlesque, 1883), 24
Galatea 2.2 (novel, Powers), 21, 26, 29, 48, 145–46, 164–73
Galatea Again (poem, Taggard), 97
Galatea Before the Mirror [Galatea Ante el Espejo] (poem, Alegría), 97
Galatea in Sonnet (poem, Hickey), 99
Galateas. *See also* performance, Galatean; Pygmalionism; Pygmalion myth
　agency of, 100
　Frankenstein's creature compared with, 159
　in *Galatea 2.2*, 165–73
　gaze of, 92–93, *94*
　name of, 20–21, 224–25nn30–33
　perspective of, 96–101
　speech of, 19–26, 100
　in *The Triptych of Agata Schwarzkobler*, 90–95
Galatea to Pygmalion (poem, Montgomery), 97
Galatea to Pygmalion (poem, Stryker), 100
Gall, France, 24
games, AI competing in, 17, 177, •203
Garland, Alex, 109–11
geminoid robots, 134–35, 239n23

Gemsouls (Chinese virtual being company), 18
gender. *See also* women writers
　in Agata Schwarzkobler novels, 90–91
　in *Galatea 2.2*, 167–68, 171–72
　and Pygmalion myth, 14, 24–25, 28, 88–89, 99–100, 223n24
　women as machines/machines as women, 12–13, 15, 39
generative adversarial networks (GANs), *66–68*, 248n19
Genlis, Stephanie Felicite de, 99
Geoghegan, Bernard Dionysius, 44
Gérôme, Jean-Léon, *22*
Gibson, John, 116
Gibson, William, 136
Gilbert, W. S., 20
Giles, Martin, 66
Gillespie, Craig, 125
'The Girl Who Was Plugged In' (short story, Sheldon), 130–32, 138
Goering, Sara, 138
Goethe, Johann Wolfgang von, 170–71
'The Golden Touch' (Hawthorne), 8–9
golems, 25, 85
Golem XIV (Lem), 25, 103–4
Good, Irving John (Isadore Jacob), 63–64
Goodfellow, Ian, 66
Google
　AlphaGo Zero (AI), 203
　BERT (Bidirectional Encoder Representations from Transformers, LLM), 179
　Duplex (virtual assistant), 43
　Google Assistant (virtual assistant), 55, 56
　Google DeepMind, 203
　Google Search, 206
　LaMDa (text-based language model), 45, 51, 139
　and LLM development, 178–79
GPT-1 (LLM, OpenAI), 179
GPT-2 (LLM, OpenAI), 166, 179
GPT-3 (LLM, OpenAI), 124, 179–80, 192
　novel co-written with, 199, 200, 201–2
GPT-4 (LLM, OpenAI), 155
Gračner, Nataša Barbara, 92
Gradiva (Jensen), 118–19
gramophone, invention of, 9–10

Graves, Robert, 100
'The Great Automatic Grammatisator' (Dahl), 189–91
Greatley-Hirsch, Brett, 192
The Guardian (newspaper), 174
Gunderson, Keith, 40
Guthrie, Thomas Anstey, 116
Guy-Bray, Stephen, 97

Hall, Eliza Calvert, 99
Halle, Morris, 150
hallucination, by AI agents, 120
Hamann, Johann Georg, 149
Hamilton, Melissa, 117
Handke, Peter, 172
Hanson Robotics, 130
　BINA48 (robot), 84
　Sophia (social robot), 78–84, 239n24
Haraway, Donna, 109, 160–61, 217
Harbisson, Neil, 136
Harbou, Thea von, 86
Harris, Anita M., 120
Hartley, Ralph, 184
Hartree, Douglas R., 16
Hawel, Rudolf, 85
Hawking, Stephen, 134
Hawthorne, Nathaniel, 8–9
Hayles, N. Katherine, 70, 172
Heine, Heinrich, 115
'Helen O'Loy' (short story, del Rey), 169
Helens, in literature, 169–71
Henry, Joseph, 13
Hepburn, Audrey, 78–79
Her (film, Jonze, 2013), 105–8, 112, 206
Herder, Johann Gottfried von, 98, 149, 234n31
Hermann, Isabella, 211
Heti, Sheila, 48
Hickey, Emily Henrietta, 99
Hinton, Geoffrey, 174
history
　of computing, 229n33
　of language, 29, 146–52
　of LLMs, 182–84
　of machine writing, 188–91, 241n5
　of Pygmalion myth, 17–19, 223nn20–22
　of robots, 85, 142, 231n7
　and what artificial humanities offers to STEM, 212, 214–15

The Hitchhiker's Guide to the Galaxy (Adams), 70
Hoffmann, E. T. A., 23, 159, 229n30
Holmes, Ronald, 117
The House of Mirth (novel, Wharton), 100
'How to write like Roberto Bolano in less than an hour' (short story, Tomažin), 196–97
Hubbard, Mabel Gardiner, 14
Hugo (film, 2011), 25
human exceptionalism, 40–41, 195, 197–98
humanities, the. *See* artificial humanities
humanity. *See also* hybrids/humanoids/monsters/cyborgs
 in *Galatea 2.2*, 165–66, 172–73
 and language-centeredness, 60–61, 147, 148–49, 150, 158
 in *The Mask*, 103
 modern concept of, 18, 21
 in Shaw's *Pygmalion*, 56–59
human-nonhuman relationships. *See* Pygmalionism; relationality
hybrids/humanoids/monsters/cyborgs, 210–11. *See also* Galateas; humanity
cyborgs, human, 136
cyborgs, in short stories, 128–32
Frankenstein, 158–64
hyper-structuralism, 182

IBM
 Watson (AI), 177
'I didn't know how to write about my sister's death—so I had AI do it for me.' (Vara), 124
Imaginary Magnitude (Wielkość Urojona) (Lem), 104
imitation game. *See* Turing test
ImportAI (newsletter, Clark), 205
Im Reich der Homunkuliden [In the Kingdom of Homunculids] (Hawel), 85
incest, 118, 119
industrialization, 85–86, 189
InflectionAI (generative AI company), 122
information technology, what humanities brings to, 2
information theory, 150, 182–83, 184
interdisciplinarity, and what artificial humanities offers to STEM, 212, 215–16

International Classification of Diseases (ICD-11), 117, 118
Ishiguro, Hiroshi, 134–35
Ishiguro, Kazuo, 105

Jakobson, Roman, 150
Jasanoff, Sheila, 206, 216
Jensen, Wilhelm, 118–19
Jentsch, Ernst, 18
Jiajia, Zheng, 125
Johansson, Scarlett, 106, 235nn47–48
Jonze, Spike, 106
Joshua, Essaka, 24, 42, 97, 98, 232–33n26
Journal of the Neurological Sciences, 133
Joyal, Christian C., 118
Jurjaševič, Boris, 92

Kant, Immanuel, 149
Kapor, Mitchell, 49
Katchadjian, Pablo, 197
Kazemi, Darius, 194
Kehlmann, Daniel, 30, 199, 200–201
Keller, Helen, 168–69, 244nn30–31
Kempelen, Wolfgang von, 11
Kennedy, Philip, 136
Kermauner, Taras, 95
killer robot trope, 103, 109, 210
Kim, Sang-Hyun, 216
Kirschenbaum, Matthew, 188
Kittler, Friedrich A., 217
Klopčič, Matjaž, 92
Kondziella, Daniel, 133
Konior, Bogna, 85, 104, 230n35
Kons 33 (poem, Kosovel), 86
Kosovel, Srečko, 86
Kovach, Steve, 84
Krafft-Ebing, Richard Freiherr von, 115
Krajewski, Markus, 137
Kurzweil, Ray, 49, 222n7
Kuyda, Eugenia, 106, 122–23, 206, 238n18
Kypriaka [History of Cyprus] (Philostephanus), 8, 113, 222n10, 236n2

'Lackeys, Heroes, and AI' ['Hlapci, heroji in umetna inteligenca'] (short story, Tomažin), 194–96, 197–99
LaMDa (text-based language model, Google), 45, 51, 139

Lang, Fritz, 86
language, 144–75. *See also* large language
    models (LLMs); machine writing
  acquisition of, 165–66, 226n5
  conceptual history of, 29, 146–52
  human exclusivity in, 153–58
  in Lem's imaginary, 104
  machine/nonhuman/synthetic, 187
  and meaning, 153–54, 184
  and ontology, 147
  as prosthetic, 160
  resilience of, 207–8
  and thought/reason, 39, 147, 148–49
  and Turing test, 42
language-centeredness in AI, 60–64
language enhancement, 69–74, 230n38
  defined, 69–70
Language Test (Descartes), 41
large language models (LLMs), 176–88.
    See also ChatGPT; machine writing
  appreciating innate abilities of, 203–4
  challenges of, 184
  and creativity, 176–77, 187
  defined, 178
  and ethics, 154–55, 246–47nn8–9
  excitement about, 180, 186
  history of, 182–84
  hyper-structuralist logic of, 182
  and language, 144–45, 153–56
  language acquisition by, 165–66
  and literary market, 188–91, 192
  meta-analysis by, 179–80
  renaming of, 182, 184
  skepticism about, 180–81
  speed of change in field, 186–87, 215
  summarizing by, 192–93
  useful applications of, 181–82
Lars and the Real Girl (film, Gillespie,
    2007), 125–27, *126*
larynx, artificial, 10–11
'The Last Dream' (Weizenbaum), 50
Latour, Bruno, 217–18
Law, Helen, 20, 225n33
LeCun, Yann, 152, 173, 174, 175
Leibniz, Gottfried Wilhelm, 149
Lem, Stanisław, 102–4
  Golem XIV, 25, 103–4
  Imaginary Magnitude (Wielkość Urojona),
    104

The Mask [Maska], 102–3, 204
Solaris, 104
Summa Technologiae, 45, 104, 230n35
Lemoine, Blake, 51, 139
linguistics, 39, 41, 150–52
literacy
  in *Frankenstein,* 162–63
  in *Galatea 2.2,* 165–66, 171–72
literary market, and LLMs, 188–91, 191,
    192
literary studies, role of, 216–19
The Little Mermaid [Den lille havfrue]
    (story, Andersen), 23
LLMs. *See* large language models (LLMs)
Llull, Ramon, 149
Locke, John, 20, 21, 148–49, 228n20
locked-in syndrome, 132–36, 239n23, 239n27
logos, 147–48
London Times (newspaper), 188
loneliness, 124
Lovelace, Ada, 14–15, 16, 163–64

Ma, Ricky, 106
machine learning, 62, 65, 75, 155, 179, 211.
    See also large language models (LLMs)
machine reading, 192–93
machine speech training, 64–68
machine writing, 29–30
  in Dahl's story, 191–93
  history of, 188–91, 241n5
  McCann with CTRL, 199–201
  of novels, 193–94
  Pharmako-AI, 199, 201–2
  of poetry, 188, 193
  in Tomažin's stories, 194–99
Madama Butterfly (opera, Puccini), 23
Makavejev, Dušan, 86–90
  *Anthony's Broken Mirror [Antonijevo
    razbijeno ogledalo]* (film, 1957),
    86–*87, 88*
  *Don't Believe in Monuments [Spomenicima
    ne treba verovati]* (film, 1958), 86,
    88–*89,* 224n24
Manet, Édouard, *60*
The Mannequin [Le Mannequin] (play, de
    Staël, 1811), 23, 99–100, 159
Mark 1 (robot, Ma), 106
Markov, Andrey, 183
Markov process, 183

Marlowe, Christopher, 170
marriage, 119
Marshall, Gail, 116
masculine/male humanoids, 25–26
The Mask [Maska] (short story, Lem), 102–3, 204
'A Mathematical Theory of Communication' (Shannon), 182–83, 184
mathematics, 179, 183–84, 185, 190
McArthur, Neil, 119
McCaffrey, Anne, 23
McCann, Bryan
    CTRL (AI), 199, 200–201
McCarthy, John, 45, 61, 221n1
McClelland, James, 152
McLaughlin, Steve, 193
meaning, in communication, 153–54, 184
meaning, lack of, 153–54, 194–95, 203
Mechanical Turk (Amazon microwork/crowdsourcing platform), 11, 85, 207
Mechanical Turk (chess-playing automaton), 11
Media Equation theory, 50
Medical Eponyms dictionary, 117
medicalization, 71
medical treatment, 112, 230n38. *See also* disability; Pygmalionism, in techno-medical lens
Medusa, 101
Meller, Aidan, 84
Mérimée, Prosper, 210
Merlin, John Joseph, 15
Metamorphoses (Ovid)
    Galatea in, 20
    Narcissus in, 222n9
    Prometheus in, 222n8
    Pygmalion myth in, 8, 31, 58, 59, 113, 159, 222nn11–12
metaverse, concept of, 121
Metropolis (film, 1927), 86
Metropolis (novel, von Harbou), 86
Mialet, Hélène, 134
Microsoft
    Cortana (virtual assistant), 55
Midas, King, 8–9
Mind Over Machine (Dreyfus and Dreyfus), 198
monsters. *See* hybrids/humanoids/monsters/cyborgs

Montaigne, Michel de, 118
Montgomery, Roselle Mercier, 97
Moore, Catherine Lucille (C. L.), 127–30, 138
Moreau de Tours, Paul, 114
Morgan, Piers, 84
Morris, William, 99
Mufwene, Salikoko, 160
Murakami, Haruki, 207–8
music, 23, 24, 198
'My Algorithm and Me' ['Mein Algorithmus und Ich'] (essay, Kehlmann), 199
My Fair Ladies (Wosk), 101, 216
My Fair Lady (film, 1964), 23, 54, 74, 78–79, 100, 225n1
mythology. *See also Metamorphoses* (Ovid); Pygmalion myth
    artificial humans in, 7–8, 123

Nass, Clifford, 50
National Novel Generation Month (NaNoGenMo), 193–94
National Novel Writing Month (NaNoWriMo), 193–94
natural language processing (NLP), 52, 65, 153, 186
Nature, 15
Nešković, Zoran, 95–96
neural networks, 62–63. *See also* large language models (LLMs)
    deep learning in, 65
    in *Galatea 2.2*, 29, 145–46, 165–73
    generative adversarial networks (GANs), 66–68, 248n19
Neuromancer (Gibson), 136
neuroprostheses, 132, 135–36
New York Paper, 12
New York Times, 63, 120, 235n46, 247n11
Ní Chuilleanáin, Eiléan, 101
Nietzsche, Friedrich, 151
Nixon, Marni, 79
nominalism, 148
nonhumans. *See* hybrids/humanoids/monsters/cyborgs
Norvig, Peter, 186
Novelist as Vocation (Murakami), 207
novels
    Galatea 2.2 (Powers), 21, 26, 48, 145–46, 164–73

novels (*Continued*)
　machine writing in, 193–94
　Pharmako-AI (Allado-McDowell with GPT-3), 199, 200, 202
　The Triptych of Agata Schwarzkobler [Triptih Agate Schwarzkobler] (Šeligo), 90–91, 93–95
'No Woman Born' (short story, Moore), 24, 128–30, 138

Oedipus complex, 119
Offenbach, Jacques, 23
Of the Affection of Fathers to Their Children (Montaigne), 118
Olympia (Manet, 1865), 60
Only the Eyes Say Yes: A Love Story [Putain de Silence] (Vigand), 134
'On the Danger of Stochastic Parrots: Can Language Models be Too Big?' (Bender et al.), 153
ontology, 147, 161
OpenAI, 207
　GPT-1 (LLM), 179
　GPT-2 (LLM), 166, 179
　GPT-3 (LLM), 124, 179–80, 192, 199, 200, 201–2
　GPT-4 (LLM), 155
　and LLM development, 179
　Sky (virtual assistant voice), 106
The Order of Things (Foucault), 151
Orientalism, 12, 44
Osgood, Frances Sargent Locke, 98, 233–34n30
Oulipo group, 190
'The Oval Portrait' (Poe), 18, 233n30
Ovid. See *Metamorphoses* (Ovid)
Ozaki, Masayuki, 125–27, *126*

Parallel Distributed Processing (Rumelhart and McClelland), 152
paralysis, 96, 112
paraphilias, 117–18, 237n8, 238n14
Parmenides, 147
parrots/parroting, 41–42
　Alex the African gray, 157
　stochastic parrots, 153, 156
PARRY (chatbot, Colby), 47
Passages from the Life of a Philosopher (Babbage), 15
perceptrons, 62–63

performance, Galatean, 23–24
　automata exhibitions, 11–13
　by chatbots, 55–56
　hallucination by AI agents, 120
　in Shaw's *Pygmalion*, 35–36, 79
　by social robots, 79–84
　of Turing test, 38–39, 43–44
personhood, 172, 242n13, 244n29
Peter, John, 11
Pharmako-AI (novel, Allado-McDowell with GPT-3), 199, 200, 202
Philosophical Thoughts (Diderot), 41
philosophy of language, 146–52
Philostephanus, 8, 113, 222n10, 222n11, 236n2
phonetic alphabets, 33–35, 225n2
phonograph, invention of, 9–10
Picard, Rosalind, 50
Pirjevec, Dušan, 90
plagiarism, 192, 197. See also machine writing
Plato, 147
Plum, Fred, 132–33
Poe, Edgar Allen, 18, 233n30
poetry
　artificial, 180, 245–46n4
　brief consolation regarding, 207
　concepts of, 173–74
　and Eureka machine, 11
　and lack of meaning, 203
　LLMs' structure for, 179
　machine writing in, 188, 193
　and Turing test, 217
　women-authored, Galatea in, 96–100
Posner, Jerome, 133
posthumanism, 5, 160–61, 172
postmodernism, 150–51
Powers, Richard
　Galatea 2.2, 21, 26, 29, 48, 145–46, 164–73
prediction, in LLM development, 182–83
Primate Visions (Haraway), 160–61
progress, belief in, 57
progress, relentless advance of, 215
Prometheus myth, 145, 158–59, 222n8
Propoetides, 58
prosthetics
　of intimacy, 107
　language as, 160
　for locked-in syndrome, 132, 134–36
　in science fiction, 128–32
prostitution, 58–59, 107, 115

Psychopathia Sexualis (Krafft-Ebing), 115
Puccini, Giacomo, 23
Pyggy (chatbot in improv theater), 79, *80*
Pygmalion (film, 1938), 54, *73*, *81*
Pygmalion (king of Cyprus), 118
Pygmalion (play, Rousseau, 1762/1770), 20, 159
Pygmalion (play, Shaw, 1912), 21, 23, 27, 32, 33–37
  doubling in, 36
  and the Eliza effect, 45–47
  feminism of, 37, 54
  humanity in, 56–59
  inspiration for, 33–34
  and language enhancement, 71–72, 73–74
  and machine speech training, 65–67
  medical treatment in, 112
  paralysis in, 112
  and phonetics, 33–36
  and relationality, 52–54
  and the Turing test, 41–44, 45–47
Pygmalion, ou la Statue animée (Boureau-Deslandes), 19–20
Pygmalion and Galatea (play, Gilbert, 1871), 20, 24
Pygmalion and Galatea, or the statue animated for twenty-four hours [Pygmalion et Galatee, ou la statue animee depuis vingt-quatre heures] (play, de Genlis, 1790s), 99
'Pygmalion and the Image' (poem, Morris), 99
Pygmalion Bride (poem, Coleridge), 100
Pygmalion et Galatée (Gérôme, 1890), *22*
Pygmalionism, 28–29
  in Central European fictions, 86–96
  in mythology and folklore, 123
  and relationality, 54–55
  and robotics, 75–77
  in Shaw's play, 53–54
Pygmalionism, in techno-medical lens, 112–75
  cyborgs, in short stories, 128–32
  and *Frankenstein*, 158–64
  and *Galatea 2.2*, 164–73
  and law, 117–18
  locked-in syndrome, 132–36
  as mental illness, 117, 118–19
  and psychology, 118–20

relationships with robots, 125–27
and sexology, 114–16
and virtual beings, 120–24
Pygmalion myth, 4–5, 8–9. *See also* Galateas
  in *A.I. Rising*, 95–96
  and gender, 14, 24–25, 99–100
  history of, 17–19, 223nn20–22
  in Makavejev's films, 86–90
  reversal of, 88–89
  in Šeligo's novel, 90–91
  and sexuality, 113
Pygmalion poem/myth, in Ovid's *Metamorphoses*, 8, 31, 58, 59, 113, 159, 222nn11–12
Pygmalion's Bride (poem, Duffy), 96–97
Pygmalion's Image (poem, Ní Chuilleanáin), 101
Pygmalion to Galatea (poem, Graves), 100

racial/ethnic bias, 71–72, 84
rationalism, 148
Ray, Johnny, 136
reading, by machines, 192–93
reason, 21, 40, 147, 148–49. *See also* thought
Rees, Tobias, 188
Reeves, Byron, 50
reinforcement learning, 65–66, 75, 155
Reinhold, Meyer, 20, 225n33
reistic style, 91–92
relational agents. *See* virtual beings
relationality, 52–56, 108–9
  in *Her*, 105–8
  human-computer interactions, 51–52, 55–56, 63–64, 119–20, 230n33
  with robots, 125–27
  in Shaw's *Pygmalion*, 52–54
  and virtual beings, 56, 120–24, 141
Replika (virtual being), 56, 106, 121–23, 141, 206, 238n18
Reynolds, Emily, 130
Rhee, Jennifer, 140
Richardson, Kathleen, 106
Rime (AI accent conversion startup), 72–73
'Robbie' (short story, Asimov), 25
The Robotic Imaginary (Rhee), 140
robotic perspectives, 105
  in *Ex Machina*, 109–11
  in *Her*, 107–8

robotics
  Asimov's Laws of, 138–39, 240n33
  centering of whiteness in, 84, 106
  for paralysis, 134–35
  and Pygmalionism, 75–77
robots. *See also* chatbots
  anthropomorphization of, 28, 79–81
  BINA48 (Hanson Robotics), 84
  geminoid, 134, 239n23
  killer robot trope, 103, 109, 210
  in Lem's *The Mask*, 102–3
  lineage/history of, 85, 142, 231n7
  Mark 1 (Ma), 106
  Pygmalionesque relationships with, 125–27
  Sophia (Hanson Robotics), 78–84, 239n24
Ronell, Avital, 162
Rosenblatt, Frank, 62–63
Rousseau, Jean Jacques, 20, 159
Rowe, Charles J., 100
Rumelhart, David, 152
R.U.R. (Rossum Universal Robots) [Rossumovi Univerzalni Roboti] (play, Čapek, 1920), 85, 169–70, 218
Russ, Joanna, 159
Russell, Stuart J., 186

Sanas (company), 71, 73
'The Sandman' ['Der Sandmann'] (short story, Hoffmann), 23, 159, 229n30
Sapir-Whorf hypothesis, 70
'Sarrasine' (de Balzac), 23
Schaffer-Goddard, Jennifer, 139–40
Schölkopf, Bernard, 205
Schuring, Martin, 116
science fiction, 205, 206, 237n13
Sculpture: Some Observations on Shape and Form from Pygmalion's Creative Dream (Herder), 98
Searle, John, 45, 201, 226n6
Seemingly Human (Ward), 60
Šeligo, Rudi, 90–95
semantics, 64, 150
  "post-semantic literature," 194–95
semiotics, 150
serfdom, 85
servants, 55, 72, 137
sexology, 113, 114–16, 237n13
Sexuale Neuropathie (Eulenburg), 115

sexual harassment, 91
Sexual Selection in Man (Ellis), 115
Shakespeare, William, 171
Shannon, Claude, 45, 150, 182–83, 184
Shaw, George Bernard, 21, 25. *See also Pygmalion* (play, Shaw, 1912)
  Back to Methuselah, 50
  on English language, 32–33, 34
  and Mrs. Patrick Campbell, 36
  Shavian alphabet, 34
  What Happened Afterwards, 54
Sheldon, Alice (James Tiptree Jr.), 127–28, 130–32, 138
Shelley, Mary, 25–26, 145, 163
Shelley, Percy Bysshe, 173–74
The Ship Who Sang (novel, McCaffrey), 23
Shoemaker, Martin, 105
shorthand, 34–35
short stories
  'El Aleph' (Borges), 197
  'Before the evening it is not at all possible…' ['Predveče se nikako ne može…'] (Nešković), 95–96
  'The Girl Who Was Plugged In' (Sheldon), 130–32, 138
  'Helen O'Loy' (del Rey), 169
  'How to write like Roberto Bolano in less than an hour' (Tomažin), 196–97
  'Lackeys, Heroes, and AI' ['Hlapci, heroji in umetna inteligenca'] (Tomažin), 194–96, 197–99
  LLMs' structure for, 179
  The Mask [Maska] (Lem), 102–3, 204
  'No Woman Born' (Moore), 24, 128–30, 138
  'Robbie' (Asimov), 25
  'The Sandman' ['Der Sandmann'] (Hoffmann), 23, 159, 229n30
  'Story of Your Life' (Chiang), 70
  La Vénus d'Ille (Mérimée), 210
Silver Lady automaton, 15
Silverman, Robert, 128
Singhal, Amit, 206
singing, 23, 24, 78–79
singularity, trope of, 108
Siri (virtual assistant, Apple), 55–56
Sky (virtual assistant voice, OpenAI), 106
Slovenian language, 90

Smith, Will, 84
social biases, 4, 7
socialism, in Makavejev's films, 88–90
social robots, 28. *See also* chatbots
  category of, 141
  Sophia (Hanson Robotics), 78–84, 239n24
social sciences, the, 216
Solaris (novel, Lem), 104
Sophia (social robot, Hanson Robotics), 78–84, 239n24
sound spectograms, 67
'Speculations Concerning the First Ultraintelligent Machine' (Good), 63–64
speculative fiction, 218
speech, 90
  speaking machines, 9–14, 64–68
  through neuroprostheses, 136
  and Turing test, 44
stable diffusion, 186
Star Trek, 206
statues
  and Pygmalionism in medical/sexological field, 114–16, 117
  in Pygmalion myth, 8, 17, 31, 59
The Statue to Pygmalion (poem, Osgood), 98
Steinthal, Heymann, 151
stenography, 10
Stevens, Brett, 190
Stiegler, Bernard, 218
stochasticism, 153, 156
'Story of Your Life' (short story, Chiang), 70
'The Storyteller' (essay, Benjamin), 162
Strachey, Christopher, 189
structuralism, 150–51, 182, 194
Stryker, Leonora Clawson, 100
STS (science and technology studies; also science, technology, and society), 216
stuttering, 10–11
Sullivan, Anne, 168
summarizing, by LLMs, 192–93
Summa Technologiae (Lem), 45, 104, 230n35
supervised learning, 65
Sweet, Henry, 34
Switzky, Lawrence, 43, 53
symbolic AI, 61–62, 151, 152, 185
Symonds, Eliza Grace, 14

Syntactic Structures (Chomsky), 151
syntax analysis, 155–56
Synthesia (AI video generating platform), 71

Taggard, Genevieve, 97
The Tales of Hoffmann [Les Contes du Hoffmann] (opera, Offenbach), 23
Tarnowsky, Benjamin, 115, 117
Tavčar, Ivan, 90
techno-medicine. *See* Pygmalionism, in techno-medical lens
telephone, invention of, 9–10, 33
The Tempest (Shakespeare), 171
Temple of Nature (E. Darwin), 10
theory, and what artificial humanities offers to STEM, 214–15
Thérèse Raquin (Zola), 132
Thesiger, Ernest, 36
Thomsen, Mads Rosendahl, 204, 221n2
thought
  and embodiment, 40, 43, 44–45
  and language, 39, 147, 148–49, 174
  writing as embodiment of, 205
The Tinted Venus (Guthrie), 116
Tiptree, James Jr. (Alice Sheldon), 127–28, 130–32, 138
Tomažin, Andrej, 194–97
  Anonymous Technology [Anonimna tehnologija], 194, 196
  'How to write like Roberto Bolano in less than an hour,' 196–97
  'Lackeys, Heroes, and AI' ['Hlapci, heroji in umetna inteligenca'], 194–96, 197–99
Towes, Rob, 144
transformer architecture, 178
transformer models. *See* large language models (LLMs)
transhumanism, 6, 69–70, 222n7
translation, 70, 203
'Transmission of Information' (Hartley), 184
The Triptych of Agata Schwarzkobler (film, Jurjašević, 1979), 92
The Triptych of Agata Schwarzkobler (film, Klopčič, 1996), 92–93, 94
The Triptych of Agata Schwarzkobler [Triptih Agate Schwarzkobler] (novel, Šeligo), 90–91, 93–95
Tsing, Anna, 109

Turing, Alan, 16–17. *See also* Turing test
  'Computing Machinery and Intelligence,' 16, 38–39, 43, 166–67, 169, 216–17
  on machine writing, 188
  and Wittgenstein, 226n4
Turing test, 27, 38–45
  and anthropomorphization of robots, 81
  creativity in, 217
  criticisms of, 45
  and the Eliza effect, 45–47, 48–50
  literature as, in fiction, 162, 165, 171–72
  machine writing in, 188
Turkle, Sherry, 124
Twist, Markie L. C., 119
2001: A Space Odyssey (film, 1968), 49, 64, 211

Ubi Sunt (Agüera y Arcas), 146, 166
uncanny, the, 18, 81
unsupervised learning, 65

value alignment, 154, 155, 187, 246–47n8
Vara, Vauhini, 124
Varley, Rosemary, 39
Vendler, Helen, 207
La Vénus d'Ille (short story, Mérimée), 210
Vidan, Aida, 87, 89
videos, AI-generated, 71
Vigand, Philippe, 134, 135–36, 240n29
Vigand, Stéphane, 134
Villiers de l'Isle-Adam, Auguste, 9, 21, 229n30
virtual assistants, 229n28. *See also* chatbots
  Alexa (Amazon), 55, 123
  category of, 141
  Cortana (Microsoft), 55
  Duplex (Google), 43
  Eliza Doolittle as precursor of, 52–53
  Google Assistant (Google), 55, 56
  lineage/history of, 142
  lineage of, 52
  and relationality, 54–55
  Siri (Apple), 55–56
virtual beings, 28, 56, 120–24, 238n15
  and building ethically, 141–42
  category of, 141
  ChatGPT for emotional support, 238n16
  in *Her*, 105–8
  lineage/history of, 142

Replika, 56, 106, 121–23, 141, 206, 238n18
Xiaoice, 56, 121
Visible Speech (phonetic alphabet), 14, 33, 225n1
Visible Speech (Potter, Kopp, and Kopp), 67
The Visoko Chronicle [Visoška kronika] (novel, Tavčar), 90–91
visual storytelling, 186
Vojnov, Dimitrije, 95

Ward, Elizabeth Stuart Phelps, 98
Ward, Megan, 60, 216
Watson (AI, IBM), 177
Weightman, John, 160
Weizenbaum, Joseph
  on AI, 47, 49–50
  ELIZA (chatbot), 27, 47–48, 49–51, 228n23
  'The Last Dream,' 50
Wharton, Edith, 100
What Happened Afterwards (Shaw), 54
Wheatstone, Charles, 11
White, Lewis, 73
White, Murray, 115, 116
whiteness, centering of, 71–72, 84, 106
Wiener, Norbert, 61
Wiesing, Urban, 70
Wilk, Elvia, 202
women as machines/machines as women, 12–13, 15, 39. *See also* Galateas
women writers
  drama on Galatean perspective, 99–100
  on Galatean paralysis, 127–32
  poetry on Galatean perspective, 96–99, 100–101
word embeddings, 185
Working Group on Sexual Disorders and Sexual Health, 117–18
Wosk, Julie, 101, 216
Wyman, Thomas, 129

Xiaoice (virtual being), 56, 121

Yeates, Amelia, 101, 116, 232n26
Yuste, Rafael, 139

Zeavin, Hannah, 120, 124
Zola, Èmile, 133